A History of
Latin America

A History of Latin America

Fourth Edition

Volume I
Ancient America to 1910

Benjamin Keen

Professor Emeritus
Northern Illinois University

HOUGHTON MIFFLIN COMPANY   Boston   Toronto

Dallas   Geneva, Illinois   Palo Alto   Princeton, New Jersey

Cover credit:

School of Miguel Cabrara, *THE CASTES: De Español, y
Mulata, Morisco* (detail), ca. 1750, Mexico, oil on canvas.
Was once either mounted on an "estuche de viaje"
(rolled travelling frame) or was part of a "biombo"
(folding screen). Denver Art Museum Collection.

Maps by Dick Sanderson.
        Patty Isaacs, *Parrot Graphics.*

Sponsoring Editor: John Weingartner
Project Editor: Linda Hamilton
Cover Designer: Sandra Gonzalez
Production Coordinator: Renée Le Verrier
Manufacturing Coordinator: Marie E. Barnes
Marketing Manager: Diane Brow Gifford

Printed in the U.S.A.

Library of Congress Catalog Card Number: 91-71983

ISBN 0-395-60138-X

ABCDEFGHIJ-D-9987654321

Contents

Contents

List of Maps

Preface

The fourth edition of *A History of Latin America* has two major objectives. First, it seeks to make available to teachers and students of Latin American history a text based on the best recent scholarship and enriched with data and concepts drawn from the sister social sciences of economics, anthropology, and sociology. Because the book is a history of Latin American *civilization,* it devotes considerable space to the way of life at different periods of the area's history. To enable students to deepen their own knowledge of Latin American history on their own, it includes an updated annotated bibliography, "Suggestions for Further Reading," limited to titles in English.

A second objective has been to set Latin American history within a broad interpretive framework. This framework is the "dependency theory," the most influential theoretical model for social scientists concerned with understanding Latin America. Not all followers of the theory understand it precisely the same way, but most probably agree with the definition of *dependency* offered by the Brazilian scholar Theotonio dos Santos: "A situation in which the economy of certain countries is conditioned by the development and expansion of another economy to which the former is subject." In recent years the theory has come under scattered fire from some scholars, mostly North American, who charge its followers with serious faults of omission and commission, such as the claim that capitalist development is impossible on the Latin American periphery. But, as Peter Evans pointed out in a thoughtful survey of several "postdependency" writings (*Latin American Research Review,* 20, No. 2 [1985]), Fernando Henriques Cardoso, himself a founder and leading theoretician of the dependency school, had attacked such claims "with vitriolic effectiveness" more than a decade earlier. Evans concluded that the dependency approach had established itself as one of the "primary lenses through which scholars, both North American and Latin American, analyze the interaction of classes and the state in the context of an increasingly internationalized economy," and that "it is hard to argue that this approach has been or is likely to be replaced by some new overarching paradigm." Since Evans wrote those words, Latin America has experienced deepening economic and social crises that have given new relevance to the dependency approach.

A word about the organization of this text. In its planning, the decision was made to reject the approach that tries to cover the post-independence history of the twenty Latin American republics in detail, including mention of every general who ever passed through a presidential palace. Most teachers will agree that this approach discourages students by miring them in a bog of tedious facts. Accordingly, it was decided to limit coverage of the national period in the nineteenth century to Mexico, Argentina, Chile, and Brazil, whose history seemed to illustrate best the major issues and trends of the period. In addition to these four countries, the survey of the twentieth century broadened to include the central Andean area, with a special concentration on Peru, and Cuba, the scene of a socialist revolution with continental repercussions. The second edition added a chapter on Central America, where a revolutionary storm, having toppled the U.S.–supported Somoza tyranny in Nicaragua, threatened the rickety structures of oligarchical and military rule in El Salvador and Guatemala.

To accommodate alternative course configurations, the fourth edition of *A History of Latin America* is being published in two volumes, as well as in the complete version. Volume 1 includes Latin American history from ancient times to 1910, and volume 2 covers Latin American history from independence to the present.

This present edition recognizes the political and economic importance of the Bolivarian lands of Venezuela and Colombia by including a chapter on the modern history of countries. Venezue-

lan history, like that of Mexico, demonstrates that great oil wealth will not, by itself, ensure escape from dependency and mass poverty. The violent history of Colombia, complicated by its recent emergence as principal supplier of cocaine to the United States, reflects an accumulation of political and social problems that still awaits solution.

The colonial chapters, in particular, have been extensively revised and expanded, with new material on ancient America, the discovery of America in historical perspective, colonial labor struggles, and colonial women, among other subjects. The book has also been updated to cover recent events and to incorporate current scholarship. The chapter on United States-Latin American relations, for example, includes sections on the invasion of Panama and the impact of the Gulf crisis and war on Latin America.

The book has also benefited from the careful scrutiny of the third edition by colleagues who made valuable suggestions for revision:

Margaret Chowning, California State University—Hayward
Donald B. Cooper, Ohio State University
Mariano Diaz-Miranda, University of Rhode Island
René De La Pedraja, Canisius College
Jane M. Rausch, University of Massachusetts, Amherst
John Jay TePaske, Duke University
Thomas Zoumaras, Northeast Missouri State University

Many but not all of these colleagues' suggestions were adopted; they bear no responsibility for any remaining errors of fact or interpretation. I wish to recall, too, the many students, graduate and undergraduate, who helped me to define my views on Latin American history through the give-and-take of classroom discussion and the reading and discussion of their papers and theses. In particular, I wish to thank two former students, Professors Steven Niblo and Keith Haynes, for sharing with me the findings of their important research on the political economy of the *Porfiriato* and the ideology of the Mexican revolution, respectively.

B.K.

Introduction

The Geographical Background of Latin American History

Latin America, a region of startling physical contrasts, stretches 7,000 miles southward from the Mexican-U.S. border to the tip of Tierra del Fuego on Cape Horn. The widest east–west point, across Peru and Brazil, spans 3,200 miles. This diverse geography has helped produce distinctive development of each Latin American nation.

Latin America has two dominant physical characteristics: enormous mountains and vast river systems. The often snow-capped and sometimes volcanic mountain ranges—the three Sierra Madre ranges in Mexico and the 4,000-mile-long Andes in South America making a western spine from Venezuela to Tierra del Fuego—form the backbone of the landmass. Nearly impassable for most of their length, these mountain ranges boast many peaks of over 22,000 feet. The mountains have presented a formidable barrier to trade and communications in Mexico and the nations of the southern continent. Not only do the mountain ranges separate nations from each other, they divide regions within nations.

The enormous rivers most often lie in lightly populated areas. Three mammoth river systems (the Amazon, the Orinoco, and the Río de la Plata) spread over almost the entire South American continent east of the Andes. The size of the Amazon River Basin and the surrounding tropics—the largest such area in the world—have posed another impediment to the development of transportation and human settlement, although some rivers are navigable for long distances. Only with the advent of modern technology—railroads, the telegraph, telephones, automobiles, and airplanes—has geographic isolation been partly overcome, a condition that has helped create markets and forge independent states.

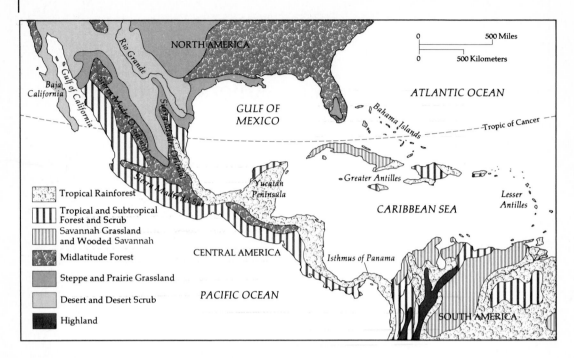

THE MAPS ON THESE FACING PAGES FORM AN OVERALL PICTURE OF THE NATURAL GEOGRAPHIC FEATURES OF LATIN AMERICA; MIDDLE AMERICA (ABOVE) COMPRISED OF MEXICO, CENTRAL AMERICA, AND THE CARIBBEAN REGION; AND SOUTH AMERICA (OPPOSITE).

Latin America encompasses five climatological regions: high mountains, tropical jungles, deserts, temperate coastal plains, and temperate highlands. The first three are sparsely populated, while the latter two tend to be densely inhabited. With the exception of the Mayan, all the great ancient civilizations arose in the highlands of the Andes and Mexico.

The varied climate and topography of South America, Mexico, and Central America have helped produce this highly uneven distribution of population. Three notable examples, the gargantuan Amazonian region of mostly steamy tropical forests and savannah, the vast desert of Patagonia in southern Argentina, and the northern wastelands of Mexico, support few inhabitants. In contrast to these inhospitable regions, a thin strip along Brazil's coast, the plain along the Río de la Plata estuary in Argentina, and the central plateau of Mexico contain most of the people in these countries. Thus these nations are over-populated and underpopulated at the same time.

In western South America the heaviest concentration of people is found on the inland plateaus. None of the major cities—Santiago, Chile; Lima, Peru; Quito, Ecuador; and Bogotá and Medellín, Colombia—are ports; there are few good natural harbors on the west coast. In contrast, in eastern South America the major cities—Buenos Aires, Argentina; Montevideo, Uruguay; and São Paulo–Santos, Rio de Janeiro, Bahia, and Recife, Brazil—are situated on the Atlantic coast. The preponderance of people in Argentina, Brazil, and Uruguay reside on the coastal plains. Mexico City, Guadalajara, and Monterrey, Mexico's largest cities, are inland. Almost all these cities in Latin America have a population of over one million, with Mexico City, the largest, having over fifteen million.

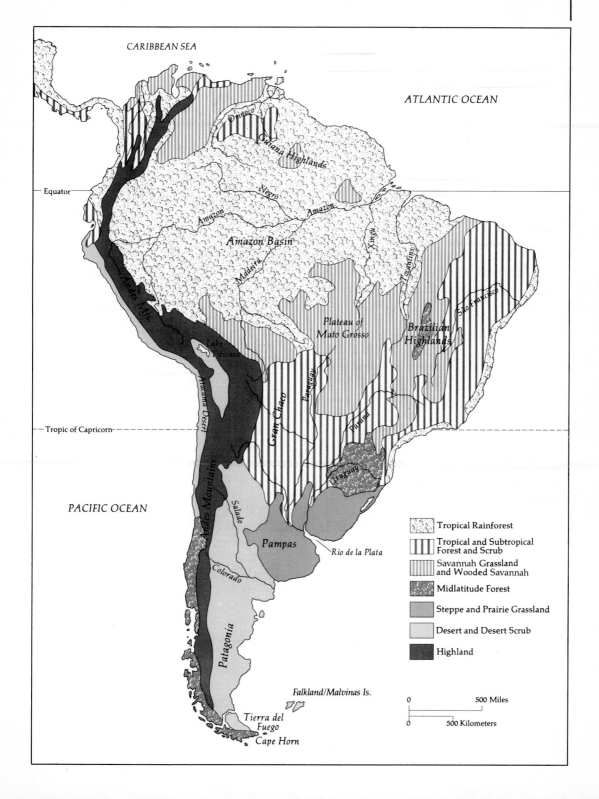

The number of waterways and the amount of rainfall vary greatly from region to region. Mexico has no rivers of importance, while Brazil contains the huge Amazon network. Lack of rain and rivers for irrigation in large areas makes farming impossible. Barely 10 percent of Mexico's land is fertile enough to farm; rainfall is so uncertain in some cultivable areas that drought strikes often and for years at a time. Mexico, with too little water, contrasts with Brazil with too much. Much of Brazil's vast territory, however, is equally uncultivable as its tropical soils have high acidity and have proved infertile and incapable of sustaining agricultural crops.

On the other hand, Latin America has enormous natural resources for economic development. Mexico and Venezuela rank among the world's largest oil producers. Mexico may have the biggest petroleum reserves of any nation other than Saudi Arabia. Bolivia, Ecuador, Colombia, and Peru also produce oil. Over the centuries, Latin American nations have been leading sources of copper (Mexico and Chile), nitrate (Chile), silver (Peru and Mexico), gold (Brazil), diamonds (Brazil), and tin (Bolivia). Much of the world's coffee is grown on the fertile highlands of Central America, Colombia, and Brazil. Much of the world's cattle have been raised on the plains of northern Mexico, southern Brazil, and central Argentina. Argentina's immense plains, the Pampas, are among the planet's most fertile areas, yielding not only cattle but sheep and wheat as well. Over the past five centuries, the coastal plains of Brazil have produced enormous amounts of sugar. In addition, human ingenuity has converted geographical obstacles into assets. Some extensive river systems have potential for hydroelectric power and provide water for irrigation as well, as has been done in Mexico's arid regions.

The historical record shows that the richness of Latin America's resources has had a significant impact on the economic and political development of Europe and North America. The gold and silver of its New World Empire fueled Spain's wars and diplomacy in Europe for four hundred years. Many scholars trace the origins of the Industrial Revolution in such nations as Great Britain and the Netherlands to resources extracted from Latin America by its colonial masters, Spain and Portugal.

Latin America's resources have affected economic development elsewhere, but how these resources have been developed and by whom and in which ways has profoundly changed the history of the nations in this area. Geography has perhaps narrowed historical alternatives in Latin America, but the decisions of people determined its development. Going back to the colonization by Spain and Portugal, Latin America's history has been marked by exploitation of its peoples and its natural resources. Imperial Spain's policy to drain the lands it conquered of gold, silver, and other resources fixed the pattern for later exploiters. With European dominance came the decisions to subjugate the indigenous peoples and often force them to labor under subhuman conditions in mines and large estates, where many died. In the more recent era, there has been the decision to grow bananas on the coastal plains of Central America, instead of corn or other staples of the local diet; this has made export profitable, usually for North American concerns, but this land-use has left many, like the Guatemalans, without sufficient food.

The book that follows is a history of the development of Latin America's economy, politics, and society viewed primarily from the perspective of ordinary people, who were exploited and oppressed, but who resisted and endured. It is the story of the events and forces that produced the alternatives from which Latin Americans created their world.

A History of
Latin America

Part 1

The Colonial Heritage of Latin America

For most North Americans, perhaps, the colonial past is a remote, picturesque time that has little relevance to the way we live now. The situation is very different in Latin America. "Even the casual visitor to Latin America," says the historian Woodrow Borah, "is struck by the survival of institutions and features that are patently colonial." The inventory of colonial survivals includes many articles and practices of everyday life, systems of land use and labor, and a wealth of social relations and attitudes.

Characteristic of the Latin American scene is the coexistence and mingling of colonial and modern elements: the digging stick, the foot plow, and the handloom coexist with the tractor, the conveyor belt, and the computer. In Latin America the colonial past is not a nostalgic memory but a harsh reality. It signifies economic backwardness; political arbitrariness, corruption, and nepotism; a hierarchical social order and attitudes of condescension and contempt on the part of elites toward the masses.

We begin our survey of the colonial period of Latin American history with some account of Ancient America, the name we give to that long span of time during which the Indians—the first Americans—developed their cultures in virtual isolation from the Old World. The Indian past profoundly influenced the character of the colonial era. By no accident, the chief capitals of the Spanish Empire in America arose in the old Indian heartlands—the Mexican and Peruvian areas—the homes of millions of industrious natives accustomed to performing tribute labor for their ruling classes. The Indians, the Spaniards well knew, were the true wealth of the Indies. Territories that held few Indians failed to attract them or remained marginal in the Spanish colonial scheme of things.

Equally decisive for the character of the colonial period was the Hispanic background. The conquistadors came from a Spain where seven centuries of struggle against the Moslems had made warfare almost a way of life and had created a large *hidalgo* (noble) class that regarded manual labor with contempt. To some the conquest of America appeared to be an extension of the reconquest of Spain from the Moors. "The conquest of Indians," wrote the Spanish chronicler Francisco López de Gómara, "began when the conquest of the Moors had ended, in order that Spaniards may always war against the infidels." Spain's economic backwardness and immense inequalities of wealth, which sharply limited opportunities for advancement or even a decent livelihood for most Spaniards, help explain the desperate valor of the conquistadors; they also help explain the harshness in dealing with the Indians, and sometimes with each other, and the dog-eat-dog atmosphere of the Conquest. It seems significant that many great captains of the Conquest—Cortés, Pizarro, Valdivia, Balboa—came from the bleak land of Estremadura, Spain's poorest province.

Another factor that may help to explain the peculiarly ferocious and predatory character of the Conquest is the climate of violence that existed in contemporary Spain—a clear legacy of the reconquest and social conditions and values it generated. In his *Spanish Character: Attitudes and Mentalities from the Sixteenth to the Nineteenth Century,* Bartolomé Bennassar notes how widespread and accepted was the incidence of violence in Spain of the sixteenth and seventeenth centuries. According to Bennassar, assassins proliferated, and he illustrates the cheapness of life by the survival of the ancient practice of issuing writs of pardon in return for the payment of blood money—usually a small amount—for the murder of individuals of humble social status. To concede that the historical background had created this climate of violence is not to ascribe to Spaniards a unique capacity for cruelty or deviltry. We know all too well that colonial or imperialist wars and civil wars are replete with atrocities and horrors of every kind. Indeed, what distinguishes Spain among the colonial powers of history is the fact that it produced a minority of men who denounced in the face of the world the crimes of their own countrymen and did all in their power to stop what Bartolomé de Las Casas called "the destruction of the Indies."[1]

On the ruins of the old Indian societies Spain laid the foundations of a new colonial order. Two important aspects of that order need to be stressed. One is the mixture of capitalist and feudal elements in its economic structure, its social organization, and its ideology. This blend of feudal and capitalist elements formed part of Spain's (and Portugal's) legacy to independent Latin America and serves to explain the tenacious hold of some anachronistic institutions on the area today.

The other important aspect of that order is the continual struggle, sometimes open, sometimes muffled, between the Spanish crown and the conquistadors and their descendants for control of Indian labor and tribute. In that struggle the colonists gradually gained the upper hand. Spain's decline in the seventeenth century contributed to this shift in the balance of power in favor of the colonists. The emergence in the sixteenth and seventeenth centuries of a hereditary colonial aristocracy rich in land and peons represented a defeat for the crown and for the Indian community whose interests, however feebly and vacillatingly, the crown defended. When in the late eighteenth century Spain's kings sought to tighten their control over the colonies, exclude creoles (American-born Spaniards) from high official posts, and institute reforms that sometimes clashed with creole-vested interests, it was too late. These policies only alienated a powerful colonial elite whose members already felt a dawning sense of nationality and dreamed of the advantages of a free trade with the outside world.

A parallel development occurred during the same period in the relations between Portugal and Brazil. Between 1810 and 1822, American elites, taking advantage of Spain's and Portugal's distresses, seized power in most of Spanish America and Brazil. These aristocratic rebels wanted no radical social changes or economic diversification; their interests as producers of staples for export to western Europe required the continuance of the system of large estates worked by peons or slaves. As a result, independent Latin America inherited almost intact the colonial legacy of a rigidly stratified society and an externally oriented economy dependent on foreign countries for capital and finished goods.

---

[1] From the sixteenth century to the present, defenders of Spain's colonial record have charged Las Casas and other accusers with bias and exaggeration, claiming that they created a "Black Legend" of Spanish cruelty and intolerance. In the process these defenders created a counterlegend, a "White Legend" of Spain's benevolent and enlightened colonial rule; under the Fascist dictatorship of Francisco Franco this became the official version of Spain's work in America.

In fact, every colonial power has its own Black Legend that is no legend but a dismal reality. The brutality of the Spanish Conquest is easily matched, for example, by that of the genocidal Indian wars waged by the United States in the nineteenth century. The Filipino revolt against the imposition of American rule, between 1899 and 1902, was violently repressed with massacres, use of "water torture" to elicit information, and incarceration of civilian populations in concentration camps. General J. Franklin Bell, who took part in that repression, estimated that in Luzon alone over 600,000 people had been killed or died from disease as a result of the war.

Chapter 1

Ancient America

A great number of Indian groups, speaking many different languages and having different ways of life, occupied America at the time of its discovery by Columbus. For at least ten thousand years before European discovery, the New World had existed in virtual isolation from the Old. Sporadic and transient contacts between America and Asia no doubt occurred, and some transfer of culture traits, mainly stylistic embellishments, probably took place through trans-Pacific diffusion. But there is no convincing evidence that people or ideas from China, India, or elsewhere significantly influenced the cultural development of Indian America.

Environment and Culture in Ancient America

During its thousands of years of isolation, America was a unique social laboratory in which the Indians worked out their own destinies, adapting in various ways to their special environments. By 1492 this process had produced results that suggest that the patterns of early human cultural evolution are basically similar the world over. The first Europeans found native groups in much the same stages of cultural development through which parts of the Old World had once passed: Old Stone Age hunters and food gatherers, New Stone Age farmers, and empires as complex as those of Bronze Age Egypt and Mesopotamia.

Racially, the inhabitants of Ancient America were blends of several Asiatic physical types and shared with the modern Indian the typical physical features of dark eyes, straight or wavy black hair, and yellowish or copper skin. Their remote ancestors had probably come from Asia across the Bering Strait in waves of migration that began perhaps as early as forty thousand years ago and continued until about 10,000 B.C.[1] These first-comers brought with them little more than fire, the domesticated dog, a few stone tools and weapons, and some kind of clothing.

Two waves of migrations appear to have taken place. The first brought extremely primitive groups who lived by gathering wild fruit, fishing, and hunting small game. A recent archaeological discovery suggests that these primitive hunters and gatherers passed through Peru about twenty-two thousand years ago. The second series of invasions brought big-game hunters who, like their predecessors, spread out through the continent. By 9000 B.C., these Asiatic invaders or their descendants had reached Patagonia, the southern tip of the continent.

This first colonization of America took place in the last part of the great geological epoch known as the Pleistocene, a period of great climatic changes. Glacial ages, during which blankets of ice covered extensive areas of the Old and New Worlds, alternated with periods of thaw, when temperatures rose to approximately present-day levels. Even in ice-free areas, precipitation often increased markedly during the glacial ages, creating lush growth of pastures and woodlands that supported many varieties of game. Consequently, large sections of America in this period were a hunter's paradise. Over its plains and through its forests roamed many large prehistoric beasts. The projectile points of prehistoric hunters have been found near the remains of such animals from one end of America to the other.

Around 9000 B.C., the retreat of the last great glaciation (the Wisconsin), accompanied by drastic climate changes, caused a crisis for the Indian hunting economy. A warmer, drier climate settled over vast areas. Grasslands decreased, and the large animals that had pastured on them gradually died out. The improved techniques of late Pleistocene hunting also may have contributed to the disappearance of these animals. The hunting folk now had to adapt to their changing environment or vanish with the animals that had sustained them.

Southwestern United States, northern Mexico, and other areas offer archaeological evidence of a successful adjustment to the new conditions. The Indians increasingly turned for food to smaller animals, such as deer and jack rabbits, and to edible wild plants, especially seeds, which were ground into a palatable meal. This new way of life eventually led to the development of agriculture. At first, agriculture merely supplemented the older pursuits of hunting and food collecting; its use hardly constituted an "agricultural revolution." The shift from food gathering to food producing was more likely a gradual accumulation of more and more domesticated plants that gradually replaced the wild edible plants. Over an immensely long period, time and energy formerly devoted to hunting and plant collecting were diverted to such agricultural activities as clearing, planting, weeding, gardening, picking, harvesting, and food preparation. But in the long run, agriculture, in the New World as in the Old, had revolutionary effects: people began to lead a more disciplined and sedentary life, the food

[1] Much controversy surrounds the problem of the approximate date of the first human habitation in America. Some archaeologists argue that no firm evidence exists to refute the traditional view, based on the dating of so-called Folsom stone projectile points found throughout North and South America, that such habitation began about 12,000 years ago. Revisionists point to the discoveries made in recent decades, especially in Chile and Brazil, that suggest a much earlier occupation. Especially startling is the recent discovery of elaborate rock paintings in rock shelters of northeast Brazil. Found by French and Brazilian archaeologists, these paintings are dated 17,000 years ago and other artifacts are dated from 32,000 years ago. In 1989 a new report on these sites claimed that carbon dating and geological analysis indicated that they were occupied by successive groups of people from 45,000 to 5,000 years ago. A factor contributing to the controversy about these discoveries is the difficulty of determining whether the stone and bone artifacts, much cruder than the Folsom points, were actually made by humans or shaped by water or other natural forces.

supply increased, population grew, and division of labor became possible.

In caves in the Mexican highlands, archaeologists have found the wild plants that the Indians gradually domesticated; among the more important are pumpkins, beans, and maize. Domestication of these plants probably occurred between 7000 and 2300 B.C. Among these achievements, none was more significant than the domestication of maize, the mainstay of the great cultures of Ancient America. Manioc (a starchy root cultivated in the tropics as a staple food) and the potato (in Peru) were added to the list of important Indian domesticated plants between 5000 and 1000 B.C.

From its place or places of origin, agriculture swiftly spread over the American continents. By 1492 maize was under cultivation from the northern boundary of present-day United States to Chile. But not all Indian peoples adopted agriculture as a way of life. Some, like the Indians who inhabited the bleak wastes of Tierra del Fuego at the far tip of South America, were forced by severe climatic conditions either to hunt and collect food or starve. Others, like the prosperous, sedentary Indians of the Pacific northwest coast, who lived by waters teeming with fish and forests filled with game, had no reason to abandon their good life in favor of agriculture.

Where agriculture became the principal economic activity, its yield depended on such natural factors as soil fertility and climate and on the farming techniques employed. Forest tribes usually employed the slash-and-burn method of cultivation. Trees and brush were cut down and burned, and maize or other staples were planted in the cleared area with a digging stick. Because this method soon exhausted the soil, the clearing had to be left fallow and a new one made. After this process had gone on long enough, the whole village had to move to a new site or adopt a dispersed pattern of settlement that would allow each family group sufficient land for its needs. Slash-and-burn agriculture thus had a structural weakness that usually sharply limited the cultural development of the Indian peoples who em-

ployed it. That a strong controlling authority could at least temporarily overcome the defects of this method is suggested by the success of the Maya: their brilliant civilization arose in a tropical forest environment on a base of slash-and-burn farming directed by a powerful priesthood, but there is now abundant evidence that from very early times this was supplemented by more intensive methods of agriculture.

A more productive agriculture developed in the rugged highlands of Middle America and the Andean altiplano and on the desert coast of Peru. In such arid or semiarid country, favored with a temperate climate and a naturally rich soil, the land could be tilled more easily and its fertility preserved longer with digging-stick methods. Most important, food production could be increased with the aid of irrigation, which led to larger populations and a greater division of labor. The need for cooperation and regulation on irrigation projects favored the rise of strong central governments and the extension of their authority over larger areas. The Aztec and Inca empires arose in natural settings of this kind.

Finally, the vast number of human groups inhabiting the American continents on the eve of the Spanish Conquest can be classified by their subsistence base and the complexity of their social organization into three levels or categories— tribe, chiefdom, and state. These categories correspond to stages in general cultural evolution. The simplest or most primitive, the *band* and *tribal* level, usually correlated with difficult environments (such as dense forests, plains, or extremely wet, dry, or frigid areas) that sharply limited productivity. The band and tribal level comprises all those small, egalitarian groups based on hunting, fishing, and collecting; on a shifting agriculture; or on a combination of these activities. Hunting and gathering groups were typically nonsedentary, migrating within a given territory in a cyclical pattern according to the seasonal availability of game and edible plants. Groups that supplemented hunting, fishing, and gathering with slash-and-burn agriculture, which usually required making a new clearing after two

egalitarianism of hunting / gathering bands

or three seasons, were semisedentary. The often precarious nature of the subsistence base tended to keep band and tribal population densities low and hinder development of division of labor. The social unit on this level was an autonomous band or a village; a loose association of bands or villages, linked by ties of kinship, real or fictitious, formed a tribe. Social stratification was unknown; all members of the group had access to its hunting and fishing grounds and its land. Village and tribal leaders or chiefs owed their authority to their prowess in battle or other outstanding abilities; the exercise of their authority was limited to the duration of a hunt, a military operation, or some other communal activity.

Typical of these egalitarian societies were many Brazilian tribes of the Amazon basin. A frequent feature of their way of life was constant intertribal warfare whose purpose was to capture prisoners. After being kept for weeks or months the captured warriors were ritually executed and their flesh was cooked and eaten by members of the tribe to gain spiritual strength and perpetuate the tribal feud. The sixteenth-century French philosopher Michel de Montaigne, who read about their customs in travel accounts and met some Brazilian Indians brought to France, was much impressed by their democratic spirit and freedom from the familiar European contrasts of extreme poverty and wealth. He used these impressions to draw an influential literary portrait of the noble savage, the innocent cannibal, who represents a type of moral perfection free from the vices of civilization.

(2) The *chiefdom,* the second category of Indian social organization, represented an intermediate level between primitive tribal societies and more advanced societies featured by social stratification and the state. Most commonly the subsistence base of the chiefdom was intensive farming, which supported a dense population living in large villages. These villages had lost their autonomy and were ruled from an elite center by a paramount chief, who was aided by a hierarchy of subordinate chiefs. Ranking was an important element in chiefdom social organization, but it was defined in kinship terms. Persons were ranked according to their genealogical nearness to the paramount chief, who was often assigned a sacred character and attended by a large retinue of officials and servants. The paramount chief siphoned off the surplus production of the group by requiring tribute payment and forced donations; he used much of this surplus for selective redistribution to officials, retainers, and warriors, thereby enhancing his own power. Warfare between chiefdoms was very common and probably played a decisive role in their origin and expansion through the absorption of neighboring villages. Warfare, leading to the taking of captives who were enslaved and made to labor for their owners, also contributed to the growth of incipient social stratification.

Numerous chiefdoms existed in ancient America on the eve of the Spanish Conquest, with the largest number in the Circum-Caribbean area (including Panama, Costa Rica, northern Colombia, and Venezuela; and the islands of Hispaniola, Puerto Rico, Jamaica, and Cuba). The Cauca Valley of Colombia alone contained no less than eighty chiefdoms.

The complex, densely populated Chibcha or Muisca chiefdoms, located in the eastern highlands of Colombia, may serve to illustrate this level of social and political integration. They rested on a subsistence base of intensive agriculture and fishing, and hunting was an important supplementary activity. The agricultural techniques most likely included terracing and ridged planting beds (raised above wet basin floors to control moisture) as well as slash-and-burn methods. In addition to maize these chiefdoms cultivated potatoes, *quinoa* (a hardy grain resembling buckwheat), and a wide variety of other plants. The crafts—pottery, weaving, and metallurgy—were highly developed. Their magnificent gold work ranks among the finest such work in ancient America.

At the time of the Spanish Conquest, most of the Muisca territory was dominated by two rival chiefdoms, centered at Bogotá and Tunja respectively; the population of the area has been esti-

8

mated at about one and a half million. The Muisca lived in large villages of several hundred to several thousand persons. Each village consisted of pole-and-thatch houses and was surrounded by a palisade. The society was divided into commoners and elites, and membership in both sectors entailed differential rights and obligations. Commoners owed tribute in goods and in labor for the support of the chiefs and nobles, who controlled the distribution and consumption of surplus production.

The chiefdom marks the transition to the next and highest stage of organization, sometimes called *civilization* or more simply the *state* level of social and political integration. The dividing line between the two stages, especially in the case of larger and more complex chiefdoms, is difficult to draw, since the state reflected an expansion and deepening of tendencies already present in the chiefdom. There was a growth of division of labor and specialization, indicated by the formation of artisan groups who no longer engaged in farming, the rise of a priesthood in charge of religious and intellectual activities, the rise of a distinct warrior class, and a bureaucracy entrusted with the administration of the state. These changes were accompanied by intensified social stratification and corresponding ideological changes. The kinship ties that in fact or in theory had united the paramount chief and the elite with the commoners became weakened or dissolved, and there arose a true class structure, with a ruling group claiming a separate origin from the commoners whose labor supported it. At the head of the state stood a priest-king or emperor who was sometimes endowed with divine attributes.

The state level of organization required a technological base of high productivity, usually an intensive agriculture that made large use of irrigation, terracing, and other advanced techniques. The state differed from the chiefdom in its larger size and population, the increased exchange of goods between regions, sometimes accompanied by the emergence of a professional merchant class, and the rise of true cities. In ad-

dition to being population, administrative, and industrial centers, these cities were cult centers often featured by a monumental architecture not found in chiefdoms. The Aztec, Maya, and Inca societies offer the best-known examples of the state level of organization.

What were the decisive factors in the qualitative leap from the chiefdom to the state in ancient America? Scholars do not agree on this point. Some regard warfare leading to territorial conquest as the prime mover in this process; others believe that the state arose primarily as a coercive mechanism to resolve internal conflict between economically stratified classes. Others stress the importance of religious ideology in promoting centralized control by elites over populations and their resources. All these factors played a part in the process of state formation.

What appears certain is that, as we noted above, certain environmental conditions are more favorable than others for the formation of early states, especially of their highest form, empire. Indeed, it is more than doubtful that such states could have arisen in such natural settings as the grassy plains of North America, whose hard sod was impervious to Indian digging sticks, or the Amazonian rain forests, completely unsuitable for farming other than transient slash-and-burn clearings. Specialists often refer to the favored region that combined the necessary environmental conditions for the rise of states and empires as Nuclear America.

Nuclear America

Mexico and Peru were the centers of an extensive Indian high culture area that included central and southern Mexico, Central America, and the Andean zone of South America. This is the heartland of Ancient America, the home of its first agricultural civilizations. Evidence of early village life and the basic techniques of civilization—agriculture, pottery, weaving—has been found in almost every part of this territory.

In recent decades, this region has been the scene of major archaeological discoveries. In the Valley of Mexico, in southern Mexico and on its gulf coast, on the high plateau of Bolivia, and in the desert sands of coastal Peru, excavations have uncovered the remains of splendid temples, mighty fortresses, large cities and towns, and pottery and textiles of exquisite artistry. Combining the testimony of the spade with that provided by Indian and Spanish historical accounts, specialists have attempted to reconstruct the history of Nuclear America. The framework for this effort is a sequence of stages based on the technology, social and political organization, religion, and art of a given period. To this sequence of stages specialists commonly assign the names Archaic, Formative or Preclassic, Classic, and Postclassic. This scheme is tentative in detail, with much chronological overlap between stages and considerable variation in the duration of some periods from area to area.

The *Archaic* stage began about nine thousand years ago when a gradual shift from food gathering and hunting to agriculture began in many parts of Nuclear America. This incipient agriculture, however, did not cause revolutionary changes in Indian society. For thousands of years, people continued to live in much the same primitive fashion as before. Social groups were small and probably seminomadic. Weaving was unknown, but a simple pottery appeared in some areas toward the end of the period.

Between 2500 and 1500 B.C., a major cultural advance in various regions of Nuclear America opened the *Formative,* or *Preclassic,* period. Centuries of haphazard experimentation with plants led to the selection of improved, high-yield varieties. These advances ultimately produced an economy solidly based on agriculture and sedentary village life. Maize and other important domesticated plants were brought under careful cultivation; irrigation came into use in some areas; a few animals were domesticated. By the end of the period, pottery and weaving were highly developed. Increased food production enabled villagers to support a class of priests who acted as intermediaries between people and gods. More abundant food also released labor for the construction of ceremonial sites—mounds of earth topped by temples of wood or thatch.

The social unit of the Formative period was a village community composed of one or more kinship groups, but by the end of the period small chiefdoms uniting several villages had appeared. Since land and food were relatively plentiful and populations small, warfare must have been infrequent. Religion centered on the worship of water and fertility gods; human sacrifice was probably absent or rare.

The advances of the Formative period culminated in the *Classic* period, which began around the opening of the Christian era and lasted until approximately A.D. 1000. The term Classic refers to the flowering of material, intellectual, and artistic culture that marked this stage. There was no basic change in technology, but the extension of irrigation works in some areas caused increases in food production and freed manpower for construction and technical tasks. Population also increased, and in some regions genuine cities arose. Architecture, pottery, and weaving reached an impressive level of style. Metallurgy flourished in Peru, as did astronomy, mathematics, and writing in Mesoamerica (central and south Mexico and adjacent upper Central America). The earlier earth mounds gave way to huge stone-faced pyramids, elaborately ornamented and topped by great temples. The construction of palaces and other official buildings nearby made each ceremonial center the administrative capital of a state ruled by a priest-king. Social stratification was already well developed, with the priesthood the main ruling class. However, the growing incidence of warfare in the late Classic period (perhaps caused by population pressure, with greater competition for land and water) brought more recognition and rewards to successful warriors. Religion became an elaborate polytheism served by a large class of priests.

Typical cultures of the Classic period were the Teotihuacán civilization of central Mexico, the Monte Albán culture in southwestern Mexico,

10

and the lowland Maya culture of southern Yucatán and northern Guatemala. The Olmec civilization of the Mexican gulf lowlands displays some Classic features, but falls within the time span usually allotted to the Formative. In Peru the period is best represented by the brilliant Mochica and Nazca civilizations of the coast. The available evidence suggests that the Classic stage was limited to Mesoamerica, the central Andean area (the highlands and coasts of Peru and Bolivia), and the Ecuadorian coast.

The Classic era ended abruptly in both the northern and southern ends of Nuclear America. Shortly before or after A.D. 1000 most of the great Classic centers in Mesoamerica and Peru were abandoned or destroyed by civil war or foreign invasion. Almost certainly, the fall of these civilizations came as the climax of a longer period of decline. Population pressure, soil erosion, and peasant revolts caused by excessive tribute demands are among the explanations that have been advanced for the collapse of the great Classic city-states and kingdoms.

A Time of Troubles, of obscure struggles and migrations of peoples, followed these disasters. Then new civilizations arose on the ruins of the old. The *Postclassic* stage, from about A.D. 1000 to 1500, seems to have repeated on a larger, more complex scale, the rise-and-fall pattern of the previous era. Chronic warfare, reflected in the number of fortifications and fortified communities, and an increased emphasis on urban living were distinguishing features of this stage. Another was the formation of empires through the subjugation of a number of states by one powerful state. The dominant state appropriated a portion of the production of the conquered people, primarily for the benefit of its ruling classes. The Aztec and Inca empires typify this era.

No important advances in technology occurred in the Postclassic period, but in some regions the net of irrigation works was extended. The continuous growth of warfare and the rise of commerce sharpened economic distinctions between nobles and commoners, between rich and poor. The warrior class replaced the priesthood

as the main ruling class. Imperialism also influenced the character of religion, enhancing the importance of war gods and human sacrifice. The arts and crafts showed some decline from Classic achievements; there was a tendency toward standardization and mass production of textiles and pottery in some areas.

After reaching a peak of power, the empires displayed the same tendency toward disintegration as their Classic forerunners. The Tiahuanaco civilization and the Inca Empire in Peru may have represented two cycles of empire growth, while the first true Mexican imperial cycle, that of the Aztec conquests, had not ended when the Spaniards conquered America.

Three high civilizations, the Aztecs of Mexico, the Maya of Central America, and the Incas of Peru, have held the center of attention to the virtual exclusion of the others. This partiality is understandable. We know more about these peoples and their ways of life. The Aztec and Inca civilizations still flourished at the coming of the Spaniards, and some conquistadors wrote vivid accounts of what they saw. The colorful story of the Conquest of Mexico and Peru and the unhappy fate of their emperors Moctezuma (Montezuma) and Atahualpa have also served to focus historical and literary attention on the Aztecs and the Incas. Unfortunately, the fame and glamour surrounding these peoples have obscured the achievements of their predecessors, who laid the cultural foundations on which the Maya, Aztecs, and Incas built.

The Aztecs of Mexico

At the opening of the sixteenth century, most of central Mexico, from the fringes of the arid northern plateau southward to the lowlands of Tehuantepec, paid tribute to the Aztecs of the Valley of Mexico. These Aztecs were latecomers in a region that had been the home of highly developed civilizations for almost a thousand years before their arrival.

The Olmec culture of the Mexican gulf lowlands produced powerful stone sculpture that featured colossal heads—like this one found at San Lorenzo, Veracruz. (From *Mexico* by Michael D. Coe. Published by Thames & Hudson Inc. Copyright © 1962, 1977, and 1984 Michael D. Coe. Reprinted by permission.)

Pre-Aztec Civilizations

As early as 1000 B.C., the inhabitants of the Valley of Mexico lived in small villages set in the midst of their maize, bean, and squash fields. They cultivated the land with slash-and-burn methods, produced a simple but well-made pottery, and turned out large numbers of small clay figures that suggest a belief in fertility goddesses. By the opening of the Old World's Christian era, small flat-topped mounds appeared, evidence of a more formal religion and directing priesthood.

Much earlier (perhaps spanning the period 1500 to 400 B.C.), arose the precocious and enigmatic Olmec civilization of the gulf coast lowlands, whose influence radiated widely into the central Mexican plateau and Central America.

The origins, development, and disappearance of the Olmec culture remain a mystery.

Important elements of the Olmec civilization were its ceremonial centers, monumental stone carving and sculpture (including the famous colossal heads whose significance is conjectural), hieroglyphic writing, and probably a calendrical system. The principal Olmec sites are La Venta and Tres Zapotes, in the modern state of Veracruz. Discovery of Olmec culture and evidence of the wide diffusion of its art style have made untenable the older view that Maya civilization was the first in Mesoamerica. It seems likely that Olmec culture was the mother civilization of Mesoamerica.

12

The technical, artistic, and scientific advances of the Formative period made possible the climactic cultural achievements of the Classic era. In Mexico's central highlands, the Classic period opened in splendor. About the beginning of the Christian era, at Teotihuacán, some twenty-eight miles from Mexico City, arose the mighty pyramids later given the names of the Sun and the Moon, which towered over clusters of imposing temples and other buildings. The stone sculpture used in the decoration of the temples, as well as the marvelous grace and finish of the cement work and the fresco painting, testify to the high development of the arts among the Teotihuacáns. The ancient water god, known to the Aztecs as Tlaloc, seems to have been the chief deity. But the feathered serpent with jaguar fangs, later known as Quetzalcóatl, is also identified with water and fertility and appears prominently in the greatest temple. There is little evidence of war or human sacrifice until a relatively late phase. Priests in benign poses and wearing the symbols of their gods dominate the mural paintings.

This great ceremonial center at Teotihuacán was sacred ground. Probably only the priestly nobility and their servants lived here. Farther out were the residential quarters inhabited by officials, artisans, and merchants. Teotihuacán is estimated to have had a population of at least 50,000. On the outskirts of the city, which covered an area of seven square miles, lived a large rural population that supplied the metropolis with its food. It is likely that an intensive agriculture using canal irrigation and terracing on hillslopes formed the economic foundation of the Teotihuacán civilization. Despite the predominantly peaceful aspect of its religion and art, Teotihuacán seems to have been not only a major trading center but also a military state that directly controlled regions as remote as highland Guatemala.

Contemporary with Teotihuacán, but overshadowed by that great city, were other centers of Classic culture in Mesoamerica. To the southwest, at Monte Albán in the rugged mountains of Oaxaca, the Zapotecs erected a great ceremonial center that was also a true city. One of their achievements, probably of Olmec origin, was a complicated system of hieroglyphic writing. In the same period, the Maya Classic civilization flowered in the Petén region of northern Guatemala.

By A.D. 800, the Mesoamerican world had been shaken to its foundations by a crisis that seemed to spread from one Classic center to another. Teotihuacán, Rome of that world, itself perished at the hands of invaders, who burned down the city sometime between A.D. 650 and 800. Toward the latter date, the great ceremonial center at Monte Albán was abandoned. And by A.D. 800, the process of disintegration had reached the Classic Maya heartland of southern Yucatán and northern Guatemala, whose deserted or destroyed centers reverted one by one to the bush.

From this Time of Troubles in Mesoamerica (approximately A.D. 700 to 1000) a new Postclassic order emerged, sometimes appropriately called Militarist. Whereas priests and benign nature gods may have sometimes presided over Mesoamerican societies of the Classic era, warriors and terrible war gods clearly dominated the states that arose on the ruins of the Classic world. In central Mexico the sway of Teotihuacán, probably based above all on cultural and economic supremacy, gave way to strife among new states that warred with one another for land, water, and tribute.

The most important of these, successor to the power of Teotihuacán, was the Toltec "empire," with its capital at Tula, about fifty miles from present-day Mexico City. Lying on the periphery of the Valley of Mexico, Tula may have once been an outpost of Teotihuacán, guarding its frontiers against the hunting tribes of the northern deserts. Following the collapse of Teotihuacán, one such tribe, the Toltecs, swept down from the north, entered the Valley of Mexico, and overwhelmed the pitiful survivors among the Teotihuacán people.

Toltec power and prosperity reached its peak under a ruler named Topiltzin, who moved his capital to Tula in about 980. Apparently renamed Quetzalcóatl in his capacity of high priest of the ancient god worshiped by the Teotihuacáns, Topiltzin-Quetzalcóatl reigned for nineteen years with such splendor that he and his city became legendary. The Song of Quetzalcóatl tells of the wonders of Tula, a true paradise on earth where cotton grew colored and the soil yielded fruit of such size that small ears of corn were used, not as food, but as fuel to heat steam baths. The legends of ancient Mexico celebrate the Toltecs' superhuman powers and talents; they were described as master artisans, as creators of culture. Over this Golden Age presided the great priest-king Quetzalcóatl, who thus revived the glories of Teotihuacán.

Toward the end of Quetzalcóatl's reign, Tula seems to have become the scene of an obscure struggle between two religious traditions. One was associated with the worship of Tezcatlipoca, a Toltec tribal god pictured as an all-powerful and capricious deity who demanded human sacrifice. The other was identified with the cult of the ancient god Quetzalcóatl, who had brought men and women maize, all learning, and the arts. In a version of the Quetzalcóatl legend that may reflect post-Conquest Christian influence, the god demanded of them only the peaceful sacrifice of jade, snakes, and butterflies. This struggle found fanciful expression in the native legend that tells how the black magic of the enchanter Tezcatlipoca caused the saintly priest-king Quetzalcóatl to fall from grace and drove him into exile from Tula.

Whatever its actual basis, the Quetzalcóatl legend, with its promise that an Indian Redeemer would someday return to reclaim his kingdom, profoundly impressed the people of ancient Mexico and played its part in the destruction of the Aztec Empire. By a singular coincidence, the year in the Aztec cycle of years in which Quetzalcóatl promised to return was the very year in which Cortés landed at Veracruz. Aztec belief in the legend helps to explain the vacillation and contradictory moves of the doomed Moctezuma.

Topiltzin-Quetzalcóatl was succeeded by lesser kings, who vainly struggled to solve the growing problems of the Toltec state. The causes of this crisis are obscure: tremendous droughts may have caused crop failure and famines, perhaps aggravated by Toltec neglect of agriculture in favor of collection of tribute from conquered peoples. A series of revolutions reflected the Toltec economic and social difficulties. The last Toltec king, Huemac, apparently committed suicide about 1174, and the Toltec state disappeared with him. In the following year, a general dispersion or exodus of the Toltecs took place. Tula itself fell into the hands of barbarians in about 1224.

The fall of Tula, situated on the margins of the Valley of Mexico, opened the way for a general invasion of the valley by Nahuatl-speaking northern peoples. These newcomers, called Chichimecs, may be compared to the Germanic invaders who broke into the dying Roman Empire. Like them, the Chichimec leaders respected and tried to absorb the superior culture of the vanquished people. They were eager to intermarry with the surviving Toltec royalty and nobility.

These invaders founded a number of succession-states in the lake country at the bottom of the Valley of Mexico. Legitimately or not, their rulers all claimed the honor of Toltec descent. In artistic and industrial development, the Texcocan kingdom, organized in 1260, easily excelled its neighbors. Texcocan civilization reached its climactic moment two centuries later in the reign of King Nezahualcoyotl (1418–1472), distinguished poet, philosopher, and lawgiver, perhaps the most remarkable figure to emerge from the mists of Ancient America.

The Arrival of the Aztecs

Among the last of the Chichimec tribes to arrive in the valley were the Aztecs, or Mexica. The date of their departure from the north was probably about A.D. 1111. Led by four priests and a woman who carried a medicine bundle housing the spirit of their tribal god, Huitzilopochtli, they arrived in the Valley of Mexico in about 1218 after obscure wanderings. The traditional belief that they were basically a hunting and gathering people who were only "half-civilized" but had some acquaintance with agriculture, has recently been questioned by some scholars. Some now hold that by the time of their arrival the Aztecs were typically Mesoamerican in culture, religion, and economic and social organization. Finding the most desirable sites occupied by other tribes, they had to take refuge on marshy lands around Lake Texcoco. Here in 1344 or 1345, they began to build the town of Tenochtitlán. At this time, the Aztec tribe was composed of a small number of kinship groups called *calpulli.*

The patches of solid ground that formed the Aztec territory were gradually built over with huts of cane and reeds. They were followed later by more ambitious structures of turf, adobe, and light stone. As the population increased, a larger cultivable area became necessary. For this purpose the Aztecs borrowed from their neighbors the technique of making *chinampas*—artificial garden beds formed of masses of earth and rich sediment dredged from the lake bed and held in place by wickerwork. Eventually the roots, striking downward, took firm hold in the lake bottom and created solid ground. On these chinampas the Aztecs grew maize, beans, and other products.

For a long time, the Aztecs were subservient to their powerful neighbors in Azcapotzalco, the dominant power in the lake country in the late fourteenth and early fifteenth centuries. A turning point in Aztec history came in 1428. Led by their new war chief Itzcoatl, the Aztecs joined the rebellious city-state of Texcoco and the smaller town of Tlacopan to destroy the tyranny of Azcapotzalco. Their joint victory (1430) led to the rise of a Triple Alliance for the conquest first of the valley, then of much of the Middle American world. Gradually, the balance of power shifted to the aggressive Aztec state. Texcoco became a junior partner, and Tlacopan was reduced to a satellite. The strong position of their island fortification and a shrewd policy of forming alliances and sharing the spoils of conquest with strategic mainland towns, which they later came to dominate, help to explain Aztec success in gaining control of the Valley of Mexico. In turn, conquest of the valley offered a key to the conquest of Middle America. The valley possessed the advantages of short internal lines of communication surrounded by easily defensible mountain barriers. Openings to the north, east, west, and south gave Aztec warriors easy access to adjacent valleys.

Conquest of Azcapotzalco gave the Aztecs their first beachhead on the lakeshore. Most of the conquered land and the peasantry living on it were assigned to warrior-nobles who had distinguished themselves in battle. Originally assigned for life, these lands tended to become fiefs held in permanent inheritance. Thus, warfare created new economic and social cleavages within Aztec society. In the process the kinship basis of the calpulli was partly eroded and it lost most of its autonomy, becoming primarily a social and territorial administrative unit. Composed mostly of *macehualtin* (commoners) who owed tribute, labor, and military service to the Aztec state, the calpullis continued to be governed by hereditary elite families who were completely subject to superior Aztec officials whose orders they carried out. The communal landownership traditionally associated with the calpulli also suffered erosion as a result of growing population pressure on land and internal economic differentiation; by the time of the Conquest landlessness and tenant farming appear to have become fairly widespread, with *mayeques* (unfree peasants) forming perhaps 30 percent of the Aztec population. The growing cleavage between commoners and nobles found ideological reflection in the origin myth that claimed a separate divine origin (from the god Quetzalcóatl) for the Aztec nobility.

Other ideological changes included the elevation of the tribal god Huitzilopochtli to a position of equality with, or supremacy over, the great gods traditionally worshiped in the Valley of Mexico, the burning of the ancient picture writings because these books slighted the Aztecs, and the creation of a new history that recognized the Az-

These drawings, which are taken from Fray Sahagún's sixteenth-century *History of the Things of New Spain,* Codex Florentino, show how this Aztec farmer used a digging stick to sow his seeds and harvest the crop. The drawing on the left shows the farmer arranging a display of his produce for sale. (From *The Cities of Ancient Mexico,* Jeremy A. Sabloff. Thames and Hudson. Reprinted by permission of the publisher.)

tec grandeur. A new emphasis was placed on capturing prisoners of war to use as sacrifices on the altars of the Aztec gods in order to assure the continuance of the universe.[2]

[2] Some social scientists have attempted to explain the Aztec practice of mass human sacrifice and its accompaniment of ritual cannibalism by the lack of protein in the Aztec diet. This theory is contradicted by the variety of animal foods available to the Aztecs and by the fact that neither Indian nor Spanish sources refer to the practice of cannibalism during the great famine that hastened the end of Aztec resistance to the Spanish conquest. For the rest, the sacramental feast, designed to let participants share the grace of the god to whom the prisoner was sacrificed, was simplicity itself; and the captor could not eat of his flesh because of an assumed mystical kinship relationship between the captor and his prisoner.

The successors of Itzcoatl, sometimes individually, sometimes in alliance with Texcoco, extended Aztec rule over and beyond the Valley of Mexico. By the time Moctezuma II became ruler in 1502, the Triple Alliance was levying tribute on scores of towns, large and small, from the fringes of the arid northern plateau to the lowlands of Tehuantepec, and from the Atlantic to the Pacific. Within this extensive area only a few states or kingdoms, like the fierce Tarascans' state or the city-state of Tlaxcala, retained complete independence. Others, like Cholula, were left at peace in return for their benevolent neutrality or cooperation with the Aztecs. According to some controversial modern estimates, the Aztecs and their allies ruled over a population of perhaps 25 million.

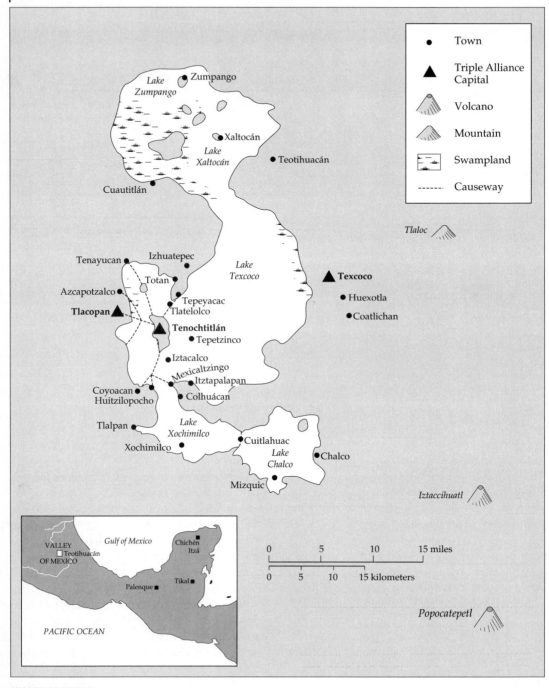

VALLEY OF MEXICO

The Aztecs waged war with or without cause. Refusal by a group to pay tribute to the Aztec ruler was sufficient pretext for invasion by the Aztecs. Injuries to the far-ranging Aztec merchants by people of the region they visited sometimes served as motive for invasion. Aztec merchants also prepared the way for conquest by reporting on the resources and defenses of the areas in which they traded; sometimes they acted as spies in hostile territory. If they returned home safely, these valiant merchants were honored by the ruler with amber lip plugs and other gifts. If their enemies discovered them, however, the consequences were horrid. "They were slain in ambush and served up with chili sauce," says a native account.

Victory in war always had the same results: Long lines of captives made the long journey to Tenochtitlán to be offered up on the altars of the gods. In addition, periodic tribute payments of maize, cotton mantles, cacao beans, or other products—depending on the geography and resources of the region—were imposed on the vanquished. Certain lands were also set aside to be cultivated by them for the support of the Aztec crown, priesthood, and state officials or as fiefs given to warriors who had distinguished themselves in battle. A steward or tribute collector, sometimes assisted by a resident garrison, was stationed in the town. For the rest, as a rule the conquered people continued to enjoy autonomy in government, culture, and customs.

Because of its nonintegrated character—reflected in the relative autonomy enjoyed by vanquished peoples and the light Aztec political and military presence in conquered territories—the Aztec empire has traditionally been regarded as an inferior or deficient political organization in comparison with the Inca empire, with its centralized administration, standing armies, massive transfers of populations, and other integrative policies. Recently, however, it has been argued that rather than inferior the Aztec imperial system represented an alternative—but no less efficient—approach to the problem of extracting surplus from tributary peoples at a minimal administrative and military cost. The Aztec army mobilized only for further conquests and the suppression of rebellions. By leaving the defeated regimes in place and avoiding direct territorial control, the Aztec state was spared the expense, inherent in a more integrated empire, of maintaining provincial administrations, standing armies, permanent garrisons, and fortifications.

Aztec Culture and Society

The Aztec capital of Tenochtitlán had a population estimated to be between 150,000 and 200,000. An Indian Venice, the city was an oval island connected to the mainland by three causeways that converged at the center of the city and served as its main arteries of traffic. There were few streets; their place was taken by numerous canals, thronged with canoes and bordered by footpaths giving access to the thousands of houses that lined their sides. An aqueduct in solid masonry brought fresh water from the mountain springs of Chapultepec.

On the outlying chinampas, the Aztec farmers, who paddled their produce to town in tiny dugouts, lived in huts with thatched roofs resting on walls of wattle smeared with mud. Inside each hut were a three-legged *metate* (grinding stone), a few mats that served as beds and seats, some pottery, and little more. The majority of the population—artisans, priests, civil servants, soldiers, and entertainers—lived in more imposing houses. These were sometimes built of adobe, sometimes of a reddish *tezontli* lava, but they were always lime-washed and painted. Far more pretentious than most were the houses of calpulli leaders, merchants, and nobles.

As in housing, Aztec clothing differed according to the individual's economic and social status. For men the essential garments were a loincloth with broad flaps at front and back, usually decorated with fringes and tassels as well as embroidery work, and a blanket about two yards by one in size. This blanket hung under the left arm and was knotted on the right shoulder. Commoners wore plain blankets of maguey fiber or coarse cotton; rich merchants and nobles displayed very elaborate cotton mantles adorned with symbolic designs. Women wore shifts, wraparound skirts of white cotton tied with a narrow belt, and loose, short-sleeved tunics. Both shifts and tunics were decorated with vivid embroidery. Men wore sandals of leather or woven maguey fiber; women went barefoot.

As with dress, so with food: wealth and social position determined its abundance and variety. The fare of the ordinary Aztec consisted of ground maize meal, beans, and vegetables cooked with chili. Meat was rarely seen on the commoner's table, but on festive occasions a dog might be served. It was otherwise with the nobility. A native account of the foods eaten by the lords includes many varieties of tortillas and tamales, roast turkey hen, roast quail, turkey with a sauce of small chilies, tomatoes, and ground squash seeds, venison sprinkled with seeds, many kinds of fish and fruits—and such delicacies as maguey grubs with a sauce of small chilies, winged ants with savory herbs, and rats with sauce. They finished their repast with chocolate, a divine beverage forbidden to commoners.

Education among the Aztecs was highly formal and served the dual purpose of preparing the child for his or her duties in the world and of indoctrinating him or her with the ideals of the tribe. Boys were sent to school at the age of ten or twelve. Sons of commoners, merchants, and artisans attended the *Telpochcalli* (House of Youth), where they received instruction in religion, good usage, and the art of war. The *Calmecac* (Priests' House), a school of higher learning, was reserved in principle for the sons of the nobility, but there is evidence that at least some children of merchants and commoners were admitted. Here, in addition to ordinary training, students received instruction that prepared them to be priests, public officials, and military leaders. The curriculum included what we would today call rhetoric, or a noble manner of speaking, study of religious and philosophical doctrines as revealed in the divine songs of the sacred books,

the arts of chronology and astrology, and training in history through study of the *Xiuhamatl* (Books of the Years). The *tlamatinime* (sages) who taught in the Aztec schools were also concerned with the formation of "a true face and heart," the striking Nahuatl metaphor for personality. Self-restraint, moderation, devotion to duty, a stoic awareness that "life is short and filled with hardships, and all comes to an end," an impeccable civility, modesty: these were among the qualities and concepts that the Aztec sages instilled in their charges.

Girls had special schools where they were taught such temple duties as sweeping, offering incense three times during the night, and preparing food for the idols; weaving and other womanly tasks; and general preparation for marriage. Education for the men usually terminated at the age of twenty or twenty-two; for girls, at sixteen or seventeen. These were also the ages at which marriage was contracted.

In a society with such a complex economic and social life, disputes and aggressions inevitably arose and necessitated the development of an elaborate legal code. A hierarchy of courts was topped by two high tribunals that met in the royal palace in Tenochtitlán. The punishments of the Aztecs were severe. Death was the penalty for murder, rebellion, wearing the clothes of the other sex, and adultery; theft was punished by slavery for the first offense, by hanging for the second.

Economic life in Aztec Mexico rested on a base of intensive and extensive agriculture. Intensive irrigation was practiced in areas with reliable water sources; its most notable form was that of the chinampas. Slash-and-burn cultivation, with field rotation, was the rule in other areas, but everywhere maize and beans were the principal crops. In the absence of large domesticated animals to produce manure, night soil was regularly used as fertilizer in chinampa agriculture in the Valley of Mexico. To prevent contamination of the valley's two freshwater lakes by flows of water from the saline ones that were harmful to chinampa agriculture, and to maintain the fairly constant water level that it required, the construction of an elaborate system of dikes, canals, and aqueducts was begun during the reign of King Itzcoatl. This led to the creation of large chinampa areas producing foodstuffs for Tenochtitlán. Productive as they were, however, it is estimated that they accounted for only 5 percent of the city's subsistence needs, and their expansion was limited by the salinity of the remaining lakes. For the balance of its food needs, therefore, Tenochtitlán had to rely on imports obtained by way of tribute and trade. An elaborate, state-controlled trade and transportation network based on regional and metropolitan markets, the *tlameme* (professional carrier) system of portage, and an efficient canoe traffic that linked the entire lake system of the Valley of Mexico funneled a vast quantity of foodstuffs and other bulk goods into Tenochtitlán. Manufactured goods were then exported from Tenochtitlán to its hinterlands, forming a core-periphery relationship.

The vast scale on which the exchange of goods and services was carried on in the great market of Tenochtitlán aroused the astonishment of the conquistador Cortés, who gave a detailed account of its immense activity. "Each kind of merchandise is sold in its respective street," he wrote, "and they do not mix their kinds of merchandise of any species; thus they preserve perfect order." The Aztecs lacked a unitary system of money, but cacao beans, cotton mantles, quills filled with gold dust, and small copper axes were assigned standardized values and supplemented a barter system of exchange. The Aztecs had no scales; goods were sold by count and measure. The market was patrolled by officials who checked on the fairness of transactions; a merchants' court sat to hear and settle disputes between buyers and sellers.

As the above account implies, by the time of the Conquest division of labor among the Aztecs had progressed to the point where a large class of artisans no longer engaged in agriculture. The artisan class included carpenters, potters, stonemasons, silversmiths, and featherworkers. In the same category belonged such specialists as fishermen, hunters, dancers, and musicians. All these specialists were organized in guilds, each with its guildhall and patron god; their professions were probably hereditary. The artist and the craftsman enjoyed a position of high honor and responsibility in Aztec society. Assigning the origin of all their arts and crafts to the Toltec period, the Aztecs applied the name Toltec to the true or master painter, singer, potter, or sculptor.

Advances in regional division of labor and the growth of the market for luxury goods also led to the emergence of a merchant class, which was organized in a very powerful guild. The wealth of this class and its important military and diplomatic services to the Aztec state made the merchants a third force in Aztec society, ranking only after the warrior nobility and the priesthood. The wealth of the merchants sometimes aroused the distrust and hostility of the Aztec rulers and nobility. Popular animosity toward the merchants is reflected in the words of a native account: "The merchants were those who had plenty, who prospered; the greedy, the well-fed man, the covetous, the niggardly, the miser, who controlled wealth and family ... the mean, the stingy, the selfish."

The priesthood was the main integrating force in Aztec society. Through its possession of a sacred calendar that regulated the performance of agricultural tasks, it played a key role in the life of the people. The priesthood was also the repository of the accumulated lore and history of the Aztec tribe. By virtue of his special powers of intercession with the gods, his knowledge and wisdom, the priest was called on to intervene in every private or collective crisis of the Aztec. Celibate, austere, continually engaged in the penance of bloodletting, priests wielded an enormous influence over the Aztec people.

The priesthood shared authority and prestige with the nobility, a class that had gained power through war and political centralization. In addition to many warriors, this class consisted of a large bureaucracy made up of tribute collectors, judges, ambassadors, and the like. Such office-holders were rewarded for their services by the revenue from public lands assigned to support them. Their offices were not hereditary. They were, however, normally conferred on sons of fathers who had held the same positions.

The wealth of the warrior nobility consisted chiefly of landed estates. Originally granted for life, these lands eventually became private estates that were handed down from father to son and could be sold or exchanged. The former free peasants on these lands were probably transformed into mayeques, farm workers or tenant farmers tied to the land. With the expansion of the Aztec Empire, the number of private estates steadily grew.

On the margins of Aztec society was a large class of slaves. Slavery was the punishment for a variety of offenses, including failure to pay debts. Slavery was sometimes assumed by poor people in return for food. Slave owners frequently brought their chattels to the great market at Atzcapotzalco for sale to rich merchants or nobles for personal service or as sacrificial offerings to the gods.

The Aztec political system on the eve of the Conquest was a mixture of royal despotism and theocracy. Political power was concentrated in a ruling class of priests and nobles, over which presided an absolute ruler resembling an Oriental despot. Originally, the ruler had been chosen by the whole Aztec tribe, assembled for that purpose. Later he was chosen by a tribal council or electoral college dominated by the most important priests, officials, and warriors, including close relatives of the king. The council, in consultation with the kings of Texcoco and Tlacopan, selected the monarch from among the sons, brothers, or nephews of the previous ruler. The new ruler was assisted by a council of four great nobles. At the time of the Conquest the emperor was the luckless Moctezuma II, who succeeded his uncle Ahuitzotl.

Barbaric splendor and intricate ceremonies prevailed in Moctezuma's court. The great nobles of the realm took off their rich ornaments of feather, jade, and gold before entering his presence; barefoot, eyes on the ground, they approached the basketry throne of their king. Moctezuma dined in solitary magnificence, separated by a wooden screen from his servitors and the four great lords with whom he conversed.

This wealth, luxury, and ceremony revealed the great social and economic changes that had taken place in the small, despised Aztec tribe that came to live in the marshes of Lake Texcoco less than two centuries before. The Aztec Empire had reached a peak of pride and power. Yet the Aztec leaders lived in fear; the Aztec chronicles register a deep sense of insecurity. The mounting demands of the Aztec tribute collectors caused revolts on the part of tributary towns. Though repressed, they broke out afresh. The haunted Aztec imagination saw portents of evil on earth and in the troubled air. A child was born with two heads; the volcano Popocatepetl became unusually active; a comet streamed across the sky. The year 1519 approached, the year in which according to Aztec lore the god-king Quetzalcóatl might return to reclaim the realm from which he had been driven centuries before by the forces of evil.

The Maya of Central America

If the Aztecs excelled in war and conquest, the Maya were preeminent in cultural achievement. Certainly, no other Indian group ever demonstrated such extraordinary abilities in architecture, sculpture, painting, mathematics, and astronomy.

The ancient Maya lived in a region comprising portions of modern-day southeastern Mexico, almost all of Guatemala, the western part of Honduras, all of Belize, and the western half of El Salvador. But the Maya civilization attained its highest development in the tropical forest lowland area whose core is the Petén region of Guatemala, at the base of the Yucatán Peninsula. This

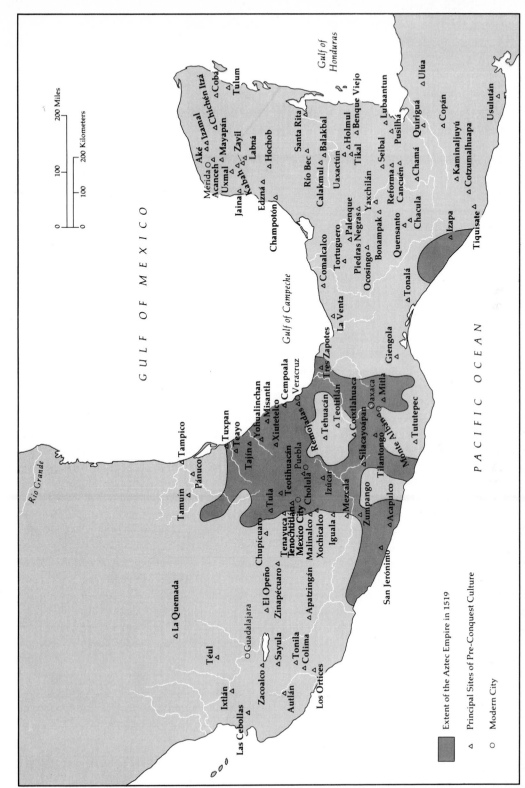

PRINCIPAL SITES OF PRE-CONQUEST CULTURE IN MESOAMERICA

was the primary center of Maya Classic civilization from about A.D. 250 to 900.[3] The region was rich in wild game and building materials (limestone and fine hardwoods). In almost every other respect it offered immense obstacles to the establishment of a high culture. Clearing the dense forests for planting and controlling weeds were extremely difficult tasks with the primitive implements available. There was no metal, the water supply was uncertain, and communication facilities were poor. Yet it was here that the Maya built some of their largest ceremonial centers.

The contrast between the forbidding environment and the Maya achievement led some specialists to speculate that Maya culture was a transplant from some other, more favorable area. This view has been made obsolete by the discovery of long Preclassic sequences at lowland sites. There is, however, linguistic and archaeological evidence that the lowland Maya were descendants of groups who lived in or near the Olmec area before 1000 B.C. and who brought with them the essential elements of Mesoamerican civilization. In time they developed these elements into their own unique achievements in the sciences, art, and architecture.

Just as puzzling as the rise of the Maya lowland culture in such an inhospitable setting is the dramatic decline that led to a gradual cessation of building activity and eventual abandonment of the ceremonial centers after A.D. 800. Specialists have advanced various explanations for this decline. They include soil exhaustion as a result of slash-and-burn farming, invasion of cornfields by grasslands from the same cause, failure of the water supply, peasant revolts against the ruling priesthood, and the disruptive effects of the fall of Teotihuacán, which had close commercial and

political ties with the Maya area. None of these explanations by itself, however, appears completely satisfactory.

Recently a more complex explanation of the Classic Maya collapse has emerged. According to this theory, the cessation of political and commercial contacts with Teotihuacán after about A.D. 550 led to a breakdown of centralized authority—perhaps previously exerted by Tikal, the largest and most important ceremonial center of the southern lowlands—and increased autonomy of local Maya elites. These elites expressed their pride and power by constructing ever more elaborate ceremonial centers, which added to the burdens of commoners. Growing population size and density strained food resources and forced the adoption of more intensive agricultural methods. These, in turn, increased competition for land, which was reflected in the growth of warfare and militarism. Improved agricultural production relieved population pressures for a time and made possible the late Classic flowering (A.D. 600–800), marked by a revival of ceremonial center construction, architecture, and the arts. But renewed population pressures, food shortages, and warfare between regional centers, perhaps aggravated by external attacks, led to a severe cultural and social decline in the last century of the Classic period. The build-up of pressure—so runs the theory—"resulted in a swift and catastrophic collapse accompanied by widespread depopulation through warfare, malnutrition, and disaster, until those who survived were again able to achieve a stable agricultural society at a much lower level of population density and social organization."[4]

No such decline occurred in northern Yucatán, a low, limestone plain covered in most places with dense thickets of thorny scrub forest. This area had been occupied by the Maya fully as long as the south, although with less impressive cultural achievements. But here, too, there arose

[3] Recent archaelogical discoveries, however, are revolutionizing the dates traditionally assigned to the Maya Classic period. The newly discovered city of Nakbé in the dense tropical forest of northern Guatemala, containing extensive stone monuments and temples, is dated from 600 to 400 B.C., pushing the Classic era back into the time span commonly assigned to the Formative or Preclassic period.

[4] Norman Hammond, *Ancient Maya Civilization* (New Brunswick, N.J.: Rutgers University Press, 1982), p. 140.

great ceremonial centers complete with steep pyramids, multistoried palaces, and large quadrangles. Into this area, in about 900, poured invaders from the central Mexican highlands, probably Toltec emigrants from strife-torn Tula. Toltec armies overran northern Yucatán and established their rule over the Maya, governing from the temple city of Chichén Itzá. The invaders introduced Toltec styles in art and architecture, including colonnaded halls, warrior columns, and the reclining stone figures called Chac Mools. Toltec influence was also reflected in an increased obsession with human sacrifice. After 1200, Maya cultural and political influence revived. Chichén Itzá was abandoned, and power passed to the city-state of Mayapan, a large, walled town from which Maya rulers dominated much of the peninsula, holding tribal chiefs and their families as hostages to exact tribute from surrounding provinces. But in the fifteenth century, virtually all centralized rule disappeared. A successful revolt overthrew the tyranny of Mayapan and destroyed the city itself in 1441. By this time, Maya civilization was in full decline. By the arrival of the Spaniards, all political unity or imperial organization in the area had disappeared.

Maya Economy and Society

Archaeological discoveries of the past three decades have radically revised our notions about the subsistence base of the ancient Maya. Until recently, the prevailing view assumed the primary role of maize in the diet and the almost exclusive reliance on the slash-and-burn (swidden) system of agriculture. Since this system excluded the possibility of such dense populations as were found at Teotihuacán and other Mesoamerican Classic or Postclassic centers, the traditional interpretation assumed a dispersed peasant population whose houses—typically one-room pole-and-thatch structures—were widely scattered or grouped in small hamlets across the countryside between the ceremonial and administrative centers. These centers, containing temples, pyramids, ritual ball courts, and other structures,

were denied the character of true "cities"; it was believed that only the Maya elites—a few priests, nobles, and officials and their attendants—lived in them. The rural population, on the other hand, living out among their *milpas* (farm plots), only visited these centers for religious festivals and other special occasions.

This traditional view began to be seriously questioned in the late 1950s, when detailed mapping of the area around the Tikal ceremonial precinct revealed that dense suburbs spread out behind the center for several miles. Similar dense concentrations of house clusters were later found at other major and even minor centers of the Classic period. In the words of Norman Hammond, "the wide-open spaces between the Maya centers, with their scattered bucolic farmers, suddenly became filled with closely packed and hungry suburbanites."

These revelations of the size and density of Classic Maya settlements forced a reassessment of the economic system that supported them. It has now been clearly established that, in addition to slash-and-burn farming, the Maya practiced an intensive and permanent agriculture that included highly productive kitchen gardens with root crops as staples, arboriculture, terracing, and raised fields—artificial platforms of soil built up from low-lying areas.

The evidence of dense suburban populations around ceremonial centers like Tikal has also provoked a debate about the degree of urbanism present in the Maya lowlands. The traditional view that the Classic Maya centers were virtually deserted for most of the year has become untenable. There is, however, no agreement as to whether they were "cities" in the sense that Teotihuacán was clearly a city. Tikal, in the heart of the Petén, was certainly a metropolitan center with a population of perhaps 50,000 and a countryside heavily populated over an area of some fifty square miles. There is also evidence of some genuine urbanization in northern Yucatán during the Postclassic period, possibly a result of Toltec influence and the tendency to develop the city or town as a fortified position. Chichén Itzá, an old

Ritual ball courts were for a game in which the players used their hips, thighs, and arms to knock a heavy rubber ball through a stone ring located about twenty-five feet above the court. In this picture, from the Codex Magliabecchi, the stone rings are shown outside the court. (From *The Cities of Ancient Mexico,* Jeremy A. Sabloff. Thames and Hudson. Reprinted by permission of the publisher.)

Classic ceremonial center, was greatly enlarged under Toltec influence, while Mayapan, which succeeded Chichén Itzá as a political and military center, constituted a large urban zone encircled by a great wall.

Awareness of the large size and density of Classic Maya populations, the intensive character of much of their agriculture, and the strict social controls that such complex conditions require has also led to a reassessment of Maya social organization. The older view that the ruling class was a small theocratic elite that ruled over a dispersed peasant population from basically

empty ceremonial centers has been abandoned. Increased ability to decipher glyphs on the stelae (carved monuments) periodically erected at Classic Maya centers has contributed to a better understanding of the Maya social order. It was once believed that the content of these inscriptions was exclusively religious and astronomical. In recent decades, however, evidence has accumulated that many of the glyphs carved on stelae, lintels, and other monuments record accessions, wars, and other milestones in the lives of secular rulers. The new interpretation assumes a very complex social order with large distance between the classes. At the apex of the social pyramid stood a hereditary ruler who combined the political, military, and religious leadership of the state. He was surrounded by an aristocracy or nobility, from which were drawn the administrative and executive bureaucracy. Intellectual specialists such as architects, priests, and scribes may have formed another social level. Below them were the numerous artisans required for ceremonial and civil construction—potters, sculptors, stoneworkers, painters, and the like. At the bottom of the social pyramid were the common laborers and peasant farmers who supplied the labor and food that supported this massive superstructure. The weight of their burdens must in time have become crushing, and their discontent may have ignited revolts that brought about the ultimate collapse of the lowland Maya civilization.

Archaeological investigations have thrown new light on Classic Maya family and settlement patterns. The fact that the residential platforms on which most Maya houses rested occur in groups of three or more suggests that the Maya family was extended rather than nuclear. It probably consisted of two or more nuclear families spanning two or more generations with a common ancestor. Male predominance is suggested by the richer furnishings of male graves and the preeminence of men in monumental art, leading to the conclusion that descent was patrilineal, from father to son. Maya dress and diet, like its housing, reflected class distinctions. Maya clothing was much the same as the Aztec: cotton loincloths, leather sandals, and sometimes a mantle knotted about the shoulder for men; and wraparound skirts of cotton and blouses with holes for the head and arms for the women. The same articles of clothing, more ornately decorated, were worn by the upper classes.

Maya Religion and Learning

The great object of Maya religion, as the Spanish bishop Diego de Landa concisely put it, was "that they [the gods] should give them health, life, and sustenance." The principal Maya divinities, like those of the Aztecs, represented those natural forces and objects that most directly affected the material welfare of the people. The supreme god in the Maya pantheon was Itzam Na, a creator god who incorporated in himself the aspects of many other gods; not only creation, but fire, rain, crops, and earth were among his functions or provinces. Other important divinities were the sun god, the moon goddess, the rain god, the maize god, and the much-feared god of death. Like the Aztecs, the Maya believed that a number of worlds had successively appeared and been destroyed; this present world, too, would end in catastrophe.

The Maya view of the afterlife also closely resembled that of the Aztecs. They believed in an Upper World constituted of thirteen layers and an Under World of nine. Over each layer presided a certain god; over the lowest layer of the Under World presided the God of Death, Ah Puch. In common with the Aztecs and other peoples of Middle America, the Maya worshiped and placated the gods with a variety of ritual practices that included fasting, penance by bloodletting, the burning of incense, and human sacrifice. Human sacrifice on a large scale already existed in the late Classic period, marked by growing political turbulence and strife among the lowland Maya states, but may have increased in the Postclassic period under Toltec influence.

The Maya priests were obsessed with time, to which they assigned an occult or magical content. They developed a calendar that was more accurate than ours in making adjustments in the exact length of the solar year. Maya theologians thought of time as burdens carried on the backs of the gods. At the end of a certain period one god laid down his burden for another god to pick up and continue on the journey of time. A given day or year was lucky or unlucky depending on whether the god-bearer was benevolent or malevolent. Thus, the Maya calendars were primarily divinatory in character; that is, they were used to predict conditions in a particular time period.

Like the Aztecs, the Maya had two almanacs. One was a sacred round of 260 days, corresponding to the pattern of ceremonial life. This calendar was composed of two intermeshing and recurrent cycles of different length: one of thirteen days, recorded as numbers; and the second of twenty days, recorded as names. The name of the fourteenth day-name began with one again. A second cycle was the solar year of 365 days, divided into eighteen "months" of twenty days each, plus a final period of five unlucky days during which all unnecessary activity was banned. Completion of these two cycles coincided every fifty-two years. The Aztecs awaited the end of the fifty-two-year period with great anxiety because they believed that the world might come to an end at this time. A similar belief may have existed among the Maya. Stelae bearing hieroglyphic texts indicating the date and other calendrical data, such as the state of the moon, the position of the planet Venus, and so on, were frequently erected at the end of the fifty-two-year cycle and at other intervals.

The Maya developed the science of mathematics further than any of their Middle American neighbors. Their units were ones, fives, and twenties, with ones designated by dots, fives by bars, and positions for twenty and multiples of twenty. Place-value numeration, based on a sign for zero, was perhaps the greatest intellectual development of Ancient America. In this system, the position of a number determined its value, making it possible for a limited quantity of symbols to express numbers of any size. Its simplicity made it far superior to the contemporary western European arithmetical system, which employed the cumbersome Roman numeration consisting of distinct symbols for each higher unit. It remained for the Arabs to bring their numeration concept to Europe from India, the only other place where it had been invented. However, Maya mathematics appears to have been applied chiefly to calendrical and astronomical calculation; there is no record of Maya enumeration of people or objects.

Until recently it was believed that Maya hieroglyphic writing, like the mathematics, chiefly served religious and divinatory rather than utilitarian ends. We now have abundant evidence that many of the glyphs carved on the monuments are historical, recording milestones in the lives of Maya rulers. In addition to the inscriptions that appear on stone monuments, lintels, stairways, and other monumental remains, the Maya had great numbers of sacred books or codices, of which only three survive today. These books were painted on folding screens of native paper made of bark. Concerned above all with astronomy, divination, and other related topics, they reveal that Maya astronomers made observations and calculations of truly astounding complexity.

The Maya had no alphabet, properly speaking; that is, the majority of their characters represent ideas or objects rather than sounds. But Maya writing, like the Aztec, had reached the stage of syllabic phonetics through the use of rebus writing, in which the sound of a word is represented by combining pictures or signs of things whose spoken names resemble sounds in the word to be formed. Thus, the Maya word for drought, *kintunyaabil,* was written with four characters, the signs of sun or day (*kin*), stone or 360-day unit of time (*tun*), solar year (*haab*), and the affix *il.* Certain Russian scholars have advanced a theory that Maya writing was truly syllabic and hence can be deciphered by matching the most frequent sound elements in modern Maya to the most frequent signs in the ancient writing, using computers to speed the process of decipherment. The existence of purely phonetic glyphs in the Maya script is now generally accepted by scholars, but they seem to be relatively rare in the deciphered material.

Maya writing was not primarily used to record literature or history, but the Maya, like the Aztecs, had a large body of myth, legends, poetry, and traditional history that was transmitted orally from generation to generation. Examples of such material are found in the *Popol Vuh,* the so-called Sacred Book of the Quiche Maya of Guatemala. This book deals, among other matters, with the adventures of the heroic twins Hunahpu and Xbalanque, who after many exploits ascended into heaven to become the sun and the moon. It was written in post-Conquest times in the Spanish alphabet by a native who drew on the oral traditions of his people.

In certain types of artistic activity the Maya surpassed all other Middle American peoples. The temples and pyramids at Teotihuacán and Tenochtitlán were often larger than their Maya counterparts but lacked their grace and subtlety. A distinctive feature of Maya architecture was the corbeled vault, or false arch. Other Middle American peoples used horizontal wooden beams to bridge entrances, producing a heavy and squarish impression. The Maya solved the same problem by having the stones on either side of the opening project farther and farther inward, bridging the two sides at the apex by a capstone. Other characteristics of the Maya architectural style were the great façades richly decorated with carved stone and high ornamental roof combs in temples and palaces. Inner walls were frequently covered with paintings, a few of which have survived. The most celebrated of these paintings are the frescoes discovered in 1946 at Bonampak, an isolated site in the tropical forests of the northeastern corner of the Mexican state of Chiapas. They date from about A.D. 800. These frescoes completely cover the inner walls of a small building of three rooms. They tell a story that begins with a ritual dance, goes on to portray an expedition to obtain sacrificial victims, which is followed by a battle scene, and ends with a human sacrifice, ceremonies, and dance. Despite the highly conventionalized and static style, the absence of perspective and shading, and obvious errors in the human figure, there is an effect of realism that is often missing from Aztec or Toltec art.

Students of the Maya have frequently testified to the admirable personal qualities of the people who, with a very limited technology and in a most forbidding environment, created one of the greatest cultural traditions of all time. Bishop Diego de Landa, who burned twenty-seven Maya codices as "works of the devil," nevertheless observed that the Maya were very generous and

hospitable. No one could enter their houses, he wrote, without being offered food and drink. Modern anthropologists confirm Landa's judgment; mildness, generosity, and honesty, they report, are prominent traits of contemporary Maya Indians.

The Incas of Peru

In the highlands of modern Peru in the mid-fourteenth century, a small tribe rose from obscurity to create by 1500 the mightiest empire of Ancient America. From the time of the discovery and conquest of Peru by Pizarro to the present, the Inca achievements in political and social organization have attracted intense interest. Soon after the Conquest a debate began on the nature of Inca society that has continued almost to the present day. For some it was a "socialist empire"; others viewed it as a forerunner of the "welfare state" of our own time; for still others the Inca realm anticipated the totalitarian tyrannies of the twentieth century. Only recently has more careful study of the evidence, especially the evidence of colonial provincial records of official economic and social inquiries, litigation, wills, and the like, provided a more correct picture of Inca society and banished the traditional labels.

The physical environment of the central Andean area offers a key to the remarkable cultural development of this region. In Peru high mountains rise steeply from the sea, leaving a narrow coastal plain that is a true desert. The Humboldt Current runs north along the coast from the Antarctic, making the ocean much colder than the land; hence the rains fall at sea. But lack of rainfall is compensated for by short rivers that make their precipitous way down from the high snowfields. These rivers create oases at intervals along the coast and provide water for systems of canal irrigation. The aridity of the climate preserves the great natural wealth of the soil, which in areas of heavy rainfall is leached away. The coastal waters of Peru are rich in fish, and its off-shore islands, laden in Inca times with millions of tons of guano, made available an inexhaustible source of fertilizer for agriculture.

To be sure, the rugged highlands of modern Peru and Bolivia offer relatively little arable land. But the valleys are fertile and well watered and support a large variety of crops. Maize is grown at lower levels (up to about eleven thousand feet), potatoes and quinoa at higher altitudes. Above the agricultural zone the *puna* (plateau) provides fodder for herds of llamas and alpacas, domesticated members of the camel family, which were important in Inca times as a source of meat and wool. Potentially, this environment offered a basis for large food production and a dense population.

Origins of Inca Culture

Like the Aztecs of ancient Mexico, the Incas of Peru were heirs to a cultural tradition of great antiquity. This tradition had its origin not in the highlands but on the coast. By 2500 B.C., a village life, based chiefly on fishing and food gathering and supplemented by the cultivation of squash, lima beans, and a few other plants, had arisen about the mouths of rivers in the coastal area. Maize, introduced into Peruvian agriculture about 1500 B.C, did not become important until many centuries later.

The transition from the Archaic to the Preclassic period seems to have come later and more suddenly in Peru than in Mesoamerica. After long centuries of the simple village life just described, a strong advance of culture began on the coast about 900 B.C. This advance seems to have been associated with progress in agriculture, especially greater use of maize, and with a movement up the river valleys from the littoral (coastal area), possibly as a result of population pressure. Between 900 and 500 B.C., a distinctive style in building, art, ceramics, and weaving, known as Chavín (from the name of the site of a great ceremonial center discovered in 1946), spread along the coast and even into the highlands. The most distinctive feature of Chavín is its art style, which features a feline being, presumably a deity, whose cult spread over the area of Chavín influence.

The Classic period that emerged in Peru at or shortly before the beginning of the Old World's Christian era reflected further progress in agriculture, notably in the use of irrigation and fertilization. The brilliant culture called Nazca displaced the Chavín along the coast and highlands of southern Peru at this time. Nazca pottery is distinguished by its use of color. Sometimes there are as many as eleven soft pastel shades on one pot. The lovely Nazca textiles display an enormous range of colors.

Even more remarkable was the Mochica culture of the northern Peruvian coast. The Mochica built pyramids and temples, roads and large irrigation canals, and evolved a complex, highly stratified society with a directing priesthood and a powerful priest-king. Metallurgy was well developed, as evidenced by the wide use of copper weapons and tools and the manufacture of alloys of gold, copper, and silver. But as craftsmen and artists the Mochica are best known for their red and black pottery, never surpassed in the perfection of its realistic modeling. The so-called portrait vases, apparently representing actual individuals, mark the acme of Mochica realism. The pottery was also frequently decorated with realistic paintings of the most varied kind, including erotic scenes, which today are collectors' items. The pottery frequently depicts war scenes, suggesting chronic struggles for limited arable land and sources of water. The aggressive Mochica were themselves finally conquered by invaders who ravaged their lands, and a time of turbulence and cultural decline came to northern Peru.

About A.D. 600, the focus of Andean civilization shifted from the coast to the highlands. At the site called Tiahuanaco, just south of Lake Titicaca on the high plateau of Bolivia, there arose a great ceremonial center famed for its megalithic architecture, which was constructed with great stone blocks perfectly fitted together, and for its monumental human statuary. Tiahuanaco seems to have been the capital of a military state that eventually controlled all of southern Peru from Arequipa south to highland Bolivia and Chile. Another people, the Huari, embarked on a career of conquest from their homeland near modern Ayacucho; their territory ultimately included both the coast and highlands as far north as Cajamarca and south to the Tiahuanaco frontier. After a few centuries of domination, the Huari Empire broke up about A.D. 1000. At about the same time the Tiahuanaco sway also came to an end. The disintegration of these empires was followed by a return to political and artistic regionalism in the southern Andean area.

By A.D. 1000, a number of Postclassic states, differing from their predecessors in their greater size, had established their control over large portions of the northern Peruvian coast. Their rise was accompanied by the growth of cities. Each river valley had its own urban center, and an expanded net of irrigation works made support of larger populations possible. The largest of these new states was the Chimu kingdom. Its capital, Chanchan, was an immense city spread over eight square miles, with houses made of great molded adobe bricks grouped into large units or compounds. The Chimu kingdom survived until its conquest by the Inca in the mid-fifteenth century.

Inca Economy and Society

In the highlands, meanwhile, where less settled conditions prevailed, a new power was emerging. The Incas (so called after their own name for the ruling lineage) made a modest appearance in history as one of a number of small tribes that inhabited the Cuzco region in the Andean highlands and struggled with each other for possession of land and water. A strong strategic situation in the Valley of Cuzco and some cultural superiority over their neighbors favored the Incas as they began their career of conquest. Previous empires—Huari, Tiahuanaco, and Chimu—no doubt provided the Incas with instructive precedents for conquest and the consolidation of conquest through a variety of political and socio-economic techniques. Like other imperialist nations of antiquity, the Incas had a body of myth and legend that ascribed a divine origin to their rulers and gave their warriors a comforting assurance of supernatural favor and protection.

True imperial expansion seems to have begun in the second quarter of the fifteenth century, in the reign of Pachacuti Inca, who was crowned in 1438. Together with his son Topa Inca, also a great conqueror, Pachacuti obtained the submission of many provinces by the skillful use of claims of divine aid, fair promises, threats, and naked force. Reputed to be a great organizer as well as a mighty warrior, Pachacuti is credited with many reforms and innovations, including the establishment of the territorial divisions and elaborate administrative bureaucracy that made the wheels of the Inca Empire go round. By 1527, the boundary markers of the Children of the Sun rested on the modern frontier between Ecuador and Colombia to the north and on the Maule River in Chile to the south. A population of perhaps 9 million people owed allegiance to the emperor. When the Spaniards arrived, the ruler was Atahualpa, who had just won the imperial mantle by defeating his half-brother Huascar.

The Incas maintained their authority with an arsenal of devices that included the spread of their Quechua language (still spoken by five-sixths of the Indians of the central Andean area) as the official language of the empire, the imposition of a unifying state religion, and a shrewd policy of incorporating chieftains of conquered regions into the central bureaucracy. An important factor in the Inca plan of unification was the policy of resettlement, or colonization. This consisted of deporting dissident populations and replacing them with loyal *mitimaes* (colonists) from older provinces of the empire. An excellent network of roads, or rather footpaths, linked administrative centers and made it possible to send armies and messengers quickly from one part of the empire to another. Some roads were paved, others were cut into solid rock. Where the land was marshy, the roads passed over causeways; suspension bridges spanned gorges, and pontoon bridges of buoyant reeds were used to cross rivers. The Incas had no system of writing, but they possessed a most efficient means of keeping records in a memory aid called the *quipu,* a stick or cord with a number of knotted strings tied to it. Strings of different colors represented different articles, people, or districts; knots tied in the strings ascended in units representing ones, tens, hundreds, thousands, and so on.

The economic basis of the Inca Empire was its intensive irrigation agriculture capable of supporting without serious strain not only the producers but the large Inca armies, a large administrative bureaucracy, and many other persons engaged in nonproductive activities. The Incas did not develop this agriculture. By the time of their rise, the original coastal irrigation systems had probably been extended over all suitable areas in coastal and highland Peru. But along with their political and religious institutions, the Incas introduced the advanced practices of irrigation, terracing, and fertilization among conquered peoples of more primitive culture. Terracing was widely used to extend the arable area and to prevent injury to fields and settlements in the narrow Andean valleys from run-off from the steep slopes during the rainy season. Irrigation ditches, sometimes mere trenches, sometimes elaborate stone channels, conducted water to the fields and pastures where it was needed.

Agricultural implements were few and simple. They consisted chiefly of a foot plow, used to break up the ground and dig holes for planting, and a hoe with a bronze blade for general cultivation. As previously noted, the potato and quinoa were staple crops in the higher valleys; maize was the principal crop at lower altitudes; and a wide variety of plants, including cotton, coca, and beans, was cultivated in the lower and hotter valleys. A major function of the Inca state was to regulate the exchange of the products of these multiple environments, primarily through the collection of tribute and its redistribution to various groups in Inca society. The Inca state also promoted self-sufficiency by allowing members of a given community to exploit the re-

sources of different levels of the Andean "vertical" economy.

The basic unit of Inca social organization was the *ayllu,* a kinship group whose members claimed descent from a common ancestor and married within the group. A village community typically consisted of several ayllu. Each ayllu owned certain lands, which were assigned in lots to heads of families. Each family head had the right to use and pass on the land to male descendants but not to sell or otherwise dispose of it. Villagers frequently practiced mutual aid in agricultural tasks, in the construction of dwellings, and in other projects of a private or public nature. The Inca rulers took over this communal principle and utilized it for their own ends in the form of corvée, or unpaid forced labor. In the words of the anthropologist Nathan Wachtel, "the imperial Inca mode of production was based on the ancient communal mode of production which it left in place, while exploiting the principle of reciprocity to legitimate its rule."

Before the Inca conquest, the ayllu were governed by *curacas* (hereditary chiefs) assisted by a council of elders, with a superior curaca or lord (*jatun curaca*) ruling over the whole people or state. Under Inca rule, the kinship basis of ayllu organization was weakened through the planned removal of some of its members and the settlement of strangers in its midst (the system of mitimaes). A varying amount of land was taken from the villages and vested in the Inca state and the state church. In addition to working their own lands and those of their curaca, ayllu members were required to till the Inca state and church lands. The Inca government also used the forced labor of villagers to create new arable land by leveling and terracing slopes. This new land was often turned over as private estates to curacas and Inca military leaders and nobles who had rendered conspicuous service to the Inca state. The Inca himself possessed private estates, and others were owned by the lineages of dead emperors and used to maintain the cult of these former rulers. These private estates were not worked by ayllu members but by a new servile

Machu Picchu, an Inca fortress-city located high in the Andean Mountains, includes over one hundred acres of stone buildings. With a Sun Temple, central plaza, public buildings, a defensive wall, water system, baths and fountains, and terraced hillsides for intensive agricultural production, Machu Picchu probably served as a retreat for the last Inca rulers after their defeat by the Spanish rulers in the 1500s. (Carl Frank/Photo Researchers)

class, the *yanacona*,[5] defined by Spanish sources as "permanent servants"; each ayllu had to contribute a number of such servants or retainers, who also worked in the Inca temples and palaces and performed personal service.

In addition to agricultural labor, ayllu members had to work on roads, irrigation channels, and fortresses, in the mines, and so on, in a

system called the *mita,* later adopted by the Spaniards for their own purposes. Another requirement was that villages produce specified quantities of cloth for the state to use in clothing soldiers and retainers. All able-bodied commoners between certain ages were subject to military service. There is no trace of socialism or a welfare state in these arrangements, which favored not the commoners but the Inca dynasty, nobility, priesthood, warriors, and officials. Many of the activities cited as reflecting the benevolence

---

[5] A plural term in Quechua but treated by the Spaniards as singular.

32

and foresight of the Inca state were actually traditional village and ayllu functions. One such activity was the maintenance of storehouses of grain and cloth by the community for times of crop failure. The Inca state merely took over this principle, as it had taken over the principle of cooperative labor for communal ends, and established storehouses containing the goods produced by the peasants' forced labor on state and church lands. The cloth and grain stored in these warehouses were used primarily to clothe and feed the army, the crown artisans, the conscript labor for public works, and the officials who lived in Cuzco and other towns.

The relations between the Inca and the peasantry were based on the principle of reciprocity, expressed in an elaborate system of gifts and countergifts. The peasantry cultivated the lands of the Inca, worked up his wool and cotton into cloth, and performed various other kinds of labor for him. The Inca, the divine, universal lord, in turn permitted them to cultivate their communal lands, and in time of shortages released to the villages the surplus grain in his storehouses. Since the imperial gifts were the products of the peasants' own labor, this "reciprocity" amounted to intensive exploitation of the commoners by the Inca rulers and nobility. We must not underestimate, however, the hold of this ideology, buttressed by a religious world view that regarded the Inca as responsible for defending the order and very existence of the universe, on the Inca peasant mentality.

At the time of the Conquest, a vast gulf separated the regimented and laborious life of the commoners from the luxurious life of the Inca nobility. At the apex of the social pyramid were the Inca and his kinsmen, composed of twelve lineages. Members of these lineages had the privilege of piercing their ears and distending the lobes with large ornaments; hence the name *orejones* (big ears) assigned to the Inca kinsmen by the Spaniards. The orejones were exempt from tribute labor and military service; the same was true of the curacas, who had once been chieftains

in their own right, and of a numerous class of specialists—servants, retainers, quipu keepers and other officials, and entertainers. Side by side with the Inca state, which drained off the peasants' surplus production, regulated the exchange of goods between the various regions, and directed vast public works, there arose the incipient feudalism of the Inca nobility and curacas. Their loyalty and services to the Inca were rewarded with rich gifts of land, llamas, and yanacona. Their growing resources enabled them to form their own local clienteles, achieve a certain relative independence of the crown, and play an important role in the disputes over the succession that sometimes followed the emperor's death.

Inca rule over the peasant masses was largely indirect, exercised through local chieftains. It probably did not seriously affect the round of daily life in the villages. The typical peasant house in the highlands was a small hut with walls of fieldstone or adobe and a gable roof thatched with grass. The scanty furniture consisted of a raised sleeping platform, a clay stove, and some clay pots and dishes. A man's clothing consisted of a breechcloth, a sleeveless tunic, and a large cloak over the shoulders with two corners tied in front; the fineness of the cloth used and the ornamentation varied according to social rank. A woman's dress was a wraparound cloth extending from beneath the arms to the ankles, with the top edges drawn over the shoulders and fastened with straight pins. An ornamented sash around the waist and a shoulder mantle completed the woman's apparel. Men adorned themselves with earplugs and bracelets; women wore necklaces and shawl pins.

On the eve of the Spanish Conquest, the Inca state appeared all-powerful. But, like the Aztec Empire, it was rent by deep contradictions. Frequent revolts by conquered peoples were put down with ferocious cruelty. Even the outwardly loyal curacas, former lords of independent states, chafed at the vigilant Inca control and dreamed of regaining their lost freedom.

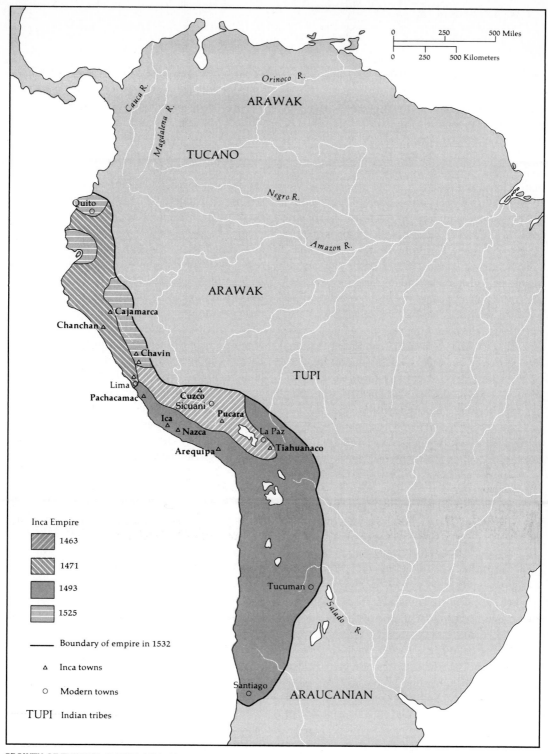

Inca Empire

▨	1463
▨	1471
▨	1493
▨	1525

—— Boundary of empire in 1532

△ Inca towns

○ Modern towns

TUPI Indian tribes

GROWTH OF THE INCA EMPIRE, 1460–1532

Inca Religion and Learning

The Inca state religion existed side by side with the much older ancestor cults and the worship of innumerable *huacas* (local objects and places). Chief of the Inca gods was a nameless creator called Viracocha and Pachayachachic (lord and instructor of the world). His cult seems to have been a philosophical religion largely confined to the priesthood and nobility. First in importance after Viracocha was the Sun God, claimed by the Inca royal family as its divine ancestor. Other notable divinities were the Thunder God, who sent the life-giving rain, and the Moon, wife of the Sun, who played a vital role in the regulation of the Inca festival calendar. The Inca idols were housed in numerous temples attended by priests who directed and performed ceremonies that included prayer, sacrifice, confession, and the rite of divination. Another priestly function was the magical cure of disease. The priests were assisted in their religious duties by a class of *mamacuna* (holy women) who had taken vows of permanent chastity. Human sacrifice was performed on very momentous occasions, such as an important victory or some great natural calamity.

Inca art was marked by a high level of technical excellence. The architecture was solid and functional, characterized by massiveness rather than beauty. The stone sculpture, more frequent in the highlands than on the coast, has been described as ponderous and severe. But the tapestries of Inca weavers are among the world's textile masterpieces, so fine and intricate is the weaving. Inca metallurgy was also on a high technical and artistic plane. Cuzco, the Inca capital, abounded in gold objects: the imperial palace had gold friezes and panels of gold and silver, and the Temple of the Sun contained a garden with lifelike replicas of plants and animals, all made of hammered gold.

Although the Incas had no system of writing and hence no written literature, narrative poems, prayers, and tales were handed down orally from generation to generation. The Inca hymns and prayers that have been preserved are notable for their lofty thought and beauty of expression. Of the long narrative poems that dealt with Inca mythology, legends, and history, there remain only summaries in Spanish prose.

A melancholy and nostalgic spirit pervades many of the traditional Inca love songs, and the same plaintiveness characterizes the few examples of their music that have come down to us. Based on the five-toned, or pentatonic, scale, this music was performed with an assortment of instruments: flutes, trumpets, and whistles; gongs, bells, and rattles; and several kinds of skin drums and tambourines. The dances that accompanied the music sometimes represented an elementary form of drama.

Spanish conquistadors destroyed Inca political organization and dealt shattering blows to all aspects of Inca civilization, but elements of that culture survive everywhere in the central Andean area. These survivals, tangible and intangible, include the Quechua speech of great numbers of Indians; the numerous Indian communities, or ayllu, still partly based on cooperative principles; the widespread pagan beliefs and rites of the people; and of course the monumental ruins of Sacsahuaman, Ollantaytambo, Machu Picchu, Pisac, and Cuzco itself. Inca civilization also lives in the writings of Peruvian historians, novelists, and statesmen who evoke the vanished Inca greatness and praise the ancient virtues of their people. In the 1960s, one Peruvian president, Fernando Belaúnde Terry, urged his nation to imitate the industry, energy, and foresight of its Indian forebears in order to make Peru once again the flourishing garden that it was under the Incas. In the 1970s, his successor, the military reformer Juan Velasco Alvarado, gave the name Inca to his program for the economic, social, and political reconstruction of Peru. For many Peruvians, the great technical achievements and social engineering of the Incas, ensuring a modest well-being for all, offer proof of the inherent capacity of their native peoples and a prospect of what the poverty-ridden, strife-torn Peru of today may yet become.

New Light on Ancient America

As a result of the patient researches by anthropologists and historians, the volume of information on Ancient America is growing at an extremely rapid rate. Students are more and more impressed with the complexity of the civilizations of Ancient America and commonly compare them with such advanced Old World cultures as ancient Egypt and Mesopotamia. As the frontiers of our knowledge and understanding of the subject advance, traditional generalizations have had to be discarded in favor of concepts and explanations that conform more closely to what is known. Our understanding of the Maya economic, social, and political structures, for example, has been revolutionized in recent decades. We have gained a new respect for Aztec culture, and the traditional view of the Aztec empire as "inferior" or "primitive" in comparison with the Inca imperial model is now disputed. Furthermore, the stereotypes of the Inca empire as a "socialist," "totalitarian," or "welfare" state have been definitively banished and replaced by a more sophisticated interpretation that brings into clear perspective the magnificent achievements of the ancient Andean peoples in economic, social, and political engineering.

Recent studies of the population history of Ancient America have contributed to the rising respect for the Indian cultural achievement. If we assume, as many social scientists do, that population density is correlated with a certain technological and cultural level, then a high estimate of the Indian population of America in 1492 is in some measure a judgment on the old Indian societies and on the colonial societies that arose on their ruins.

Beginning in the 1940s, three professors at the University of California, Woodrow Borah, Sherburne Cook, and Lesley B. Simpson, opened a new line of inquiry into the demographic history of Ancient America with a remarkable series of studies focusing on central Mexico. Using a variety of Indian and Spanish records and sophisticated statistical methods, the Berkeley school projected backward from a base established from Spanish counts of the Indians for tax purposes and arrived at a population figure of 25.3 million for central Mexico on the eve of the Conquest.

Later, Cook and Borah extended their inquiries into other areas. Particularly striking are their conclusions concerning the population of Hispaniola in 1492. Previous estimates of the island's population had ranged from a low of 60,000 to the 3 to 4 million proposed by the sixteenth-century Spanish friar Bartolomé de Las Casas, but those high figures had long been regarded as the patent exaggerations of a pro-Indian enthusiast. After careful study of a series of statements and estimates on the aboriginal population of Hispaniola (modern Haiti and the Dominican Republic) made between 1492 and 1520, Cook and Borah not only confirmed the reliability of Las Casas's figures but offered even higher probable figures of from 7 to 8 million.

Aside from Borah's suggestion in 1964 that the population of America in 1492 may have been "upwards of 100 million," the Berkeley school did not attempt to estimate the pre-Columbian population of the continent as a whole. A systematic effort of this kind was made by the American anthropologist Henry Dobyns. Assuming that the Indian population was reduced by roughly 95 percent after contact with the Europeans, he estimated a pre-Conquest population of between 90 and 112 million; of this number he assigned 30 million each to central Mexico and Peru.

The methods and findings of the Berkeley school and Dobyns have provoked some bitter dissent, and the debate continues. In general, however, the evidence of the last quarter-century of research in this field quite consistently points to larger populations than were accepted previously. One effort to generalize from this evidence, taking account both of the findings of the Berkeley school and its critics, is that of Professor William M. Denevan (1976), who postulates a total population of 57.3 million—a far cry from the 1939 estimate of 8.5 million by the American anthropologist A. L. Kroeber.

Chapter 2

The Hispanic Background

Conquest was a major theme of Spanish history from very remote times. The prehistoric inhabitants of the peninsula, whose unknown artists produced the marvelous cave paintings of Altamira, were overrun by tribes vaguely called Iberians and by the Celts, who are believed to have come from North Africa and central Europe, respectively, probably before 1000 B.C. New waves of invasion brought the Phoenicians, Greeks, and Carthaginians, commercial nations that established trading posts and cities on the coast but made no effort to dominate the interior. Still later, Spain became a stake of empire in the great struggle for commercial supremacy between Rome and Carthage that ended with the decisive defeat of the latter in 201 B.C. For six centuries thereafter, Rome was the dominant power in the peninsula.

Unlike earlier invaders, the Romans attempted to establish their authority throughout Spain (the name comes from the word *Hispania,* applied by the Romans to the whole peninsula) and to impose their language and institutions on the native peoples. From Latin, made the official language, sprang the various dialects and languages still spoken by the Hispanic peoples. Roman law replaced the customary law of the Celts, Iberians, and other native groups. Native tribal organization was destroyed through forced changes of residence, concentration in towns, and the planting of Roman colonies that served as agencies of pacification and assimilation. Agriculture, mining, and industry developed, and Roman Spain carried on an extensive trade in wheat, wine, and olive oil with Italy. Roman engineers constructed great public roads and aqueducts, some of which are still in use. Roman education and literary culture were brought to Spain, and a number of Spaniards by birth or residence (the satirical poet Martial, the epic poet Lucan, and the philosopher Seneca) made notable contributions to Latin literature.

Early in the fifth century A.D., as a result of the decline of Roman military power, a number of barbarian peoples of Germanic origin invaded Spain. By the last half of the century, one group of invaders, the Visigoths, had gained mastery over most of the peninsula. As a result of long contact with the empire, the Visigoths had already lost part of their barbarism. Their assimilation of Roman culture continued in Spain through contact with the Hispano-Romans. The Visigothic kingdom was Christian; its speech became Latin with a small admixture of Germanic terms; in administration it followed the Roman model. But the succession to the kingship followed Germanic tradition in being elective, a frequent source of great internal strife.

Spain's Medieval Heritage

The divisions among the Goths caused by struggles over kingship played into the hands of the new Muslim power in North Africa. In 711 the Muslims crossed the straits and decisively defeated Roderic, the last Gothic king. Within a few years, all of Spain, aside from the remote region north of the Cantabrian Mountains, had fallen into Muslim hands. But the Muslims' hold on the bleak uplands of Castile was never strong; they preferred the fertile plains and delightful climate of southern Spain, which they called Al-Andalus, the land of Andalusia.

The Muslims, heirs to the accumulated cultural wealth of the ancient Mediterranean and Eastern worlds, enriched this heritage with their own magnificent contributions to science, arts, and letters. In the tenth and eleventh centuries, Muslim Spain, with its capital at Córdoba, was an economic and intellectual showplace from which

fresh knowledge and ideas flowed into Christian lands. Spanish agriculture gained by the introduction of new irrigation and water-lifting devices and new crops: sugar, saffron, cotton, silk, and citrus fruits. Industry was broadened through the introduction of such products as paper and glass, hitherto unknown to the West. Muslim metalwork, pottery, silk, and leatherwork were esteemed throughout Europe. Many Muslim rulers were patrons of literature and learning; the scholar-king Al-Haquem II built up a library said to have numbered four hundred thousand volumes.

As a rule, the Muslim conquerors did not insist on the conversion of the vanquished Christians, preferring to give them the option of accepting the Islamic faith or paying a special poll tax. The relatively tolerant Muslim rule was favorable to economic and cultural advance. The Jews, who had suffered severe persecution under the Visigoths, enjoyed official protection and made major contributions to medicine, philosophy, and Talmudic studies. The condition of the peasantry probably improved, for the conquerors distributed the vast estates of the Visigothic lords among the serfs, who paid a certain portion of the produce to the Muslim lords and kept the rest for themselves. But in later centuries, these trends were reversed; great landed estates again arose, taxation increased, and severe persecution of Jews and Mozárabes (Christians who had adopted Arab speech and customs) drove many to flee to Christian territory.

Despite its noble achievements, Muslim civilization rested on insecure foundations. The Arab conquerors never fully threw off the tribal form of social organization under which they began their prodigious advance, and the Muslim world was torn by fierce political and religious feuds over control of the empire. In Spain these internal differences were complicated by conflicts between the Arabs and the North African Berbers, recent converts to Islam who were more fanatically devout than were their teachers. By the mid-eleventh century, the caliphate of Córdoba

38

had broken into a large number of *taifas* (states) that constantly warred with each other. These discords enabled the petty Christian kingdoms that had arisen in the north to survive, grow strong, and eventually launch a general advance against the Muslims. In the west, Portugal, having achieved independence from Castile by the mid-twelfth century, attained its historic boundaries two centuries later. In the center, the joint realm of León and Castile pressed its advance; to the east, the kingdom of Aragon steadily expanded at the expense of the disunited Muslim states.

The Reconquest began as a struggle of Christian kings and nobles to regain their lost lands and serfs; only later did it assume the character of a crusade. Early in the ninth century, the tomb of St. James, supposedly found in northwest Spain, became the center of the famous pilgrimage of Santiago de Compostela and gave Spain a warrior patron saint who figured prominently in the Reconquest and the conquest of the New World. But the career of the famous Cid (Ruy Díaz de Vivar), to whom the Arabic title of "lord" was given by his Muslim soldiers, illustrates the absence of religious fanaticism in the first stage of the struggle. True to the ideals of his time, the Cid placed feudal above religious loyalties, and as a vassal of the Muslim kings of Saragossa and Valencia fought Moorish and Christian foes alike. When he captured Valencia for himself in 1094, he allowed the Muslims to worship freely and retain their property, requiring only the payment of tributes authorized by the Koran.

The Muslims vainly sought to check the Christian advance by calling on newly converted, fanatically religious Berber tribes in North Africa to come to their aid. The Christian victory at Las Navas de Tolosa (1212) in Andalusia over a large Berber army marked a turning point in the Reconquest. Ferdinand III of Castile captured Córdoba, the jewel of Muslim Spain, in 1236; the surrender of Seville in 1248 gave him control of the mouth of the Guadalquivir River and communication with the sea. By the time of Ferdinand's death in 1252, the Muslim territory in Spain had

been reduced to the small kingdom of Granada. The strength of its position, protected by steep mountains and impassable gorges, and the divisions that arose within the Christian camp gave Granada two and a half more centuries of independent life.

Castile

Castile, the largest and most powerful of the Spanish kingdoms, played the leading role in the Reconquest. The great movement left an enduring stamp on the Castilian character. Centuries of struggle against the Moor made war almost a Castilian way of life and created a large class of warrior-nobles who regarded manual labor with contempt. In the Castilian scale of values, the military virtues of courage, endurance, and honor took the first place. Not only the nobles but the commoners accepted these values. The lure of plunder, land, and other rewards drew many peasants and artisans into the armies of the Reconquest and diffused militarist and aristocratic ideals throughout Castilian society. To these ideals the crusading spirit of the Reconquest, especially in its later phase, added a strong sense of religious superiority and mission.

The Reconquest also helped to shape the character of the Castilian economy. As the Muslims fell back, vast tracts of land came into the possession of the crown. The kings assigned the lion's share of this land to the nobility, the church, and the three military orders of Calatrava, Alcántara, and Santiago. As a result, Castile, especially the area from Toledo south (New Castile), became a region of enormous estates and a very wealthy, powerful aristocracy.

The Reconquest also insured the supremacy of sheep raising over agriculture in Castile. In a time of constant warfare, of raids and counterraids, the mobile sheep was a more secure and valuable form of property than land. With the advance of the Christian frontier, much new territory—frequently too arid for easy agricultural use—was opened to the sheep industry. The introduction of the merino sheep into Spain from North Africa around 1300, coinciding with a sharply increased demand in northern Europe for Spanish wool, gave a marked stimulus to sheep raising. By the late thirteenth century, there had arisen a powerful organization of sheep raisers, the *Mesta.* In return for large subsidies to the crown, this organization received extensive privileges, including the right to move great flocks of sheep across Spain from summer pastures in the north to winter pastures in the south, with frequent injury to the farmlands and woods in their path. The great nobles dominated the sheep industry as well as agriculture. Their large rents and the profits from the sale of their wool gave them an economic, social, and military power that threatened the supremacy of the king.

The Castilian towns represented the only counterpoise to this power. The advance of the Reconquest and the need to consolidate its gains promoted municipal growth. To attract settlers to the newly conquered territory, the king gave generous *fueros* (charters of liberties) to the towns that sprang up one after another. These charters endowed the towns with administrative autonomy and vast areas of land that extended their jurisdiction into the surrounding countryside. The towns were governed by elected judicial officials known as *alcaldes* and by members of the town council, called *regidores.* The economic expansion of the thirteenth and fourteenth centuries and the growth of the wool trade, above all, made the Castilian towns bustling centers of industry and commerce. The wealth of the towns gave them a peculiar importance in the meetings of the consultative body, or parliament, known as the Cortes. Since the nobles and the clergy were exempt from taxes, the deputies of the towns had to vote the money needed by the king. Their price for voting it became the redress of grievances presented in the form of petitions that royal approval transformed into laws.

The Castilian towns had their time of splendor, but in the last analysis the middle class remained small and weak; it was overshadowed by the enormous power of the great nobles. Aware of their weakness, the towns joined their forces in *hermandades,* military associations that resisted the aggressions of the nobles and sometimes of the king. But the posture of the towns was essentially defensive. Without the aid of the king, they could not hope to impose their will on the aristocracy.

As the Muslim power waned, the great nobles turned from fighting the infidel to battling the king, the towns, and each other. In the course of the fourteenth and fifteenth centuries, the nobles gained the upper hand in their struggle with the king, usurping royal lands and revenues and often transforming the monarch into their pawn. The degradation of the crown reached its lowest point in the reign of Henry IV (1454–1474), when there was an almost total breakdown of central government and public order. Beneath this anarchy, however, the continued expansion of economic life inspired a growing demand for a strong monarchy capable of establishing peace and order.

Aragon

The medieval history of the smaller, less populous kingdom of Aragon differed in important ways from that of Castile. The king of Aragon ruled over three states: Aragon, Valencia, and Catalonia, each regarded as a separate *reino* (kingdom), each having its own Cortes. The upland state of Aragon was the poorest, most backward of the three. Valencia was the home of a large Moorish peasant population subject to a Christian landowning nobility. The dominant role in the union was played by Catalonia and its great city of Barcelona, which had given Aragon its dynasty and most of its revenues. A thriving industry and powerful fleets had made Barcelona the center of a commercial empire based on the export of textiles. Catalan arms had also won Sardinia and Sicily for the crown of Aragon. In Aragon, therefore, the ruling class was not the landed nobility, which was relatively poor, but the commercial and industrial oligarchy of Barcelona. The constitutional system of Aragon reflected the supremacy of this class by giving legislative power to the Cortes of Catalonia and by providing special watchdog committees of the Cortes, which guarded against any infringement of the rights and liberties of the subjects.

In the fourteenth and fifteenth centuries, the prosperity of Barcelona was undermined by the ravages of the Black Death, agrarian unrest in the Catalan countryside, struggles between the merchant oligarchy and popular elements in Barcelona, and above all by the loss of traditional Catalan markets to Genoese competitors. This economic decline sharpened Catalan internal struggles, in which the crown joined on the side of the popular elements. The result was the civil war of 1462–1472, which ended in a qualified victory for the king, John II, but which completed the ruin of Catalonia. The weakness of Aragon on the eve of its union with Castile insured Castilian leadership of the coming new Spain.

The chain of events leading to Spanish unity began with the secret marriage in 1469 of Isabella, sister of Henry IV of Castile, and Ferdinand, son of John II of Aragon. This match was the fruit of complex intrigues in which the personal ambitions of the young couple, the hostility of many Castilian nobles to their king, and the desire of John II to add Castile to his son Ferdinand's heritage all played their part. On the death of Henry IV in 1474, Isabella proclaimed herself queen of Castile with the support of a powerful faction of Castilian nobles and towns that declared that Henry's daughter Juana was illegitimate. This claim led to a dynastic war in which Portugal supported Juana. By 1479 the struggle had ended in Isabella's favor. In the same year, John II died and Ferdinand succeeded to his dominions. Ferdinand and Isabella now became joint rulers of Aragon and Castile, but the terms of their marriage contract carefully subordinated Ferdinand to Isabella in the government of Castile and excluded Isabella from the administration of Aragon. The process of Spanish unification, however, had begun. Under the leadership of Castile, Spain

embarked on a remarkable career of domestic progress and imperial expansion.

The Spain of Ferdinand and Isabella

Restoration of Order

The young monarchs faced an urgent problem of restoring peace and order in their respective kingdoms. Catalonia was still troubled by struggles between feudal lords and serfs determined to end their legal servitude. Ferdinand intervened to bring about a solution relatively favorable to the peasantry. His ruling of Guadalupe (1486) ended serfdom in Catalonia and enabled fifty thousand peasants to become small landowners. But he made no effort to reform Aragon's archaic constitutional system, which set strict limits on the royal power. As a result, Castile and Aragon, despite their newfound unity, continued to move along divergent political courses.

The task of restoring order was greater in Castile. The age of anarchy under Henry IV had transformed cities into battlefields and parts of the countryside into a desert. To eradicate the evils of banditry and feudal violence, Isabella counted above all on the support of the towns and the middle classes. The Cortes of Madrigal (1476) forged a solid alliance between the crown and the towns for the suppression of disorder. Their instrument was the *Santa Hermandad,* a police force paid for and manned principally by the towns but under the direct control of the crown. The efficiency of this force and the severe and prompt punishments meted out by its tribunals gradually restored peace in Castile.

But Isabella's program went beyond this immediate goal. She proposed to bend to the royal will all the great institutions of medieval Castile: the nobility, the church, and the towns themselves. The Cortes of Toledo of 1480 reduced the power of the grandees (nobles of the first rank) in various ways. An Act of Resumption compelled them to return to the crown about half the rev-

Isabella and Ferdinand transformed Spain into one of the strongest European kingdoms of the fifteenth century. (Granada Cathedral. Oronoz Photo Archives)

enues they had usurped since 1464.[1] Another reform reorganized the Council of Castile, the central governing agency of the kingdom. This reform reduced the grandees who had dominated the old royal council to holders of empty dignities. It vested effective responsibility and power

[1] Stephen Haliczer, *The Comuneros of Castile: The Forging of a Revolution, 1475–1521* (Madison: University of Wisconsin Press, 1981), p. 39, points out, however, that in the majority of cases the *mercedes* (grants of annuities) that were recovered "were not from the nobility . . . but from tax farmers [individuals entrusted with the collection of taxes who paid the crown a fixed sum and retained the moneys collected], who had been cheating the merced holders and the Crown." The nobility were confirmed in possession of the remaining, most valuable annuities. The episode illustrates the royal policy of simultaneously seeking to weaken and conciliate the great nobility.

in *letrados* (officials usually possessed of legal training), who were drawn from the lower nobility, the middle class, and *conversos* (converted Jews). The same end of curbing aristocratic power was served by the establishment of a hierarchy of courts and magistrates that ascended from the *corregidor* (the royal officer who watched over the affairs of a municipality) through the *cancillerías* (the high law courts of Castile) up to the Council of Castile, the highest court as well as the supreme administrative body of the country. At all levels, the crown asserted its judicial primacy, including the right of intervention in the feudal jurisdiction of the nobility.

The vast wealth of the military orders made them veritable states within the Castilian state. The crown determined to weaken their power by securing for itself control of these orders. When

42

the grand mastership of Santiago fell vacant in 1476, Isabella personally appeared before the dignitaries of the order to insist that they confer the headship on her husband; they meekly assented. When the grand masterships of Calatrava and Alcántara fell vacant, they too were duly conferred on Ferdinand. By these moves, the crown gained new sources of revenue and patronage.

The towns had served the crown well in the struggle against anarchy, but in the past two centuries their democratic traditions had declined, and many had fallen under the control of selfish oligarchies. Some, like Seville, had become battlefields of aristocratic factions. These disorders provided Isabella with pretexts for resuming the policy, initiated by some of her predecessors, of intervening in municipal affairs by introducing *corregidores* into the towns. These officials combined administrative and judicial functions and steadily usurped the roles of the *alcaldes* and *regidores*. Ferdinand and Isabella also carried forward another practice begun by their predecessors. The offices of *alcalde* and *regidor* in towns with royal charters were made appointive by the crown instead of elective by the householders. *Villas de señorío* (towns under noble or ecclesiastical jurisdiction) were permitted to function under the traditional system, but with the right of royal intervention if necessary.

The taming of the towns was accompanied by a decline in the importance of the Cortes. An important factor in this decline was the large increase in revenues from royal taxes, such as the *alcabala* (sales tax), which freed the crown from excessive dependence on the grants of the Cortes. The increased supervision of the crown over the municipalities also decreased the likelihood of resistance by their deputies in the Cortes to royal demands. The sovereigns summoned the Castilian Cortes only when they needed money. When the treasury was full or when peace prevailed they ignored them.

Religious and Economic Reforms

In their march toward absolute power, the monarchs did not hesitate to challenge the church.

Under their pressure, the weak popes of this period yielded to them the right of *patronato* (the right of appointment to all major ecclesiastical benefices in the Spanish realms). Although, unlike Henry VIII of England, Ferdinand and Isabella never despoiled the church of its vast landed possessions, they did drain off for themselves a part of the ecclesiastical wealth by taking one-third of all the tithes paid to the Castilian church and the proceeds from the sale of indulgences.

To ensure the loyalty of the church, to make it an effective instrument of royal policy, the sovereigns had to purge it of abuses that included plural benefices, absenteeism, and concubinage. The pious Isabella found a strong ally in the work of reform in a dissident faction of the regular clergy (those belonging to a monastic order or religious community). This group, who called themselves Observants, protested against the worldliness of their colleagues and demanded a return to the strict simplicity of the primitive church. The struggle for reform began within the Franciscan order under the leadership of the ascetic Francisco Jiménez de Cisneros, whom Isabella appointed archbishop of Toledo in 1495, and spread to the other orders. It grew so heated that four hundred Andalusian friars preferred moving to North Africa and becoming Muslims, rather than accept the new rule. The dispute ended in the complete victory of the Observants over their more easygoing brethren.

Isabella was less successful in efforts to reform the secular (or nonmonastic) clergy, but here too an improvement took place. The great ecclesiastical offices ceased to be a monopoly of the aristocracy. Isabella preferred to select prelates from the lower nobility and the middle class, taking account of the morals and learning of the candidates. The Isabelline religious reform had a special meaning for the New World: it insured that the Faith would be carried to the Indies by an elite force of clergy often distinguished for their zeal, humanity, and learning.

The sovereigns also gave attention to the need for economic reform. They attempted to promote Castilian industry and commerce by protectionist measures. They forbade the export of gold and silver, sporadically barred the import of cloth that competed with native products, and encouraged Italian and Flemish artisans to settle in Spain. They promulgated navigation acts that gave preference to domestic shipping and subsidies to domestic shipbuilding. They suppressed all the internal tolls that had been established in Castile since 1464 and made an effort to standardize weights and measures. Under Isabella's predecessors, a serious depreciation of the currency had taken place. To restore the credit of the coinage, Isabella suppressed all private mints and struck an excellent money that equaled foreign coins in value. All these measures contributed to an economic expansion and consequently to a rapid increase of crown revenues, from 885,000 *reales* in 1474 to 26,283,334 *reales* in 1504.

Despite their basically pragmatic outlook, the sovereigns had broad intellectual and artistic interests. To their court they summoned Italian humanists like Alessandro Geraldini, Lucio Marineo Siculo, and Peter Martyr de Anghera to tutor their children and the sons of the greatest houses of Spain. Enlightened prelates like Archbishop Jiménez de Cisneros founded new schools and universities to rival the famed University of Salamanca. Spain herself produced some distinguished practitioners of the new learning, such as Antonio de Nebrija, grammarian, historian, and lexicographer, who in 1492 published and presented to Isabella a Castilian grammar—the first grammar of any modern European language. The vitality of the Castilian language and life found expression in a realistic masterpiece, the novel *La Celestina* (1499) by Fernando de Rojas. Meanwhile, Spanish architecture and sculpture developed its own style, known as plateresque, an ornamental blend of Moorish arabesques, flowers, foliage, and Renaissance motifs.

Foreign Policy

The restoration of domestic peace enabled the sovereigns to turn their attention to questions of foreign policy. For the Castilian Isabella, the conquest of Granada came first. Hardly had their au-

thority been firmly restored when the sovereigns demanded of the Granadan ruler the tribute paid by his predecessors to Castile. Abdul Hassan replied that his mints now coined steel, not gold. The wealth of the Granadan kingdom and its mountainous terrain enabled the Moors to hold out for ten years. But the superior Spanish military power, especially the formidable new arm of artillery, finally broke the Muslim resistance. In January 1492, Granada surrendered to Ferdinand and Isabella, on whom Pope Alexander VI bestowed the title "The Catholic Sovereigns" in honor of their crusading piety.

Whereas Isabella's heart was set on the conquest of Granada, Ferdinand, heir to Aragon's Mediterranean empire and the traditional rivalry between France and Aragon, looked eastward to Aragon's borders with France and to Italy. He achieved most of his goals after Isabella's death in 1504. Employing an adroit blend of war and diplomacy, he obtained the return of two Aragonese provinces lost to France by previous rulers, the incorporation of the kingdom of Naples into the Aragonese empire, and the checkmating of French designs in Italy. In the course of Ferdinand's Italian wars, his commanders, especially the "Great Captain," Gonzalo de Córdoba, created a new-style Spanish army armed with great firepower and strong offensive and defensive weapons. The new system, first tested in Italy, established Spain's military supremacy in Europe. Before his death, Ferdinand rounded out his conquests with the acquisition of Navarre (1512), which gave Spain a strongly defensible frontier with France.

The Catholic Sovereigns rendered major services to the Spanish people. They tamed the arrogant nobility, defeated the Moors, and united the Spanish kingdoms in the pursuit of common goals. They encouraged the growth of trade and industry and showed themselves to be intelligent patrons of learning and the arts. Their prudent diplomacy gave Spain a place among the first powers of Europe. In the same period, America was discovered under Castilian auspices, the Caribbean became a Spanish lake, and Spanish explorers and adventurers, by the end of the

SPAIN IN THE TIME OF CHRISTOPHER COLUMBUS

reign, were at the approaches to the great Indian empires of Mexico and Peru. Small wonder that monarchs who presided over such victories became for succeeding generations of Spaniards the objects of a national cult and legend.

Reappraisal of Ferdinand and Isabella's Policies

For modern historians, the fame of the Catholic Sovereigns has lost some of its luster. These his-

torians charge Ferdinand and Isabella with mistaken policies that nullified much of the sound part of their work. One of these errors was a definite bias in favor of the economic and social interests of the aristocracy. If the nobility lost most of its political power under Ferdinand and Isabella, nothing of the kind happened in the economic sphere. Concentration of land in noble hands actually increased during their reign. The Cortes of 1480, which forced the nobility to surrender about half the lands and revenues usurped from the crown since 1464, explicitly authorized the nobles to retain the vast holdings acquired prior to that date. A policy of assigning a lion's share of the territory reconquered from the Muslims to the grandees also favored the growth of land monopoly. After the War of Granada, moreover, the great nobles used their private armies and increased political influence to expand their territories and seigneurial control. This "aristocratic offensive" met with little resistance from the crown. As a result, about 2 or 3 percent of the population owned 95 percent of the land by 1500.

This land monopoly reduced the great majority of the Castilian peasants to the condition of tenants heavily burdened by rents, seigneurial dues, tithes, and taxes. True, serfdom in the strict sense had apparently disappeared from most parts of Castile by 1480; the Castilian peasant was legally free to leave his village and move elsewhere at will. But since the nobility owned virtually all the land, the peasant's liberty was, as the Spanish historian Jaime Vicens Vives puts it, the liberty "to die of hunger."

The royal policy of favoring sheep raising over agriculture was equally harmful to long-range Spanish economic interests. Like their predecessors, the Sovereigns were influenced by the taxes and export duties paid by the sheep farmers and by the inflow of gold in payment for Spanish wool. As a result, they granted extensive privileges to the sheep raisers' guild, the Mesta. The climax of these favors was a 1501 law that reserved in perpetuity for pasture all land on which the migrant flocks had ever pastured. This measure barred vast tracts of land in Andalusia and Estremadura from being used for agriculture. The privilege granted the shepherds to cut branches from trees for fuel or to make fences and to trim or even fell trees whenever pasturage was scarce, together with the practice of burning the trees in autumn to produce better spring pasturage, contributed heavily to deforestation and soil erosion. Moreover, the overflow of sheep from their legal passage caused much damage to crops and soil. In a time of growing population, these policies and conditions inevitably produced serious food deficits. Chronic shortages climaxed in

a devastating food crisis in the early sixteenth century.

Modern historians also question the traditional view that Spanish industry made spectacular advances under the Catholic Sovereigns. These historians claim that the only true industries of the period were the iron industry of the Basque provinces and the cloth industry of the Castilian central zone, which received a strong stimulus from the discovery of America and the opening of American markets. The resulting industrial prosperity lasted until shortly after the middle of the sixteenth century. But the level of industrial production never reached that of England, the Low Countries, and Italy. The abject poverty of the peasantry, which composed 80 percent of the population, sharply limited the effective market for manufactured goods. Shortages of capital and skilled labor also acted as a brake on industrial expansion. Other obstacles to industrial growth were the excessive costs of transport by mule train and oxcarts across the rugged peninsula and the customs barriers that continued to separate the Spanish kingdoms. Nor were the paternalistic measures of the sovereigns invariably helpful to industry. Through Ferdinand's influence, a guild system modeled on the rigid Catalan model was introduced into the Castilian towns. In this the Sovereigns did Castilian industry no service, for they fastened the straitjacket of guild organization on it precisely at the time when the discovery and colonization of America, the influx of American gold and silver, and the resulting economic upsurge challenged Spanish industry to transform its techniques, lower costs, increase output and quality, and thereby establish Spanish economic as well as political supremacy in Europe.

No policy of the Sovereigns has come under harsher attack than their anti-Semitic measures. During the early Middle Ages, the Jews formed an influential and prosperous group in Spanish society. Down to the close of the thirteenth century, a relatively tolerant spirit prevailed in Christian Spain. Relations among Jews, Christians, and Muslims were so close and neighborly as to provoke protests by the church. In the fourteenth

46

century, these relations began to deteriorate. Efforts by the clergy to arouse hatred of the Jews and popular resentment of such specialized Jewish economic activities as usury and tax farming, which caused severe hardship for peasants and other groups, contributed to this process. The rise of anti-Semitism led to the adoption of repressive legislation by the crown and to a wave of attacks on Jewish communities. To save their lives, many Jews accepted baptism; they came to form a very numerous class of conversos.

Religious intolerance reached a peak during the reigns of Ferdinand and Isabella. In 1492, the Sovereigns ordered all Jews who refused to be baptized to leave Spain. In the picture below, a Jew kneeling before wealthy religious and secular authorities submits to an interrogation. (*Interrogation of the Jew.* Anonymous. Museo de Bellas Artes/Laurie Platt Winfrey, Inc.)

The converts soon achieved a marked prosperity and influence as tax farmers, court physicians, counselors, and lawyers. Wealthy, unhampered by feudal traditions, intellectually curious, intensely ambitious, the conversos incurred the hostility not only of peasants but of the church and of many nobles and burghers. Whether heretics or not, they posed a threat to the feudal order based on landed wealth, hereditary status, and religious orthodoxy. The envy and hostility they aroused help to explain why the Sovereigns, who had surrounded themselves with Jewish and converso advisers, and one of whom (Ferdinand) had Jewish blood in his veins, established the Inquisition and expelled the Jews from Spain. When the crown had tamed the nobility and the towns, when it had acquired large new sources of revenue, its dependence on the Jews and conversos was reduced; these groups became dispensable. The sacrifice of the Jews and conversos sealed the alliance between the absolute monarchy and the church and nobility.

The conversos first felt the blows of religious persecution with the establishment of the Spanish Inquisition in Castile in 1478. The task of this tribunal was to detect, try, and punish heresy, and its special target was the mass of conversos, many of whom were suspected of secretly adhering to Judaism. As a result of the Inquisition's activities, some two thousand conversos were burned at the stake; a hundred and twenty thousand fled abroad. As certain Spanish towns pointed out in memorials protesting the establishment of the Inquisition, the purge had a disastrous effect on the Spanish economy by causing this great flight of the conversos and their capital.

The Jews had a breathing space of twelve years during the costly War of Granada, for they were among the largest contributors to the royal finances. The surrender of Granada, however, brought near a decision on the fate of the Jews. The conquest of a rich territory and an industrious Moorish population, ending the drain of the war, meant that the Jews were no longer financially indispensable. After some hesitation, the Sovereigns yielded to anti-Semitic pressure and, on March 30, 1492, signed the edict giving the Jews the choice of conversion or expulsion.

The destruction or flight of many conversos and the expulsion of the Jews certainly contributed to the dreary picture presented by the Spanish economy at the close of the sixteenth century. The purge of the conversos eliminated from Spanish life its most vital merchant and artisan elements, the groups that in England and Holland were preparing the ground for the Industrial Revolution. The flight of converso artisans dealt Spanish industry a heavy blow and was directly responsible for royal edicts (1484) inviting foreign artisans to settle in Castile with exemption from taxes for ten years.

The anti-Semitic policies of the Sovereigns also harmed Spanish science and thought in general. The Inquisition helped to blight the spirit of free inquiry and discussion in Spain at a time when the Renaissance was giving an extraordinary impulse to the play of European intellect in all fields. The Sovereigns, who laid the foundations of Spain's greatness in so short a time, bear much of the responsibility for its premature decline. But the contradictions in their policies, the incorrect decisions that nullified much of the sound part of their work, resulted from more than personal errors of judgment; they reflected the structural weakness and backwardness of Spanish society as it emerged from seven centuries of struggle against the Moor.

The Hapsburg Era: Triumph and Tragedy

Isabella's death in 1504 placed all of the Iberian Peninsula except Portugal under the rule of Ferdinand. Isabella's will had named her daughter Juana as successor, with the provision that Ferdinand should govern in case Juana proved unable. Since Juana's growing mental instability made her unfit to govern, Ferdinand assumed the regency. Juana's husband, Philip the Handsome of Burgundy, supported by a number of Castilian nobles, challenged Ferdinand's right to rule Cas-

tile, but Philip's sudden death in 1506 left Ferdinand undisputed master of Spain. Ferdinand himself died in 1516. To the Spanish throne ascended his grandson Charles, eldest son of Juana and Philip. Through his maternal grandparents, Charles inherited Spain, Naples and Sicily, and the Spanish possessions in Africa and America. Through his paternal grandparents, Marie of Burgundy and the Holy Roman emperor Maximilian, he inherited the territories of the house of Burgundy, which included the rich Netherlands, and the German possessions of the house of Hapsburg.

The Reign of Charles V

A solemn youth with the characteristic jutting underjaw of the Hapsburgs, Charles (first of that name in Spain and fifth in the Holy Roman Empire) had been born and reared in Flanders and knew no Spanish. Ferdinand had hoped that his younger grandson of the same name, who had been educated in Spain, would succeed him on the throne, but on his deathbed the old king had reluctantly consented to rescind his previous will and name Charles his heir. As the result of the accession of Charles to the throne of Spain, the course of Spanish history underwent a decisive change.

The Catholic Sovereigns, whatever their errors, had attempted to foster Spain's economic development and its partial unity; their prudent diplomacy set for itself limited goals. They had advanced toward absolute monarchy discreetly, respecting both the sensitivities of their peoples and those traditions that did not stand in the way of their designs. Charles, reared at the court of Burgundy in a spirit of royal absolutism, had a different notion of kingship. On his arrival in Spain he immediately alienated his subjects by his haughty manner and by the greed of his Flemish courtiers, whom he placed in all key positions. He aroused even greater resentment by attempting to make the Castilians pay the bill for his election as Holy Roman emperor to succeed his grandfather Maximilian. Having achieved his ambition by expending immense sums of money,

48   which placed him deeply in debt to the German banking house of Fugger, Charles hurried off to Germany.

For Castilians the election appeared to mean an absentee king and heavier tax burdens. Popular wrath burst forth in the revolt of the Castilian towns, or communes, in 1520–1521. The revolt of the *Comuneros* has been called the first bourgeois revolution in Europe, but it began as an essentially conservative movement: the rebels demanded that Charles return to Spain and make his residence there, that the drain of money abroad end, that no more foreigners be appointed to offices in Spain. Many nobles supported the rebellion at this stage, although the grandees remained neutral or hostile. But the leadership of the revolution soon fell into more radical hands. Simultaneously, there arose in Valencia a revolt of the artisans and middle classes against the great landowners. As a result of these developments, the Comunero movement lost almost all aristocratic support. In April 1521 the Comunero army suffered a total defeat, and the revolt began to fall apart. In July 1522, Charles was able to return to Spain, with four thousand German troops at his side. The last effort of the Spanish people to turn the political clock back, to prevent the final success of the centralizing and absolutist policies initiated by the Catholic Sovereigns, had failed.

For a time, at least, the dazzling successes of Charles V in the New and the Old Worlds reconciled the Spanish people to the new course. Spaniards rejoiced over the conquests of Cortés and Pizarro and the victories of the invincible Spanish infantry in Europe. They set to dreaming of El Dorados, universal empires, and a universal church. The poet Hernando de Acuña gave voice to Spain's exalted mood:

One Fold, one Shepherd only on the earth . . .
One Monarch, one Empire, and one Sword.

War dominated Charles's reign: war against France, against the Protestant princes of Germany, against the Turks, even against the pope, whose holdings in central Italy were threatened by Spanish expansionism. Actually, only one of these wars vitally concerned Spain's national interests; this was the struggle with the Turkish Empire, whose growing naval power endangered Aragon's possessions in Italy and Sicily and even threatened Spain's coasts with attack. Yet Charles, absorbed in the Protestant problem and his rivalry with France, pursued this struggle against the infidel less consistently than the others; in the end, it declined to a mere holding operation.

The impressive victories of Spanish arms on land and sea had few tangible results, for Charles, embroiled in too many quarters, could not take full advantage of his successes. In 1556, Charles renounced the Spanish throne in favor of his son Philip. Charles had failed in all his major objectives. The Protestant heresy still flourished in the north; the Turks remained solidly entrenched in North Africa, and their piratical fleets prowled the Mediterranean. Charles's project of placing his son Philip on the imperial throne had broken on the opposition of German princes, Protestant and Catholic, and of Charles's own brother Ferdinand, who wished to make the title of Holy Roman emperor hereditary in his own line. Charles's other dream of bringing England into the empire by marrying Philip to Mary Tudor collapsed when Mary died in 1558.

Meanwhile, Spaniards groaned under a crushing burden of debts and taxes, with Castile bearing the main part of the load. German and Italian merchant-princes and bankers, to whom an ever-increasing part of the royal revenue was pledged for loans, took over important segments of the Spanish economy. The Fuggers assumed the administration of the estates of the military orders and the exploitation of the mercury mines of Almadén. Their rivals, the Welsers, took over the Galician mines and received the American province of Venezuela as a fief whose Indians they barbarously exploited. To find money for his fantastically expensive foreign enterprises, Charles resorted to extraordinary measures: he extracted ever larger grants from the Cortes of Castile and Aragon; he multiplied royal taxes; he appropriated remittances of American treasure to private individuals, compensating the victims with *juros* (bonds). When his son Philip came to the throne in 1556, Spain was bankrupt.

The Reign of Philip II and the Remaining Hapsburgs

The reign of Philip (1556–1598) continued in all essential respects the policies of his father, with the same general results. Spain won brilliant military victories, which Philip failed to follow up from lack of funds or because some new crisis diverted his attention to another quarter. His hopes of dominating France by playing on the divisions between Huguenots and Catholics were frustrated when the Protestant Henry of Navarre entered the Catholic church, a move that united France behind Henry and forced Philip to sign a peace with him. The war against the Turks produced the great sea victory of Lepanto (1571), which broke the Turkish naval power, but when Philip's reign ended, the Turks remained in control of most of North Africa. In the prosperous Netherlands, the richest jewel in his imperial crown, Philip's policies of religious repression and absolutism provoked a great revolt that continued throughout his reign and imposed a terrible drain on the Spanish treasury. War with England flowed from the accession of the Protestant Elizabeth to the throne, from her unofficial support to the Dutch rebels, and from the encroachments of English corsairs and smugglers in American waters.

The crushing defeat of the Invincible Armada in 1588 dealt a heavy blow to Spain's self-confidence and virtually sealed the doom of Philip's crusade against the heretical north. Philip succeeded in another enterprise, the annexation of Portugal (1580), which gave Spain considerably more naval strength and a long Atlantic seaboard to use in a struggle against the Protestant north. But Philip failed to exploit these strategic opportunities, and Portugal, whose colonies and ships now became fair game for Dutch and English seafarers, grew increasingly discontent with a union whose disadvantages exceeded its gains.

At his death in 1598, Philip II left a Spain in which the forces of disintegration were at work but which was still powerful enough militarily and territorially to be feared and respected. Under his successors, Spain entered a rapid decline. This decline first became visible in the area of diplomacy and war. The truce of 1609 with the Dutch, which tacitly recognized Dutch independence, was an early sign of waning Spanish power. The defeat of the famous Spanish infantry at the battle of Rocroi (1643) revealed the obsolescence of Spanish military organization and tactics and marked the end of Spanish military preponderance on the Continent. By the third quarter of the century, Spain, reduced to the defensive, had been compelled to sign a series of humiliating treaties by which she lost the Dutch Netherlands, part of Flanders, Luxembourg, and a string of lesser possessions.

The crisis existed at home as well as abroad. Efforts to make other Spanish kingdoms bear part of the burdens of the wars in which Castile had been so long engaged caused resentment and resistance. The able but imprudent favorite of Philip IV, Count Olivares, aroused a storm by his efforts to billet troops in Catalonia and otherwise make Catalonia contribute to the Castilian war effort at the expense of the ancient fueros, or privileges, of the principality. In 1640 a formidable revolt broke out; it continued for twelve years and shattered the economy of Catalonia. In the same year, Portugal, weary of a union that brought more losses than gains, successfully revolted against Spanish rule. Lesser insurrections took place in Biscay, Andalusia, Sicily, and Naples.

A decline in the quality of Spain's rulers no doubt contributed to this political decline. Philip II, "a glorious failure," had worked diligently to achieve his goals of Spanish predominance in Europe and the liquidation of Protestantism. His successors, Philip III (1598–1621) and Philip IV (1621–1665), were weak and incompetent kings who preferred to leave the work of government in the hands of favorites. The last Hapsburg king of Spain, Charles II (1665–1700), was a pathetic imbecile, totally incapable of ruling.

50

The Waning Economy and Society

The quality of the rulers of Spain had less to do with its decay than the crumbling of the economic foundations on which the empire rested. By the 1590s, the Castilian economy had begun to crack under the strain of costly Hapsburg adventures in foreign policy. Philip II several times resorted to bankruptcy to evade payments of debts to foreign bankers. His successors, lacking Philip's resources, were driven to currency inflation, which caused a flight of gold and silver abroad, until the national currency consisted largely of copper. But the development that contributed most to the Spanish economic crisis was a drastic decline in the inflow of American treasure in the middle decades of the seventeenth century—from about 135 million pesos in the decade from 1591 to 1600 to 19 million pesos in the decade from 1651 to 1660 (the complex causes of this decline will be discussed in Chapter 4).

By the end of the first quarter of the seventeenth century, signs of economic decline were on every hand. In the reign of Charles V, Seville had sixteen thousand looms producing silk and wool; at the death of Philip III in 1621, only four hundred remained. Toledo had fifty woolen manufacturing establishments in the sixteenth century; it had thirteen in 1665. The plight of agriculture was shown by a chronic shortage of foodstuffs, sometimes approaching famine conditions, and by the exodus of peasants from the countryside. Castile became a land of deserted villages. In the period from 1600 to 1700, Spain also suffered an absolute loss of population, from about 8 million to 6 million. The ravages of epidemics, aggravated by near-famine conditions; the expulsion of the Moriscos, or converted Moors. between 1609 and 1614; and emigration to the Indies contributed to this heavy loss.

The economic decline caused a contraction of Spain's artisan and merchant class, strengthened the domination of aristocratic values, and fostered the growth of parasitism. In the seventeenth century, ambitious young Spaniards looked above all to the church and the court for an assured living. In 1626, Spain had nine thousand monasteries; at the end of the century, there were about 200,000 monks and priests in a population of 6 million. The nobility formed another very large unproductive class. At the end of the century, according to one calculation, Spain had four times as many nobles as France with its much larger population. The highest rung of the ladder of nobility was occupied by a small number of grandees—counts, dukes, marquis—who possessed enormous wealth and immense prerogatives; the lowest was occupied by a great number of hidalgos, petty nobles whose sole capital often was their honor and the precious letters patent that attested to their rank and their superiority over base *pecheros* (taxpayers), peasants, artisans, and burghers. The noble contempt for labor infected all classes. The number of vagabonds steadily grew; meanwhile, agriculture lacked enough laborers to till the land.

Literary and Artistic Developments

Spreading into all areas of Spanish life, the *decadencia* (decadence) inspired moods of pessimism, fatalism, and cynicism. Spanish society presented extreme contrasts: great wealth and abject poverty, displays of fanatical piety and scandalous manners, desperate efforts to revive the imperial glories of a past age by kings who sometimes lacked the cash to pay their servants and supply the royal table. The paradoxes of Spanish life, the contrast between the ideal and the real, stimulated the Spanish literary imagination. In this time, so sterile in other respects, Spain enjoyed a Golden Age of letters. As early as 1554, the unknown author of *Lazarillo de Tormes,* first of the picaresque novels, captured the seamy reality of a Spanish world teeming with rogues and vagabonds. Its hero relates his adventures under a succession of masters—a blind beggar, a stingy priest, a hungry hidalgo; he finally attains his highest hope, a sinecure as a town crier, secured for him by a priest whose mistress he had married.

The picaresque genre reached its climax in the *Guzmán de Alfarache* of Mateo de Alemán (1599), with its note of somber pessimism: "All steal, all lie. . . . You will not find a soul who is man unto man." The cleavage in the Spanish soul, the conflict between the ideal and the real, acquired a universal meaning and symbolism in the *Don Quijote* (1605) of Miguel Cervantes de Saavedra. The corrosive satires of Francisco Quevedo (1580–1645) gave voice to the despair of many seventeenth-century intellectuals. "There are many things here," wrote Quevedo, "that seem to exist and have their being, and yet they are nothing more than a name and an appearance."

By contrast, Spanish drama of the Golden Age only faintly reflected the national crisis. The plays of Lope de Vega (1562–1645) are rich in invention, sparkling dialogue, and melodious verse; his gallant hidalgos, courageous and clever heroines, and dignified peasants evoke the best traditions of Spain's past with a curious disregard for the dismal present. The dramas of Calderón de la Barca (1600–1681), however, suggest the defeatist temper of late seventeenth-century Spain by their tragic view of life and their stress on the illusory nature of reality: *"La vida es sueño, y los sueños sueño son"* ("Life is a dream, and our dreams are part of a dream").

Spanish painting of the Golden Age, like the literature, mirrors the transition from the confident and exalted mood of the early sixteenth century to the disillusioned spirit of the late seventeenth century. The great age of painting began with El Greco (1541–1616), whose work blends naturalism, deliberate distortion, and intense emotion to convey the somber religious passion of the Spain of Philip II. Yet some of El Greco's portraits are done with a magnificent realism. The mysticism of El Greco is completely absent from the canvases of Diego Velázquez (1599–1660). With a sovereign mastery of light, coloring, and movement, Velázquez captured for all time the palace life of two Spanish kings, presenting with the same detachment the princes and princesses and the dwarfs and buffoons of the court.

As we shall see in Chapter 5, the seventeenth-century Spanish *decadencia* profoundly influenced the relations between Spain and its American colonies. The loosening of economic and political ties between the mother country and the colonies,

In the portrait *Grand Inquisitor Don Fernando Niño de Guevara,* by El Greco, the majestic robes of the Inquisitor and the intensity of his gaze help to convey the religious passion of Spain's Golden Age. (The Metropolitan Museum of Art, Bequest of Mrs. H. O. Havemeyer, 1929. The H. O. Havemeyer Collection)

along with growing colonial self-sufficiency and self-consciousness, produced a shift in the balance of forces in favor of the colonists—a change that Spain's best efforts could not reverse.

The death of the wretched Charles II in 1700 brought the Hapsburg era to its end. Even before that symbolic death there had been some signs of a Spanish demographic and economic revival, notably in Catalonia, which by the 1670s had made a strong recovery from the depths of the great depression. Under a new foreign dynasty, the Bourbons, who were supported by all the progressive elements in Spanish society, Spain was about to begin a remarkable, many-sided effort at national reconstruction.

Chapter 3

The Conquest of America

The European discovery of America resulted from efforts to find a sea road to the East that would break the monopoly of Egypt and Venice over the lucrative trade in spices and other Oriental products. The drain of their scanty stock of gold and silver into the pockets of Italian and Levantine middlemen had grown increasingly intolerable to the merchants and monarchs of western Europe. Portugal took a decisive lead in the race to find a waterway to the land of spices. It had important advantages over its rivals: a long Atlantic seaboard with excellent harbors, a large class of fishermen and sailors, and an aristocracy that early learned to supplement its meager revenue from the land with income from trade and shipbuilding. Earlier than any other European country, Portugal became a unified nation-state under an able dynasty, the house of Avis, which formed a firm alliance with the merchant class and took a personal interest in the expansion of commerce. This fact helps explain Portugal's head start in the work of discovery. The Portuguese victory of Aljubarrota (1385), gained with English support, ended for a time Castile's efforts to absorb its smaller neighbor and released Portuguese energies for an ambitious program of overseas expansion.

The Great Voyages

Exploration Under Prince Henry

The famous Prince Henry (1394–1460) initiated the Portuguese era of exploration and discovery. Henry, somewhat misleadingly known as "the Navigator" since he never sailed beyond sight of land, united a medieval crusading spirit with the more modern desire to penetrate the secrets of unknown lands and seas and reap the profits of expanded trade. In 1415, Henry participated in the capture of the Moroccan seaport of Ceuta, a great Muslim trading center from which caravans crossed the desert to Timbuktu, returning with ivory and gold obtained by barter from the blacks of the Niger basin. Possession of the African beachhead of Ceuta opened up large prospects for the Portuguese. By penetrating to the sources of Ceuta gold, they could relieve a serious Portuguese shortage of the precious metal; Henry also hoped to reach the land of the fabled Christian ruler Prester John. Prester John was already identified with the emperor of Abyssinia, but no one knew how far his empire extended. An alliance with this ruler, it was hoped, would encircle the Muslims in North Africa with a powerful league of Christian states.

Efforts to expand the Moroccan beachhead, however, made little progress. If the Portuguese could not penetrate the Muslim barrier that separated them from the southern sources of gold and the kingdom of Prester John, could they not reach these goals by sea? In 1419, Henry set up a headquarters at Sagres on Cape St. Vincent, the rocky tip of southeast Portugal. Here he assembled a group of expert seamen and scientists. At the nearby port of Lagos, he began the construction of stronger and larger ships, equipped with the compass and the improved astrolabe. Beginning in 1420, he sent ship after ship to explore the western coast of Africa. Each captain was required to enter in his log data concerning currents, winds, and calms and to sketch the coastline. An eminent converso map maker, Jehuda Crespes, used these data to produce ever more detailed and accurate charts.

The first decade of exploration resulted in the discovery of the Madeiras and the Azores. But progress southward was slow; the imaginary barriers of a flaming torrid zone and a green sea of darkness made sailors excessively cautious. Passage in 1434 around Cape Bojador, the first major landmark on the West African coast, proved these fears groundless. Before Henry's death in 1460, the Portuguese had pushed as far as the Gulf of Guinea and had begun a lucrative trade in gold dust and slaves captured in raids or bought from coastal chiefs. Henry's death brought a slackening in the pace of exploration. But the advance down the African coast continued, under private auspices and as an adjunct to the slave trade—the first bitter fruit of European overseas expansion. In 1469 a wealthy merchant, Fernão Gomes, secured a monopoly of the trade to Guinea (the name then given to the whole African coast), on condition that he explore farther south at the rate of a hundred miles a year. Complying with his pledge, Gomes sent his ships eastward along the Gold, Ivory, and Slave coasts and then southward almost to the mouth of the Congo.

The Sea Route to the East

Under the energetic John II, who came to the throne in 1481, the crown resumed control and direction of the African enterprise. At Mina, on the Gold Coast, John established a fort that became a center of trade in slaves, ivory, gold dust, and a coarse black pepper, as well as a base for further exploration. If Henry had dreamed of finding gold and Prester John, the project of reaching India by rounding Africa was now uppermost in John's mind. In 1483 an expedition commanded by Diogo Cão discovered the mouth of the Congo River and sailed partway up the mighty stream. On a second voyage in 1484, Cão pushed as far south as Cape Cross in southwest Africa. The Portuguese monarch sensed that victory was near. In 1487 a fleet headed by Bartholomeu Dias left Lisbon with orders to pass the farthest point reached by Cão and if possible sail round the tip of Africa. After he had cruised farther south than any captain before him, a providential gale blew Dias's ships in a wide sweep around the Cape of Good Hope and to a landfall on the coast of East Africa. He had solved the problem of a sea road to the Indies and returned to Lisbon to report his success to King John.

The route to the East lay open. But domestic and foreign problems distracted John's attention from the Indian enterprise. He died in 1495 without having sent the expedition for which he had made elaborate preparations. His successor,

Manuel I, known as the Fortunate, carried out John's plan. In 1497 a fleet of four ships, commanded by the tough, surly nobleman Vasco da Gama, sailed from Lisbon on a voyage that inaugurated the age of European imperialism in Asia. After rounding the Cape, da Gama sailed into the Indian Ocean and up the coast of East Africa. At Malinda, in modern Kenya, he took on an Arab pilot who guided the fleet to Calicut, the great spice trade center on the west coast of India. Received with hostility by the dominant Arab traders and with indifference by the local Indian potentate, who scorned his petty gifts, the persistent da Gama managed to load his holds with a cargo of pepper and cinnamon and returned to Lisbon in 1499 with two of the four ships with which he had begun his voyage. A new fleet, commanded by Pedro Álvares Cabral, was quickly outfitted and sent to India. Swinging far west in the south Atlantic, Cabral made a landfall on the coast of Brazil in early 1500 and sent one ship back to Lisbon to report his discovery before continuing to India. He returned to Portugal with a cargo of spices and a story of severe fighting with Arab merchants determined to resist the Portuguese intruders.

The great soldier and administrator Afonso de Albuquerque, who set out in 1509, completed the work begun by da Gama. He understood that in order to squeeze out the Egyptian and Venetian competition and gain a total monopoly of the spice trade he must conquer key points on the trade routes of the Indian Ocean. Capture of Malacca on the Malay Peninsula gave the Portuguese control of the strait through which East Indian spices entered the Indian Ocean. Capture of Muscat and Ormuz barred entrance to the Persian Gulf and closed that route to Europe to other nations' ships. The Portuguese strategy was not completely successful, but it diverted to Lisbon the greater part of the spice supply.

For a time, Portugal basked in the sun of an unprecedented prosperity. But the strain of maintaining its vast Eastern defense establishment was too great for Portugal's limited manpower and financial resources, and expenses began to outrun revenues. To make matters worse,

under Spanish pressure King Manuel decreed the expulsion of all unbaptized Jews in 1496. As a result, Portugal lost the only native group financially capable of exploiting the investment opportunities offered by the Portuguese triumph in the East. Florentine and German bankers quickly moved in and diverted most of the profits of the Eastern spice trade abroad. Lisbon soon became a mere depot. Cargoes arriving there from the East were shipped almost at once to Antwerp or Amsterdam, better situated as centers of distribution to European customers. In time, Dutch and English rivals snatched most of the Asiatic colonies from Portugal's failing hands.

The Voyages of Columbus

The search for a sea road to the Indies inspired more than one solution. If some believed that the route around Africa offered the answer to the Eastern riddle, others favored sailing due west across the Atlantic. This view had the support of an eminent authority, the Florentine scientist Paolo Toscanelli, who in 1474 advised the Portuguese to try the western route as "shorter than the one which you are pursuing by way of Guinea." His letter came to the attention of an obscure Italian seafarer, Christopher Columbus, who had been reflecting on the problem, and helped to confirm his belief that such a passage from Europe to Cipangu (Japan) and Cathay (China) would be easy. This conception rested on a gross underestimate of the earth's circumference and an equal overestimate of the size and eastward extension of Asia. Since all educated Europeans believed that the world was round, that question never entered into the dispute between Columbus and his opponents. The main issue was the extent of the ocean between Europe and Asia, and on this point the opposition was right.

For Columbus the idea of reaching the East by sailing west acquired all the force of an obsession. A figure of transition from the dying Middle Ages to the world of capitalism and science, a curious combination of mystic and practical man, Columbus became convinced that God himself had revealed to him "that it was feasible to sail from here to the Indies, and placed in me a burning desire to carry out this plan."

About 1484, Columbus, who then resided in Lisbon, offered to make a western voyage of discovery for John II, but a committee of experts who listened to his proposal advised the king to turn it down. Undismayed by his rebuff, Columbus next turned to Castile. After eight years of discouraging delays and negotiation, Isabella—in a last-minute change of mind—agreed to support the "Enterprise of the Indies." The *capitulación* (contract) made by the queen with Columbus named him admiral, viceroy, and governor of the lands he should discover and promised him a generous share in the profits of the venture.

On August 3, 1492, Columbus sailed from Palos with three small ships, the *Pinta,* the *Santa María,* and the *Niña,* manned not by the jailbirds of legend but by experienced crews under competent officers. The voyage was remarkably prosperous, with fair winds the whole way out. But the great distance beyond sight of land began to worry some of the men, and by the end of September there was grumbling aboard the *Santa María,* Columbus's flagship. According to Columbus's son Ferdinand, some sailors proposed to heave the admiral overboard and return to Spain with the report that he had fallen in while watching the stars. Columbus managed to calm his men, and soon floating gulfweed and bosun birds gave signs of land. On October 12, they made landfall at an island in the Bahamas that Columbus named San Salvador.[1]

Cruising southward through the Bahamas, Columbus came to the northeast coast of Cuba, which he took for part of Cathay. An embassy sent to find the Great Khan failed in its mission but returned with reports of a hospitable reception by natives who introduced the Spaniards to the use of "certain herbs the smoke of which they inhale"—an early reference to tobacco. Next Columbus sailed eastward to explore the northern coast of an island (present-day Dominican Republic and Haiti) he named Española (Hispaniola). Here the Spaniards were cheered by the discovery of some alluvial gold and gold ornaments, which the natives bartered for Spanish trinkets.

From Hispaniola, on whose coast Columbus lost his flagship, he returned to Spain to report his supposed discovery of the Indies. The Sovereigns received him with signal honors and ordered him to prepare immediately a second expedition to follow up his discovery. In response to Portuguese charges of encroachment on an area in the Atlantic reserved to Portugal by a previous treaty with Castile, Ferdinand and Isabella appealed for help to Pope Alexander VI, himself a Spaniard. The pontiff complied by issuing a series of bulls in 1493 that assigned to Castile all lands discovered or to be discovered by Columbus and drew a line from north to south a hundred leagues west of the Azores and Cape Verdes; west of this line was to be a Spanish sphere of exploration. To John II this demarcation line seemed to threaten Portuguese interests in the south Atlantic and the promising route around Africa to the East. Yielding to Portuguese pressure, Ferdinand and Isabella signed in 1494 the Treaty of Tordesillas, which established a boundary 270 leagues farther west. Portugal obtained exclusive rights of discovery and conquest east of this line; Castile gained the same rights to the west.

Columbus returned to Hispaniola at the end of 1493 with a fleet of seventeen ships carrying twelve hundred people, most of them artisans and peasants, with a sprinkling of "caballeros, hidalgos, and other men of worth, drawn by the fame of gold and the other wonders of that land."

[1] Precisely where Columbus made landfall has long been the subject of controversy, recently rekindled by the approaching quincentenary of the Discovery. For a fascinating account of a five-year search for the landfall island by "a company of varied talents and kindred spirits," see Joseph Judge and James L. Stanfield, "The Island of Landfall," *National Geographic* (November 1986), pp. 566-599. The authors conclude that a "reasoned chain of evidence" leads not to previously favored Watling Island but only to Samana Cay, sixty-five miles north of Watling in the eastern Bahamas, but their conclusions have encountered much criticism.

The settlers soon gave themselves up to gold hunting and preying on the Indians. A foreigner of obscure origins, Columbus lacked the powers and personal qualities needed to control this turbulent mass of fortune hunters.

After founding the town of Isabella on the north coast of Hispaniola, Columbus sailed again in quest of Cathay. He coasted down the southern shore of Cuba almost to its western end. The great length of the island convinced him that he had reached the Asiatic mainland. To extinguish all doubts he made his officers and crews take solemn oath, "on pain of a hundred lashes and having the tongue slit if they ever gainsaid the same," that Cuba was the mainland of Asia. In 1496 he returned to Spain to report his discoveries and answer charges sent by disgruntled settlers to the court. He left behind his brother Bartholomew, who removed the settlement from Isabella to a healthier site on the south shore, naming the new town Santo Domingo.

The first two voyages had not paid their way, but the sovereigns still had faith in Columbus and outfitted a third fleet in 1498. On this voyage he discovered Trinidad and the mouths of the Orinoco. The mighty current of sweet water discharged by the great river made Columbus conclude that he was on the shores of a continent, but his crotchety mysticism also suggested that the Orinoco was one of the four rivers of Paradise and had its source in the Garden of Eden.

Columbus arrived in Hispaniola to find chaos. The intolerable demands of the greedy Castilian adventurers had provoked the peaceable Taino Indians to the point of war. The Spaniards, disappointed in their hopes of quick wealth, blamed the Columbus brothers for their misfortunes and rose in revolt under a leader named Roldán. To appease the rebels Columbus had to issue pardons and grant land and Indian slaves. Meanwhile, acting on a stream of complaints against Columbus, the sovereigns had sent out an agent, Francisco de Bobadilla, to supersede Columbus and investigate the charges against the discoverer. Arriving at the island, the irascible Bobadilla seized Columbus and his brother and sent them to Spain in chains. Although Isabella immediately disavowed Bobadilla's arbitrary actions, Columbus never again exercised the functions of viceroy and governor in the New World.

Still gripped by his great illusion, Columbus continued to dream of finding a western way to the land of spices. He was allowed to make one more voyage, the most difficult and disastrous of all. He was now convinced that between the mainland he had recently discovered and the Malay Peninsula shown on ancient maps there must be a strait that would lead into the Indian Ocean. In 1502 he sailed in search of this strait and a route to southern Asia. From Hispaniola, where he was not permitted to land, he crossed the Caribbean to the coast of Central America and followed it south to the Isthmus of Panama. Here he believed he was ten days' journey from the Ganges River. In Panama he found some gold, but the hoped-for strait continued to elude him. He finally departed for Hispaniola with his two remaining ships but was forced to beach the worm-riddled craft on Jamaica, where he and his men were marooned for a year awaiting the arrival of a relief ship. In November 1504, Columbus returned to Europe. Broken in health, convinced of the ingratitude of princes, he died in 1506 a rich but embittered man.

The Discovery of America in Historical Perspective

The approach of the five hundredth anniversary of the discovery of America in 1992 produced an outpouring of writings seeking to throw new light on that momentous event. There has long been agreement that the Discovery had prodigious consequences, but also dispute as to whether they should cause jubilation or regret. The Spanish chronicler Francisco López de Gómara, filled with imperialist pride, had no doubts on that score. "The greatest event since the creation of the world (excluding the incarnation of Him who created it)," he wrote in 1552, "is the discovery of the Indies." But the radical Italian philosopher Giordano Bruno, who was burned for heresy in 1600, strongly dissented, assailing Columbus as one of those "audacious navigators" who only "disturbed the peace of others . . . increased the vices of nations, spread fresh follies by violence, and . . . taught men a new art and means of tyranny and assassination among themselves." In his *The Wealth of Nations* (1776), Adam Smith, the father of capitalist economic thought, echoed Gómara when he observed that "the discovery of America and that of a passage to the East Indies by the Cape of Good Hope, are the two greatest and most important events recorded in the history of mankind." Almost a century later (1867), in a famous passage of his *Capital,* Karl Marx proclaimed that

the discovery of gold and silver in America, the extirpation, enslavement, and entombment in the mines of the aboriginal population, the beginning of the conquest and looting of the East Indies, the turning of Africa into a warren for the commercial hunting of black-skins, signalized the rosy dawn of capitalist production.

Smith and Marx—one primarily interested in the mighty stimulus given by the discovery of America to economic progress and the other concerned as well with its immense cost in human lives and suffering—illustrate two opposed viewpoints in a continuing debate about the Discovery in terms of its contribution to human welfare or misery.

Until recently, however, few Europeans and Americans questioned the splendor and value of Columbus's achievement. In the course of the nineteenth century the Discovery came to be viewed as a harbinger and cause of the great movement of Western economic expansion and domination of the globe that was then under way. Celebrations of the Discovery were especially exuberant in the United States, where a mystic link was seen between that event and the spectacular rise of the great republic of the West. In this period Columbus was transformed into an almost mythic hero, a larger-than-life figure who overcame all the obstacles placed in his path by prejudiced and ignorant adversaries in order to complete his providential task.

Until well into the twentieth century this view of the Discovery as an event that should inspire

unalloyed pride and satisfaction was rarely challenged. Only the immense political and economic changes caused by World War II and the anticolonial revolutions unleashed by the conflict led to a new way of looking at the Discovery and its repercussions. That new frame of reference is commonly known as "the Vision of the Vanquished" because it takes as its point of departure the impact of the Discovery not on Europe but on the peoples and cultures of the Americas. Awareness of the ethnocentric, Eurocentric connotations of the term "discovery" has even led many scholars to replace it with the more neutral term "encounter" (*encuentro* in Spanish). America, after all, was not an empty continent when the first Europeans arrived; its true "discoverers" were the people who had crossed over from Asia by way of the Bering Strait many thousands of years before. But the word "encounter," with its suggestion of a peaceful meeting of peoples and cultures, hardly fits the grim reality of the European invasion of Indian America, so we shall continue to use "discovery" for lack of a better word.

"The Vision of the Vanquished" initiated a more balanced assessment of the discovery of America and its consequences. Such an assessment begins by noting that, for the native peoples of America, the Discovery and its sequel of the Conquest were an unmitigated disaster. The combination of new diseases to which the Indians had no acquired immunity, their brutal exploitation, and the resulting social disorganization and loss of will to live led to perhaps the greatest demographic catastrophe in recorded history, with an estimated loss of between 90 and 95 percent of the native population between 1492 and 1575. The Discovery and the Conquest also cut short the independent development of brilliant civilizations like the Aztec and Inca empires, which, many scholars believe, had not exhausted their possibilities for further cultural advance and flowering.

The impact of the Discovery on Europe and its long-term development was much more positive. That impact, as noted long ago by Adam Smith and Karl Marx, is clearest in the realm of economics. Historians may debate the impact of

American precious metals on Europe's sixteenth-century "price revolution" or the contribution of the slave trade to the "primitive accumulation" of capital in Europe. It is beyond dispute, however, that the combination of these and other events flowing from the discovery of America gave an immense stimulus to Europe's economic modernization and the rise of capitalism, which in turn hastened and facilitated its domination of the rest of the globe.

The intellectual impact of the Discovery on Europe is more difficult to measure, but it seems indisputable that the expansion of geographical horizons produced by the discovery of America was accompanied by an expansion of mental horizons and the rise of new ways of viewing the world that significantly contributed to intellectual progress. One of the first casualties of the great geographic discoveries was the authority of the ancients and even of the church fathers. Thus the Spanish friar Bartolomé de Las Casas (1484–1566), writing on the traditional belief in uninhabitable zones, in one paragraph managed to demolish the authority of Saint Augustine and the ancients, who, "after all, did not know very much." In the writings of Las Casas and other chroniclers who had actually traveled in America, such phrases as "I can testify from personal experience" or "This I saw with my own eyes" replace the medieval citing of authority as decisive proofs of truthful reporting of the facts.

The discovery of America and its peoples also produced disputes about the origins and nature of the Indians that led to the founding of the science of anthropology. The desire to prove the essential humanity and equality of the Indians inspired some sixteenth-century Spanish missionaries to make profound investigations of Indian culture. One of the greatest of these friar-anthropologists was, again, Bartolomé de Las Casas, one of whose works is an immense accumulation of ethnographic data used to demonstrate that the Indians fully met the requirements laid down by Aristotle for the good life. Las Casas, resting his case above all on experience and observation, offered an environmentalist explanation of cultural differences and regarded with scientific detachment such deviations from European standards as Indian human sacrifices and ritual cannibalism.

Reflection on the apparent novelty and strangeness of some Indian ways, and the effort of pro-Indian friar-anthropologists to understand and explain those ways, also led to the development of a cultural relativism that, like the rejection of authority, represented a sharp break with the past. Las Casas, for example, subjected the term "barbarian" to a careful semantic analysis that robbed it, as applied to advanced Indian cultures like the Aztec or the Inca, of most of its sting. Michel de Montaigne, who avidly read accounts of Indian customs, observed in his famous essay on the Brazilian Indians, "Of Cannibals": "I think there is nothing barbarous and savage in this nation, from what I have been told, except that each man calls barbarian whatever is not his own practice."

The discovery of America and its peoples also inspired some Europeans, troubled by the follies and social injustices of Renaissance Europe, to propose radical new schemes of political and economic organization. In 1516, for example, Thomas More published his *Utopia,* portraying a pagan, socialist society whose institutions were governed by justice and reason, so unlike the states of contemporary Europe, which More described as a "conspiracy of the rich" against the poor. More's narrator, who tells about the Utopians and their institutions, claims to be a sailor who made three voyages with Amerigo Vespucci. The principal source of More's ideas about the evils of private property and the benefits of popular government appears to be a key passage about Indian customs and beliefs in Vespucci's *Second Letter:*

Having no laws and no religious doctrine, they live according to nature. They understand nothing of the immortality of the soul. There is no possession of private property among them, for everything is in common. They have no king, nor do they obey anyone. Each is his own master. There is no administration of justice, which is unnecessary to them. . . .

But if the Discovery had a beneficial impact on European intellectual life, reflected in the new rejection of authority, the growth of cultural relativism, and the impulse it gave to unorthodox social and political thought, it also reinforced the negative European attitudes of racism and ethnocentrism. The great Flemish map maker Abraham Ortelius gave clear expression to these attitudes in his 1579 world atlas. To the map of Europe Ortelius attached a note proclaiming Europe's historic mission of world conquest, in process of fulfillment by Spain and Portugal, "who between them dominate the four parts of the globe." Ortelius declared that the Europeans had always surpassed all other peoples in intelligence and physical dexterity, thus qualifying them to govern the other parts of the globe.

The broad vision of Las Casas, who proclaimed that "all mankind is one," and of Montaigne, who furiously denounced European wars and atrocities against the Indians and proposed a "brotherly fellowship and understanding" as the proper relationship between Europeans and the peoples of the New World, was not typical of contemporary thinking on the subject. Colonial rivals might condemn Spanish behavior toward the Indians, but they usually agreed in regarding them as tainted with vices, and as "poor barbarians."

The perspective of "The Vision of the Vanquished" and new approaches in historical research combine to give us a better understanding of the man Columbus and his dealings with the people he wrongly called "Indians." A curious blend of medieval mystic and modern entrepreneur, Columbus revealed the contradictions in his thought by his comment on gold: "O, most excellent gold! Who has gold has a treasure with which he gets what he wants, imposes his will on the world, and even helps souls to paradise." In his *Conquest of America,* Tźvetan Todorov subjects the ideology of Columbus (which represented the ideology of the European invaders) to a careful and subtle dissection that reveals other contradictions. Sometimes Columbus views the Indians as "noble savages"; sometimes, according to the occasion, he sees them as "filthy dogs." Todorov explains that both myths rest on

a common base: scorn for the Indians and refusal to admit them as human beings with the same rights as himself. In the last analysis, Columbus regards the Indians not as human beings but as objects. This is well illustrated by a letter he wrote to the Spanish monarchs in September 1498:

We can send from here in the name of the Holy Trinity, all the slaves and brazilwood that can be sold. If my information is correct, one could sell 4000 slaves that would bring at least twenty millions. . . . And I believe that my information is correct, for in Castile and Aragon and Italy and Sicily and the islands of Portugal and Aragon and the Canary Islands they use up many slaves, and the number of slaves coming from Guinea is diminishing. . . . And although the Indian slaves tend to die off now, this will not always be the case, for the same thing used to happen with the slaves from Africa and the Canary Islands.

Columbus, of course, wrote from the background of a sea captain and trader who had lived in Portugal and was very familiar with the conduct of Portugal's African slave trade when slavery, under certain conditions, was almost universally regarded as licit and proper. His callous lack of concern for the life and death of the Indians he enslaved does not make him a monster. If he ardently desired gold it was not from vulgar greed but in order to promote the universal triumph of Christianity; he repeatedly urged his royal masters to use the revenues from the Indies for a crusade to wrest the Holy Land from Muslim hands. To assess the significance of Columbus's achievement properly, it must be understood that he was the instrument of historical forces of which he was unaware, forces of transition from the dying Middle Ages to the rising world of capitalism, whose success required the conquest of the world and the creation of a world market. That process in turn required an ideological justification, a proud conviction of the superiority of white Europeans over all other peoples and races. Columbus's work in the Caribbean represents the first tragic application of that ideology in the New World.

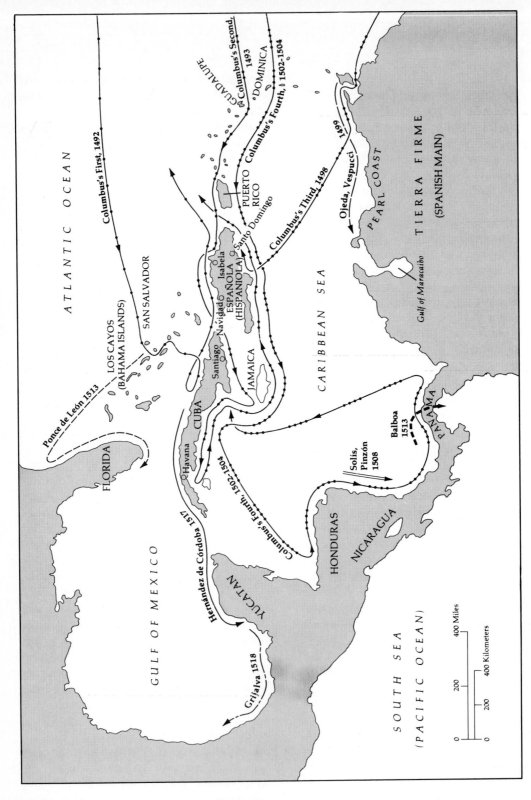

EARLY SPANISH VOYAGES IN THE CARIBBEAN

Balboa and Magellan

Other explorers followed in the wake of Columbus's ships and gradually made known the immense extent of the mainland coast of South America. In 1499, Alonso de Ojeda, accompanied by the pilot Juan de la Cosa and the Florentine Amerigo Vespucci, sailed to the mouths of the Orinoco and explored the coast of Venezuela. Vespucci took part in another voyage in 1501–1502 under the flag of Portugal. This expedition, sent to follow up the discovery of Brazil by Pedro Álvares Cabral in 1500, explored the Brazilian coast from Salvador da Bahia to Rio de Janeiro before turning back. Vespucci's letters to his patrons, Giovanni and Lorenzo de' Medici, reveal an urbane, cultivated Renaissance figure with a flair for lively and realistic description of the fauna, flora, and inhabitants of the New World. His letters were published and circulated widely in the early 1500s. One (whose authenticity is disputed) told of a nonexistent voyage in 1497 and gave him the fame of being the first European to set foot on the South American continent. A German geographer, Martin Waldseemuller, decided to honor Vespucci by assigning the name America to the area of Brazil in a map of the newly discovered lands. The name caught on and presently was applied to the whole of the New World.

A growing shortage of Indian labor and the general lack of economic opportunities for new settlers on Hispaniola incited Spanish slave hunters and adventurers to explore and conquer the remaining Greater Antilles. Puerto Rico, Jamaica, and Cuba were occupied between 1509 and 1511. In the same period, efforts to found colonies on the coast of northern Colombia and Panama failed disastrously, and the remnants of two expeditions were united under the energetic leadership of the conquistador Vasco Núñez de Balboa to form the new settlement of Darien on the Isthmus of Panama. Moved by Indian tales of a great sea, south of which lay a land overflowing with gold, Balboa led an expedition across the forests and mountains of Panama to the shores of the Pacific. He might have gone on to discover the Inca Empire of Peru if he had not aroused the jealousy of his terrible father-in-law, the "two-legged tiger," Pedrarias Dávila, sent out by Charles V in 1514 as governor of the isthmus. Charged with treason and desertion, the discoverer of the Pacific was tried, condemned, and beheaded in 1519.

The discovery of the "South Sea" confirmed Columbus's reports on his fourth voyage of a narrow isthmus beyond which lay a sea that led to India. Although further exploration was required to dispel the lingering belief that the whole American landmass was a peninsula projecting from southeast Asia, the work of discovery after 1513 centered on the search for a waterway to the East through or around the American continent. Ferdinand Magellan, a Portuguese who had fought in India and the East Indies, was convinced that a short passage to the East existed south of Brazil. Failing to interest the Portuguese king in his project, Magellan turned to Spain, with greater success. The resulting voyage of circumnavigation of the globe, 1519–1522, the first in history, represented an immense navigational feat and greatly increased Europe's stock of geographical knowledge. But, aside from the acquisition of the Philippines for Spain, Magellan's exploit had little practical value, for his new route to the East was too long to have commercial significance. The net result was to enhance the value of America in Spanish eyes. Disillusioned with the dream of easy access to the riches of the East, Spain turned with concentrated energy to the task of extending her American conquests and to the exploitation of the human and natural resources of the New World.

The Conquest of Mexico

Early Contact with Moctezuma

A disturbing report reached the Aztec capital of Tenochtitlán in 1518. Up from the coast of the Gulf of Mexico hurried the tribute collector Pinotl to inform King Moctezuma of the approach from

62
the sea of winged towers bearing men with white faces and heavy beards. Pinotl had communicated with these men by signs and had exchanged gifts with their leader. Before departing, the mysterious visitors had promised (so Pinotl interpreted their gestures) to return soon and visit Moctezuma in his city in the mountains.

Indian accounts agree that the news filled Moctezuma with dismay. Could the leader of these strangers be the redeemer-god Quetzalcóatl, returning to reclaim his lost kingdom? According to one Aztec source, Moctezuma exclaimed: "He has appeared! He has come back! He will come here, to the place of his throne and canopy, for that is what he promised when he departed!"

The "winged towers" were the ships of the Spanish captain Juan de Grijalva, sent by Governor Diego Velázquez of Cuba to explore the coasts whose existence the slave-hunting expedition of Francisco Hernández de Córdoba (1517) had already made known. Córdoba had discovered the peninsula of Yucatán, inhabited by Maya Indians whose cotton cloaks and brilliant plumes, stone pyramids, temples, and gold ornaments revealed a native culture far more advanced than any the Spaniards had hitherto encountered. Córdoba met with disastrous defeat at the hands of the Maya and returned to Cuba to die of his wounds. He brought back enough gold and other signs of Indian wealth, however, to encourage Velázquez to outfit a new venture, which he entrusted to his kinsman Juan de Grijalva.

Grijalva sailed from Santiago in April 1518, touched at the island of Cozumel on the northeastern corner of Yucatán, then coasted down the peninsula, following Córdoba's route. In June they reached the limits of Moctezuma's empire. At a river that Grijalva named Banderas they were greeted by natives waving white flags and inviting them by signs to draw near. Here Grijalva's flagship was boarded by the Aztec official Pinotl, whose report was to cause so much consternation in Tenochtitlán. A lively trade developed, with Indians bartering gold for Spanish green beads. Grijalva was now convinced that he had come to a wealthy kingdom filled with many large towns. Near the present port of Veracruz, Grijalva sent Pedro de Alvarado back to Cuba with the gold that had been gained by barter. Alvarado was to report to Velázquez what had been accomplished, request authority to found a colony, and seek reinforcements. Grijalva himself sailed on with three other ships, perhaps as far as the river Pánuco, which marked the northern limits of the Aztec Empire. Then he turned back and retraced his course, arriving in Cuba in November 1518.

Cortés-Quetzalcóatl

Velázquez was already planning a third expedition to conquer the Mexican mainland. He passed over his kinsman Grijalva and chose as leader of the expedition the thirty-four-year-old Hernando Cortés, a native of Medellín in the Spanish province of Estremadura. Cortés was born in 1485 into an hidalgo family of modest means. At the age of fourteen he went to Salamanca, seat of a great Spanish university, to prepare for the study of law, but left some years later, determined on a military career. He had to choose between Italy, the great battlefield of Europe, where Spanish arms were winning fame under the great captain Gonzalo de Córdoba, and the Indies, land of gold, Amazons, and El Dorados. In 1504, aged nineteen, he embarked for Hispaniola.

Soon after arriving on the island he participated in his first military exploit, the suppression of a revolt of Indians made desperate by Spanish mistreatment. His reward was an *encomienda* (a grant of Indian tribute and labor). In 1511 he served under Velázquez in the easy conquest of Cuba. The following year he was appointed alcalde of the newly founded town of Santiago in Cuba. In 1518 he persuaded Velázquez to give him command of the new expedition to the Mexican mainland. At the last moment the distrustful governor decided to recall him, but Cortés simply disregarded Velázquez's messages. In February 1519, he sailed from Cuba with a force of some six hundred men. Because Velázquez had not completed negotiations with the emperor

Charles for an agreement authorizing the conquest and settlement of the mainland, Cortés's instructions permitted him only to trade and explore.

Cortés's fleet first touched land at the island of Cozumel, where they rescued a Spanish castaway, Jerónimo de Aguilar, who had lived among the Maya for eight years. In March 1519, Cortés landed on the coast of Tabasco, defeated local Indians in a sharp skirmish, and secured from them along with pledges of friendship the Mexican girl Malinche, who was to serve him as interpreter, adviser, and mistress. In April he dropped anchor near the site of modern Veracruz. He had contrived a way to free himself from Velázquez's irksome authority. In apparent deference to the wishes of a majority of his followers, who claimed that conquest and settlement would serve the royal interest better than mere trade, Cortés founded the town of Villa Rica de la Vera Cruz and appointed its first officials, into whose hands he surrendered the authority he had received from Velázquez. These officials then conferred on Cortés the title of captain general with authority to conquer and colonize the newly discovered lands. Cortés thus drew on Spanish medieval traditions of municipal autonomy to vest his disobedience in a cloak of legality.

Some days later, Moctezuma's ambassadors appeared in the Spanish camp. The envoys brought precious gifts, the finery of the great gods Tlaloc, Tezcatlipoca, and Quetzalcóatl. Reverently, they arrayed Cortés in the finery of Quetzalcóatl. On his face they placed a serpent mask inlaid with turquoise, with a crossband of quetzal feathers and a golden earring hanging down on either side. On his breast they fastened a vest decorated with quetzal feathers; about his neck they hung a collar of precious stones with a gold disc in the center. They fastened a mirror encrusted with turquoises to his hips, placed a cloak with red borders about his shoulders, and adorned his feet with greaves set with precious stones and hung with little bells. In his hand they placed a shield with ornaments of gold and mother-of-pearl and a fringe and pendant of quetzal feathers. They also set before him sandals of fine, soft rubber, black as obsidian.

The Aztec account relates that the god was not satisfied. "Is this all?" Cortés is said to have asked. "Is this your gift of welcome? Is this how you greet people?" The stricken envoys departed and returned with gifts more to the god's liking, including a gold disc in the shape of the sun, as big as a cartwheel, an even larger disc of silver in the shape of the moon, and a helmet full of small grains of gold.

The envoys reported to Moctezuma what they had heard and seen, supplementing their accounts with painted pictures of the gods and their possessions. They described the firing of a cannon, done on Cortés's order to impress the Aztec emissaries:

A thing like a ball of stone comes out of its entrails; it comes out shooting sparks and raining fire. The smoke that comes out with it has a pestilent odor, like that of rotten mud. . . . If the cannon is aimed against a mountain, the mountain splits and cracks open. If it is aimed against a tree, it shatters the tree into splinters.

Vividly, they described other weapons, the armor, and the mounts of the Spaniards.

Of the terrible war dogs of the Spaniards the envoys said:

Their dogs are enormous, with flat ears and long dangling tongues. The color of their eyes is burning yellow; their eyes flash fire and shoot off sparks. Their bellies are hollow, their flanks long and narrow. They are tireless and very powerful. They bound here and there, panting, with their tongues hanging out. And they are spotted like an ocelot.[2]

Moctezuma's envoys assured Cortés that they would serve him in every way during his stay on the coast but pleaded with him not to seek

---

[2] Miguel Leon-Portilla, ed., *The Broken Spears: The Aztec Account of the Conquest of Mexico* (Boston: Beacon Press, 1962), pp. 30-31.

64

a meeting with their king. This pleading was part of Moctezuma's pathetic strategy of plying Cortés-Quetzalcóatl with gifts in the hope that he would be dissuaded from advancing into the interior and reclaiming his lost throne. Suavely, Cortés informed the ambassadors that he had crossed many seas and journeyed from very distant lands to see and speak with Moctezuma and could not return without doing so.

The March to Tenochtitlán

Becoming aware of the bitter discontent of tributary towns with Aztec rule, Cortés began to play a double game. He encouraged the Totonac Indians of the coast to seize and imprison Moctezuma's tax collectors but promptly obtained their release and sent them to the king with expressions of his regard and friendship. He took two other steps before beginning the march on Tenochtitlán. To Spain he sent a ship with dispatches for the emperor Charles in which he sought to obtain approval for his actions by describing the great extent and value of his discoveries. To help in gaining the emperor's goodwill, Cortés persuaded his men to send Charles not only his *quinto* (royal fifth) but all the treasure received from Moctezuma. In order to stiffen the resolution of his followers by cutting off all avenues of escape, he scuttled and sank all his remaining ships on the pretext that they were not seaworthy. Then Cortés and his small army began the march on Mexico-Tenochtitlán.

Advancing into the sierra, Cortés entered the territory of the tough Tlaxcalan Indians, traditional enemies of the Aztecs. The Spaniards had to prove in battle the superiority of their weapons and their fighting capacity before they obtained an alliance with this powerful tribe. Then Cortés marched on Cholula, an ancient center of Classic cultural traditions and the cult of Quetzalcóatl. Here, claiming that the Cholulans were conspiring to attack him, Cortés staged a mass slaughter of the Cholulan nobility and warriors after they had assembled in a great courtyard. When news of this event reached Tenochtitlán, terror spread throughout the city.

The Spaniards continued their inexorable advance:

They came in battle array, as conquerors, and the dust rose in whirlwinds on the roads. Their spears glinted in the sun, and their pennons fluttered like bats. They made a loud clamor as they marched, for their coats of mail and their weapons clashed and rattled. Some of them were dressed in glistening iron from head to foot; they terrified everyone who saw them.[3]

Moctezuma's fears and doubts had by now reduced him to a hopelessly indecisive state of mind. He wavered between submission and resistance, between the conviction that the Spaniards were gods and half-formed suspicions that they were less than divine. He sent new envoys, who brought rich gifts to Cortés but urged him to abandon his plan of visiting the Aztec capital. Moctezuma's naive efforts to bribe or cajole the terrible strangers who "longed and lusted for gold," who "hungered like pigs for gold," in the bitter words of an Indian account, proved vain. As Moctezuma's doom approached, his own gods turned against him. A group of sorcerers and soothsayers sent by the king to cast spells over the Spaniards were stopped by the young god Tezcatlipoca, who conjured up before their terrified eyes a vision of Mexico-Tenochtitlán burning to the ground. His forces spent, Moctezuma ended by welcoming Cortés at the entrance to the capital as a rightful ruler returning to his throne. The Aztec king completed his degradation by allowing himself to be kidnaped from his palace by Cortés and a few comrades and taken to live as a hostage in the Spanish quarters.

The Aztec nation had not said its last word. In Cortés's absence from the city—he had set off for the coast to face an expedition sent by Governor Velázquez to arrest him—his lieutenant Pedro de Alvarado ordered an unprovoked massacre of the leading Aztec chiefs and warriors as they celebrated with song and dance a religious festival in honor of Huitzilopochtli. The result was a popular uprising that forced the Spaniards to retreat

[3] Ibid., p. 41.

to their own quarters. This was the situation that Cortés, having won over most of the newcomers and defeated the rest, found when he returned to Tenochtitlán to rejoin his comrades. His efforts to pacify the Aztecs failed. The tribal council deposed the captive Moctezuma and elected a new chief, who launched heavy attacks on the invaders. As the fighting raged, Moctezuma died, killed by stones cast by his own people as he appealed for peace, according to Spanish accounts; strangled by the Spaniards themselves, according to Indian sources. Fearing a long siege and famine, Cortés evacuated Tenochtitlán at a heavy cost in lives. The surviving Spaniards and their Indian allies at last reached friendly Tlaxcala.

Strengthened by the arrival of Spanish reinforcements from Cuba and by thousands of Indians who joined the fight against their old masters, Cortés again marched on Tenochtitlán in December 1520. A ferocious struggle began in late April 1521. On August 23, after a siege in which the Aztecs fought for four months with extraordinary bravery, their last king, Cuauhtemoc, surrendered amid the laments of his starving people. Cortés took possession of ruins that had been the city of Tenochtitlán.

Cuauhtémoc surrenders to Cortés after a futile attempt to escape capture. (From *Escenas de la Conquista,* Rafael Lopez Castro y Felipe Garrido [Ediciones del Ermitaño]. Reprinted by permission)

66

The Aftermath of Conquest

From the Valley of Mexico the process of conquest was extended in all directions. Guatemala was reduced by Pedro de Alvarado, Honduras by Cortés himself. In 1527, Francisco de Montejo began the conquest of Yucatán, but as late as 1542 the Maya rose in a desperate revolt that was crushed with great slaughter. Meanwhile, expeditions from Darien subjugated the Indians of Nicaragua. Thus did the two streams of Spanish conquest, both originally starting from Hispaniola, come together again.

For a brief time, Cortés was undisputed master of the old Aztec Empire, renamed the Kingdom of New Spain. He made grants of encomienda to his soldiers, reserving for himself the tributes of the richest towns and provinces. The crown rewarded his services by granting him the title of marquis of the Valley of Oaxaca and the tributes of twenty-three thousand Indian vassals; he lived in almost kingly style, dining "with minstrels and trumpets." But royal distrust of the great conquerors soon asserted itself. He was removed from his office of governor, his authority was vested in an *audiencia* (high court), pending the appointment of a viceroy, and all his actions came under close legal scrutiny. In 1539 he returned to Spain and served with distinction in the expedition against Algiers in the following year, but he was ignored and snubbed by the king. Filled with bitterness, he retired to live in seclusion in Seville. He died in 1547, leaving his title and estates to his eldest legitimate son, Martín Cortés.

The Conquest of Peru

The conquest of Mexico challenged other Spaniards to match the exploits of Cortés and his companions. The work of discovering a golden kingdom rumored to lie beyond the "South Sea" was begun by Balboa but cut short by his death at the hands of Pedrarias Dávila. In 1519, Dávila founded the town of Panama on the western side of the isthmus, and this town became a base for explorations along the Pacific coast. Three years later, Pascual de Andagoya crossed the Gulf of San Miguel and returned with more information concerning a land of gold called "Biru."

Pizarro and Atahualpa

Dávila entrusted direction of a voyage of discovery southward to Francisco Pizarro, an illiterate soldier of fortune little of whose early history is known. Pizarro recruited two partners for the Peruvian venture: Diego de Almagro, an adventurer of equally obscure origins, and Hernando de Luque, a priest who acted as financial agent for the trio. Two preliminary expeditions, fitted out from Panama in 1524 and 1526, yielded enough finds of gold and silver to confirm the existence of the elusive kingdom. Pizarro now left for Spain to obtain royal sanction for the enterprise of Peru. He returned to Panama with the titles of captain general and *adelantado* (commander), accompanied by his four brothers and other followers. Almagro, dissatisfied with the allotment of titles and other rewards in the royal contract, accused Pizarro of slighting his services to the king. The quarrel was patched up, but it contained the seeds of a deadly feud.

In December 1531, Pizarro again sailed from Panama for the south with a force of some two hundred men and landed several months later on the Peruvian coast. On arrival the Spaniards learned that civil war was raging in the Inca Empire. Atahualpa, son of the late emperor Huayna Capac by a secondary wife, had risen against another claimant of the throne, his half-brother, Huascar, defeated him in a war marked by great slaughter, and made him prisoner. Atahualpa was advancing toward the imperial capital of Cuzco when messengers brought him news of the arrival of white strangers. After an exchange of messages and gifts between the leaders, the two armies advanced to a meeting at the town of Cajamarca, high in the mountains.

Perhaps in direct imitation of Cortés, Pizarro proposed to win a quick and relatively bloodless victory by seizing the Inca Atahualpa, through whom he may have hoped to rule the country, much as Cortés had done with Moctezuma. In one important respect, however, the Peruvian story differs from that of Mexico. If Moctezuma's undoing was his passive acceptance of the divinity of the invaders, Atahualpa's mistake was to underestimate the massed striking power of the small Spanish force. He had been led to believe that the swords were no more dangerous than women's weaving battens, that the firearms were capable of firing only two shots, and that the horses were powerless at night. This last delusion apparently led to his delayed entry into Cajamarca at dusk, instead of noon, as Pizarro had been told to expect.

When Atahualpa and his escort appeared for the rendezvous in the square of Cajamarca, he found it deserted, for Pizarro had concealed his men in some large buildings opening on the square. Then the priest Vicente de Valverde came forward, accompanied by an interpreter, to harangue the bewildered Inca concerning his obligations to the Christian God and the Spanish king until the angry emperor threw down a Bible, which Valverde had handed him. At a signal from Pizarro, his soldiers, supported by cavalry and artillery, rushed forward to kill hundreds of the terrified Indians and take the Inca prisoner. "It was a very wonderful thing," wrote a Spanish observer, "to see so great a lord, who came in such power, taken prisoner in so short a time."

Atahualpa vainly sought to gain his freedom by offering to fill his spacious cell higher than a man could reach with gold objects as the price of his ransom. Pizarro accepted the offer, and hundreds of llama-loads of gold arrived from all parts of the empire until the room had been filled to the stipulated height. But Pizarro had no intention of letting the emperor go; he remained in "protective custody," a puppet ruler who was to insure popular acceptance of the new order. Soon, however, the Spaniards began to suspect that Atahualpa was becoming the focal point of a widespread conspiracy against them and decided that he must die. He was charged with treason and

Atahualpa, last of the independent Incan emperors, grandly displayed his regal power with an array of golden objects. The litter on which he rode was sheathed in gold and he wore a golden headband and earplugs. (Courtesy, Sotheby Parke-Bernet)

condemned to death by burning, a sentence commuted to strangling on his acceptance of baptism.

After the death of the Inca, the Spaniards marched on the Inca capital of Cuzco, which they captured and pillaged in November 1533. A major factor in the success of this and later Spanish campaigns was the military and other assistance given by the late Huascar's branch of the Inca royal family and by curacas who, seeing an opportunity to regain their lost independence and power, rallied to the Spanish side after the capture of Atahualpa. The gold and silver looted from Cuzco, together with Atahualpa's enormous ransom of gold, was melted down and divided among the soldiers. Hernando Pizarro, Francisco's brother, was sent to Spain with Emperor Charles's share of the plunder. Hernando's arrival with his load of gold and silver caused feverish excitement, and a new wave of Spanish fortune hunters sailed for the New World. Meanwhile, Francisco Pizarro had begun construction of an entirely new Spanish capital, Lima, the City of the Kings, conveniently near the coast for communication with Panama.

Post-Conquest Troubles

After Atahualpa's death, Pizarro, posing as the defender of the legitimate Inca line, proclaimed Huascar's brother Manco as the new Inca. But Manco was not content to play the role of a Spanish puppet. A formidable insurrection, organized and led by Manco himself, broke out in many parts of the empire. A large Indian army laid siege to Cuzco for ten months but failed by a narrow margin to take the city. Defeated by superior Spanish weapons and tactics and by food shortages in his army, Manco retreated to a remote stronghold in the Andean mountains, where he and his successors maintained a kind of Inca government-in-exile until 1572, when a Spanish military expedition entered the mountains, broke up the imperial court, and captured the last Inca, Tupac Amaru, who was beheaded in a solemn ceremony at Cuzco.

The Indian siege of Cuzco had barely been broken when fighting began between a group of the conquerors headed by the Pizarro brothers and a group led by Diego de Almagro over possession of the city of Cuzco. Defeated in battle, Almagro suffered death by strangling but left behind him a son and a large group of supporters to brood over their poverty and supposed wrongs. Twelve of them, contemptuously dubbed by Pizarro's secretary "the knights of the cape" because they allegedly had only one cloak among them, planned and carried out the assassination of the conqueror of Peru in June 1541. But their triumph

was of short duration. From Spain came a judge, Vaca de Castro, sent by Charles V to advise Pizarro concerning the government of his province. Assuring himself of the loyalty of Pizarro's principal captains, Vaca de Castro made war on Almagro's son, defeated his army on the "bloody plains of Chupas," and promptly had him tried and beheaded as a traitor to the king.

Presently, fresh troubles arose. Early in 1544, a new viceroy, Blasco Núñez Vela, arrived in Lima to proclaim the edicts known as the New Laws of the Indies. These laws regulated Indian tribute, freed Indian slaves, and forbade forced labor by the Indians. They evoked outraged cries and appeals for their suspension from the Spanish landowners in Peru. When these pleas were not heeded, the desperate conquistadors rose in revolt and found a leader in Gonzalo Pizarro, brother of the murdered Francisco.

The first phase of the great revolt in Peru ended auspiciously for Gonzalo Pizarro with the defeat and death of the viceroy Núñez Vela in a battle near Quito. Pizarro now became the uncrowned king of the country. The rebel leader owed much of his initial success to the resourcefulness and demoniac energy of his eighty-year-old field commander and principal adviser, Francisco de Carbajal. To these qualities Carbajal united an inhuman cruelty that became legendary in Peru.

After his victory over the viceroy, Carbajal and other advisers urged Pizarro to proclaim himself king of Peru. But Pizarro, a weaker man than his iron-willed lieutenant, hesitated to avow the revolutionary meaning of his actions. The arrival of a smooth-tongued envoy of the crown, Pedro de la Gasca, who announced suspension of the New Laws and offered pardons and rewards to all repentant rebels, caused a trickle of desertions from Pizarro's ranks that soon became a flood. As his army melted away, Carbajal is said to have hummed the words of an old Spanish song: "These my hairs, mother, two by two the breeze carries them away."

Finally, the rebellion collapsed almost without a struggle, and its leaders were executed. Before the civil wars in Peru had run their course, four of the Pizarro "brothers of doom" and the Almagros, father and son, had met violent deaths; a viceroy had been slain; and numberless others had lost their lives. Peace and order were not solidly established in the country until the administration of Viceroy Francisco de Toledo, who came out in 1569, a quarter-century after the beginning of the great civil wars.

The Quest for El Dorado

Exploration in North America

From its original base in the West Indies and from the two new centers of Mexico and Peru, the great movement of Spanish exploration radiated in all directions. While Spanish ships were launched on the waters of the Pacific to search for the Spice Islands, land expeditions roamed the interior of North and South America in quest of new golden kingdoms.

The North American mainland early attracted the attention of Spanish gold hunters and slave hunters based in the West Indies. In 1513, Ponce de León, governor of Puerto Rico, sailed west and discovered a subtropical land to which he gave the name La Florida. His subsequent efforts to colonize the region ended with his death at the hands of Indians. In the 1520s another expedition, ineptly led by Pánfilo de Narváez, met with disaster in the vast, indefinite expanse of La Florida. Only four survivors of the venture, among them its future chronicler, the honest and humane Alvar Núñez Cabeza de Vaca, reached Mexico safely after a great, circuitous trek over the plains of Texas. In the last stages of his journey, Cabeza de Vaca was followed by thousands of adoring Indians, "clouds of witnesses" to his reputation as a medicine man of great powers.

Cabeza de Vaca's tales of adventure, with their hints of populous cities just beyond the horizon, inspired the conquistador Hernando de Soto, a veteran of the conquest of Peru, to try his fortune in La Florida. In 1542, after three years of unprofitable wanderings and struggles with Indians in the great area between modern-day South Carolina and Arkansas, the discoverer of the Mississippi died in the wilderness of a fever.

The strange tales told by Cabeza de Vaca and his three companions on their arrival in Mexico in 1536, and the even stranger story told by a certain Fray Marcos, who claimed to have seen in the far north one of the Seven Cities of the mythical golden realm of Cibola (from a great distance, it was true), persuaded Viceroy Antonio de Mendoza in 1540 to send an expedition northward commanded by Francisco Vásquez de Coronado. For two years, Spanish knights in armor pursued the elusive realm of gold through the future states of Arizona, New Mexico, Colorado, Oklahoma, Kansas, and possibly Nebraska. Disillusioned by the humble reality of the Zuñi pueblos of Arizona, the apparent source of the Cibola myth, Coronado went on to discover the Grand Canyon of the Colorado and then pushed east in search of still another El Dorado, this time called Quivira. Intruders who left no trace of their passage, the Spaniards were repelled by the immensity of the great plains and returned home bitterly disappointed with their failure to find treasure.

Further Exploration in South America

The golden will-o'-the-wisp that lured Spanish knights into the deserts of the Southwest also beckoned to them from South America's jungles and mountains. From the town of Santa Marta, founded in 1525 on the coast of modern Colombia, an expedition led by Gonzalo Jiménez de Quesada set out in 1536 on a difficult journey up the Magdalena River in search of gold and a passage to the Pacific. They suffered incredible hardships before they finally emerged onto the high plateau east of the Magdalena inhabited by the Chibcha. These Indians were primarily farmers, were skillful in casting gold and copper ornaments, lived in palisaded towns, and were ruled by a chieftain called the Zipa. After defeating them in battle, Jiménez de Quesada founded in

EARLY SPANISH OVERLAND EXPEDITIONS

1538 the town of Santa Fé de Bogatá, future capital of the province of New Granada. The immense treasure in gold and emeralds looted from the Chibcha fired Spanish imaginations and inspired fantasies about yet other golden kingdoms. The most famous of these legends was that of El Dorado (the Golden Man).

The dream of spices also played its part in inspiring the saga of Spanish exploration and conquest. Attracted by accounts of an eastern land where cinnamon trees grew in profusion, Gonzalo Pizarro led an expedition in 1539 from Quito in modern Ecuador across the Andes and down the forested eastern slopes of the mountains. Cinnamon was found, but in disappointingly small quantities. Lured on by the customary Indian tall tales of rich kingdoms somewhere beyond the horizon, designed to trick the intruders into moving on, the treasure hunters plunged deep into the wilderness. Gonzalo's lieutenant, Francisco de Orellana, sent with a party down a certain stream in search of food, found the current too strong to return and went on to enter a great river whose course he followed in two makeshift boats for a distance of eighteen hundred leagues, eventually emerging from its mouth to reach Spanish settlements in Venezuela. Meanwhile, the disgruntled Pizarro and his men made their way back home as best they could. On the banks of the great river, Orellana fought Indians whose women joined the battle. For this reason, he gave the river its Spanish name of Amazonas—an illustration of the myth-making process among the Spaniards of the Conquest.

Among others who pursued phantom kingdoms in the wilderness of the Amazon and Orinoco river systems was Sir Walter Raleigh, wise in other things but naive and credulous in the matter of El Dorado. Raleigh staked and lost his head on his promise to find a gold mine for King James of England. His description of the "Rich and Beautiful Empire of Guiana" incorporated just about all the elements of the legend of El Dorado, including the themes of lost Inca treasure, the Golden Man who was anointed with gold dust, which he washed off in a sacred lake, and a warlike tribe of women.

In the southern reaches of the continent, which possessed little gold or silver, new agricultural and pastoral settlements arose. In 1537, Pizarro's comrade and rival, Diego de Almagro, made a fruitless march across the rugged Andean altiplano and the sun-baked Chilean desert in search of gold. He returned, bitterly disappointed, to a final confrontation with Pizarro. Two years later, Pizarro authorized Pedro de Valdivia to undertake the conquest of the lands to the south of Peru. After crossing the desert of northern Chile, Valdivia reached the fertile Central Valley and founded there the town of Santiago. In constant struggle with the Araucanian Indians, Valdivia laid the foundations of an agricultural colony based on the servile labor of other, more pacific Indians. He was captured and killed by the Araucanians during an expedition southward in 1553.

In the same period (1536), the town of Buenos Aires was founded on the estuary of the Rio de la Plata by the adelantado Pedro de Mendoza, who brought twenty-five hundred colonists in fourteen ships. But Buenos Aires was soon abandoned by its famished inhabitants, who moved almost a thousand miles upstream to the newly founded town of Asunción in Paraguay, where a genial climate, an abundance of food, and a multitude of docile Guarani Indians created more favorable conditions for Spanish settlement. Asunción became the capital of Paraguay and all the Spanish territory in southeastern South America. Not until 1580 was Buenos Aires permanently resettled by colonists coming from Asunción.

The Conquistadors

What sort of men were the conquistadors? The conquest of America attracted a wide variety of types. There was a sprinkling of professional soldiers, some with backgrounds of service in the Italian wars and some with pasts that they preferred to forget. The old conquistador Gonzalo Fernández de Oviedo had such men in mind

72

when he warned the organizers of expeditions against "fine-feathered birds and great talkers" who "will either slay you or sell you or forsake you when they find that you promised them more in Spain than you can produce." In one of his *Exemplary Tales,* Cervantes describes the Indies as "the refuge and shelter of the desperate men of Spain, sanctuary of rebels, safe-conduct of homicides." No doubt men of this type contributed more than their share of the atrocities that stained the Spanish Conquest. But the background of the conquistadors was extremely varied, running the whole gamut of the Spanish social spectrum. The majority were commoners, but there were many marginal hidalgos, poor gentlemen who wished to improve their fortunes; some were *segundones* (second sons), disinherited by the Spanish laws of primogeniture and entail. Of the 168 men who captured Atahualpa at Cajamarca in 1532, 38 were hidalgos and 91 plebeians, with the background of the rest unknown or uncertain. According to James Lockhart, who has studied the men of Cajamarca, 51 members of the group were definitely literate and about 76 "almost certainly functioning literates." The group included 19 artisans, 12 notaries or clerks, and 13 "men of affairs."

Of the Spanish kingdoms, Castile provided the largest contingent, with natives of Andalusia predominating in the first, or Caribbean, phase of the Conquest; men from Estremadura, the poorest region of Spain, made up the largest single group in the second, or mainland, phase. Cortés, Pizarro, Almagro, Valdivia, Balboa, Orellana, and other famous conquistadors all came from Estremadura. Foreigners were not absent from the Conquest. Oviedo, in an attempt to clear Spaniards of sole responsibility for the crimes committed in the Indies, assures us that men had come there from every part of Christendom: there were Italians, Germans, Scots, Englishmen, Frenchmen, Hungarians, Poles, Greeks, Portuguese, and men "from all the other nations of Asia, Africa, and Europe."

By the 1520s, an institution inherited from the Spanish *Reconquista,* the *compaña* (warrior band), whose members shared in the profits of conquest according to certain rules, had become the principal instrument of Spanish expansion in the New World. At its head stood a military leader who usually possessed a royal capitulación, which vested him with the title of adelantado and with the governorship of the territory to be conquered. Sometimes these men were wealthy in their own right and contributed large sums or incurred enormous debts to finance the expedition. Italian, German, and Spanish merchant capitalists and royal officials grown wealthy through the Indian slave trade or other means provided much of the capital needed to fit out ships, acquire horses and slaves, and supply arms and food.

The warrior band was in principle a military democracy, with the distribution of spoils carried out by a committee elected from among the entire company. After subtracting the quinto and the common debts, the remaining booty was divided into equal shares. In the distribution of Atahualpa's treasure, there were 217 such shares, each worth 5,345 gold pesos—a tidy sum for that time. Distribution was made in accordance with the individual's rank and contribution to the enterprise. The norm was one share for a *peón* or foot soldier, two for a *caballero* or horseman (one for the rider, another for the horse), and more for a captain.

Despite its democratic aspect, the captains, large investors, and royal officials dominated the enterprise of conquest and took the lion's share for themselves. Some of the men were servants or slaves of the captains and investors, and their shares went entirely or in part to their employers or masters; in other cases, conquistadors had borrowed or bought on credit to outfit themselves, and the greater part of their earnings went to their creditors. Contemporary accounts complain of the predatory ways of some captains, who sold supplies to their men in time of need at profiteering prices. At a later stage of each conquest came the distribution of encomiendas. Craftsmen and other plebeians received encomiendas after the conquest of Mexico and

Peru; later, however, only the leaders and hidalgo members of expeditions were rewarded with such grants.

Bravery, tenacity, and an incredible capacity for enduring hardships were among the conspicuous virtues of the conquistador. The legendary Castilian austerity prepared the conquistador for the difficulties he encountered in the New World. The Spanish common soldier of the War of Granada ate only once a day, fortifying himself occasionally with swigs of the thin, sharply bitter wine he carried in a leather bottle. His single meal was a salad of onions, garlic, cucumbers, and peppers chopped very finely and mixed with bread crumbs, olive oil, vinegar, and water. Soldiers with such traditions were capable of marching a day's journey on a handful of toasted corn.

A fierce nationalism and a religious fanaticism—more often manifested in a brutal contempt for the Indian than in a desire for his or her conversion—were essential elements in the psychological make-up of the conquistador. Add to these traits the quality of romanticism. The Reconquest, filled with a thousand combats, raids, and ambushes, had heated the Spanish imagination to an incandescent pitch. Spanish romanticism found expression in a rich literature of romances, popular ballads that celebrated the exploits of the frontier wars against the Moors and that were frequently on the lips of the conquistadors. The literate soldiers of the Conquest were also influenced by their reading of classic literature, especially of the romances of chivalry with their prodigious line of perfect knights and their mythical islands, Amazons, and giants, which the fantasy of the conquistadors placed in one or another part of the Indies. The conquistador was romantically conscious of his historical role. Some of Cortés's soldiers boasted to him that neither the Romans nor Alexander had ever performed deeds equal to theirs, to which Cortés replied that "far more will be said in future history books about our exploits than has ever been said about those of the past."

Of the trinity of motives (God, Gold, and Glory) commonly assigned to the Spanish conquistador,

the second was certainly uppermost in the minds of most. "Do not say that you are going to the Indies to serve the king and to employ your time as a brave man and an hidalgo should," observed Oviedo in an open letter to would-be conquerors, "for you know the truth is just the opposite; you are going solely because you want to have a larger fortune than your father and your neighbors." Pizarro put it even more plainly in his reply to a priest who urged the need for spreading the Faith among the Indians. "I have not come for any such reasons. I have come to take away from them their gold." The conquistador and chronicler of the conquest of Mexico, Bernal Díaz del Castillo, ingenuously declared that the conquerors died "in the service of God and of His Majesty, and to give light to those who sat in darkness— and also to acquire that gold which most men covet." But the worthy Bernal wrote with the self-serving end of gaining additional rewards for his "great and notable service" to the king, and his book was meant for their grave worships, the members of the Royal Council of the Indies.

Most conquistadors dreamed of eventually returning to Spain with enough money to found a family and live in a style that would earn them the respect and admiration of their neighbors. Only a minority, chiefly large merchants and *encomenderos,* acquired the capital needed to fulfill this ambition, and not all of them returned to Spain. The majority, lacking encomiendas or other sources of wealth, remained and often formed ties of dependency with more powerful Spaniards, usually encomenderos whose service they entered as artisans, military retainers, or overseers of their encomiendas or other enterprises. After 1535, as more and more would-be conquistadors came to the Indies while the opportunities for joining profitable conquests diminished, the problem of a large number of unemployed and turbulent Spaniards, many of whom wandered about, robbing and abusing the Indians, caused serious concern to royal officials and to the crown itself.

Most conquistadors and other early Spanish settlers in the Indies were single young males, with a sprinkling of married men who had left their wives at home while they sought their fortunes. Aside from an occasional mistress or camp follower, few Spanish women accompanied the expeditions. Once the fighting had stopped, however, a small stream of Spanish women began to cross the Atlantic. Some were wives coming to rejoin their husbands (there were laws, generally unenforced, requiring that a married man must have his wife come to live with him or be deported to Spain); others were mothers, sisters, or nieces of the settlers. Marriages with Indian women were not uncommon; even hidalgos were happy at the opportunity to marry a wealthy Indian noblewoman like Moctezuma's daughter, Tecuixpo (Isabel Moctezuma), who was wed to three Spanish husbands in turn. After mid-century, however, most Spaniards of all social levels tended to marry Spanish women, either immigrants or those born in the Indies. By the last quarter of the century, the Spanish family and household, based on strong clan and regional loyalties, had been reconstituted in the Indies.

Of the thousands of bold captains and their followers who rode or marched under the banner of Castile to the conquest of America, few lived to enjoy in peace and prosperity the fruits of their valor, their sufferings, and their cruelties. "I do not like the title of adelantado," wrote Oviedo, "for actually that honor and title is an evil omen in the Indies, and many who bore it have come to an evil end." Of those who survived the battles and the marches, a few received the lion's share of spoils, land, and Indians; the majority remained in modest or worse circumstances, and frequently in debt. The conflict between the haves and the have-nots among the conquerors contributed significantly to the explosive, tension-ridden state of affairs in the Indies in the decades following the Conquest.

Lope de Aguirre: An Underdog of the Conquest

That conflict was a major ingredient in the devil's brew of passions that produced three decades of

murderous civil wars and revolts among the Spaniards in Peru following the fall of the Inca empire. The defeat of the great revolt of Gonzalo Pizarro in 1548 brought no lasting peace to Peru, for it left seething with discontent the many adventurers who had flocked from all parts of the Indies to join the struggle against Pizarro. These men had hoped to be fittingly rewarded for their services to the crown. Instead Pizarro's wily conqueror, La Gasca, added to the encomiendas of the rich and powerful friends who had abandoned Pizarro and come over to the royal side. The sense of betrayal felt by many rank-and-file conquistadors was expressed by Pero López, who charged that La Gasca had left "all His Majesty's servants poor, while he let many of His Majesty's foes keep all they had and even gave them much more."

The Viceroy Cañete clearly defined the economic essence of the problem in a letter that he wrote to Emperor Charles V in 1551; he reported that there were only 480 encomiendas in Peru, whereas the number of Spaniards was 8,000. Including the jobs that the colonial administration could provide, only 1,000 Spaniards could "have food to eat." Cañete's only solution to rid Peru of the plague of unemployed conquistadors was to send them off on new conquests, "for it is well known that they will not work or dig or plow, and they say that they did not come to these parts to do such things." The emperor agreed; permission for new conquests, he wrote the viceroy in December 1555, would serve "to rid and cleanse the country of the idle and licentious men who are there at present and who would leave to engage in that business. . . ." Accordingly, Charles revoked a decree of 1549, issued at the urging of Las Casas, which prohibited new Indian conquests.

The career of the famous Lope de Aguirre, "the Wanderer," casts a vivid light on the psychology and mentality of the disinherited conquistador host. A veteran conquistador, Aguirre was fifty, lame in one leg as a result of wounds, and had spent a quarter-century in a fruitless search for fortune in the Indies when the rumor of a new El

Dorado in the heart of the Amazon wilderness caused feverish excitement in Peru. Whether or not the legendary realm existed, it provided a convenient means of solving a potentially explosive social problem. In 1559 Viceroy Andrés Hurtado de Mendoza authorized Pedro de Ursúa to lead an expedition to search for the province of "Omagua and Dorado." Lope de Aguirre, accompanied by his young mestiza daughter, formed part of the expedition when it sailed down the Huallaga River, a tributary of the Amazon, in quest of the new golden realm. Ursúa proved to be a poor leader and unrest, aggravated by intolerable heat, disease, and lack of food, soon grew into a mutiny whose ringleader was Lope de Aguirre. Ursúa was murdered and, although the rebels raised a Spanish noble named Fernando de Guzmán to be their figurehead "prince," Aguirre soon became the expedition's undisputed leader.

He had devised an audacious new plan that had nothing to do with the quest for El Dorado. It called for the conquest of Peru, removal of its present rulers, and rewards for old conquistadors like himself

for the labors we have had in conquering and pacifying the native Indians of those kingdoms. For although we won those Indians with our persons and effort, spilling our blood, at our expense, we were not rewarded. . . . Instead the Viceroy exiled us with deception and falsehood, saying that we were coming to the best and most populous land in the world, when it is in fact bad and uninhabitable. . . .

Having constructed two large boats on the banks of the Amazon, the expedition sailed off down the great river, bound for the conquest of Peru. Aguirre's distrust of Guzmán soon led to the killing of the "lord and Prince of Peru," his mistress, and followers. By the time Aguirre and his men entered the Atlantic in July 1561 other killings had reduced the number of Spaniards from 370 to 230. Sailing past the shores of Guiana, they reached the island of Margarita off the Venezuelan coast on July 21. Having seized the island and

killed its governor, Aguirre first planned to sail for Panama, capture Nombre de Dios (later Portobelo), and raise an army of discontented soldiers for an invasion of Peru. Finding this plan impracticable, he decided to sail to the mainland and advance over the northern Andes toward Peru. In September he landed on the coast of Venezuela, captured the town of Valencia, and proclaimed a "cruel war of fire and sword" against King Philip II of Spain. But by now the alarm had gone out in all directions and overwhelming royal forces were moving against him. His small army, already much diminished by his summary executions of suspected traitors, began to melt away as a result of growing desertions. On October 27, 1561, after a number of his most trusted followers had fled to the royalist camp, Aguirre ran his sixteen-year-old daughter through with his sword to save her, he said, from going through life as the daughter of a rebel. Shortly after he was killed by arquebus shots fired by two of his former soldiers.

Some weeks before his death, Aguirre had written a remarkable letter to King Philip. Written by a man who had nothing to lose, who had staked his head on the triumph of a wildly improbable project and therefore was free to express his most audacious and subversive ideas, the letter is marked by "the originality and barbaric power of its style," in the words of one critic. Aguirre makes a compelling impression of intimacy, sincerity, and frankness. Although his letter offers a conquistador's vision of the Conquest and the world it created, it is not the vision of the great captains in the heroic mold of Cortés. It is the vision of the underdogs of the Conquest, bitter over their betrayal by the great captains, the viceroys, cunning letrados (officials with legal training) or judges like La Gasca, and their king. Aguirre insists that he is of Old Christian descent and of noble blood, but admits that he was born of "middling parents," an admission that he was probably one of the many poor hidalgos who came to the Indies in search of fame and fortune.

Aguirre mingles an account of the services that he and his comrades had rendered to the crown in the Indies with fierce attacks on the king's ingratitude and the great injustices that they had suffered at the hands of his corrupt and greedy ministers:

Consider, King and Lord, that you cannot justly take any profits from this land, where you risked nothing, until you have properly rewarded those who labored and sweated there in your service. . . . Few kings go to hell, because there are so few of you, but if there were many none would go to heaven. I hold it for certain that even in hell you would be worse than Lucifer, for your whole ambition is to quench your insatiable thirst for human blood.

Despite this blasphemously revolutionary sentiment, Aguirre expresses the horror that he and his comrades feel for the Lutheran heresy and assures the king that, sinners though they be, they accept completely the teachings of the Holy Mother Church of Rome. But Aguirre denounces the scandalous dissolution and pride of the friars in the Indies. "Their whole way of life here is to acquire material goods and sell the sacraments of the church for a price. They are enemies of the poor—ambitious, gluttonous, and proud—so that even the meanest friar seeks to govern and rule these lands." Mockingly, Aguirre wrote that the life the friars led was very bitter and burdensome; by way of penance each had a dozen Indian girls working in his kitchen and as many boys employed in fishing, hunting partridges, and gathering fruit.

Aguirre was also harsh in his comments on the royal officials in Peru. He noted that each royal *oidor* (judge) received an annual salary of 4,000 pesos plus 8,000 pesos of expenses, yet at the end of three years of service each had saved 60,000 pesos and acquired estates and other possessions to boot. Moreover, they were so proud that "whenever we run into them they want us to drop on our knees and worship them like Nebuchadnezzar." Aguirre advised the king not to entrust the discharge of his royal conscience to these judges, for they spent all their time planning marriages for their children, and their com-

mon refrain was, "To the left and to the right, I claim all in my sight."

Aguirre closed his revealing letter by wishing King Philip good fortune in his struggle against the Turks and the French and all others "who wish to make war on you in those parts. In these, God grant that we may obtain with our arms the reward rightfully due us, but which you have denied." He signed himself, "son of your loyal Basque vassals and rebel till death against you for your ingratitude, Lope de Aguirre, the Wanderer."[4]

How a Handful of Spaniards Won Two Empires

The fact of Spanish Conquest raises a question: how did small groups of Spaniards, initially numbering a few hundred men, conquer the Aztec and Inca empires, which had populations in the millions, large armies, and militarist traditions of their own? Here we have a paradox. With relative ease the Spaniards conquered the Aztecs and the Incas, peoples who were organized on the state level, lived a sedentary life based on intensive agriculture, and were ruled by emperors to whom they owed complete obedience. On the other hand, tribes of marginal culture such as the nomadic Chichimec Indians of the northern Mexican plains or the Araucanians of Chile, who practiced a simple shifting agriculture and herding, were indomitable; the Araucanians continued to battle white invaders for hundreds of years until 1883.

A sixteenth-century Spanish soldier and chronicler of uncommon intelligence, Pedro Cieza de León, reflecting on the contrast between the swift fall of the Inca Empire and the failure of the Span-

[4] I am grateful to Professor Thomas Holloway of the History Department of Cornell University for calling my attention to the peculiar interest of the Aguirre episode and for allowing me to use his translation of Aguirre's letter to Philip II.

iards to conquer the "uncivilized" tribes of the Colombian jungles, found an explanation in the simple social and economic organization of the tribes, which made it possible for the people to flee before a Spanish advance and soon to rebuild village life elsewhere. In contrast, the mass of the Inca population, docile subjects, accepted their emperor's defeat as their own and quickly submitted to the new Spanish masters. For these people, flight from the fertile valleys of the Inca to the deserts, bleak plateaus, and snow-capped mountains that dominate the geography of the region would have been unthinkable.

Cieza's comments are insightful but do not satisfactorily explain the swift fall of the great Indian empires. At least four other factors contributed to that outcome.

1. Spanish firearms and cannon, though primitive by modern standards, gave the invaders a decided superiority over Indians armed with bows and arrows, wooden lances and darts, slings, Inca war clubs with stone or bronze heads, and Aztec wooden swords tipped with obsidian points. Even more decisive for the Spanish was the horse, an animal unknown to the Indians, who at least initially regarded it with awe. The Spanish cavalryman, armed with lance and sword, clad in armor and chain mail, had a striking force comparable to that of the modern tank. Time and time again, a small Spanish squadron of cavalry routed a much larger number of Indian warriors.

2. Diseases, notably smallpox, unwittingly introduced by the invaders became effective Spanish allies. To give one instance, smallpox raged in Tenochtitlán during the Spanish siege of the city, killing King Cuitlahuac and many Aztec soldiers and civilians, and thereby contributed to its fall.

3. The Spaniards were Renaissance men and the Indians were Upper Stone Age people, together with all the cultural differences and associations that these terms imply. Certainly the conquistadors were in part inspired by religious zeal. However, for the Spanish, war was basically a science or art based on centuries of European study and practice of military strategy and tactics. For the Aztecs and the Incas, war had a large religious component. The Aztec method of waging war, for example, emphasized capturing Spaniards and dragging them off to be sacrificed to the Indian gods instead of killing them on the spot. Indian warfare also included elaborate ceremonies and conventions that required giving proper notice to a people targeted for attack. The Spaniards did not limit themselves with such conventions.[5]

4. Internal division was a major factor in the swift collapse of the Indian empires. Hatred of the Aztecs by tributary peoples or unvanquished peoples like the Tlaxcalans explains why Indian auxiliaries formed a majority of Cortés's forces during the last struggle for Tenochtitlán. In what is now Peru, the conflict between two claimants of the Inca throne and their followers played directly into Pizarro's hands. Also, the Inca Empire was a mosaic of states, some quite recently incorporated into the empire, and the former lords or curacas of these states, eager to regain their independence, rallied to the Spanish side. All too late, these Indians discovered that they had exchanged one oppressor for a worse one.

Thus, the sophisticated, highly organized Indian empires fell to the Spaniards because of their superior armament, the decimating diseases that they brought, their cultural superiority, and the internal divisions within the empires themselves.

---

[5] One exception was the *Requerimiento,* or Requirement, a document designed to satisfy Spanish royal conscience. It contained Spanish demands that must be read to and rejected by Indians before making war on them. For the farcical use of this document, see Chapter 4.

Chapter 4

The Economic Foundations of Colonial Life

From the first days of the Conquest, the Spanish government faced a problem of harmonizing the demand of the conquistadors for cheap Indian labor, which they frequently employed in a wasteful and destructive manner, with the crown's interest in the preservation of a large, tribute-paying Indian population. The first decades of colonial experience demonstrated that the Indians, left to the tender mercies of the colonists, might either become an extinct race, as actually happened on the once densely populated island of Hispaniola, or rise in revolts threatening the very existence of the Spanish Empire in America. The crown naturally regarded these alternatives with distaste.

The Indian question had other facets. There was a political issue, for excessive concentration of land and Indians in the hands of colonists might lead to the rise of a class of feudal lords independent of royal authority, a development the Spanish kings were determined to prevent. The church also had a major interest in the Indian problem. If the Indians died out as a result of Spanish mistreatment, the great task of saving pagan souls would remain incomplete and the good name of the church would suffer. Besides, who then would build churches and monasteries and support the servants of God in the Indies?

The dispute over Indian policy immediately assumed the dramatic outward form of a struggle of ideas. For reasons deeply rooted in Spain's medieval past, Spanish thought of the sixteenth century had a strongly legalistic and scholastic character. At a time when scholasticism[1] was dying in

---

[1] A system of theological and philosophical doctrine and inquiry that predominated in the Middle Ages. It was based chiefly on the authority of the church fathers and of Aristotle and his commentators.

other Western lands, it retained great vitality in Spain as a philosophic method and as an instrument for the solution of private and public problems. The need "to discharge the royal conscience," to make the royal actions conform to the natural and divine law, helps to explain Spanish preoccupation with the doctrinal foundations of Indian policy. What was the nature of the Indians? What was their cultural level? Were they the slaves by nature described by Aristotle, a race of subhumans who might properly be conquered and made to serve the Spaniards? What rights and obligations did the papal donation of America to the Spanish monarchs confer on them? Summoned by the monarchs to answer these and similar questions, jurists and theologians waged a battle of books in which they bombarded each other with citations from Aristotle, the church fathers, and medieval philosophers. Less frequently, they supported their positions with materials based on direct observation or written accounts of Indian life.

Tribute and Labor in the Spanish Colonies

Behind the subtle disputations over Spain's obligations to the Indians, however, went on a complex struggle over the question of who should control Indian labor and tribute, the foundations of the Spanish Empire in America. The main parties to this struggle were the crown, the church, and the colonists.

The Encomienda and Slavery

Hispaniola was the first testing ground of Spain's Indian policy. The situation created on the island by the arrival of Columbus's second expedition has been aptly summed up by Samuel Eliot Morison in the phrase "Hell on Hispaniola." Eager to prove to the crown the value of his discoveries, Columbus compelled the natives to bring in a daily tribute of gold dust. When the hard-pressed Indians revolted, they were hunted down, and hundreds were sent to Spain as slaves. Later,

yielding to the demands of rebellious settlers, Columbus distributed the Indians among them, with the grantees enjoying the right to use the forced labor of the natives.

This temporary arrangement, formalized in the administration of Governor Nicolás de Ovando and sanctioned by the crown, became the encomienda. This system, which had its origin in the Spanish medieval practice of granting jurisdiction over lands and people captured from the Moors to leading warriors, consisted in the assignment to a colonist of a group of Indians who were to serve him with tribute and labor. He in turn assumed the obligation of protecting his Indians, paying for the support of a parish priest, and helping to defend the colony. In practice, the encomienda in the West Indies proved a hideous slavery. Basically as a result of this mistreatment and the disorganization of Indian society, the Indian population of Hispaniola dwindled from several million to 29,000 within two decades. This decline was not the result of epidemic disease, for there is no record of any epidemic among the Indians of the Antilles before 1518.

The first voices raised against this state of affairs were those of a company of Dominican friars who arrived in Hispaniola in 1510. Their spokesman was Father Antonio Montesinos, who on Advent Sunday, 1511, ascended the church pulpit to threaten the Spaniards of the island with damnation for their offenses against the natives. The angry colonists and the Dominicans soon carried their dispute to the court. King Ferdinand responded by approving a code of Spanish-Indian relations, the Laws of Burgos (1512–1513). For all its fine-sounding phrases, however, the code did little more than sanction and regularize the existing situation.

The agitation begun by the Dominicans raised the larger question of the legality of Spain's claim to the Indies. To satisfy the royal conscience, a distinguished jurist, Dr. Juan López de Palacios Rubios, drew up a document, the *Requerimiento,* which the conquistadors were supposed to read to the Indians before making war on them. This curious manifesto called on the natives to acknowledge the supremacy of the church and the

A post-Conquest Indian codex presents a fanciful version of Spanish conquistadors attempting to wade ashore on the Mexican coast and battling Aztec warriors. (From *Codex Azcatitlan*. Instituto Nacional de Antropología e Historia/Studio Beatrice Trueblood)

pope and the sovereignty of the Spanish monarchs over their lands by virtue of the papal donation of 1493, on pain of suffering war and enslavement. Not until they had rejected those demands, which were to be made known to them by interpreters, could war be legally waged against them. Some conquistadors took the Requirement lightly, mumbling it into their beards before an attack or reading it to captured Indians after a raid; the chronicler Oviedo relates that Palacios Rubios himself laughed heartily when told of the strange use made of the document by these captains.

Bartolomé de Las Casas, the former encomendero who had repented of his ways and later turned friar, now joined the struggle against Indian slavery and the doctrines of Palacios Rubios. Of the Requirement, Las Casas said that on reading it he could not decide whether to laugh or weep. Las Casas argued that the papal grant of America to the crown of Castile had been made solely for the purpose of conversion; it gave the Spanish crown no temporal power or possession in the Indies. The Indians had rightful possession of their lands by natural law and the law of nations. All Spanish wars and conquests in the New

World were illegal. Spain must bring Christianity to the Indians by the only method "that is proper and natural to men . . . namely, love and gentleness and kindness."

Las Casas hoped for a peaceful colonization of the New World by Spanish farmers who would live side by side with the Indians, teach them to farm and live in a civilized way, and gradually bring into being an ideal Christian community. A series of disillusioning experiences, including the destruction of an experiment along those lines on the coast of Venezuela (1521) by Indians who had suffered from the raids of Spanish slave hunters, turned Las Casas's mind toward more radical solutions. His final program called for the suppression of all encomiendas, liberation of the Indians from all forms of servitude except a small voluntary tribute to the crown in recompense for its gift of Christianity, and the restoration of the ancient Indian states and rulers, the rightful owners of those lands. Over these states the Spanish king would preside as "Emperor over many kings" in order to fulfill his sacred mission of bringing the Indians to the Catholic faith and the Christian way of life. The instruments of that mission should be friars, who would enjoy special jurisdiction over the Indians and protect them from the corrupting influence of lay Spaniards. Although Las Casas's proposals appeared radical, they in fact served the royal aim of curbing the power of the conquistadors and preventing the rise of a powerful colonial feudalism in the New World. Not humanitarianism but self-interest, above all, explains the partial official support that Las Casas's reform efforts received in the reign of Charles V (1516–1556).

The question of Indian policy became crucial with the discovery and conquest of the rich, populous empires of Mexico and Peru. The most elementary interests of the crown demanded that the West Indian catastrophe should not be repeated in the newly conquered lands. In 1523, Las Casas appeared to have won a major victory. King Charles sent Cortés an order forbidding the establishment of encomiendas in New Spain (the name given to the former Aztec Empire), because "God created the Indians free and not subject."

Cortés, who had already assigned encomiendas to himself and his comrades, did not enforce the order. Backed by the strength and needs of his hard-bitten soldiers, he argued so persuasively for the encomienda system as necessary for the welfare and security of the colony that the royal order was revoked. Encomienda tribute and labor continued to be the main source of income for the colonists until the middle of the sixteenth century. The labor of encomienda Indians was supplemented by that of Indian slaves captured in wars or obtained from Indian slave owners.

The New Laws of the Indies and the Encomienda

Despite its retreat in the face of Cortés's disobedience, the crown renewed its efforts to bring Indian tribute and labor under royal control. Cautiously, it moved to curb the power of the conquistadors. The second audiencia (high court) of New Spain was established in 1531–1532 after a stormy period of rule by the first "gangster" audiencia, which devoted itself to despoiling Cortés and mercilessly oppressing the Indians. Taking the first steps in the regulation of Indian tribute and labor, the second audiencia moderated the tribute paid by many Indian towns, provided for registration of tribute assessments, and forbade, in principle, the use of Indians as carriers without their consent. The climax of royal intervention came with proclamation of the New Laws of the Indies (1542). These laws appeared to doom the encomienda. They prohibited the enslavement of Indians, ordered the release of slaves to whom legal title could not be proved, barred compulsory personal service by the Indians, regulated tribute, and declared that existing encomiendas were to lapse on the death of the holder.

In Peru the New Laws provoked a great revolt; in New Spain they caused a storm of protest by the encomenderos and a large part of the clergy. Under this pressure the crown again retreated. The laws forbidding Indian slavery and forced labor were reaffirmed, but the right of inheritance by the heir of an encomendero was recognized and even extended by stages to a third, fourth, and sometimes even a fifth life. Thereafter, or earlier in the absence of an heir, the encomienda reverted to the crown. In the natural course of events, the number of encomiendas steadily diminished and that of crown towns increased.

By about 1560, the encomienda had been partially "tamed." Royal intervention had curbed the power of the encomenderos and partially stabilized the tribute and labor situation, at least in areas near the colonial capitals. Tribute was now assessed in most places by the audiencias, which made a continuing effort to adjust it to the fluctuations of population and harvests on appeal from the Indians. The institution of *visita* and *cuenta* was employed to make such adjustments. The visita (inspection of an Indian town) yielded information concerning its resources or capacity to pay, which was needed to determine its per capita quota. The cuenta (count), made at the same time, gave the number of tribute payers. About 1560, the annual tribute paid to the king or to an encomendero by each married tributary Indian in New Spain was usually one silver peso and four-fifths of a bushel of maize or its equivalent in other produce.

This mechanism of assessment and copious protective legislation did not bring significant or enduring relief to the Indians. Padding of population counts and other abuses by encomenderos and other interested parties were common. More important, recounts and reassessments consistently lagged behind the rapidly shrinking number of tribute payers, with the result that the survivors had to bear the tribute burdens of those who had died or fled. Moreover, from the accession to the throne of Philip II (1556), the dominant motive of Spain's Indian policy became the increase of royal revenues in order to relieve the crown's desperate financial crisis. Indian groups hitherto exempt from tribute lost their favored status, and the tribute quota was progressively raised. As a result of these measures and the gradual reversion of encomiendas to the crown, the amount of royal tribute collected annually in New Spain rose from about 100,000 pesos to well over 1 million pesos between 1550 and the close of the eighteenth century. (These figures do not take account of the impact on the tribute's value due to the considerable rise in prices during the same period.)

For the colonists, however, the encomienda steadily declined in economic value. They lost the right to demand labor from their tributaries (1549); they also lost their fight to make the encomienda perpetual. The heaviest blow of all to the encomendero class was the catastrophic decline of the Indian population in the second half of the sixteenth century. In central Mexico, the Indian population dropped from perhaps 25 million in 1519 to slightly over 1 million in 1605. On the central coast of Peru, the tributary population seems to have fallen by 1575 to 4 percent of what it had been before the Conquest. For reasons that remain unclear, the rates of population decline in both Mexico and Peru appear to have been considerably higher on the coast than in the highlands. Disease, especially diseases of European origin against which the Indians had no acquired immunity, was the major direct cause of this demographic disaster. But overwork, malnutrition, severe social disorganization, and the resulting loss of will to live underlay the terrible mortality associated with the great epidemics and even with epidemic-free years. In Peru the great civil wars and disorders of the period from 1535 to 1550 undoubtedly contributed materially to Indian depopulation.

As the number of their tributaries fell, the encomenderos' income from tribute dropped proportionately, while their expenses, which included the maintenance of a steward to collect tribute, support of a parish priest, and heavy taxes, remained steady or even increased. As a result, many encomenderos, as well as other Spaniards without encomiendas, began to engage in the more lucrative pursuits of agriculture, stock raising, and mining. The decline of the Indian population, sharply reducing the flow of foodstuffs and metals, stimulated a rapid growth of *haciendas* (Spanish estates) producing grain and meat.

Thus, in central Mexico by the 1570s, and in the northern and central Andean highlands by the end of the sixteenth century, the encomienda had lost its original character of an institution based on the use of Indian labor without payment. Its importance as a source of revenue to Spanish colonists had greatly diminished, and it had been placed in the way of extinction through the progressive reversion of individual encomiendas to the crown. These changes, however, did not take place everywhere. In areas that lacked precious metals or where Indian agricultural productivity was low, and where consequently there was little danger of the colonists acquiring excessive power, the crown permitted encomenderos to continue exploiting the forced labor of the Indians. This was the case in Chile, where the encomienda based on personal service continued until 1791; in Venezuela, where it survived until the 1680s; and in Paraguay, where it still existed in the early 1800s. The crown also allowed the encomienda as a labor system to continue in such areas of New Spain as Oaxaca and Yucatán.

The Repartimiento, Yanaconaje, and Free Labor

In the key areas of central Mexico and the Andean highlands, however, a new system, the *repartimiento,* replaced forced labor under the encomienda after 1550. Under this system, all adult male Indians had to give a certain amount of their time in rotation throughout the year to work in Spanish mines and workshops, on farms and ranches, and on public works. By this means, the crown sought to regulate the use of an ever-diminishing pool of Indian labor and give access to such labor to both encomenderos and the growing number of Spaniards without encomiendas. The Indians received a token wage for their work, but the repartimiento, like the encomienda, was essentially disguised slavery. Indians who avoided service and community leaders who failed to provide the required quotas were imprisoned, fined, and physically punished.

In Peru, where the condition of the Indians seems to have been generally worse than in New Spain, the repartimiento (here known as the *mita*) produced especially disastrous effects. Un-

der this system, developed by Viceroy Francisco de Toledo in the 1570s, all able-bodied Indian men in the provinces subject to the mita were required to work for six-month periods, one year in seven, at Potosí or other mining centers, or were assigned to other Spanish employers. The silver mines of Potosí and the Huancavelica mercury mine were notorious deathtraps for Indian laborers under the mita. In Peru and Bolivia, the mita remained an important source of labor in mining and agriculture to the end of the colonial period.

In the Andean area, the repartimiento was supplemented by another institution taken over from Inca society—the system of *yanaconas,* Indians who were separated from their communities and served Spaniards as personal servants or were attached to their estates. Like European serfs, the yanaconas were transferred from one landowner to another together with the estate. It is estimated that by the end of the sixteenth century the number of yanaconas on Spanish haciendas was almost equal to the number of Indians who lived in their own communities.

Although the repartimiento offered a temporary solution for the critical labor problem, many Spanish employers found it unsatisfactory, for it did not provide a dependable and continuing supply of labor. From an early date, mine owners and *hacendados* in New Spain turned increasingly to the use of free or contractual Indian wage labor. The heavy weight of tribute and repartimiento obligations on a diminishing native population and Spanish usurpation of Indian communal lands induced many Indians to accept an hacendado's invitation to become farm laborers working for wages, mostly paid in kind. Some traveled back and forth to work from their communities; others became resident peons on the haciendas. Other Indians were drawn to the northern silver mines by the lure of relatively high wages.

By 1630, when the crown abolished the agricultural repartimiento in central Mexico, the move provoked little or no protest, for most landowners relied on free labor. The mining repartimiento continued longer in New Spain. It was still

84

employed intermittently in the eighteenth century but had little importance, for the mines of New Spain operated mainly with contractual labor. In Peru and Bolivia, where the mita, supplemented by *yanaconaje,* was the dominant labor system, providing a mass of cheap workers for the high-cost silver mines, free labor was less important. However, there were as many as forty thousand free Indian miners (known as *mingas*) employed at the Potosí mines in the seventeenth century.[2]

From the first, this so-called free labor was often associated with debt servitude. The second half of the seventeenth century saw the growth of the system of *repartimiento* or *repartimiento de mercancías,*[3] the compulsory purchase by Indians of goods from district governors (corregidores, alcaldes mayores). In combination with their other burdens, repartimiento was a powerful inducement for Indians to accept advances of cash and goods from Spanish hacendados; the tribute payment was usually included in the reckoning. An Indian so indebted had to work for his employer until the debt was paid. Despite its later evil reputation, peonage, whether or not enforced by debts, had definite advantages for many Indians. It usually freed them from the recurrent tribute and repartimiento burdens of the Indian community and often gave some security in the form of a plot of land the Indian could work for himself and his family. But if the hacienda offered some Indians escape from their intolerable conditions, it aggravated the difficulties of those who remained on their ancestral lands. The hacienda expanded by legal or illegal means at the expense of the Indian pueblo, absorbing whole towns and leaving others without enough land for their people when the long population decline finally ended in the first half of the seventeenth century and a slow recovery began. The hacienda also lured laborers from the pueblo, making it difficult for the Indian town to meet its tribute and repartimiento obligations. Between the two *repúblicas* (commonwealths), the *república de indios* and the *república de españoles,* as Spanish documents frequently called them, stretched a gulf of hostility and distrust.

The importance of debt servitude as a means of securing and holding labor seems to have varied according to the availability of free labor. It was used extensively in northern Mexico, where such labor was scarce, but appears to have been less important in central Mexico, where it was more abundant. Some recent studies stress that debt peonage was "more of an inducement than a bond," with the size of advances reflecting the bargaining power of labor in dealing with employers and that hacendados sometimes made no special effort to recover their peons who had fled without repayment of loans. But the evidence for such relative lack of concern about fugitive peons comes chiefly from late-eighteenth-century Mexico, when labor was increasingly abundant. For earlier, labor-scarce periods, there is much evidence of strenuous efforts to compel Indians to remain on estates until their debts had been paid off. Indeed, hacendados and officials sometimes likened Mexican peons to European serfs who were bound to their estates, with the right to their services passing with the transfer of the land from one owner to another.

Widely used in agriculture and mining, debt servitude assumed its harshest form in the numerous *obrajes* (workshops) producing cloth and other goods that sprang up in many areas in the sixteenth and seventeenth centuries. Convict labor, assigned to employers by Spanish judges, was early supplemented by the "free" labor of Indians who were ensnared by a variety of devices. Indians were often tempted into these workshops by an offer of liquor or a small sum of money and, once inside the gates, were never let out again.

[2] In the early seventeenth century the growing shortage of Indian labor, due to the ravages of epidemic disease and the flight of Indians from communities subject to the mita, gave rise to a system whereby the delivery of mita labor was replaced by deliveries of silver collected from Indian communities and raised through the operation of economic enterprises supervised by the curacas. Mine owners used this silver to cover minga costs and to hire minga substitutes for mita labor (*mitayos*) not received in person.

[3] The term *repartimiento* was also applied to the periodic conscription of Indians for labor useful to the Spanish community.

"In this way," wrote a seventeenth-century observer, "they have gathered in and duped many married Indians with families, who have passed into oblivion here for twenty years, or longer, or their whole lives, without their wives or children knowing anything about them; for even if they want to get out, they cannot, thanks to the great watchfulness with which the doormen guard the exits."[4]

Black Slavery

Side by side with the disguised slavery of repartimiento and debt servitude existed black slavery. For a variety of reasons, including the fact that Spaniards and Portuguese were accustomed to the holding of black slaves, the tradition that blacks were descendants of the biblical Ham and bore his curse, and the belief that they were better able to support the hardships of plantation labor, Spanish defenders of the Indian did not display the same zeal on behalf of the enslaved Africans.

In fact, the rapid development of sugar cane agriculture in the West Indies in the early 1500s brought an insistent demand for black slave labor to replace the vanishing Indians. There arose a lucrative slave trade, chiefly carried on by foreigners under a system of *asiento* (contract between an individual or company and the Spanish crown). The high cost of slaves tended to limit their use to the more profitable plantation cultures or to domestic service in the homes of the wealthy. Large numbers lived on the coasts of Venezuela and Colombia, where they were employed in the production of such crops as cacao, sugar, and tobacco, and in the coastal valleys of Peru, where they labored on sugar and cotton plantations, but smaller concentrations were found in every part of the Indies. In Chapter 5, we shall consider the much disputed question

whether African slavery in Hispanic America was "milder" than in other European colonies.

In summary, all colonial labor systems rested in varying degrees on servitude and coercion. Although contractual labor gradually emerged as the theoretical norm, all the labor systems just described coexisted throughout the colonial period. Indian slavery, for example, was abolished in 1542, but Indian wars and enslavement continued in frontier areas on various pretexts into the eighteenth century. Which labor system dominated at a given time and place depended on such factors as the area's natural resources, the number of Europeans in the area and the character of their economic activities, the size and cultural level of its Indian population, and the crown's economic and political interests. Finally, it should be noted that in the course of the sixteenth and seventeenth centuries the labor pool was gradually expanded by the addition of mestizos (mixtures of Indians and whites), free blacks and mulattos, and poor whites. Since most of these people were exempt from encomienda and repartimiento obligations, they usually worked for wages and enjoyed freedom of movement, but like the Indians were subject to control through debts. In Chapter 7, we will discuss eighteenth-century changes in the labor system.

The Colonial Economy

The Conquest disrupted the traditional subsistence-and-tribute economy of the Indians. War and disease took a heavy toll of lives, to the detriment of production; in some areas the complex irrigation networks established and maintained by Indian centralized authorities were destroyed or fell into ruin. The Conquest also transformed the character and tempo of Indian economic activity. When the frenzied scramble for treasure had ended with the exhaustion of the available gold and silver objects, the encomienda became the principal instrument for the extraction of wealth from the vanquished. The peoples of the

[4] Antonio Vasquez de Espinosa, *Compendium and Description of the West Indies,* tr. by C. U. Clark (Washington, D.C.: The Smithsonian Institution, 1942), p. 134.

Aztec and Inca empires were accustomed to paying tribute in labor and commodities to their rulers and nobility. But the tribute demands of the old ruling classes, although apparently increasing on the eve of the Conquest, had been limited by custom and by the capacity of Indian ruling groups to utilize tribute goods. The greater part of such tribute was destined for consumption or display, not for trade. The demands of the new Spanish masters, on the other hand, were unlimited. Gold and silver were the great objects; if these could not be obtained directly, the encomenderos proposed to obtain them by sale in local or distant markets of the tribute goods produced by their Indians. Driven by visions of infinite wealth, the Spaniards took no account of what the Indians had formerly given in tribute and exploited them mercilessly. A compassionate missionary, writing in 1554, complained that before the Conquest the Indians in his part of Mexico

never used to give such large loads of mantas [*pieces of cotton cloth*]*, nor had they ever heard of beds, fine cotton fabrics, wax, or a thousand other fripperies like bed sheets, tablecloths, shirts, and skirts. All they used to do was cultivate the fields of their lords, build their houses, repair the temples, and give of the produce of their fields when their lords asked for it.*[5]

Cortés as a Businessman

The business career of Hernando Cortés illustrates the large variety and scale of the economic activities of some encomenderos. By 1528, Cortés was already worth 500,000 gold pesos. Part of this wealth represented Cortés's share of the loot taken in Tenochtitlán and other places during and immediately after the Conquest. But his chief source of income was his encomienda

holdings. To himself he assigned the richest tribute areas in the former Aztec Empire. At the time of his death in 1547, although many of his encomiendas had been drastically reduced and tribute assessments lowered, he was still receiving 30,000 gold pesos annually from this source. He received large quantities of gold dust, textiles, maize, poultry, and other products from encomienda towns. The pueblo of Cuernavaca (near Mexico City) alone gave as part of its annual tribute cloth worth 5,000 gold pesos. Cortés's agents sold the tribute cloth and other products to traders who retailed them in Mexico City and other Spanish towns. Cortés had his own extensive real estate holdings in Mexico City. On or near the central square he erected shops, some of which he used for his own trading interests, others of which he rented out.

Cortés was an empire builder in the economic as well as political sense of the word. He invested the capital he acquired from encomienda tribute and labor in many enterprises. Mining attracted his special attention. In the Oaxaca and Michoacán districts, he had gangs of Indian slaves, more than a thousand in each, panning gold; many of these slaves died from hard labor and inadequate food. In 1529 these mining areas brought him 12,000 pesos in gold annually. In addition to his own mining properties, Cortés held others, such as silver mines in the Taxco area of Mexico, in partnerships. In such cases, his investment usually consisted of goods, livestock, or the labor of his encomienda Indians or his Indian and black slaves.

After encomienda tribute, agriculture and stock raising were Cortés's largest sources of income. He had large landholdings in various parts of Mexico, some acquired by royal grant, others usurped from Indians. He employed encomienda labor to grow maize on his land. His fields in the vicinity of Oaxaca alone produced ten to fifteen thousand bushels a year. Part of this grain he sold in the Spanish towns and at the mines, part went to feed his gangs of slaves at the gold washings and his Indian carriers. Cortés also raised great numbers of cattle and hogs, which were butchered in his own slaughterhouses. Near Te-

[5] *Life and Labor in Ancient Mexico: The Brief and Summary Relation of the Lords of New Spain by Alonso de Zorita,* tr. and ed. by Benjamin Keen (New Brunswick, N.J.: Rutgers University Press, 1963), pp. 279–280.

huantepec he had herds of more than ten thousand wild cattle, which supplied hides and tallow for export to Panama and Peru.

The restless Cortés also pioneered in the development of the Mexican sugar industry. By 1547 his plantations were producing more than three hundred thousand pounds of sugar annually, most of which was sold to agents of European merchants for export. If he was not the first to experiment with silk raising in New Spain, as he claimed, he certainly went into the business on a large scale, laying out thousands of mulberry trees with the labor of Indians paid in cash or cacao beans. In this venture, however, he suffered heavy losses. Nonetheless, the variety and extent of Cortés's business interests suggest how misleading is the familiar portrait of the conquistador as a purely feudal type devoted only to war and plunder, disdainful of all trade and industry.

The Growth of the Haciendas

Among the first generation of colonists, large-scale enterprises such as those of Cortés were rare. The typical encomendero was content to occupy a relatively small land grant and draw tribute from his Indians, who continued to live and work in large numbers on their ancestral lands. The major shift from reliance on encomienda tribute to the development of Spanish commercial agriculture and stock raising came after 1550 in response to the massive Indian population decline and the crown's restrictive legislation, which combined to deprive the encomienda of much of its economic value. Acute food shortages in the Spanish towns created new economic opportunities for Spanish farmers and ranchers. Simultaneously, the reduction of Indian populations left vacant large expanses of Indian land, which Spanish colonists hastened to occupy for wheat raising or, more commonly, as sheep or cattle ranges.

By the end of the sixteenth century, the Spanish-owned hacienda was responsible for the bulk of agricultural commercial production and

pressed ever more aggressively on the shrinking Indian sector of the colonial economy. Spanish colonists used various methods to "free" land from Indian occupation: purchase, usurpation, and *congregación* (forced concentration of Indians in new communities, ostensibly to facilitate control and Christianization). Although Spain's declared policy was to protect Indian community land, the numerous laws forbidding encroachment on such land failed to halt the advance of the hacienda. The power of the hacendados, whose ranks included high royal officials, churchmen, and wealthy merchants, usually carried all before it.

In the seventeenth century, the crown, facing an acute, chronic economic crisis, actually encouraged usurpation of Indian lands by adopting the device of *composición* (settlement), which legalized the defective title of the usurper through payment of a fee to the king. Not only Indian communities but communities of Spanish or mestizo small farmers saw their lands devoured by the advancing hacienda. A striking feature of this process was that land was sometimes primarily acquired not for use but to obtain Indian day laborers and peons by depriving them of their fields or to eliminate competition by Indian or other small producers. The establishment of a *mayorazgo* (entail) assured the perpetuation of the consolidated property in the hands of the owner's descendants, but this feudal device required approval by the crown, was available only to owners of especially valuable estates, and was utilized only by a small number of very wealthy families.

A more common strategy for consolidation and preservation of holdings was marriage within the extended family, often between cousins. In the majority of cases, however, this and other strategies for ensuring the longevity of family estates were less than successful. Spanish inheritance laws requiring the equal division of estates among heirs, economic downturns, and lack of investment capital as a result of large expenditures for conspicuous consumption and donations to the church were some of the factors that made for an unstable landed elite and a high turnover rate in estate ownership. Susan Ramirez studied the collective biography of colonial elite families who lived in north coastal Peru over a period of three hundred years. She found that, contrary to tradition, this elite was "unstable, open, and in constant flux," with most families lasting no more than two or three generations. The historian Lucas Alamán, himself a member of Mexico's former colonial elite, alluded to this instability at the top, citing the Mexican proverb that said, "The father a merchant, the son a gentleman, the grandson a beggar."

The tempo of land concentration varied from region to region according to its resources and proximity to markets. In the Valley of Mexico, for example, the bulk of the land was held by great haciendas by the end of the colonial period. Indian commoners and chiefs, on the other hand, retained much of the land in the province of Oaxaca, which had limited markets for its crops. Recent studies of the colonial hacienda stress the large variations in hacienda size and productivity from one region to another. This variety in size and productivity reflects the great regional divergencies in productive potential—determined by proximity to water and quality of soil—and in access to labor and markets, among other variables, in the vast Spanish Empire in America.

Despite the long-term trend toward land concentration, there gradually arose a class of white and mixed-blood small farmers of uncertain size. In Mexico such small farmers, typically mestizos, came to be known as *rancheros* and they were interspersed among the Indian villages and commercial estates of the central and southern highlands. Some were former majordomos or foremen of large landowners from whom they rented or leased unused portions of their estates, generally raising products for sale in local markets. Their limited resources and dependence on large landowners made their situation precarious; in prosperous times of rising land values their small properties were often swallowed up by their wealthy neighbors. A less frequent occurrence, successful rancheros might expand their holdings and themselves join the ranks of the landed elite.

Spanish Agriculture in the New World

Spanish agriculture differed from Indian land use in significant ways. First, it was extensive, cultivating large tracts with plows and draft animals, in contrast with the intensive Indian digging-stick agriculture. Second, Spanish agriculture was predominantly commercial, producing commodities for sale in local or distant markets, in contrast with the subsistence character of traditional Indian agriculture. Through the need to pay tribute and other obligations in cash, the Indian farmer came under increasing pressure to produce for the market. But, as a rule, the hacendado's superior resources made it difficult for the Indian farmer to compete except in times of abundant harvests, and he tended to fall back to the level of subsistence agriculture, whose meager yield he sometimes supplemented by labor for the local hacendado.

Spanish colonial agriculture early produced wheat on a large scale for sale in urban centers like Mexico City, Lima, Veracruz, and Cartagena; maize was also grown on haciendas for the sizable Indian consumers' market in Mexico City and Lima. Sugar, like wheat, was one of Europe's agricultural gifts to America. Spaniards brought it from the Canary Islands to Hispaniola, where it soon became the foundation of the island's prosperity. By 1550 more than twenty sugar mills processed cane into sugar, which was shipped in great quantities to Spain. "The sugar industry is the principal industry of those islands," wrote José de Acosta at the end of the sixteenth century, "such a taste have men developed for sweets." From the West Indies sugar quickly spread to Mexico and Peru. Sugar refining, with its large capital outlays for equipment and black slaves, was, after silver mining, the largest-scale enterprise in the Indies.

In the irrigated coastal valleys of Peru, wine and olives, as well as sugar, were produced in quantity. The silk industry had a brief period of prosperity in Mexico, but soon declined in the face of labor shortages and competition from Chinese silk brought in the Manila galleons from the Philippines to the port of Acapulco. Spain's sporadic efforts to discourage the production of wine, olives, and silk, regarded as interfering with Spanish exports of the same products, seem to have had little effect. Other products cultivated by the Spaniards on an extensive plantation basis included tobacco, cacao, and indigo. A unique Mexican and Central American export, highly valued by the European cloth industry, was cochineal, a blood-red dye made from the dried bodies of insects parasitic on the nopal cactus.

Spain made a major contribution to American economic life with the introduction of various domestic animals—chickens, mules, horses, cattle, pigs, and sheep. The mules and horses revolutionized transport, gradually eliminating the familiar spectacle of long lines of Indian carriers loaded down with burdens. Horses and mules became vital to the mining industry for hauling and for turning machinery. Cattle and smaller domesticated animals greatly enlarged the food resources of the continent. Meat was indispensable to the mining industry, for only a meat diet could sustain the hard work of the miners. "If the mines have been worked at all," wrote a Spanish judge in 1606, "it is thanks to the plentiful and cheap supply of livestock." Indians quickly introduced meat into their diet; writing of the Valley of Mexico, Charles Gibson observes: "By 1598 it could be said that the Indian taste for meat had become fixed and unalterable." In addition to meat, cattle provided hides for export to Spain and other European centers of leather manufacture, as well as hides and tallow (used for lighting) for the domestic market, especially in the mining areas. Sheep raisers found a large market for their wool in the textile workshops that arose in many parts of the colonies.

In a densely settled region like central Mexico, the explosive increase of Spanish cattle and sheep had catastrophic consequences. A horde of animals swarmed over the land, often invading not only the land vacated by the dwindling Indian population but the reserves of land needed by the Indian system of field rotation. Cattle trampled the Indian crops, causing untold damage; torrential rains caused massive erosion on valley slopes close-cropped by sheep. By the end of the sixteenth century, however, the Mexican cattle industry had become stabilized. Exhaustion of virgin pasturelands, mass slaughter of cattle for their hides and tallow, and official efforts to halt grazing on Indian harvest lands had produced a marked reduction in the herds. The problem further abated in the seventeenth century as a result of the cumulative transfer of Indian lands in the central valley to Spaniards who established haciendas growing pulque (a fermented drink made from maguey that was very popular with the natives) and wheat. Gradually, the cattle ranches and sheep herds moved to new, permanent grazing grounds in the sparsely settled, semiarid north.

An equally rapid increase of horses, mules, and cattle took place in the empty pampas (grasslands) of the Río de la Plata (modern Argentina). Their increase in this area of almost infinite pasturage soon outstripped potential demand and utilization, and herds of wild cattle became a common phenomenon in La Plata as in other parts of Spanish America. Barred by Spanish law from seaborne trade with the outside world, the inhabitants of this remote province, lacking precious metals or abundant Indian labor, relieved their poverty by illegal commerce with Dutch and other foreign traders, who carried their hides and tallow to Europe. In addition, they also sent mules and horses, hides and tallow to the mining regions of Upper Peru (Bolivia).

Another center of the cattle industry was the West Indies. José de Acosta wrote in about 1590 that

the cattle have multiplied so greatly in Santo Domingo, and in other islands of that region that they wander by the thousands through the forests and fields, all masterless. They hunt these beasts only for their hides; whites and Negroes go out on horseback, equipped with a kind of hooked knife, to chase the cattle, and any animal that falls to their knives is theirs. They kill it and carry the hide home, leaving the flesh to rot; no one wants it, since meat is so plentiful.[6]

[6] José de Acosta, *Historia natural y moral de las Indias* (Mexico, 1940), p. 318.

Colonial Mining and Industry

Mining, as the principal source of royal revenue in the form of the quinto, or royal fifth of all gold, silver, or other precious metals obtained in the Indies, received the special attention and protection of the crown. Silver, rather than gold, was the principal product of the American mines. Spain's proudest possession in the New World was the great silver mine of Potosí in upper Peru, whose flow of treasure attained gigantic proportions between 1579 and 1635. Potosí was discovered in 1545; the rich Mexican silver mines of Zacatecas and Guanajuato were opened up in 1548 and 1558, respectively. In the same period, important gold placers (sand or gravel deposits containing eroded particles of the ore) were found in central Chile and in the interior of New Granada (Colombia). The introduction of the patio process for separating the silver from the ore with mercury (1556) gave a great stimulus to silver mining. The chief source of mercury for Potosí silver was the Huancavelica mine in Peru, where labor was "a thing of horror"; Mexican silver was chiefly processed with mercury from the Almadén mine in Spain. As in other times and places, the mining industry brought prosperity to a few, failure or small success to the great majority.

Lack of capital to finance technical improvements required by the increasing depth of mines, flooding, and similar problems, combined with shortages and the high cost of mercury (a crown monopoly), caused a precipitous decline of silver production in the viceroyalty of Peru after 1650. In Mexico production levels fluctuated, with output declining in some old centers and rising in new ones, but here the long-range trend for the seventeenth century seems to have been upward. (An older view claimed that an acute labor shortage caused by the catastrophic fall of the Indian population was the root cause of a supposed decline in silver production in New Spain, but it now appears that mine owners in general had little difficulty in filling their labor needs.) As silver production fell, colonial agriculture and stock raising, which had expanded to satisfy the demands of the mining centers for grain, meat, hides, tallow, and work animals, also entered a period of contraction. There was a shift from large-scale commercial enterprise to an emphasis on self-sufficiency. A simultaneous crisis of the European economy reduced the demand for such colonial staples as hides, sugar, and indigo.

The colonial depression was far from total, however, for the economic picture is a mixed one. It has been argued, for example, that the spectacular decline in silver remittances to Castile, cited in support of the thesis of a colonial seventeenth-century economic crisis, was caused in part by a growing colonial self-sufficiency that reduced dependence on European goods. By the start of the seventeenth century, Mexico, Peru, and Chile had become self-sufficient in grains and partly so in wine, olive oil, ironware, and furniture. This growing self-sufficiency coincided with a decay of Spanish industry that sharply curtailed the mother country's exports to the Indies.

In New Spain, proceeds from the alcabala, a significant indicator of the state of the economy, increased until 1638 and declined only slightly thereafter. Although trade with Seville declined, the same was not generally true of interprovincial trade; in the 1620s a vigorous trade in cacao, Venezuela's principal export, developed between that colony and Mexico. Trade also flourished between Chile and Peru. On balance, however, the description of the colonial seventeenth century as a century of depression is probably correct. It also seems likely that the reduced tempo of economic activity in mining and agriculture lessened the worst exploitation of Indian labor and helped to initiate the slow Indian population recovery that was under way by the last quarter of the seventeenth century.

The Spaniards found a flourishing handicrafts industry in the advanced culture areas of Mexico, Central America, and Peru. Throughout the colonial period, the majority of the natives continued to supply most of their own needs for pottery, clothing, and household goods. In the Spanish towns, craft guilds modeled on those of Spain arose in response to the high prices for all

An idealized contemporary European version of gold mining in Spanish America in the sixteenth century: Indian workers overseen by their Spanish conquerors. (Historical Pictures Service, Chicago)

Spanish imported goods. To avoid competition from Indian, black, and mestizo artisans, who quickly learned the Spanish crafts, they were incorporated into the Spanish-controlled guilds but were barred from becoming masters. The chronic shortage of skilled labor, however, soon made all such racial restrictions a dead letter. These guilds attempted to maintain careful control over the quantity and quality of production in industries serving the needs of the colonial upper class.

The period up to about 1630 saw a steady growth of factory-type establishments, the pre-viously mentioned obrajes, many of which produced cheap cotton and woolen goods for popular consumption. Most of these enterprises were privately owned, but some were operated by Indian communities to meet their tribute payments. A number of towns in New Spain (Mexico City, Puebla, Tlaxcala, among others) were centers of this textile industry. Other primitive factories produced such articles as soap, chinaware, and leather. The seventeenth-century depression seems to have blighted the once-flourishing textile industry of New Spain but does not appear to have had the same harmful effects elsewhere. To

92

some extent, the depression, by reducing the capacity to purchase foreign imports, may have promoted the growth of colonial industry. The population increase of the late seventeenth century may have also stimulated the growth of manufacturing. There is little evidence that sporadic Spanish legislative efforts to restrict the growth of colonial manufacturers achieved their purpose.

The Framework of the Economy

Was the colonial economy capitalist, feudal, or a mixture of both? Scholars have hotly debated this question in recent decades. Some deny the relevance of the concepts of feudalism and capitalism, taken from a European context, to a unique colonial reality, but most students will admit the presence of capitalist, feudal, and even more archaic elements—such as the pre-Columbian Indian communities based on communal land tenure—in the colonial economy. The feudal or quasi-feudal elements included labor systems based in varying degrees on servitude and coercion; the nonmonetary character of many economic transactions; and the technical backwardness of industry and agriculture, which reflected the very low level of investment for production by contrast with high levels of expenditure for conspicuous consumption, the church, and charities. Regulations (such as those that forbade Indians to wear European clothes or own land privately) that seriously hampered the development of a market economy also demonstrated feudal characteristics.

The colonial economy also contained capitalist elements. Although based on such noncapitalist labor systems as slavery and debt peonage, the gold and silver mines and the haciendas, ranches, and plantations producing sugar, hides, cochineal, indigo, and other commodities for external markets were fully integrated into the expanding world market. These enterprises reflected the price fluctuations and other vicissitudes of that market and promoted the accumulation of capital, not in Spain but in England and

other nations of rising capitalism. In this way the colonial economy hastened the emergence of capitalism as the dominant world economic system. Some capitalist shoots appeared in the colonies as well, notably in the great mining centers, sugar mills, and workshops that were marked by a certain development of free labor and division of labor.

But the development of colonial capitalism remained embryonic, stunted by the overwhelming weight of feudal relationships and attitudes and the continuous siphoning off of wealth to Spain, itself an economic satellite of the more developed capitalist powers of northwest Europe. The double character of the hacienda—often self-sufficient and nonmonetary in its internal relations but oriented externally toward European markets—reflected the dualism of the colonial economy. For lack of a better term, that economy may perhaps be best described as "semifeudal" or "semicapitalist."

Commerce, Smuggling, and Piracy

The Colonial Commercial System

Spain's colonial commercial system was restrictive, exclusive, and regimented in character, in conformity with the mercantilist standards of that day. Control over all colonial trade, under the Royal Council of the Indies, was vested in the Casa de Contratación (House of Trade), established in 1503 in Seville. This agency licensed and supervised all ships, passengers, crews, and goods passing to and from the Indies. It also collected import and export duties and the royal share of all precious metals and stones brought from the Indies, licensed all pilots, and maintained a *padrón real* (standard chart) to which all charts issued to ships in the Indies trade had to conform. It even operated a school of navigation that trained the pilots and officers needed to sail the ships in the transatlantic trade.

Commerce with the colonies was restricted until the eighteenth century to the wealthier merchants of Seville and Cádiz, who were organized in a guild that exercised great influence in all matters relating to colonial trade. With the aim of preventing contraband trade and safeguarding the Seville monopoly, trade was concentrated in three American ports, Veracruz in New Spain, Cartagena in New Granada, and Nombre de Dios on the Isthmus of Panama. The Seville merchant oligarchy and corresponding merchant groups in the Indies, particularly the merchant guilds in Mexico City and Lima, deliberately kept the colonial markets understocked. In general they played into each other's hands at the expense of the colonists, who were forced to pay exorbitant prices for all European goods acquired through legal channels. Inevitably, the system generated colonial discontent and stimulated the growth of contraband trade.

With the object of enforcing the closed-port policy and protecting merchant vessels against foreign attack, a fleet system was developed and made obligatory in the sixteenth century. As perfected about the middle of the century, it called for the annual sailing under armed convoy of two fleets, each numbering fifty or more ships, one sailing in the spring for Veracruz and taking with it ships bound for Honduras and the West Indies, the other sailing in August for Panama and convoying ships for Cartagena and other ports on the northern coast of South America. Veracruz supplied Mexico and most of Central America; from Portobelo goods were carried across the isthmus and shipped to Lima, the distribution point for Spanish goods to places as distant as Chile and Buenos Aires. Having loaded their returns of silver and colonial produce, the fleets were to rendezvous at Havana and sail for Spain in the spring, before the onset of the hurricane season. In the seventeenth century, as a result of Spain's economic decadence and the growing volume of contraband trade, fleet sailings became increasingly irregular.

Danger and difficulty attended the long voyage to the Indies from the time a ship left Seville to thread its careful way down the shoal-ridden Guadalquivir to the Mediterranean. Hunger and thirst, seasickness and scurvy at sea, and yellow fever and malaria in tropical harbors like Veracruz and Portobelo were familiar afflictions. Storms at sea took a heavy toll of ships; foreign pirates and privateers posed a chronic threat. Gluts of goods in the colonial markets as a result of competition from foreign smugglers, and frequent confiscation of silver by the crown, with tardy or inadequate compensation, often reduced merchants' profits to the vanishing point. But the heaviest damage to Spanish commercial interests stemmed from the activities of foreign smugglers and pirates, who seized the opportunity presented by Spain's growing economic and military weakness.

Spanish industry, handicapped by its guild organization and technical backwardness, could not supply the colonies with cheap and abundant manufactures in return for colonial foodstuffs and raw materials, as required by the implied terms of the mercantilist bargain. Indeed, it was not in the interest of the merchant monopolists of Seville and Cádiz, who throve on a regime of scarcity and high prices, to permit an abundant flow of manufactures to the colonies. Prices to the colonial consumer were also raised by a multitude of taxes: the *avería* (convoy tax), the *almojarifazgo* (import duty), and the alcabala. Inevitably, the manufacturers and merchants of the advanced industrial nations of northern Europe sought to enter by force or guile into the large and unsatisfied Spanish-American markets. The ambitious monarchs of those lands scoffed at Spain's claim of dominion over all the Western Hemisphere except that portion that belonged to Portugal; they defied Spanish edicts forbidding foreigners to navigate American waters or trade on American coasts on pain of destruction of ships and crews. The ironic query said to have been addressed by Francis I of France to the kings of Spain and Portugal summed up the foreign viewpoint: "Show me, I pray you, the will of our father Adam, that I may see if he has really made you his only universal heirs."

The English Threat and Sir Francis Drake

England soon emerged as the principal threat to Spain's empire in America. The accumulation of capital and development of manufacturing under the fostering care of the Tudor kings produced an explosion of English commercial energies in the reign of Queen Elizabeth I. The Old World did not provide sufficient outlets for these erupting energies, and England's merchant adventurers eagerly turned to America. The historic slave-trading voyage of John Hawkins to the West Indies in 1562 opened England's drive to break into the closed Spanish-American markets. Half honest trader, half corsair, Hawkins came to the Indies heavily armed and ready to compel the colonists to trade with him at cannon point, but he showed himself scrupulously honest in his business dealings with the Spaniards, even to the point of paying the royal license and customs dues. Hawkins owed the success of his first two American voyages to the needs of the Spanish settlers, who were ready to trade with a Lutheran heretic or the devil himself to satisfy their desperate need for slave labor and European wares. To cover up these violations of Spanish law, the venal local officials made a thin pretense of resistance. But by 1567 the pretense had worn too thin, the Spanish government had taken alarm, and angry orders went out to drive the English smugglers away. Stiffening Spanish resistance culminated in the near-destruction of Hawkins's trading fleet by a Spanish naval force at Veracruz in 1568.

Only two of the English ships managed to get away; one was commanded by Hawkins, the other by his cousin, Francis Drake. Four years later, Drake left England with four small ships, bound for the Isthmus of Panama. In actions marked by audacity and careful planning, he stormed and plundered the town of Nombre de Dios, escaping at dawn. Later, he made the most lucrative haul in the history of piracy by capturing the pack train carrying Peruvian silver from the Pacific side of the isthmus to Nombre de Dios.

In 1577, Drake set sail again on an expedition that had the secret sponsorship and support of Queen Elizabeth. Its objects were to "singe the King of Spain's beard" by seizing his treasure ships and ravaging his colonial towns; to explore the whole Pacific coast of America, taking possession of the regions beyond the limits of Spanish occupation; and to display English maritime prowess by means of a second circumnavigation of the globe. The expedition of 1577 led by Francis Drake achieved these goals. In the 1580s, Drake made other voyages of reprisal against Cartagena, St. Augustine, and Santo Domingo. It is small wonder that the name of Drake became a word of fear to the inhabitants of colonial coastal towns.

Inroads by Other Europeans

In the seventeenth century, piracy and smuggling were supplemented by efforts to found colonies, not only on the mainland of North America but in the forbidden waters of the Spanish Main. The Dutch, intermittently at war with Spain since 1576, launched a formidable military and commercial offensive against the Spanish West Indies. Their principal instrument was the Dutch West India Company, organized in 1621. A brilliant admiral, Piet Heyn, captured the whole homebound Veracruz treasure fleet off the coast of Cuba in 1628. That victory brought a dividend of 50 percent to the company's shareholders and financed a new company offensive against Brazil that resulted in Dutch occupation of the rich sugar-producing Brazilian northeast for a quarter-century (1630–1654).

Dutch capture of Curaçao, hard off the coast of Venezuela (1634), gave them an invaluable smuggling base and emboldened the French and English to seize both unoccupied and occupied Spanish islands—Barbados and St. Kitts, Martinique and Guadeloupe. In 1655, an English Puritan fleet, defeated in an effort to capture Santo Domingo, turned on Jamaica and easily captured the thinly settled island. In the same period, French corsairs based in the pirate lair of Tortuga began to settle the adjacent northwest corner of

Hispaniola, virtually abandoned by Spaniards since 1605. By 1665 this region had become the French colony of St. Domingue, with a governor appointed by the trading Compagnie des Indes.

The Effects of Pirates and Smugglers on Spanish Prosperity

In this period, piracy in the West Indies became a highly organized, large-scale activity often enjoying the open or covert protection of the English governors of Jamaica and the French governors of St. Domingue. Two leading figures in this unsavory business were the ferocious French pirate L'Olonnois and the equally unscrupulous English buccaneer Henry Morgan. Romantic literature has cast a false glamour about these gangsters of the sea. Unlike the nationalistic and fervently Protestant Drake, the typical pirate captain of the seventeenth century was quite free of patriotic or religious zeal and plied his trade in the calculating spirit of a businessman engaged in a likely speculation.

Piracy entered on a decline following the signing of the Treaty of Madrid in 1670 between England and Spain, by which the British government agreed to aid in the suppression of the corsairs in return for Spanish recognition of its sovereignty over the British and West Indian islands. French buccaneers, however, continued active until the signing of the Treaty of Ryswick in 1697, by which Spain formally recognized French possession of St. Domingue.

The injury inflicted on Spanish prosperity and prestige by pirates and privateers, great as it was, was dwarfed by the losses caused by the less spectacular operations of foreign smugglers. Contraband trade steadily increased in the course of the sixteenth and seventeenth centuries. European establishments in Jamaica, St. Domingue, and the Lesser Antilles became so many bases for contraband trade with the Span-

ish colonies. Buenos Aires was another funnel through which Dutch and other foreign traders poured immense quantities of goods that reached markets as distant as Peru. By the end of the seventeenth century, French companies operating behind the façades of Spanish merchant houses in Seville and Cádiz dominated even the legal trade with the Indies.

A shrewd English observer put his finger on the major source of Spain's misfortunes: her economic weakness. The Spaniards, he remarked, were said to be stewards for the rest of Europe:

Their galleons bring the silver into Spain, but neither wisdom nor power can keep it there; it runs out as fast as it comes in, nay, and faster; insomuch that the little [Swiss] Canton of Bern is really richer, and has more credit, than is the king of Spain, notwithstanding his Indies. At first sight this seems to be strange and incredible; but when we come to examine it, the mystery is by no means impenetrable. The silver and rich commodities which come from the Indies come not for nothing (the king's duties excepted) and very little of the goods or manufactures for which they come, belong to the subjects of the crown of Spain. It is evident, therefore, that the Spanish merchants are but factors, and that the greatest part of the returns from the West Indies belong to those foreigners for whom they negotiate.[7]

Spanish economists of the seventeenth century understood the causes of Spain's plight. Their writings offered sound criticisms of the existing state of affairs and constructive proposals for reform. But their arguments were powerless to change the course of Spanish policy, dictated by small mercantile and aristocratic cliques whose special interests and privileges were wholly incompatible with the cause of reform.

[7] John Campbell, *The Spanish Empire in America* (London, 1747), p. 299.

Chapter 5

State, Church, and Society

The political organization of the Spanish Empire in America reflected the centralized, absolutist regime by which Spain itself was governed. By the time of the discovery and conquest of America, Castilian parliamentary institutions and municipal liberties had lost most of their former vitality. The process of centralization begun by the Catholic Sovereigns reached its climax under the first two Hapsburgs. In Castile there arose a ponderous administrative bureaucracy capped by a series of royal councils appointed by and directly responsible to the king. Aragon, which stubbornly resisted royal encroachments on its fueros (charters of liberties), retained a large measure of autonomy until the eighteenth century. Even in Castile, however, Hapsburg absolutism left largely intact the formal and informal power of the great lords over their peasantry. In Aragon, in whose soil feudal relations were more deeply rooted, the arrogant nobility claimed a broad seigneurial jurisdiction, including the right of life and death over its serfs, as late as the last decades of the seventeenth century. This contrast between the formal concentration of authority in the hands of royal officials and the actual exercise of supreme power on the local level by great landowners was to characterize the political structure of Spanish America as well.

Political Institutions of the Spanish Empire

Formation of Colonial Administration

The pattern of Spain's administration of its colonies was formed in the critical period between 1492 and 1550. The final result reflected the steady growth of centralized rule in Spain itself and the application of a trial-and-error method to the problems of colonial government. To Columbus, Cortés, Pizarro, and other great expeditionary leaders, the Spanish kings granted sweeping political powers that made these men practically sovereign in the territories that they had won or proposed to subdue. But once the importance of these conquests had been revealed, royal jealousy of the great conquistadors was quick to show itself. Their authority was soon revoked or strictly limited, and the institutions that had been employed in Spain to achieve centralized political control were transferred to America for the same end. By the middle of the sixteenth century, the political organization of the Indies had assumed the definitive form that it was to retain, with slight variations, until late in the eighteenth century.

The Council of the Indies, originally a standing committee of the all-powerful Council of Castile but chartered in 1524 as a separate agency, stood at the head of the Spanish imperial administration almost to the end of the colonial period. Although great nobles and court favorites were appointed to the council, especially in the seventeenth century, its membership consisted predominantly of lawyers. Under the king, whose active participation in its work varied from monarch to monarch, it was the supreme legislative, judicial, and executive institution of government. One of its most important functions was the nomination to the king of all high colonial officials. It also framed a vast body of legislation for the Indies—the famous Laws of the Indies, first codified in 1681—which combined decrees of the most important kind with others of a very trivial character. Although the council was frequently staffed by conscientious and highly capable officials in the early Hapsburg period, the quality of its personnel tended to decline under the inept princes of the seventeenth century. Nonetheless, historians owe the council a particular debt for its initiative in seeking to obtain detailed information on the history, geography, resources, and population of all the colonies. The *relaciones* (reports) that incorporated this information represent a rich mine of materials for students of colonial Spanish America.

The Royal Agents

The principal royal agents in the colonies were the viceroys, the captains general, and the audiencias. The viceroys and captains general had essentially the same functions, differing only in the greater importance and extent of the territory assigned to the jurisdiction of the former. Each was the supreme civil and military officer in his realm, having in his charge such vital matters as the maintenance and increase of the royal revenues, defense, Indian welfare, and a multitude of other responsibilities. At the end of the Hapsburg era, in 1700, there were two great American viceroyalties. The viceroyalty of New Spain, with its capital at Mexico City, included all the Spanish possessions north of the Isthmus of Panama; that of Peru, with its capital at Lima, embraced all of Spanish South America except for the coast of Venezuela. Captains general, theoretically subordinate to the viceroys but in practice virtually independent of them, governed large subdivisions of these vast territories. Other subdivisions, called *presidencias,* were governed by audiencias. Their judge-presidents acted as governors, but military authority was usually reserved to the viceroy. Overlapping and shifting of jurisdiction was common throughout the colonial period and formed the subject of frequent disputes among royal officials.

A colonial viceroy, regarded as the very image of his royal master, enjoyed an immense delegated authority, which was augmented by the distance that separated him from Spain and by the frequently spineless or venal nature of lesser officials. He might be a lawyer or even a priest by background but was most commonly a representative of one of the great noble and wealthy houses of Spain. A court modeled on that of Castile, a numerous retinue, and the constant display of pomp and circumstance bore witness to

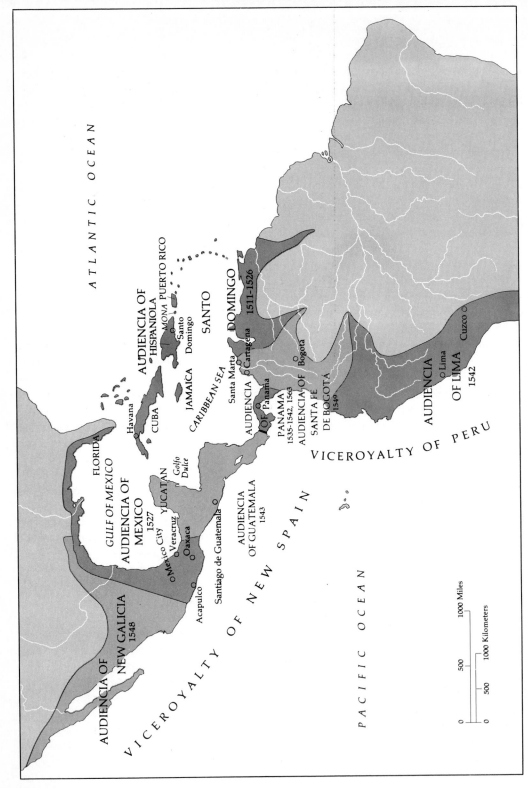

ATLANTIC OCEAN

AUDIENCIA OF HISPANIOLA

MONA PUERTO RICO

Santo Domingo

SANTO DOMINGO 1511-1526

Cartagena

JAMAICA

CARIBBEAN SEA

Havana

CUBA

Santa Marta

Bogotá

AUDIENCIA OF PANAMA 1535-1542, 1563

AUDIENCIA OF SANTA FE DE BOGOTA 1549

Cuzco

Lima

AUDIENCIA OF LIMA 1542

FLORIDA

GULF OF MEXICO

AUDIENCIA OF MEXICO 1527

YUCATAN

Golfo Dulce

Mexico City

Veracruz

Oaxaca

Santiago de Guatemala

AUDIENCIA OF GUATEMALA 1543

VICEROYALTY OF PERU

Acapulco

AUDIENCIA OF NEW GALICIA 1548

VICEROYALTY OF NEW SPAIN

PACIFIC OCEAN

0   500   1000 Miles

0   500   1000 Kilometers

VICEROYALTIES AND AUDIENCIAS IN SIXTEENTH-CENTURY SPANISH AMERICA his exalted status. In theory, his freedom of action was limited by the laws and instructions issued by the Council of the Indies, but a sensible recognition of the need to adapt the laws to existing circumstances gave him a vast discretionary power. The viceroy employed the formula *obedezco pero no cumplo*—"I obey but do not carry out"—to set aside unrealistic or unenforceable legislation.

The sixteenth century saw some able and even distinguished viceroys in the New World. The viceroy Francisco de Toledo (1569–1581), the "supreme organizer of Peru," was certainly an energetic, hardworking administrator who consolidated Spanish rule and imposed royal authority in Peru. His Indian resettlement program and his institution of *mita,* the system of forced Indian labor in the mines, however, profoundly disrupted Indian social organization and took a heavy toll of Indian lives. In New Spain, such capable officials as Antonio de Mendoza (1530–1550) and his successor, Luis de Velasco (1550–1564), wrestled with the problems left by the Conquest. They strove to curb the power of the conquistadors and to promote economic advance; sometimes they also tried, to a limited degree, to protect the interests of the Indians. But the predatory spirit of the colonists, royal distrust of excessive initiative on the part of high colonial officials, and opposition from other sectors of the official bureaucracy largely thwarted their efforts. In the seventeenth century, in an atmosphere of growing financial crisis, corruption, and cynicism at the Spanish court, the quality of the viceroys inevitably declined. In 1695, by way of illustration, the viceroyships of Peru and Mexico were, in effect, sold to the highest bidders.

Each viceroy or captain general was assisted in the performance of his duties by an audiencia, which was the highest court of appeal in its district and also served as the viceroy's council of state. The joint decisions of viceroy and audiencia, taken in administrative sessions, had the force of law, giving the audiencia a legislative character roughly comparable to that of the Council of the Indies in relation to the king. Although the viceroy had supreme executive and administrative power and was not legally obliged to heed the advice of the audiencia, its immense prestige and its right to correspond directly with the Council of the Indies made it a potential and actual check on the viceregal authority. The crown, ever distrustful of its colonial officers, thus developed a system of checks and balances that assured ample deliberation and consultation on all important questions but that also encouraged indecision and delay.

In addition to hearing appellate cases and holding consultative meetings with their viceroy or captain general, oidores were required to make regular tours of inspection of their respective provinces with the object of making a searching inquiry into economic and social conditions, treatment of the Indians, and other matters of interest to the crown. Although viceroys and oidores were well paid by colonial standards, the style of life their positions demanded was expensive, and the viceroy or oidor who did not take advantage of his office to enrich himself could expect to return to Spain poor.

Provincial Administration

Provincial administration in the Indies was entrusted to royal officials who governed districts of varying size and importance from their chief towns and who usually held the title of corregidor or alcalde mayor. Some were appointed by the viceroy (from whom they often bought their jobs), others by the crown. They possessed supreme judicial and political authority in their districts and represented the royal interest in the *cabildos* (town councils). Certain civil and criminal cases could be appealed from the municipal magistrates to the corregidor, and from him to the audiencia. If not trained as a lawyer, the corregidor was assisted by an *asesor* (legal counsel) in the trial of judicial cases.

Corregidores were of two kinds. Some presided over Spanish towns; others, *corregidores de indios,* administered Indian pueblos, or towns, which paid tribute to the crown. One of the principal duties of the corregidor de indios, who was usually appointed for three years, was to protect the natives from fraudulent or extortionate practices on the part of the whites, but there is ample testimony that the corregidor was himself the worst offender in this respect. Indian *caciques* (chiefs) often were his accomplices in these extortions. Perhaps the worst abuses of his authority arose in connection with the practice of repartimiento or repartimiento de mercancías, the mandatory purchase of goods from the corregidor by the Indians of his district. Ostensibly designed to protect the Indians from the frauds or wiles of private Spanish traders, the corregidor's exclusive right to trade with the Indians became an instrument for his own speedy enrichment at the expense of the natives.

The crown employed an arsenal of regulations to insure good and honest performance on the part of public officials. Viceroys and oidores were forbidden to engage in trade or hold land within their jurisdictions or to accept gifts or fees; even their social life was hedged about with many restrictions. All royal officials, from the viceroy down, faced a *residencia* (judicial review) of their conduct at the end of their term of office. This took the form of a public hearing at which all who chose could appear before the judge of residence to present charges or testify for or against the official in question. At the end of the process, the judge found the official guilty or innocent of part or all of the charges and handed down a sentence that could be appealed to the Council of the Indies. Another device, the visita, was an investigation of official conduct, usually made unannounced by a *visitador* specially appointed for this purpose by the crown or, in the case of lesser officials, by the viceroy in consultation with the audiencia. As a rule, the visita was no more effective than the residencia in preventing or punishing official misdeeds.

The only political institution in the Indies that satisfied to some degree local aspirations for self-rule was the town council, known as the cabildo or *ayuntamiento*. Any suggestion, however, that the cabildo had some kind of democratic character has no basis in fact. At an early date, the crown assumed the right to appoint the regidores and alcaldes. Under Philip II and his successors,

it became the established practice for the king to sell these posts to the highest bidder, with a right of resale or bequest, on condition that a certain portion of the value be paid to the crown as a tax at each transfer. In some towns, however, cabildo members elected their successors.

Throughout the colonial period, the municipal councils were closed, self-perpetuating oligarchies of rich landowners, mine owners, and merchants, who "ran the council as an exclusive club." These men frequently received no salaries for their duties and used their positions to distribute municipal lands to themselves, to assign themselves Indian labor, and in general to serve the narrow interests of their class. Their official tasks included supervision of local markets, distribution of town lands, and local taxation. They also elected the alcaldes, who administered justice as courts of first instance. Vigilantly supervised by the provincial governor, or corregidor, who frequently intervened in its affairs, the cabildo soon lost such autonomy as it may have possessed in the early days. Yet, despite its undemocratic character, inefficiency, and waning prestige and autonomy, the cabildo was not without potential significance. As the only political institution in which the creoles (American-born Spaniards) were largely represented, it was destined to play an important part in the coming of the nineteenth-century wars of independence.

The officials and agencies just described represented only a small part of the apparatus of colonial government. A large number of secretaries (*escribanos*) attended to the paperwork of the various departments. As a rule, they collected no salaries but were reimbursed by fees for their services. There was a multitude of police officers, collectors of the royal fifth, alcaldes with special jurisdiction, and the like. Under Charles V, control of such offices often lay in the hands of high Spanish officials, who sold them to persons who proposed to go to the Indies to exploit their fee-earning possibilities. Beginning with Philip II, many of these offices were withdrawn from private patronage and sold directly by the crown, usually to the highest bidder. In the second half of the seventeenth century, the sale of offices by the crown or the viceroy spread from fee-earning positions to higher, salaried posts. As a rule, the beneficiaries of such transactions sought to return to Spain rich, having made the highest possible profit on their investment. Consequently, corruption in this period became structural in the government of the Indies. Colonial officials, high and low, abused their trusts in innumerable and ingenious ways.

If the royal authority, represented by viceroys, oidores, corregidores, and other officials, was more or less supreme in the capitals and the surrounding countryside, the same was not true of more distant and isolated regions. In such areas, the royal authority was very remote, and the power of the great landowners was virtually absolute. On their large, self-sufficient estates, they dispensed justice in the manner of feudal lords, holding court and imprisoning peons in their own jails; they raised and maintained their own private armies; and they generally acted as monarchs of all they surveyed. Sometimes these powerful individuals combined their de facto military and judicial power with an official title, which made them representatives of the crown in their vicinities. Spain's growing economic and political weakness in the late seventeenth century, which loosened the ties between the mother country and her colonies, favored this decentralization of power. The contrast between the nominal concentration of power in the central government and the effective supremacy of great landowners on the local level was one of the legacies of the colonial period to independent Latin America; to this day it remains a characteristic of the political life of many Latin American republics.

Ineffectiveness of Much Spanish Colonial Law

The frequent nonobservance of Spanish colonial law was a fact of colonial political life. In considerable part, this situation reflected the dilemma of royal officials faced with the task of enforcing laws bitterly opposed by powerful colonial elites with whom they generally had close social and economic ties. This dilemma found its most acute expression in the clash between the crown's protective Indian legislation, which reflected its awareness that the conservation of the Indians—the real wealth of the Indies—was clearly in the royal interest, and the drive of colonial elites for maximum profits. The result was that the protective Indian laws were systematically flouted. The crown often closed its eyes to the violations, not only because it wished to avoid confrontation with powerful colonial elites but because those laws sometimes collided with the crown's own narrow, short-range interests (its need for revenue to finance wars and diplomacy and to support a parasitic nobility).

Hence the contradiction between that protective legislation, so often cited by defenders of Spain's work in America, and the reality of Indian life and labor in the colonies. In a report to Philip II, Alonso de Zorita, a judge who retired to an honorable poverty in 1566 after nineteen years of administrative activity in the Indies, wrote:

The wishes of Your Majesty and his Royal Council are well known and are made very plain in the laws that are issued every day in favor of the poor Indians and for their increase and preservation. But these laws are obeyed and not enforced, wherefore there is no end to the destruction of the Indians, nor does anyone care what Your Majesty decrees.[1]

Not all colonial legislation, however, was so laxly enforced. There was a considerable body of exploitative or discriminatory Indian laws that was in general vigorously enforced, including laws requiring the Indians to pay tribute and perform forced labor for token wages, permitting the forced sale of goods to them at fixed prices, and limiting Indian landownership to a low maximum figure while allowing the indefinite growth of Spanish estates.

How can the longevity of Spanish rule over its American colonies, so distant from a European

---

[1] *Life and Labor in Ancient Mexico: The Brief and Summary Relation of the Lords of New Spain by Alonso de Zorita,* tr. and ed. by Benjamin Keen (New Brunswick, N.J.: Rutgers University Press, 1963), p. 216.

country that grew steadily weaker in the course of the seventeenth century, be explained? The answer does not lie in Spain's military power, since Spain maintained few troops in the Indies until the eighteenth century. Much of the durability of Spanish rule seems to lie in a royal policy of making the large concessions needed to gain and maintain the loyalty of colonial elites. The political apparatus of viceroys, audiencias, corregidores, and the like played a decisive role in implementing this royal program. The frequent failure to enforce Indian protective legislation, the strict enforcement of the exploitative laws, the *composiciones* (settlements that legalized usurpation of Indian lands through payment of a fee to the king), and the toleration of great abuses by colonial oligarchs are illustrations of the policy. To be sure, alongside this unwritten pact between the crown and the colonial elite for sharing power and the fruits of exploitation of the Indian, black, and mixed-blood people in the Indies went a royal effort to restrain the colonists' power and ambitions. Until the eighteenth century, however, this effort did not go far enough to threaten the existing arrangements.

The Church in the Indies

The Spanish church emerged from the long centuries of struggle against the Muslims with immense wealth and an authority second only to that of the crown. The Catholic Sovereigns, Ferdinand and Isabella, particularly favored the clergy and the spread of its influence as a means of achieving national unity and royal absolutism. The Spanish Inquisition, which they founded, had political as well as religious uses, and under their great-grandson, Philip II, it became the strongest support of an omnipotent crown. While the Spanish towns sank first into political and then into economic decadence, and the great nobles were reduced to the position of a courtier class aspiring for favors from the crown, the church steadily gained in wealth and influence. Under the last Hapsburgs, it threatened the supremacy of its

royal master. It remained for the enlightened Bourbon kings of the eighteenth century to curb in some measure the excessive power of the church.

Royal control over ecclesiastical affairs, both in Spain and the Indies, was solidly founded on the institution of the *patronato real* (royal patronage). As applied to the colonies, this consisted of the absolute right of the Spanish kings to nominate all church officials, collect tithes, and found churches and monasteries in America. Under diplomatic pressure from King Ferdinand, Pope Julius II had accorded this extraordinary privilege to Spain's rulers in 1508, ostensibly to assist in converting New World heathen. The Spanish monarchs regarded the patronato as their most cherished privilege and reacted sharply to all encroachments on it.

The Spiritual Conquest of America

Beginning with Columbus's second voyage, one or more clergymen accompanied every expedition that sailed for the Indies, and they came in swelling numbers to the conquered territories. The friars formed the spearhead of the second religious invasion that followed on the heels of the Conquest. The friars who came to America in the first decades after the Conquest were, on the whole, an elite group. They were products of one of the periodic revivals of asceticism and discipline in the medieval church, especially of the reform of the orders instituted in Spain by the Catholic Sovereigns and carried out with implacable energy by Cardinal Cisneros. This vanguard group of clergy frequently combined with missionary zeal a sensitive social conscience and a love of learning. The missionaries were frequently impressed by the admirable qualities of the Indians, by their simplicity and freedom from the greed and ambitions of Europeans, by the plasticity of the Indian character. Wrote Vasco de Quiroga, royal judge and later bishop of the province of Michoacán in Mexico:

Anything may be done with these people, they are most docile, and, proceeding with due diligence,

Introducing Indians to Christianity. (By permission of the British Library)

may easily be taught Christian doctrine. They possess innately the instincts of humility and obedience, and the Christian impulses of poverty, nakedness, and contempt for the things of this world, going barefoot and bareheaded with the hair long like apostles; in fine, with very tractable minds void of error and ready for impression.[2]

Millenarian[3] and utopian ideals strongly influenced many members of the reformed clergy who came to the Indies in the first decades after the Conquest. Inspired by the vision of a multitude of Indian souls waiting to be saved, they dreamed of a fruitful fusion of Indian and Spanish cultures

under the sign of a Christianity returned to its original purity. Such men as Juan de Zumárraga, first bishop and archbishop of Mexico, Vasco de Quiroga, and Bartolomé de Las Casas were profoundly influenced by the humanist, reformist ideas of Erasmus and by Thomas More's *Utopia.* Indeed, Quiroga proposed to the Spanish crown that Indian cities be established and organized on the lines of More's ideal commonwealth, in which the Indians' natural virtues would be preserved and perfected by training in the Christian religion and culture. When the crown ignored his proposals, Quiroga used his own resources to found the pueblos or refuges of Santa Fe in Michoacán. In these communities Quiroga established collective ownership of property, systematic alternation between agricultural and craft labor, the six-hour working day, work for women, the distribution of the fruits of collective labor according to need, and the shunning of luxuries and of all occupations that were not useful. Quiroga's dream of establishing islands of charity and

[2] Quoted in Sir Arthur Helps, *The Spanish Conquest in America,* 4 vols. (London, 1902), 3:146.

[3] Millenarianism is the medieval doctrine, based on a prophecy in the Book of Revelation and widely held by the reformed clergy, that Christ would return to earth to reign for a thousand years of peace and righteousness, to be followed by the Last Judgment at the end of the world.

104

cooperative life in a sea of exploitive encomiendas and haciendas was doomed to eventual failure, but to this day the Indians of Michoacán revere the name and memory of "Tata Vasco."

The pro-Indian attitudes of the reformist clergy inevitably placed them on a collision course with the encomenderos and other lay Spaniards who sought the unchecked exploitation of the Indians and commonly described the natives as "dogs" (*perros*). To be sure, not all the religious saw eye to eye on the issue of Indian policy. Some, like the famous Franciscan Toribio de Benavente (better known by his Indian name of Motolinía), may be called "realists" or "moderates." These clergy believed that the encomienda, carefully regulated to safeguard Indian welfare, was necessary for the prosperity and security of the Indies. Others, mostly Dominicans whose leader and spokesman was Bartolomé de Las Casas, believed that the encomienda was incompatible with Indian welfare and must be put in the way of extinction.

As we have seen, during the reign of Charles V—who feared the rise of a colonial feudalism based on the encomienda—the Lascasian wing of the clergy won certain victories, capped by the passage of the New Laws of the Indies (1542). By their militant efforts to secure the enforcement of these laws, Las Casas and his disciples incurred the mortal enmity of the encomenderos. Las Casas was repeatedly threatened. The Dominican bishop Antonio de Valdivieso of Nicaragua, who had tried to enforce the abolition of Indian slavery by the New Laws, was assassinated in 1550 by a group of men led by the governor's son. These and other courageous defenders of the Indian, like Bishop Juan del Valle in Colombia and Fray Domingo de Santo Tomás in Peru, may be regarded as forerunners of today's progressive current in the Catholic church. The ideology of Las Casas, with its demand that the Spaniards "cease to be *caballeros* by grace of the blood and sweat of the wretched and oppressed," seems to anticipate today's Latin American liberation theology and its "preferential option for the poor."

Despite the partial victories won by Las Casas during the reign of Charles V, the Indianist move-ment entered on a decline when Philip II took the throne in 1556. Denial of absolution to Spaniards who had violated the laws protecting Indians—an important weapon employed by Las Casas and other pro-Indian clergy—was forbidden by various royal decrees. The church was instructed to concern itself only with questions of worship and preaching, leaving problems in the economic and social relations between Spaniards and Indians to the civil authorities. Since those authorities as a rule were ready to comply with the wishes of encomenderos, great landowners, and other ruling class groups, the descendants of the conquistadors finally obtained the direct, unchallenged dominion over the Indian for which their forebears had struggled. The encomienda (although in decline), the repartimiento or mita, and even slavery (legalized on various pretexts) remained the basic institutions in Spanish-Indian relations. The new anti-Indian political climate was marked by a growing belief in Indian constitutional inferiority, based on the Aristotelian theory of natural slavery—a theory that Las Casas and virtually all other Spanish theologians had previously condemned.

The first missionaries in the Indies did not regard their defense of the Indians against enslavement and exploitation as separate from their primary task of conversion; they reasoned that for conversion to be effective the natives must survive the shock of Conquest, multiply, and live better under the new religion than the old one. Despite the clandestine opposition of surviving pagan priests and some native nobility, the friars converted prodigious numbers of natives, who, willingly or unwillingly, accepted the new and more powerful divinities of the invaders. In Mexico, the Franciscans claimed to have converted more than a million Indians by 1531; the energetic Motoliniá asserted that he had converted more than fifteen hundred in one day! Where persuasion failed, pressures of various kinds, including force, were used to obtain conversions. Natives who had been baptized and relapsed into idolatry were charged with heresy and punished, some nobles being hanged or burned at the stake. In order to facilitate the missionary effort, the friars studied the native languages and wrote grammars and vocabularies that are still of value to scholars.

The religious, especially the Franciscans, also assigned a special importance to the establishment of schools in which Indian upper-class youth might receive instruction in the humanities, including Latin, logic, and philosophy, as well as Christian doctrine. The most notable of these centers was the Franciscan Colegio de Santa Cruz in Mexico. Before it entered on a decline in the 1560s as a result of lay hostility or disinterest and the waning fervor of the friars themselves, the school had produced a harvest of graduates who often combined enthusiasm for European culture with admiration for their own pagan past. These men were invaluable to the missionaries in their effort to reconstruct the history, religion, and social institutions of the ancient Indian civilizations.

Although some of the early friars undertook to destroy all relics of the pagan past—idols, temples, picture writings—the second generation of missionaries became convinced that paganism could not be successfully combated without a thorough study and understanding of the old pre-Conquest Indian way of life. In Mexico there arose a genuine school of ethnography devoted to making an inventory of the rich content of Indian culture. If the primary and avowed motive of this effort was to arm the missionary with the knowledge he needed to discover the concealed presence of pagan rites and practices, intellectual curiosity and delight in the discovery of the material, artistic, and social achievements of the vanished Indian empires also played a part.

The work of conversion, by the subsequent admission of the missionaries themselves, was less than wholly successful. In Mexico, concludes historian Louise M. Burkhart, the Aztecs "were able to become just Christian enough to get by in the colonial social and political setting without compromising their basic ideological and moral orientation." Here the result of the missionary effort was generally a fusion in Indian minds of old and new religious ideas, in which the cult of the Virgin Mary sometimes merged with the worship of pagan divinities. Writing half a century after the conquest of Mexico, the Dominican Diego Durán saw a persistence of paganism in every aspect of Indian life, "in their dances, in their markets, in their baths, in the songs which mourn the loss of their ancient gods." In the same period, the great scholar-missionary Sahagún complained that the Indians continued to celebrate their ancient festivals, in which they sang songs and danced dances with concealed pagan meanings. In Peru the work of conversion was even less successful. "If the Indians admitted the existence of a Christian god," writes Nathan Wachtel, "they considered his influence to be limited to the Spanish world, and looked themselves for protection to their own gods." To this day, Indians in lands like Guatemala and Peru perform ceremonies from the Maya and Inca period.

The friars had to battle not only the Indian tendency toward backsliding but divisions within

Bartolomé de Las Casas deplored the racist attitudes of the conquistadors and defended Indian culture against the scorn of Europeans. His teachings emphasized the dignity of all people. (Painting by A. Lara from 18th-century engraving. Biblioteca Colombina, Seville/MAS, Barcelona)

their own camp. Violent disputes arose among the orders over the degree of prebaptismal instruction required by Indian converts, with the Dominicans and Augustinians demanding stiffer standards than the Franciscans. Other disputes arose as to which order should have jurisdiction over a particular area or pueblo. A more serious conflict arose between the secular and the regular clergy. The pastoral and sacramental duties performed by the regular clergy in America were normally entrusted only to parish priests. Special papal legislation (1522) had been required to grant these functions to the regulars, a concession made necessary by the small number of seculars who came to the Indies in the early years. But after mid-century their number increased, and the bishops increasingly sought to create new parishes manned by seculars. These seculars were intended to replace the regulars in the spiritual direction of Indian converts. The friars resisted by every means at their disposal, but they fought a losing battle. The secular clergy had various advantages in their favor. One was a ruling of the Council of Trent that only clergy under episcopal authority could have parochial jurisdiction. Another was the preference accorded to the episcopal hierarchy by Philip II, who disliked the excessive independence of spirit shown by members of the orders in disputes over Indian policy and other matters.

In 1574 the seculars gained a decisive victory through the issuance of a royal edict giving each bishop virtual control over the number of friars in his diocese and their assignment to parishes. A subsequent decree (1583) stated the principle that secular clergy were to be preferred over friars in all appointments to parishes. But these rulings did not settle this and related questions; from first to last the colonies were a scene of unedifying strife among the clergy over their fields of jurisdiction.

Another source of division within the church was rivalry between American-born and peninsular clergy for control of the higher positions, especially in the orders. Threatened with loss of those positions in provincial elections by the growing creole majority in the seventeenth century, the peninsulars sought and obtained decrees making mandatory alternation of offices between themselves and creoles.

The Moral Decline of the Clergy and the Missionary Impulse

To the factors contributing to the decline of the intellectual and spiritual influence of the orders one must add the gradual loss of a sense of mission and of morale among the regular clergy. Apostolic fervor inevitably declined as the work of conversion in the central areas of the empire approached completion; many of the later arrivals among the clergy preferred a life of ease and profit to one of austerity and service. By the last decades of the sixteenth century, there were frequent complaints against the excessive number of monasteries and their wealth. The principal sources of this wealth were legacies and other gifts from rich donors—for a rich man not to provide for the church in his will was a matter of scandal.

Both the donor's piety and his family interest could be served by establishing a chantry to celebrate in perpetuity memorial masses for his soul. By designating a family member as chaplain, the donor ensured that control of the income from the endowment would remain in the family.

The resources acquired by the church became inalienable in the form of mortmain, or perpetual ownership. When invested in land and mortgages, this wealth brought in more wealth. The enormous economic power of the church gave it a marked advantage over competitors and enabled it to take advantage of weaker lay property owners, especially in time of recession. The last important order to arrive in Spanish America, the Society of Jesus (1572), was also the most fortunate in the number of rich benefactors and the most efficient in running its numerous enterprises, which, it should be said in its favor, were largely used to support its excellent system of *colegios* (secondary schools) and its missions.

Inevitably, this concern with the accumulation of material wealth weakened the ties between the clergy and the humble Indian and mixed-blood masses whose spiritual life they were supposed to direct. As early as the 1570s, there were many complaints of excessive ecclesiastical fees and clerical exploitation of Indian labor. A viceroy of New Spain, the Marqués de Monteclaros, assured King Philip III in 1607 that the Indians suffered the heaviest oppression at the hands of the friars and that one Indian paid more tribute to his parish priest than twenty paid to His Majesty. Hand in hand with a growing materialism went an increasing laxity of morals. Concubinage became so common among the clergy of the later colonial period that it seems to have attracted little official notice or rebuke. By the last decades of the colonial period, the morals of the clergy had declined to a condition that the Mexican historian Lucas Alamán, himself a leader of the clerical party in the period of independence, could only describe as scandalous. From this charge one must in general exclude the Jesuits, noted for their high moral standards and strict discipline; and of course men of excellent character and social conscience were to be found among both the secular and regular clergy.

The missionary impulse of the first friars survived longest on the frontier, "the rim of Christendom." Franciscans first penetrated the great northern interior of New Spain, peopled by hostile Chichimecs, "wild Indians." Franciscans accompanied the Oñate expedition of 1598 into New Mexico and dominated the mission field there until the end of the colonial period; they were also found in such distant outposts of Spanish power as Florida and Georgia. After the expulsion of the Jesuits from the Indies in 1767, the Franciscans took their place directing missionary work among the Indians of California. In addition to their pioneering efforts in California, the early Jesuits were active in the conversion and pacification of the Chichimecs of the north central plateau of Mexico and had exclusive charge of the conversion of the Indian tribes of the northwest coast of Mexico.

The mission was one of three closely linked institutions—the other two being the *presidio* (garrison) and the civil settlement—designed to serve the ends of Spanish imperial expansion and defense on the northern frontier. The mission, it was hoped, would gather the Indian converts into self-contained religious communities, train them to till the land, herd cattle, and practice various crafts, until they became fully Christianized and Hispanicized. The presidios would provide military protection for the neighboring missions and insure a cooperative attitude on the part of the Indian novices. Finally, attracted by the lure of free land, Spaniards of modest means would throng into the area, forming civil settlements that would become bustling centers of life and trade. By all these means, the frontier would be pushed back, pacified, and maintained against foreign encroachment.

This three-pronged attack on the wilderness was not very successful. Romantic literature has created a myth of an idyllic mission society in the American Southwest that does not correspond to reality. Certain tribes on the northern frontier, such as the powerful Apaches of Arizona, New Mexico, and Texas and the Comanches of Texas, never were reduced to mission life. The missionaries had greater success among such sedentary tribes as the Pueblo Indians of New Mexico, the Pima and Opata of Sonora in northwest Mexico, and the Hasinai of east Texas. Even among these peaceful tribes, however, Indian revolts and desertions were frequent. In 1680 the supposedly Christianized Pueblo Indians of New Mexico revolted, slaughtered the friars, and maintained a long, tenacious resistance against Spanish efforts at reconquest. The rise of native leaders who proclaimed that the old gods and way of life were best often sparked wholesale desertions. Mistreatment by soldiers in nearby presidios and the terror inspired by Apache and Comanche raiding parties also provoked frequent flight by mission Indians.

The authoritarian paternalism of the fathers, enforced by the use of stocks, prisons, and whipping posts, produced cultural change in the desired directions, but at the cost of reduced vitality on the part of the Indians affected. One indication of the maiming effect of mission life was the reduced birthrate among the neophytes.

Spanish census records show that the mission Indian birthrate in 1783 in Texas was far below that among the Spanish inhabitants of the province. This and desertions made necessary constant recruitment of converts, but the presence of hovering Apache and Comanche bands, mounted on swift horses introduced by the Spaniards, made this hazardous. An indication of the failure of the mission enterprise was the unwillingness of the Spanish government in the late eighteenth century to finance the search for converts.

The civil settlements proved no more successful. By the end of the colonial period, there were only a few scattered towns on the northern frontier, and the continuous raids made life and property so insecure that in New Mexico settlers who petitioned for permission to leave outnumbered recruits coming to the area. Ultimately, the whole task of defending and civilizing the future American Southwest fell on a chain of presidios stretching approximately along the present border between the United States and Mexico. Successive reverses in the open field compelled the Spanish troops to take refuge behind the security of the high presidio walls. In the end, Spain was forced to adopt a policy of neutralizing the Apaches and Comanches by periodic distribution of gifts to these warlike tribes. When the outbreak of the wars of independence stopped the flow of gifts, the hostile Indians again took to the warpath, driving by the useless line of presidios into the interior of Mexico.

The most notable instance of successful missionary effort, at least from an economic point of view, was that of the Jesuit establishments in Paraguay. In this region, favored by a genial climate and fertile soil, the Jesuits established more than thirty missions; these formed the principal field of Jesuit activity in America. Strict discipline, centralized organization, and absolute control over the labor of thousands of docile Indians producing large surpluses enabled the Jesuits to turn their missions into a highly profitable business enterprise. Great quantities of such goods as cotton, tobacco, and hides were shipped down the Paraná River to Buenos Aires for export to Europe. Rather than "Christian socialism," the Jes-

uit mission system could more correctly be described as "theocratic capitalism."

To protect the missions against slave raiders from the Portuguese colony of São Paulo, the fathers created a native militia armed with European weapons. Every effort was made to limit contact with the outside world. The life of the Indians was rigidly regimented in dress, housing, and the routines of work, play, and rest. The self-imposed isolation of the Jesuit mission empire aroused the curiosity of eighteenth-century European philosophers and literati; Voltaire gave an ironic and fanciful description of it in his witty satire on the follies and vices of the age, *Candide*.

Jesuit rule in Paraguay and Jesuit mission activity everywhere in the colonies ended when a royal decree expelled the order from the colonies in 1767. Among the motives for this action were the conflict between the nationalistic church policy of the Bourbons and Jesuit emphasis on papal supremacy, suspicions of Jesuit meddling in state affairs generally, and the belief that the Jesuit mission system constituted a state within a state. The expulsion of the Jesuits from Paraguay resulted in intensified exploitation of the Indians by Spanish officials and landowners and in a shedding by the Indians of much of the thin veneer of European culture imposed on them by the missionaries. Within a generation the previously thriving Jesuit villages were in ruins.

The Inquisition in the New World

The Inquisition formally entered the Indies with the establishment by Philip II of tribunals of the Holy Office in Mexico and Lima in 1569. Prior to that time, its functions were performed by clergy who were vested with or assumed inquisitorial powers. Its great privileges, its independence of other courts, and the dread with which the charge of heresy was generally regarded by Spaniards made the Inquisition an effective check on "dangerous thoughts," whether religious, political, or philosophical. The great mass of cases tried by its tribunals, however, had to do with offenses against morality or minor deviations from orthodox religious conduct, such as blasphemy.

As in Spain, the Inquisition in the Indies relied largely on denunciations by informers and employed torture to secure confessions. As in Spain, the damage done by the Inquisition was not limited to the snuffing out of lives and the confiscation of property but included the creation of an atmosphere of fear, distrust, and rigid intellectual conformity. Indians, originally subject to the jurisdiction of inquisitors, were later removed from their control as recent converts of limited mental capacity and hence not fully responsible for their deviations from the Faith.

The Structure of Class and Caste

The social order that arose in the Indies on the ruins of the old Indian societies was based, like that of Spain, on aristocratic or feudal principles. Race, occupation, and religion were the formal criteria that determined an individual's social status. All mechanical labor was regarded as degrading, but large-scale trade (as opposed to retail trade) was compatible with nobility, at least in the Indies. Great emphasis was placed on *limpieza de sangre* (purity of blood), meaning above all descent from "Old Christians," without mixture of converso or Morisco (Muslim) blood. Proofs of such descent were jealously guarded, and sometimes manufactured.

The various races and racial mixtures were carefully distinguished and graded in a kind of hierarchy of rank. A trace of black blood legally sufficed to deprive an individual of the right to hold public office or enter the professions, as well as depriving him of the other rights and privileges of white men. The same taint attached to the great mass of mestizos (mixtures of Indians and Spaniards). True, the Laws of the Indies assigned perfect legal equality with whites to mestizos of legitimate birth, but to the very end of the colonial period the charters of certain colonial guilds and schools excluded all mestizos, without distinction.

The lack of solid demographic information and major disagreements among historians regarding the size of pre-Conquest populations make estimates of Spanish America's population in 1650, and of the relative numerical strength of the racial groups composing that population, conjectural. It appears, however, that by that date, or even earlier, the long decline of the Indian population had ended and a slow recovery had begun. It also appears that the European element in the population was growing more rapidly than the Indian. But the groups growing most rapidly were the *castas,* the mixtures resulting from the union of whites and Indians (mestizos) and of whites and blacks (mulattos). The great majority of these mixed-bloods were born out of wedlock.

As noted above, Spanish law and opinion ranked all these racial groups in a descending order of worth and privilege, with Europeans on top and Indians, blacks, and mixtures assigned to lower levels in the social pyramid. This formal ranking did not necessarily correspond to the actual standing of individuals of different racial make-up in society, but it provided the colonial ruling groups with an ideological justification for their rule. It also created a conflict society par excellence, pitting Indians against blacks, caste against caste, inflating poor whites with a sense of their superiority over all colored groups, which hindered forging the unity of the exploited masses and thus served to maintain an oppressive social order.

The White Ruling Class

In practice, racial lines were not very strictly drawn. In the Indies, a white skin was a symbol of social superiority, roughly the equivalent of *hidalguía,* a title of nobility in Spain, but it had no cash value. Not all whites belonged to the privileged economic group. Colonial records testify to the existence of a large class of "poor whites"—vagabonds, beggars, or worse—who disdained work and frequently preyed on the Indians. A Spaniard of this group, compelled by poverty to choose his mate from the colored races, generally doomed his descendants to an inferior

110   economic and social status. The mestizo or mulatto son of a wealthy Spanish landowner or merchant, on the other hand, if acknowledged and made his legal heir, could pass into the colonial aristocracy. If traces of Indian or black descent were too strong, the father might reach an understanding with the parish priest, who had charge of baptismal certificates; it was also possible for a wealthy mestizo or mulatto to purchase from the crown a document establishing his legal whiteness. Wealth, not gentle birth or racial purity, was the distinguishing characteristic of the colonial aristocracy. Granted this fact, it remains true that the apex of the colonial pyramid was composed overwhelmingly of whites.

This white ruling class was itself divided by group jealousies and hostilities. The Spaniards brought to the New World their regional rivalries and feuds—between Old Castilians and Andalusians, between Castilians and Basques—and in the anarchic, heated atmosphere of the Indies these rivalries often exploded into brawls or even pitched battles. But the most abiding cleavage within the upper class was the division between the Spaniards born in the colonies, called creoles, and the European-born Spaniards, called peninsulars or referred to by such disparaging nicknames as *gachupín* or *chapetón* (tenderfoot). Legally, creoles and peninsulars were equal; indeed Spanish law called for preference to be given in the filling of offices to the descendants of conquistadors and early settlers. In practice, the creoles suffered from a system of discrimination that during most of the colonial period virtually denied them employment in high church and government posts and large-scale commerce. The preference shown for peninsulars over natives sprang from various causes, among them the greater access of Spaniards to the court, the fountainhead of all favors, and royal distrust of the creoles. By the second half of the sixteenth century, the sons or grandsons of conquistadors were complaining of the partiality of the crown and its officials for unworthy newcomers from Spain. The creoles viewed with envenomed spite these Johnny-come-latelies, who often won out in the scramble for *corregimientos* and other government jobs. A Mexican poet, Francisco de Terrazas, expressed the creole complaint in rhyme:

Spain: to us a harsh stepmother you have been,
A mild and loving mother to the stranger,
On him you lavish all your treasures dear,
With us you only share your cares and danger.[4]

The resulting cleavage in the colonial upper class grew wider with the passage of time. Both groups developed an arsenal of arguments to defend their positions. Peninsulars often justified their privileged status by reference to the alleged indolence, incapacity, and frivolity of the creoles, which they sometimes solemnly attributed to the American climate or other environmental conditions. The creoles responded in kind by describing the Europeans as mean and grasping parvenus (new rich). The growing wealth of the creoles from mines, plantations, and cattle ranches only sharpened their resentment at the discrimination from which they suffered. The split within the colonial upper class must be regarded as a major cause of the creole wars of independence.

The Mestizo: An Ambiguous Status

The mestizo arose from a process of racial mixture that began in the first days of the Conquest. In the post-Conquest period, when white women were scarce, the crown and the church viewed Indian-white marriages with some favor; mixed marriages were not uncommon in those years. But this attitude soon changed as the crown, for its own reasons, adopted a policy of systematic segregation of the Indians from the white community. By the first quarter of the seventeenth century, the authoritative writer on Spain's colonial legislation, Juan Solórzano Pereira, could write: "Few Spaniards of honorable position will

[4] Francisco de Terrazas, *Poesías,* ed. Antonio Castro Leal (Mexico, 1941), p. 87. From *The Aztec Image in Western Thought* by Benjamin Keen, p. 90. Copyright © 1971 by Rutgers University, the State University of New Jersey. Reprinted by permission of Rutgers University Press.

Although social rank and privileges were mostly ascribed to the white ruling class, economic advantages were enjoyed by many people with mixed racial backgrounds. This picture, although depicting late colonial society, shows colonial classes composed of Spaniards, mestizos, Indians, and mulattos. (Laurie Platt Winfrey, Inc.)

marry Indian or Negro women." Consequently, the great mass of mestizos had their origin in irregular unions between Spaniards and Indian women. The stigma of illegitimacy, unredeemed by wealth, doomed the majority to the social depths. Some became peons, resembling the Indian in their way of life; others swelled the numerous class of vagabonds; still others enrolled in the colonial militia. Mestizos also contributed to the formation of the rancheros (small farmers) and formed part of the lower middle class of artisans, overseers, and shopkeepers. Without roots in either Indian or Spanish society, scorned and distrusted by both, small wonder that the lower-class mestizo acquired a reputation for violence and instability.

112 The Indians: A Separate Nation

By contrast with the mestizo, no ambiguity marked the position of the Indian in Spanish law and practice. The Indians constituted a separate nation, the *república de indios*, which also constituted a hereditary tribute-paying caste. The descendants of the Indian rulers and hereditary nobility, however, received special consideration, partly from Spanish respect for the concept of *señor natural* (the natural or legitimate lord), partly because they played a useful role as intermediaries between the Spanish rulers and Indian tribute payers. The Indian nobles were allowed to retain all or part of their patrimonial estates and enjoyed such special privileges as the right to ride horses, wear European dress, and carry arms.

There is ample evidence that members of the Indian aristocracy were among the worst exploiters of their own race. Their role as collectors of Indian tribute for the Spaniards offered large opportunities for enrichment at the expense of the commoners. They also usurped communal lands, imposed excessive rents on their Indian tenants, and forced the commoners to labor for them. In part, as Charles Gibson points out, these inordinate demands represented a "response to strain, an effort to maintain position and security" in the face of Spanish encroachments on the lands and prerequisites of the native nobility.

By the end of the sixteenth century, the Indian aristocracy was in full decline. One cause of this decline was Spanish invasion of their lands, to which the Indian nobles responded with costly but often futile litigation. Another cause of their downfall was their responsibility for the collection of tribute from the commoners. When the number of tribute payers in a town declined because of an epidemic or other circumstances, the Indian governor had to make up the arrears on the town's fixed quota or go to jail. In order to make good the deficit, he might have to sell or mortgage his lands. However, at the end of the colonial period, especially in the Andean area, there remained a minority of Indian nobles who had grown wealthy through trade, stock raising,

or agriculture, and who enjoyed high social position. Perhaps typical of this small class of wealthy Indian or mestizo nobles was the famous late-eighteenth-century Peruvian cacique José Gabriel Condorcanqui (Tupac Amaru). Lillian Fisher writes that he lived like a Spanish nobleman, wearing "a long coat and knee-breeches of black velvet, a waistcoat of gold tissue worth seventy or eighty *duros* (dollars), embroidered linen, silk stockings, gold buckles at his knees and on his shoes, and a Spanish beaver hat valued at twenty-five duros. He kept his hair curled in ringlets that extended nearly down to his waist."[5] His source of wealth included the ownership of 350 mules, which he used to transport mercury and other goods to Potosí and other places, and a large cacao estate.

By contrast with the privileged treatment accorded to the Indian hereditary nobility, Indian commoners suffered under crushing burdens of tribute, labor, and ecclesiastical fees. Viewed as a constitutionally inferior race and hence as perpetual wards of the Spanish state, they repaid the Spanish tutelage with the obligation to pay tribute and give forced labor. *Gente sin razón* ("people of weak minds") was a phrase commonly applied to the Indians in colonial documents. Their juridical inferiority and status as wards found expression in laws (universally disregarded) forbidding them to make binding contracts or to contract debts in excess of five pesos and in efforts to minimize contact between Indians and other racial groups. These and many other restrictions on Indian activity had an ostensible protective character. But an enlightened Mexican prelate, Bishop Manuel Abad y Queipo, pointed out that these so-called privileges

do them little good and in most respects injure them greatly. Shut up in a narrow space of six hundred rods, assigned by law to the Indian towns, they possess no individual property and are obliged to work the communal lands. . . . Forbidden by law to commingle with the other castes,

[5] Lillian E. Fisher, *The Last Inca Revolt, 1780–1783* (Norman: University of Oklahoma Press, 1966), p. 23.

they are deprived of the instruction and assistance that they should receive from contact with these and other people. They are isolated by their language, and by a useless, tyrannical form of government.

He concluded that the ostensible privileges of the Indians were "an offensive weapon employed by the white class against the Indians, and never serve to defend the latter."[6]

Most of the Indians lived in their own towns, some of pre-Hispanic origin, others created by a process of resettlement of dispersed Indian populations in new towns called "reductions" or "congregations." To serve the ends of Spanish control and tribute collection, the Indian towns were reorganized on the peninsular model, with municipal governments patterned on those of Spanish towns. The Indian cabildo had its regidores, its alcaldes who tried minor cases, and its *gobernador* (governor), who was responsible for the collection and delivery of tribute to the corregidor or the encomendero. These offices as a rule became hereditary in certain aristocratic families.

The Indian town typically was composed of one or more kinship groups (calpulli in Mexico, ayllu in the Andean region), each with its hereditary elders who represented their community in intergroup disputes, acted as intermediaries in arranging marriages, supervised the allotment of land to the group's members, and otherwise served their communities. A certain degree of Hispanicization of Indian commoners took place, reflected above all in religion but also in the adoption of various tools and articles of dress and food. But the barriers erected by Spain between the two communities and the fixed hostility with which they regarded each other prevented any thoroughgoing acculturation. In response to the aggressions and injustices inflicted on it by the white world, the Indian community drew into itself and fought stubbornly not only to preserve its land but its cultural identity, speech, social organization, and traditional dances and songs. After the kinship group, the most important Indian instrumentality for the maintenance of collective identity and security was the *cofradía* (religious brotherhood), whose members were responsible for the maintenance of certain cult activities.

The Conquest and its aftermath inflicted not only heavy material damage on Indian society but serious psychological injury as well. Spanish accounts frequently cite the lament of Indian elders over the loss of the severe discipline, strong family ties, and high moral standards of the pre-Conquest regimes. The Spanish judge Zorita quoted approvingly the remark of an Indian elder that with the coming of the Spaniards to Mexico "all was turned upside down . . . liars, perjurers, and adulterers are no longer punished as they once were because the *principales* (nobles) have lost the power to chastise delinquents. This, say the Indians, is the reason why there are so many lies, disorders, and sinful women."[7] A symptom as well as cause of Indian social disorganization was widespread alcoholism.

Blacks, Mulattos, Zambos: The Lowest Class

Blacks, mulattos, and *zambos* (mixtures of Indians and blacks) occupied the bottom rungs of the colonial social ladder. By the end of the sixteenth century some 75,000 African slaves had been introduced into the Spanish colonies under the system of asiento. The infamous Middle Passage (the journey of slaves across the Atlantic) was a thing of horror; the Jesuit Alonso de Sandoval, who had charge of conversion of slaves and who wrote a book on the subject, left this harrowing description of the arrival of a cargo of slaves in the port of Cartagena in New Granada:

They arrive looking like skeletons; they are led ashore, completely naked, and are shut up in a large court or enclosure . . . and it is a great pity to see so many sick and needy people, denied all

---

[6] Cited in José María Luis Mora, *Obras sueltas*, 2 vols. (Paris, 1837), 1:55-57.

[7] Keen, *Life and Labor in Ancient Mexico*, p. 126.

care or assistance, for as a rule they are left to lie on the ground, naked and without shelter. . . . I recall that I once saw two of them, already dead, lying on the ground on their backs like animals, their mouths open and full of flies, their arms crossed as if making the sign of the cross . . . and I was astounded to see them dead as a result of such great inhumanity.

By the end of the eighteenth century some 9.5 million slaves had been brought to the Americas. Especially dense concentrations were found in Brazil and in the Caribbean area, which were dominated by plantation economies. Historians have hotly disputed the character of Latin American black slavery. What may be called the traditional view, expressed in books like Gilberto Freyre's *The Masters and the Slaves* (1946), Frank Tannenbaum's *Slave and Citizen: The Negro in the Americas* (1947), and Herbert Klein's *Slavery in the Americas: A Comparative Study of Virginia and Cuba* (1967), claimed that cultural factors tended to make slavery in Latin America milder than in the United States. Particularly influential was Tannenbaum's little book, which explained this greater leniency by such factors as medieval Iberian legislation, which recognized the unnaturalness of slavery; the church's insistence on the slave's right to marry and its protection of the slave family; and the elaborate body of Spanish law defining slave rights, including the slave's right to purchase his or her freedom and that of other family members. Marvin Harris subjected the Tannenbaum thesis to sharp criticism in his *Patterns of Race in the Americas* (1964), which argued that the supposed mildness of Latin American black slavery was a myth, that the protective legislation was often ignored, and that economic rather than cultural factors determined the specific differences between slave societies.

Recent studies generally support the view that the tempo of economic activity was decisive in determining the intensity of slave exploitation and the harshness of plantation discipline. Certainly manumission of slaves was more frequent in the Hispanic than in the English, Dutch, or French colonies, but it is likely that the unprofitability of slavery under certain conditions contributed more than cultural traditions to this result. Whatever the reasons, by the close of the colonial period slaves formed a minority of the total black and mulatto population. Whatever their treatment, slaves retained the aspiration for freedom. Fear of slave revolts haunted the white ruling class, and slaves frequently fled from their masters. Some of them formed independent communities in remote jungles or mountains that successfully resisted Spanish punitive expeditions.

This stubborn attachment of the black slaves to freedom, reflected in frequent revolts, flights, and other forms of resistance, suggests that the debate over the relative mildness or severity of black slavery in Latin America evades the main issue—the dehumanizing character of even the "mildest" slavery. Brought from Africa by force and violence, cut off from their kindred and peoples, the uprooted slaves were subjected in their new environment to severe deculturation. For reasons of security, slaveowners preferred to purchase slaves of diverse tribal origins, language, and religious beliefs and deliberately promoted tribal disunity among them. The economic interest of the planters dictated that the great majority of the imported slaves should be young, between the ages of fifteen and twenty. This contributed to the process of deculturation, for very few aged blacks, the repositories of tribal lore and traditions in African societies, came in the slaveships. The scarcity of women (the proportion of females in the slave population on Cuban plantations between 1746 and 1822 ranged between 9 and 15 percent) distorted the lives of the slaves, creating a climate of intense sexual repression and family instability. The church might insist on the right of the slave to proper Christian marriage and the sanctity of the marriage, but not until the nineteenth century was the separate sale of husbands, wives, and children forbidden in the Spanish colonies. The right of the master to sell or remove members of the slave's family and his free sexual access to slave women made difficult if not impossible a normal family life for slaves. The world of the slave plantation, resembling a prison rather than a society, left to independent Latin America a bitter heritage of racism, discrimination, and backwardness, problems that in most Latin American countries still await full solution.

Because of harsh treatment, poor living conditions, and the small number of women in the slave population, its rate of reproduction was very low. Miscegenation between white masters and slave women, on the other hand, produced a steady growth of the mulatto population. As noted above, by the end of the colonial period, for a variety of reasons, slaves formed a minority of the total black and mulatto population. Free blacks and mulattos made important contributions to the colonial economy, both in agriculture and as artisans of all kinds. Free blacks and mulattos, like Indians, were required to pay tribute.

Life in the City and on the Hacienda

In addition to the Indian communities, social life in the Spanish colonies had two major centers: the colonial city and the hacienda, or large landed estate. Unlike its European counterpart, the colonial city as a rule did not arise spontaneously as a center of trade or industry but developed in planned fashion to serve the ends of Spanish settlement and administration of the surrounding area. Sometimes it was founded on the ruins of an Indian capital, as in the case of Mexico City. More often it was founded on a site chosen for its strategic or other advantages, as in the case of Lima. By contrast with the usually anarchical layout of Spanish cities, the colonial town typically followed the gridiron plan, with a large central plaza flanked by the cathedral, the governor's *palacio,* and other public buildings. From this central square originated long, wide, and straight streets that intersected to produce uniform, rectangular blocks. This passion for regularity reflected both the influence of Renaissance neoclassical works on architecture and the regulatory zeal of the crown. In sharp contrast to the carefully planned nucleus of the colonial city was the disorderly layout of the surrounding na-

tive *barrios,* slum districts inhabited by a large Indian and mestizo population that provided the Spanish city with cheap labor and combustible material for the riots that shook the cities in times of famine or other troubles.

Into the capitals flowed most of the wealth produced by the mines, plantations, and cattle ranches of the surrounding area. In these cities, in houses whose size and proximity to the center reflected the relative wealth and social position of their owners, lived the rich mine owners and landowners of the colonies. They displayed their wealth by the magnificence of their homes, furnishings, dress, and carriages, and by the multitude of their servants and slaves. By the end of the sixteenth century, Mexico City had already acquired fame for the beauty of its women, horses, and streets, and riches of its shops, and the reckless spending, gaming, and generosity of its aristocracy. The poet Bernardo de Balbuena, in a long poem devoted to "La Grandeza Mexicana" ("The Grandeur of Mexico City"), wrote of

That lavish giving of every ilk,
Without a care how great the cost
Of pearls, of gold, of silver, and of silk.[8]

By the close of the seventeenth century, Mexico City had a population estimated to number 200,000.

Lima, founded in 1534, proud capital of the viceroyalty of Peru, and Potosí, the great Peruvian mining center whose wealth became legendary, were two other major colonial cities. By 1650, when its wealth had already begun to decline, Potosí, with a population of 160,000 inhabitants, was the largest city in South America.

Before the eighteenth century, when changes in government and manners brought a greater stability, violence was prevalent in the colonial city. Duels, assassinations, even pitched battles between different Spanish factions were events frequently mentioned in official records and private diaries. From time to time, the misery of the

---

[8] Bernardo de Balbuena, *Grandeza Mexicana* (Mexico, 1954), p. 40.

masses in the native and mixed-blood wards exploded in terrifying upheavals. In 1624 the mobs of Mexico City, goaded by famine and a decree of excommunication issued by the archbishop against an unpopular viceroy, rose with cries of "Death to the evil government" and "Long live the church." They vented their wrath in widespread destruction and looting. In 1692 similar circumstances caused an even greater explosion, which ended in many deaths, the sacking of shops, and the virtual destruction of the viceroy's palace and other public buildings.

The hacienda constituted another great center of colonial social life. We must again stress the major variations in size, productive potential, labor systems, and other aspects of the colonial hacienda. Changing economic trends brought frequent changes in the size, products, and ownership of these enterprises, with large haciendas sometimes broken up into smaller units, and vice versa. The overall trend in the course of the colonial period was toward concentration of landownership in fewer hands, usually at the expense of small Indian, mixed-blood, and European landowners. Because of the "polymorphic" nature of the colonial hacienda, however, the following description of its social life may be regarded as more characteristic of haciendas of the "traditional" type, such as were found in certain areas of Mexico and Peru, and not of haciendas everywhere.

On the haciendas lived those creole aristocrats who could not support the expense of a city establishment or whose estates were in remote provinces or frontier areas. By the end of the seventeenth century, the hacienda in many areas had become a largely self-sufficient economic unit, combining arable land, grazing land for herds of sheep and cattle, timberland for fuel and construction, and even workshops for the manufacture and repair of the implements used on the hacienda. The hacienda was often also a self-contained social unit, with a church or chapel usually served by a resident priest, a store from which workers could obtain goods charged against their wages, and even a jail to house disobedient peons. In the hacendado's large, luxu-

riously appointed house often lived not only his immediate family but numerous relatives who laid claim to his protection and support.

The hacienda often contained one or more villages of Indians who had once been owners of the land on which they now lived and worked as virtual serfs. These Indians lived in one-room adobe or thatch huts whose only furniture often was some sleeping mats and a stone used for grinding maize (called *metate* in New Spain). Unlike the independent Indian communities, which continued to resist the landowners' aggressions with strategies ranging from revolts to prolonged litigation, the resident peons had usually learned to make the appropriate responses of resigned servility to the master. The hacienda, with its characteristic economic and social organization, represented the most authentic expression of the feudal side of colonial society. Its long shadow still falls over Latin America today.

Marriage, Sexuality, and the Status of Women

Marital and familial relationships in white elite society were generally characterized by male domination, expressed in the customary right of fathers to arrange marriages for their daughters and in a double standard of sexual morality enjoining strict chastity or fidelity for wives and daughters without corresponding restrictions on husbands and sons. Both the church—the guardian of public morality—and the state—concerned with the economic and political consequences of marriage—sought to supervise and control it. Throughout the sixteenth and seventeenth centuries, the church tended to support the right of children to select their marriage partners, while conceding the right of parents to have a say in the matter. In the second half of the eighteenth century, however, when large property interests grew in importance and influence, the state and then the church gradually adopted positions supporting parental objections to marriage between "unequal" partners as prejudicial to the family's "honor." Although the royal decree of 1778 on the subject sanctioned parental opposition to only one kind of "inequality"—that arising from interracial unions—the interpretation placed upon it by high colonial courts made clear that they regarded a wealthy mulatto family as the equal of a wealthy Spanish family. "A mulatto or a descendant of mulattoes," writes Patricia Seed, "was unequal to a Spaniard only if he was poor. The trend in decision making was that economic differences tied to racial differences, rather than racial disparity alone, constituted substantial social disparity." This issue of "inequality," of course, rarely arose on the top elite level, where marriage partners were almost invariably selected with an eye to conserving or strengthening the fortunes of the aristocratic families involved.

The concept of sexual honor also underwent some change in the same period. Previously, when a young woman lost her "honor" as a result of premarital sexual activity and sued for restitution of that honor through marriage or other compensation, the church tended to hold the man responsible and require him to marry her or compensate her for her loss. In the middle of the eighteenth century, however, aristocratic parents often argued that the girl's sexual activity made her—but not him—"unequal," thereby creating a bar to marriage. "This new concept of gender-related honor," says Patricia Seed, "framed an elaborate double standard that allowed young men to take the honor of young women without damage to their reputations or matrimonial consequences, but at the same time condemned women for the identical action."

Despite the emphasis placed by the Hispanic code of honor on virginity and marital fidelity, many colonial women, including members of the elite, disregarded conventional morality and church laws by engaging in premarital and extramarital sex. Sexual relations between betrothed couples were common. Elite women who bore children out of wedlock had available a number of strategies to cover up their indiscretions and legitimate their offspring. The many lower-class women who transgressed in this way lacked the means and perhaps the will to recover their lost "honor." Illegitimacy appears to have been pervasive in colonial cities in the seventeenth and eighteenth centuries. Illegitimacy, signifying the lack of honor, could be a bar to holding public office and obstruct access to higher positions in the church, the military, and the civil service. The protection of wealthy relatives and access to education, however, could mitigate or remove the taint of illegitimacy. The chronicler Garcilaso de la Vega (1539–1616) took pride in being the natural son of a noble conquistador, and Sor Juana Inés de la Cruz (1651–1695) found her out-of-wedlock birth no obstacle to achieving a brilliant literary career, writing poetry of matchless beauty and grace.

The contrast between the formal code of sexual honor and the actual sexual conduct of colonial men and women was especially striking in a plantation area like Venezuela, where the large-scale existence of slavery and the enormous power of the great landowners tended to loosen the restraints of law and convention on such conduct. In 1770 Bishop Martí of Venezuela made a visita of his diocese. To evaluate the moral health of his subjects he invited the people of each town he visited to speak to him in confidence about their own sins and those of their neighbors. Martí's detailed record of these reports and his own investigations and judgments give an impression of sexuality run rampant. "Over fifteen hundred individuals stood accused, primarily of sexual misdeeds," writes Kathy Waldron; "nearly ten percent of the clerics in the province came under attack; and even the governor of Maracaibo was denounced. The accusations included adultery, fornication, concubinage, incest, rape, bigamy, prostitution, lust, homosexuality, bestiality, abortion, and infanticide."

The economic, social, and physical subordination of colonial women to men (prevailing church doctrine accepted a husband's right to beat disobedient or erring wives, but in moderation) is an undisputed fact. But male domination was to some extent limited by the Hispanic property law, which required equal division of estates among heirs and gave women the right to control their dowries and inheritances during and beyond marriage. We know that some colonial

118 women operated as entrepreneurs independently of their husbands; women were often appointed executors of their husbands' wills and frequently managed a husband's business after his death. Two specialists in the field, Asunción Lavrín and Edith Couturier, concluded that colonial women enjoyed more economic independence than had been supposed, "that there was repression; but repression was not the whole reality, and that it did not wholly impair women's ability of expression."

Conventual life provided an especially important means for achieving self-expression and freedom from male domination and sexual exploitation for elite and middle-class women. It was common for one or more daughters of an elite family to enter a convent; in the seventeenth century thirteen Lima convents held more than 20 percent of the city's women. The convents were self-governing institutions that gave women an opportunity to display their capacity for leadership in administration, management of resources (like other church bodies, convents invested their wealth in mortgages on urban and rural properties), and sometimes in politicking, for convents could be the scenes of stormy factional struggle for control. The convent represented a heaven-sent opportunity for a young woman like Sor Juana Inés de la Cruz, who was of a modest family background and who had no particular religious vocation. Her intellectual brilliance made it difficult for her to find a suitable marriage partner, and in any case she lacked the dowry to attract such a man. The convent, though, offered Sor Juana a way to escape the traps of sexual exploitation and cultivate her immense talents. A recent study of Hispanic women in colonial Peru by Luis Martín describes the Peruvian nunnery as "a fortress of women, a true island of women, where . . . women could protect themselves from the corroding and dehumanizing forces of Don Juanism." But a caveat is in order; the subjects of Martín's book are mostly upper-class Hispanic women, surrounded by slaves and servants, who often scorned and sometimes abused their black and Indian sisters.

Unfortunately, little as yet is known of the affairs of non-Hispanic women of the lower classes. What little is known suggests, paradoxically, that early post-Conquest society provided more opportunities for Indian females than for Indian males. The scarcity of white women forced Spaniards to take available Indian women as their mates, "allowing them to fill roles and positions that would ordinarily have been reserved for white women." Their positions in household work, sewing, and small-scale trade placed them in closer contact with Spanish society and helped strengthen their economic and social situation. With the arrival of growing numbers of white women by the late sixteenth century, however, the opportunities and mobility of Indian women became more limited.

Chapter 6

The Bourbon Reforms and Spanish America

The death of the sickly Charles II in November 1700 marked the end of an era in Spanish history and the beginning of a new and better day, although the signs under which the new day began were far from hopeful. On his deathbed the unhappy Charles, more kingly in his dying than he had ever been before, fought desperately to prevent the triumph of an intrigue for the partition of the Spanish dominions among three claimants of that inheritance, the prince of Bavaria, the archduke Charles of Austria, and Louis XIV's grandson, Philip of Anjou. In one of his last acts, Charles signed a will naming the French Philip, who became Philip V, successor to all his dominions.

English fears at the prospect of a union of France and Spain under a single ruler precipitated the War of the Spanish Succession (1702–1713). The war ended with the Treaty of Utrecht (1713), which granted to Great Britain Gibraltar and Minorca, major trade concessions in the Spanish Indies, and a guarantee against a union of the French and Spanish thrones under Philip. Another peace treaty, concluded the following year, gave the Spanish Netherlands and Spain's Italian possessions to Austria.

Reform and Recovery

Spain's humiliating losses deepened the prevailing sense of pessimism and defeatism, but there were compensations: the shock of defeat in the succession war drove home the need for sweeping reform of Spanish institutions; the loss of the Netherlands and the Italian possessions left Spain

120

with a more manageable, more truly Spanish empire, consisting of the kingdoms of Castile and Aragon and the Indies.

The War of the Spanish Succession also brought a forcible solution of the Aragonese problem, which had long plagued the Hapsburg monarchy. Fearing the authoritarian tendencies of the new Bourbon dynasty and recalling the injuries suffered at French hands during the seventeenth century, the Catalans rose in support of the Austrian claimant in 1705; Aragon and Valencia also invited and received the support of English and Austrian troops. But Aragon and Valencia fell to Philip V's armies in 1707 and suffered immediate loss of their fueros as punishment for supporting the wrong side. The Catalans, abandoned by Great Britain when it signed the peace of Utrecht in 1713, held out until September 1714, when Barcelona surrendered to the Bourbon forces. The fall of the city was followed by the destruction of Catalan liberties and autonomy, with the province being placed under a captain general who governed with the aid of a royal audiencia. The new regime made a systematic but unsuccessful effort to extinguish the Catalan language and nationality.

The Bourbon Reforms

The return of peace permitted the new dynasty to turn its attention to implementing a program of reform inspired by the French model. The reform and ensuing revival of Spain is associated with three princes of the House of Bourbon: Philip V (1700–1746) and his two sons, Ferdinand VI (1746–1759) and Charles III (1759–1788). Under the aegis of "enlightened despotism," the Bourbon kings attempted nothing less than a total overhaul of existing political and economic structures, a total renovation of the national life. Only such sweeping reform could close the gap that separated Spain from the foremost European powers and arm the country with the weapons—a powerful industry, a prosperous agriculture, a strong middle class—it needed to pre-

vent its defeat by England and her allies in the struggle for empire that dominated the eighteenth century.

The movement for reform, although carried out within the framework of royal absolutism and Catholic orthodoxy, inevitably provoked the hostility of reactionary elements within the church and the nobility. As a result, the Bourbons, although supported by such liberal grandees as the count of Floridablanca and the count of Aranda, recruited many of their principal ministers and officials from the ranks of the lesser nobility and the small middle class. These men were strongly influenced by the rationalist spirit of the French Encyclopedists,[1] although they rejected French anticlericalism and deism. They were characteristic of the Spanish Enlightenment in their rigid orthodoxy in religion and politics combined with enthusiastic pursuit of useful knowledge, criticism of defects in the church and clergy, and belief in the power of informed reason to improve society by reorganizing it along more rational lines.

The work of national reconstruction began under Philip V but reached its climax under Charles III. This great reformer-king attempted to revive Spanish industry by removing the stigma attached to manual labor, establishing state-owned textile factories, inviting foreign technical experts into Spain, and encouraging technical education. He aided agriculture by curbing the privileges of the Mesta, or stockbreeders' corporation, and by settling colonies of Spanish and foreign peasants in abandoned regions of the peninsula. He continued and expanded the efforts of his predecessors to encourage shipbuilding and foster trade and communication by the building of roads and canals. Clerical influence declined as a result of the expulsion of the Jesuits in 1767 and of decrees restricting the authority of the Inquisition. Under the cleansing influence of able and honest ministers, a new spirit of auster-

[1] Writers of the famous *Encyclopédie* (1751–1780), who were identified with the Enlightenment and advocated deism and a rationalist world outlook.

ity and service began to appear among public officials.

But the extent of the changes that took place in Spanish economic and social life under the Bourbons must not be exaggerated. The crown, linked by a thousand bonds to the feudal nobility and church, never touched the foundation of the old order, the land monopoly of the nobility, with its corollaries of mass poverty and archaic agricultural methods. As a result of these weaknesses, added to the lack of capital for industrial development and the debility of the Spanish middle class, Spain, despite marked advances in population and production, remained at the close of the era a second- or third-class power by comparison with Great Britain, France, or Holland.

The outbreak of the French Revolution, which followed by a few months the death of Charles III in December 1788, brought the reform era effectively to a halt. Frightened by the overthrow of the French monarchy and the execution of his royal kinsman, Charles IV and his ministers turned sharply to the right. The leading reformers were banished or imprisoned, and the importation of French rationalist and revolutionary literature was forbidden. Yet the clock could not be and was not entirely turned back, either in Spain or in the colonies. It was under the corrupt government of Charles IV, for example, that the expedition of Francisco Xavier Balmis sailed from Spain (1803) to carry the procedure of vaccination to the Spanish dominions in America and Asia—an act that probably saved innumerable lives.

In the field of colonial reform, the Bourbons moved slowly and cautiously, as was natural in view of the powerful vested interests identified with the old order of things. There was never any thought of giving a greater measure of self-government to the colonists or of permitting them to trade more freely with the non-Spanish world. On the contrary, the Bourbons centralized colonial administration still further, with a view to making it more efficient. In addition, their commercial reforms were designed to diminish smuggling and strengthen the exclusive commercial ties between Spain and her colonies, to "reconquer" the colonies economically for Spain.

Revival of Colonial Commerce and Breakdown of Trading Monopoly

The first Bourbon, Philip V, concentrated his efforts on an attempt to reduce smuggling and to revive the fleet system, which had fallen into decay in the late seventeenth century. With the Treaty of Utrecht, the English merchant class had scored an impressive victory in the shape of the asiento; the South Sea Company was granted the exclusive right to supply slaves to Spanish America, with the additional right of sending a shipload of merchandise to Portobelo every year. It was well known that the slave ships carried contraband merchandise, as did the provision ships that accompanied the annual ship and reloaded her with goods. Buenos Aires, where the South Sea Company maintained a trading post, was another funnel through which English traders poured large quantities of contraband goods that penetrated as far as Peru.

The Spanish government sought to check smuggling in the Caribbean by commissioning *guardacostas* (private warships), which prowled the main lanes of trade in search of ships loaded with contraband. The depredations of the guardacostas led to English demands for compensation and finally to war between England and Spain in 1739. During this war, the British again disrupted the fleet sailings Philip V had attempted to revive. In 1740 they were suspended. Their place was taken by swifter and more economical register ships, which sailed singly, under license from the crown. Ships bound for Peru used the route around Cape Horn; others sailed directly to Buenos Aires. The end of the South American fleet, known as the *galeones,* brought the death of the Portobelo Fair. The New Spain fleet was alternately revived and suspended, but abandoned in 1789. The convoy system, says John H. Parry, "had long outlived its usefulness;

in war it had become inadequate, in peace unnecessary."

The introduction of register ships did not, however, end the monopoly of the Cádiz *consulado* (merchant guild), whose members alone could load these vessels. The first breach in the wall of this monopoly came in the 1720s, with the organization of the Caracas Company, which was founded with the aid of capitalists in the Biscay region. In return for the privilege of trade with Venezuela, this company undertook to police the coast against smugglers and develop the resources of the region. The Caracas Company was on the whole a remarkable success. Dutch interlopers were driven away. Shipments of cacao to Spain doubled, and the price in Spain fell nearly to half. Exports of tobacco, cotton, dyewoods, and indigo also increased.

Biscayan and Catalan capital organized similar companies for trade with Havana, Hispaniola, and other places the old system of colonial trade had left undeveloped. These enterprises, however, were financial failures, in part because of inadequate capital, in part because of poor management. These breaches of the Cádiz monopoly brought no benefits to creole merchants, who continued to be almost completely excluded from the legal trade between Spain and her colonies.

The first Bourbons made few changes in the administrative structure of colonial government, contenting themselves with efforts to improve the quality of administration by more careful selection of officeholders. One major reorganization was the separation of the northern Andean region (present-day Ecuador, Colombia, and Venezuela) from the viceroyalty of Peru. In 1739 it became a viceroyalty, named New Granada, with its capital at Santa Fe (modern Bogotá). This change had strategic significance, reflecting a desire to provide better protection for the Caribbean coast, especially the fortress of Cartagena. It also reflected the rapid growth of population in the central highlands of Colombia. Within the new viceroyalty, Venezuela was named a cap-

taincy general, with its capital at Caracas, and became virtually independent of Santa Fe.

The movement for colonial reform, like the program of domestic reform, reached a climax in the reign of Charles III. Part of this reform had been foreshadowed in the writings of a remarkable Spanish economist and minister of finance and war under Ferdinand VI, José Campillo. Shortly before his death in 1743, Campillo wrote a memorial on colonial affairs that advocated the abolition of the Cádiz monopoly, a reduction of duties on goods bound for America, the organization of a frequent mail service to America, the encouragement of trade between the colonies, and the development of colonial agriculture and other economic activities that did not compete with Spanish manufacturers. Most of these recommendations were incorporated in a report made to Charles III by a royal commission in 1765. The shock of Spain's defeat in the Seven Years' War, which cost her the loss of Florida and almost the loss of Cuba, provided impetus for a program of imperial reorganization and reform.

In this period, the trading monopoly of Cádiz was gradually eliminated. In 1765, commerce with the West Indies was thrown open to seven other ports besides Cádiz and Seville; this reform, coming at a time when Cuban sugar production was beginning to expand, gave a sharp stimulus to the island's economy. This privilege was gradually extended to other regions until, by the famous decree of free trade of 1778, commerce was permitted between all qualified Spanish ports and all the American provinces except Mexico and Venezuela. In 1789, New Spain and Venezuela were thrown open to trade on the same terms.[2] The burdensome duties levied on this trade were also replaced by simple ad valo-

---

[2] It must be stressed, however, that these reforms did not seriously weaken the dominant role of the Cádiz monopolists and their American agents in colonial trade. As late as 1790, more than 85 percent of the trade moved through Cádiz, thanks to its superior facilities for shipping, insurance, warehousing, and communication.

rem duties of 6 or 7 percent. Restrictions on intercolonial trade were also progressively lifted, but this trade was largely limited to non-European products. A major beneficiary of this change was the Río de la Plata area, which in 1776 was opened for trade with the rest of the Indies. Meanwhile, the Casa de Contratación, symbol of the old order, steadily declined in importance until it closed its doors in 1789. A similar fate overtook the venerable Council of the Indies. As a consultative body it lasted on into the nineteenth century, but most of its duties were entrusted to a colonial minister appointed by the king.

The success of the "free trade" policy was reflected in a spectacular increase in the value of Spain's commerce with Spanish America, an increase said to have amounted to about 700 percent between 1778 and 1788. The entrance of new trading centers and merchant groups into the Indies trade and the reduction of duties and the removal of irksome restrictions had the effect of increasing the volume of business, reducing prices, and perhaps diminishing contraband (although one cannot speak with certainty here, for the easing of restrictions inevitably facilitated the activity of smugglers).

But the achievements of the Bourbon commercial reform must not be overestimated. The reform ultimately failed in its aim of reconquering colonial markets for Spain for two basic reasons: first, Spain's industrial weakness, which the best efforts of the Bourbons were unable to overcome, and, second, Spain's closely related inability to keep her sea-lanes to America open in time of war with England, when foreign traders again swarmed into Spanish-American ports. Indeed, the Spanish government openly confessed its inability to supply the colonies with needed goods in time of war by lifting the ban against foreign vessels of neutral origin (which meant United States ships, above all) during the years from 1797 to 1799 and again in the years from 1805 to 1809. This permission to trade with neutrals gave rise to a spirited United States commerce with the Caribbean area and with the Río de la Plata.

Increased Economic Activity

Perhaps the most significant result of the Bourbon commercial reform was the stimulus it gave to economic activity in Spanish America. To what extent this increased economic activity should be ascribed to the beneficial effects of the Bourbon reform and to what degree it resulted from the general economic upsurge in western Europe in the eighteenth century cannot be stated with certainty. What is certain is that the latter part of the century saw a rising level of agricultural, pastoral, and mining production in Spanish America. Stimulated by the Bourbon reform and by the growing European demand for sugar, tobacco, hides, and other staples, production of these products rose sharply in this period. There developed a marked trend toward regional specialization and monoculture in the production of cash crops. After 1770, coffee, grown in Venezuela and Cuba, joined cacao and sugar as a major export crop of the Caribbean area. The gradual increase in population also stimulated the production of food crops for local markets, notably wheat, preferred over maize by the European population. Tithe collections offer an index of agricultural growth: in the decade from 1779 to 1789, tithe collections in the principal agricultural areas were 40 percent greater than in the previous decade.

It appears, however, that agricultural prosperity was largely limited to areas producing export crops or with easy access to domestic markets. David Brading paints a gloomy picture of the financial condition of the Mexican haciendas in the eighteenth century. Except in the Valley of Mexico, the Bajío,[3] and the Guadalajara region, markets were too small to yield satisfactory returns. Great distances, poor roads, and high freight costs prevented haciendas from developing their

[3] A relatively urbanized area with a diversified economy (agriculture, mining, manufacturing) lying within the modern Mexican states of Guanajuato and Querétaro.

A typical urban market. (From Carl Nebel, *Voyage Pittoresque . . . [au] Mexique,* Paris, 1836)

productive capacity beyond the requirements of the local market. Private estates were worse off than church haciendas, because they had to pay tithes and sales taxes and bore the double burden of absentee landowners and resident administrators. Great landed families who possessed numerous estates in different regions, producing varied products for multiple markets, were more fortunate; their profits averaged from 6 to 9 percent of capital value in the late eighteenth century. However, thanks to cheap labor, even a low productivity yielded large revenues, which enabled hacendados to maintain a lavish, seigneurial style of life. Many haciendas were heavily indebted to ecclesiastical institutions, the principal bankers of the time.

The increase in agricultural production, it should be noted, resulted from more extensive use of land and labor rather than from the use of improved implements or techniques. The inefficient *latifundio* (great estate), which used poorly

paid peon labor, and the slave plantation accounted for the bulk of commercial agricultural production. The Prussian traveler Alexander von Humboldt, commenting on the semifeudal land tenure system of Mexico, observed that "the property of New Spain, like that of Old Spain, is in a great measure in the hands of a few powerful families, who have gradually absorbed the smaller estates. In America, as well as in Europe, large commons are condemned to the pasturage of cattle and to perpetual sterility."

The increasing concentration of landownership in Mexico and the central Andes in the second half of the eighteenth century reflected the desire of hacendados to eliminate the competition of small producers in restricted markets and to maintain prices at a high level. Given the low productivity of colonial agriculture, however, such natural disasters as drought, premature frosts, or excessive rains easily upset the precarious balance between food supplies and population, producing frightful famines like that of 1785–1787 in central Mexico. Thousands died of hunger or diseases induced by that famine.

What sugar, cacao, and coffee were for the Caribbean area, hides were for the Río de la Plata. The rising European demand for leather for footwear and industrial purposes and the permission given in 1735 for direct trade with Spain in register ships sparked an economic upsurge in the Plata area. The unregulated hunting of wild cattle on the open pampa soon gave way to the herding of cattle on established *estancias* (cattle ranches). By the end of the century, these were often of huge size—15 to 20 square leagues— with as many as eighty or a hundred thousand head of cattle. By 1790, Buenos Aires was exporting nearly a million and a half hides annually. The meat of the animal, hitherto almost worthless except for the small quantity that could be consumed immediately, now gained in value as a result of the demand for salt beef, processed in large-scale *saladeros* (salting plants). Markets for salt beef were found above all in the Caribbean area, especially Cuba, where it was chiefly used for feeding the slave population. The growth of cattle raising in La Plata, however, was attended by the concentration of land in ever fewer hands and took place at the expense of agriculture, which remained in a very depressed state.

The eighteenth century also saw a marked revival of silver mining in the Spanish colonies. Peru and Mexico shared in this advance, but the Mexican mines forged far ahead of their Peruvian rivals in the Bourbon era. The mine owners included creoles and peninsulars, but the Spanish merchants who financed the mining operations received most of the profits. As in the case of agriculture, the increase in silver production was not due primarily to improved technique; it resulted from the opening of many new as well as old mines and the growth of the labor force. The crown, however, especially under Charles III, contributed materially to the revival by offering new incentives to entrepreneurs and by its efforts to overcome the backwardness of the mining industry. The incentives included reductions in taxes and in the cost of mercury, a government monopoly.

In New Spain the crown promoted the establishment of a mining guild (1777) whose activities included the operation of a bank to finance development. Under this guild's auspices was founded the first school of mines in America (1792). Staffed by able professors and provided with modern equipment, it offered excellent theoretical and practical instruction and represented an important source of Enlightenment thought in Mexico. Foreign and Spanish experts, accompanied by teams of technicians, came to Mexico and Peru to show the mine owners the advantages of new machinery and techniques. These praiseworthy efforts were largely frustrated by the traditionalism of the mine owners, by lack of capital to finance changes, and by mismanagement. Yet the production of silver steadily increased. Supplemented by the gold of Brazil, it helped to spark the Industrial Revolution in northern Europe and to stimulate commercial activity on a worldwide scale. In addition, American silver helped the Bourbons meet the enormous expenses of their chronic wars.

Colonial manufacturing, after a long and fairly consistent growth, began to decline in the last part of the eighteenth century, principally because of the influx of cheap foreign wares with which the domestic products could not compete. The textile and wine industries of western Argentina fell into decay as they lost their markets in Buenos Aires and Montevideo to lower-priced foreign wines and cloth. The textile producers of the province of Quito in Ecuador complained of injury from the same cause. In the Mexican manufacturing center of Puebla, production of chinaware, of which the city had long been a leading center, slumped catastrophically between 1793 and 1802. Puebla and Querétaro, however, continued to be important centers of textile manufacturing.

Although Spain adopted mercantilist legislation designed to restrict colonial manufacturing—especially of fine textiles—this legislation seems to have been only a small deterrent to the growth of large-scale manufacturing. More important deterrents were lack of investment capital, the characteristic preference of Spaniards for land and mining as fields of investment, and a semiservile system of labor that was equally harmful to the workers and to productivity. Humboldt, who visited the woolen workshops of Querétaro in 1803, was disagreeably impressed

not only with the great imperfection of the technical process in the preparation for dyeing, but in a particular manner also with the unhealthiness of the situation, and the bad treatment to which the workers are exposed. Free men, Indians, and people of color are confounded with the criminals distributed by justice among the manufactories, in order to be compelled to work. All appear half naked, covered with rags, meagre, and deformed. Every workshop resembles a dark prison. The doors, which are double, remain constantly shut, and the workmen are not permitted to quit the house. Those who are married are only allowed to see their families on Sunday. All are unmercifully flogged, if they commit the smallest trespass on the order established in the manufactory. [4]

One of the few large-scale lines of industry was the manufacture of cigars and cigarettes. In the same town of Querétaro, Humboldt visited a tobacco factory that employed three thousand workers, including nineteen hundred women.

Labor Systems in the Eighteenth Century

Humboldt's comments testify to the persistence of servitude and coercion as essential elements of the labor system from the beginning to the end of the colonial period. Despite the Bourbons' theoretical dislike of forced labor, they sought to tighten legal enforcement of debt peonage in the Indies. Concerned with more efficient collection of Indian tribute, José de Gálvez, the reforming

minister of Charles III, tried to attach the natives more firmly to their pueblos and haciendas. In 1769, he introduced in New Spain the system of clearance certificates, documents that certified that peons had no outstanding debts and could seek employment with other landowners. The mobility of peons who lacked these papers could be restricted. Debt peonage was authorized by the Mining Ordinances of New Spain and was also practiced in the gold and silver mines of Chile, where a system of clearance certificates like that used in Mexico was employed. A recent study by James D. Riley notes a trend in Bourbon policy to make debts "considerably less coercive" in Mexico after 1785, but also notes that there was little official reluctance to pursue debtors and force them to pay up or work. On Jesuit farms in eighteenth-century Quito (Ecuador), says Nicholas Cushner, "the debt was a mechanism for maintaining a stable work force" whose wages were pitifully low. "It was an Indian analogue of black slavery," adds Cushner.

In practice, as previously noted, the importance of debt peonage and the severity of its enforcement depended on the availability of labor. In New Spain, by the late eighteenth century, the growth of the labor force through population increase and the elimination of small producers had sharply reduced the importance of debt as a means of securing and holding laborers. Eric Van Young, for example, has documented a reduction of the per capita indebtedness of resident peons in the Guadalajara area, suggesting their decreased bargaining power in dealing with employers. The new situation enabled hacendados to retain or discharge workers in line with changing levels of production. Thus in late eighteenth-century Mexico, landowners simply dismissed workers when crop failures occurred in order to save on their rations. These changes were accompanied by a tendency for real wages and rural living standards to decline.

In the Andean area, in provinces subject to the mita, it continued to play an important role in the provision of mining and agricultural labor almost to the end of the colonial period. In other prov-

[4] Alexander von Humboldt, *Political Essay on the Kingdom of New Spain,* 4 vols. (London, 1822–1823), 3:463–464.

inces, agricultural labor was theoretically free, but heavy tribute demands and the operations of the repartimiento de mercancías (the forced purchase of goods by the Indians from corregidors) created a need for cash that compelled many natives to seek employment on Spanish haciendas. These yanaconas included a large number of so-called *forasteros* ("outsiders") who had fled their native pueblos to escape the dreaded mita service and tribute burdens. In addition to working the hacendado's land, these laborers or sharecroppers and their families had to render personal service in the master's household. Theoretically free, their dependent status must have sharply limited their mobility.

Early Labor Struggles

Our knowledge of labor struggles in colonial Spanish America is fragmentary, in part because historians took little interest in the subject until recently. The first labor conflicts of a relatively modern type seem to have taken place in late eighteenth-century Mexico, the colony with the most developed and diversified economy. Strikes sometimes took place in artisan shops; in 1784, for example, the workers in the bakery of Basilio Badamler went on strike to protest "horrible working conditions." More commonly, they occurred in a few industries having large concentrations of workers and a division of labor that promoted workers' cooperation and solidarity. One such industry was the manufacture of cigars and cigarettes by the royal tobacco monopoly, whose founding was accompanied by a ruthless suppression (1773–1776) of artisan production of these goods. The immense factory operated by the monopoly in Mexico City employed about 7,000 workers of both sexes. The workers, who included Indians, mixed-bloods, and some Spaniards, were paid in cash, and the annual payroll in the 1780s and 1790s came to about 750,000 pesos. The militancy of these workers was displayed in strikes and protests and worried the authorities. In 1788 the consulado of Mexico City declared that this large assembly of workers pre-

sented a threat to public order, and cited a march on the viceroy's palace caused by a "small increase" in the length of the workday. The workers, heedless of the guards, swarmed into the palace and occupied the patios, stairs, and corridors. The viceroy, having heard their complaint, "prudently gave them a note ordering the factory's administrator to rescind that change, and so with God's help that tumult ended, the multitude left, bearing that note as if in triumph, and the viceroy decided to overlook that turbulent action, so likely to cause sedition." In 1794 the workers again marched on the viceregal palace to protest a change in the contractual arrangement that permitted them to take part of their work home to prepare for the next day's tasks.

A more dramatic labor struggle broke out in the 1780s in the Mexican silver mining industry. The scene of the conflict was the mines of Real del Monte in northern Mexico. Here, as in all other Mexican silver mines, the majority of the work force was free, but a minority of the workers were conscripted from the surrounding Indian villages through a repartimiento, or labor draft. Press gangs also picked up men charged with "idleness" or "vagrancy" to relieve the chronic shortage of labor. It was the grievances of the free skilled workers, however, that caused a series of confrontations with an arrogant unyielding employer and ultimately a work stoppage. The extreme division of labor in the silver mining industry—to get the ore out of the vein below and load it on mules above required some thirty different specialized tasks—tended to develop a sense of shared interests and cooperation among the workers.

Work in the mines was dangerous, daily exposing the miners to loss of life and limb through accidents, and even more to debilitating or fatal diseases. According to Francisco de Gamboa, the leading Mexican mining expert of the time, the miners worked "in terror of ladders giving way, rocks sliding, heavy loads breaking their backs, dripping icy waters, diseases, and the damp, hot, suffocating heat." Humboldt, who visited Mexico in the last years of the colony, claimed that Mexican miners seldom lived past the age of thirty-five. But the pay was good by colonial standards; workers who went below received four reales (fifty cents) for each twelve-hour shift (one real would buy a pound of wool or five pounds of beef or veal), more than double the pay of agricultural workers. This customary pay was supplemented by the *partido,* the skilled worker's right to a certain share of his day's haul of silver ore over an assigned quota.

Attempts by mine owner Romero de Terreros to lower wage rates of *peones* (ore carriers) from four to three reales, increase quotas, and gradually eliminate partidos provoked a series of crises culminating in the strike. A sympathetic parish priest advised the workers on legal ways to achieve their objectives and sought to mediate their dispute with the employer. (The priest was later expelled from the pueblo for his activism.) Eventually, the state intervened, aware of the critical importance of silver production to the royal treasury and of the workers' strong bargaining position because of the chronic labor shortage. Francisco de Gamboa, the leading expert on mining and mining law, was sent to arbitrate the conflict. His arbitration satisfied virtually all the workers' demands: abusive bosses were fired, the pay cuts revoked, and the right to partidos confirmed in writing.

Doris Ladd has written a brilliant, sensitive reconstruction of these events. She interprets the struggle at Real del Monte as a class struggle prior to the existence of a working class—reflecting an emerging class consciousness—and describes the workers' ideas as "radical" and "revolutionary." She cites the strikers' insistence on social and economic justice, expressed in the words of their lawyer: "It is a precept in all systems of divine, natural, and secular law that there should be a just proportion between labor and profit." But this appeal for justice had a limited scope and significance. It applied to a group of relatively privileged, skilled free workers, but did not call into question the forced labor of Indians dragged by press gangs from their homes to the mines. Thanks to a set of favorable conditions, the strikers won a victory, meaning a return to the situation that prevailed before the dispute broke out. But that victory left the conscripted Indian workers in the same intolerable conditions as before. One wonders whether ideas that accepted Indian servitude as normal can be described as truly "radical" or "revolutionary."

Political Reforms

Under Charles III, the work of territorial reorganization of the sprawling empire continued. The viceroyalty of Peru, already diminished by the creation of New Granada, was further curtailed by the creation in 1776 of the viceroyalty of the Río de la Plata, with its capital at Buenos Aires. This act reflected official Spanish concern over the large volume of contraband in the estuary. It also reflected fear of a possible foreign attack on the area by the British, who had recently entrenched themselves in the nearby Malvinas, or Falkland, Islands, or by the Portuguese who, advancing southward from Brazil, has established the settlement of Sacramento on the banks of the estuary, a base from which they threatened shipping and the town of Montevideo. To put an end to this danger the Spanish government mounted a major military expedition designed to establish full control of both banks of the river. The commander Pedro de Cevallos came out with the temporary title of viceroy of Buenos Aires. In 1778 the viceroyalty was made permanent with the appointment of the viceroy Juan José de Vértiz y Salcedo, whose rule of over a decade saw a remarkable growth in the prosperity of the area. This prosperity owed much to the decree of "free trade" of 1778, which authorized direct trade between Buenos Aires and Spain and permitted intercolonial trade. In 1783 the establishment of a royal audiencia at Buenos Aires completed the liberation of the Río de la Plata provinces from the distant rule of Lima. The inclusion of Upper Peru in the new viceroyalty, with the resulting redirection of the flow of Potosí silver from Lima to Buenos Aires, signified a stunning victory for the landowners and merchants of Buenos Aires over their mercantile rivals in Lima.

The trend toward decentralization in the administration of Spanish America, combined with a greater stress on supervision and control from Madrid, reflected not only the struggle against foreign military and commercial penetration but an enlightened awareness of the problems of communication and government posed by the great distances between the various provinces, an awareness spurred by advances in cartography and knowledge of the geography of the continent in general. Two indications of this tendency were the greater autonomy enjoyed by the captaincies general in the eighteenth century and the increase in their number. Thus, in 1777 Venezuela was raised to a captaincy general, as previously mentioned. Similarly, in 1778 Chile was raised from the status of a presidency to that of a captaincy general. The increased autonomy enjoyed by the captains general enabled an enlightened ruler like Ambrosio O'Higgins in Chile to attempt major economic reforms, stimulate mining and manufacturing, introduce new crops, and in general try to promote not only the interests of the Spanish crown but the welfare of the Chilean people.

The creation of new viceroyalties and captaincies general went hand in hand with another major political reform, the transfer to the colonies between 1782 and 1790 of the intendant system, already introduced to Spain by France. This reform was made in the interests of greater administrative efficiency and in the hope of increasing royal revenues from the colonies. The intendants, provincial governors who ruled from the capitals of their provinces, were expected to relieve the overburdened viceroys of many of their duties, especially in financial matters. Among their other duties, the intendants were expected to further the economic development of their districts by promoting the cultivation of new crops, the improvement of mining, the building of roads and bridges, and the establishment of consulados and economic societies. Under their prodding, the lethargic cabildos or town councils were in

some cases stirred to greater activity. The Ordinance of Intendants also abolished the offices of corregidor and alcalde mayor, notorious vehicles for the oppression of the natives. These officials were replaced as governors of Indian towns by men called *subdelegados,* who were nominated by the intendants and confirmed by the viceroys.

Many of the intendants at the height of the reform era were capable and cultivated men who not only achieved the objectives of increased economic activity and revenue collection but promoted education and cultural progress generally. But the same could not be said of the majority of their subordinates, the subdelegados, who, like their predecessors, soon became notorious for their oppressive practices. A common complaint was that they continued to compel the Indians to trade with them, although the repartimiento had been forbidden by the Ordinance of Intendants. The great popular revolts of the 1780s were fueled in large part by the failure of the Indian and mixed-blood populations to share in the fruits of the eighteenth-century economic advance, whose principal beneficiaries were Spanish and creole landowners, mine owners, and merchants.

Strengthening the Defenses

Increased revenue was a major objective of the Bourbon commercial and political reforms. A major purpose to which that revenue was applied was the strengthening of the sea and land defenses of the empire. Before the eighteenth century, primary dependence for defense had been placed on naval power: convoy escorts and cruiser squadrons. Before the middle of the eighteenth century, standing armed forces in the colonies were negligible, and authorities relied on local forces raised for particular emergencies. The disasters of the Seven Years' War and the loss of Havana and Manila (1762) to the English, in particular, resulted in a decision to correct the shortcomings in the defense system of the colonies. Fortifications of important American ports were strengthened and colonial armies created.

VICEROYALTIES IN LATIN AMERICA IN 1780

These included regular units stationed permanently in the colonies or rotated between peninsular and overseas service and colonial militia whose ranks were filled by volunteers or drafted recruits.

To make military service attractive to the creole upper class, which provided the officer corps of the new force, the crown granted extensive privileges and exemptions to creole youths who accepted commissions. To the lure of prestige and honors, the grant of the *fuero militar* added protection from civil legal jurisdiction and liability, except for certain specified offenses. The special legal and social position thus accorded to the colonial officer class helped to form a tradition, which has survived to the present in Latin America, of the armed forces as a special caste with its own set of interests, not subject to the civil power, that acted as the arbiter of political life, usually in the interests of conservative ruling classes. Under the Bourbons, however, the power of the colonial military was held in check by such competing groups as the church and the civil bureaucracy.

Although the expansion of the colonial military establishment under the Bourbons offered some opportunities and advantages to upper-class creole youth, it did nothing to allay the long-standing resentment of creoles against their virtual exclusion from the higher offices of state and church and from large-scale commerce. Bourbon policy in regard to the problem went through two phases. In the first half of the eighteenth century, wealthy creoles could sometimes purchase high official posts, and for a time they dominated the prestigious audiencias of Mexico City and Lima. But in the second half of the century, an anti-creole reaction took place. José de Gálvez, Charles III's colonial minister, was the very embodiment of the spirit of enlightened despotism that characterized his reign. Gálvez distrusted creole capacity and integrity and removed high-ranking creoles from positions in the imperial administration. The new upper bureaucracy, such as the intendants who took over much of the authority of viceroys and governors, was in the great majority Spanish-born.

Other Bourbon policies injured creole vested interests or wounded their sensibilities and traditions. An example was the sudden expulsion of the Jesuits (1767), who enjoyed much favor among the creole aristocracy.

Potentially more explosive was an issue that arose toward the very end of the colonial period. In 1804 the Spanish crown enacted an emergency revenue measure—the *Consolidación de Vales Reales*—that ordered church institutions in the colonies to call in all their outstanding capital, the liens and mortgages whose interest supported the charitable and pious works of the church. The proceeds were to be loaned to the crown, which would pay annual interest to the church to fund its ecclesiastical activities. Although the primary motive of the Consolidation was to relieve the crown's urgent financial needs, it had the secondary reformist aim of freeing the colonial economy from the burden of mortmain and thus promoting a greater circulation of property.

The measure, however, struck hard at two bulwarks of the colonial order, the church and the propertied elite—the numerous hacendados, merchants, and mine owners who had borrowed large sums from church institutions and now had to repay those sums in full or face loss of property or bankruptcy. Many elite families had also assigned part of the value of their estates to the church to found a chaplaincy, paying annual interest to provide the stipend of the chaplain, often a family member. Although the church had not loaned this capital, officials in charge of the Consolidation demanded that the families involved immediately turn over the value of these endowments, in cash. Many small and medium landowners and other middle-class borrowers from the church were also threatened by the Consolidation decree.

The measure caused a storm of protest, and its application was gradually softened by willingness on the part of the officials in charge to negotiate the amounts and other terms of payment. So strong was the opposition of debtors, both creoles and peninsulars, to the decree that little effort was made to implement it outside of New

132

Spain, which provided more than two-thirds of the 15,000,000 pesos collected before it was canceled in 1808 following Napoleon's invasion of Spain. The Consolidation left a heritage of bitterness, especially among individuals like Father Miguel Hidalgo, future torchbearer of the Mexican War for Independence, whose hacienda was embargoed for several years for failure to pay his debts to the Consolidation. Thus, despite and partly because of the reformist spirit of the Bourbon kings, the creoles became progressively alienated from the Spanish crown. Their alienation intensified an incipient creole nationalism that, denied direct political outlets, found its chief expression in culture and religion.

Colonial Culture and the Enlightenment

Colonial culture in all its aspects was a projection of Spanish culture of the time. If we leave aside the very important work done in the study of Indian antiquity and religions, colonial culture only faintly reflected its American milieu in respect to subject matter and treatment. At least until the eighteenth century, a neomedieval climate of opinion, enforced by the authority of church and state, sharply restricted the play of the colonial intellect and imagination. Colonial culture thus suffered from all the infirmities of its parent but inevitably lacked the breadth and vitality of Spanish literature and art, the product of a much older and more mature civilization. Despite these and other difficulties, such as the limited market for books, colonial culture left a remarkably large and valuable heritage.

The Church and Education

The church enjoyed a virtual monopoly of colonial education at all levels. The primary and secondary schools maintained by the clergy, with few exceptions, were open only to children of the white upper class and the Indian nobility. Poverty

condemned the overwhelming majority of the natives and mixed castes to illiteracy. Admission to the universities, which numbered about twenty-five at the end of the colonial era, was even more restricted to youths of ample means and pure white blood.

The universities of Lima and Mexico City, both chartered by the crown in 1551, were the first permanent institutions of higher learning. Patterned on similar institutions in Spain, the colonial university faithfully reproduced their medieval organization, curricula, and methods of instruction. Indifference to practical or scientific studies, slavish respect for the authority of the Bible, Aristotle, the church fathers, and certain medieval schoolmen, and a passion for hairsplitting debate of fine points of theological or metaphysical doctrine were among the features of colonial academic life. Theology and law were the chief disciplines; until the eighteenth century, science was a branch of philosophy, taught from the *Physics* of Aristotle.

A strict censorship of books (no book could be published in either Spain or the colonies without the approval of the Royal Council) limited the spread of new doctrines in colonial society. In recent decades it has been shown that the laws prohibiting the entry of works of fiction into the Spanish colonies were completely ineffective, but this tolerance did not extend to heretical or subversive writings. The records of the colonial Inquisition reveal many tragic cases of imprisonment, torture, and even death for individuals who were charged with the possession and reading of such writings. At least until the eighteenth century, when the intellectual iron curtain surrounding Spanish America began to lift, the people of the colonies were effectively shielded from literature of an unorthodox religious or political tendency.

Yet, within the limits imposed by official censorship and their own backgrounds, colonial scholars were able to make impressive contributions, especially in the fields of Indian history, anthropology, linguistics, and natural history. The sixteenth century was the Golden Age of Indian studies in Spanish America. In Mexico a large group of missionaries, especially members of the Franciscan order, carried out long, patient investigations of the native languages, religion, and history. With the aid of native informants, Friar Bernardino de Sahagún compiled a monumental *General History of the Things of New Spain,* a veritable encyclopedia of information on all aspects of Aztec culture; scholars have only begun to mine the extraordinary wealth of ethnographic materials in Sahagún's work. Another Franciscan, usually known by his Indian name of Motolinia (Friar Toribio de Benavente), wrote a *History of the Indians of New Spain* that is an invaluable guide to Indian life before and after the Conquest. Basing his work on Aztec picture writings and a chronicle, now lost, written by an Indian noble in his own language, Father Diego Durán wrote a history of ancient Mexico that preserves both the content and spirit of Aztec tribal epics and legends. The Jesuit José de Acosta sought to satisfy Spanish curiosity about the natural productions of the New World and the history of the Aztecs and Incas in his *Natural and Moral History of the Indies.* His book, simply and pleasantly written, displays a critical spirit rare for its time; it achieved an immediate popularity in Spain and was quickly translated into all the major languages of western Europe.

Not a few historical works were written by Indian or mestizo nobles actuated by a variety of motives: interest and pride in their native heritage joined to a desire to prove the important services rendered by their forebears to the Conquest and the validity of their claims to noble titles and land. Products of convent schools or colegios, they usually combined Christian piety with nostalgic regard for the departed glories of their ancestors. A descendant of the kings of Texcoco, Fernando de Alva Ixtlilxochitl, wrote a number of historical works that show a mastery of European historical method. These works combine a great amount of valuable information with a highly idealized picture of Texcocan civilization. Another writer of the early seventeenth century, the mestizo Garcilaso de la Vega, son of a Spanish conquistador and an Inca princess, gives in his *Royal Commentaries of the Incas,* together with much valuable information on Inca material culture and history, an idyllic picture of Peruvian life under the benevolent rule of the Inca kings. His book, written in a graceful, fluent Spanish, is more than a history; it is a first-class work of art. No other Spanish history was as popular in Europe as Garcilaso's *Royal Commentaries;* its favorable image of Inca civilization continues to influence our view of ancient Peru down to the present.

Science, Literature, and the Arts

The second half of the seventeenth century saw a decline in the quantity and quality of colonial scholarly production. This was the age of the baroque style in literature, a style that stressed word play, cleverness, and pedantry, that subordinated content to form, meaning to ornate expression. Yet two remarkable men of this period, Carlos Sigüenza y Góngora in Mexico and Pedro de Peralta Barnuevo in Peru, foreshadowed the eighteenth-century Enlightenment by the universality of their interests and their concern with the practical uses of science. Sigüenza—mathematician, archaeologist, and historian—attacked the ancient but still dominant superstition of astrology in his polemic with the Jesuit father Kino over the nature of comets; he also defied prejudice by providing in his will for the dissection of his body in the interests of science. He made careful observations of comets and eclipses of the sun and exchanged his observations with scientists in Europe. Yet the prevailing baroque spirit of fantasy appeared in his speculation that the Greek god Poseidon was the great-grandson of Noah and the forebear of the American Indians.

Peralta Barnuevo, cosmographer and mathematician, made astronomical observations that were published in Paris in the *Proceedings* of the French Royal Academy of Sciences, of which he was elected corresponding member; he also superintended the construction of fortifications in

134

Lima. Yet this able and insatiably curious man of science also sought refuge in a baroque mysticism, and in one of his last works concluded that true wisdom, the knowledge of God, was not "subject to human comprehension."

Colonial literature, with some notable exceptions, was a pallid reflection of prevailing literary trends in the mother country. The isolation from foreign influences, the strict censorship of all reading matter, and the limited audience for writing of every kind made literary creation difficult. "A narrow and dwarfed world," the discouraged Mexican poet Bernardo de Balbuena called the province of New Spain. To make matters worse, colonial literature in the seventeenth century succumbed to the Spanish literary fad of *Gongorismo* (so called after the poet Luis de Góngora)—the cult of an obscure, involved, and artificial style.

Amid a flock of "jangling magpies," as one literary historian describes the Gongorist versifiers of the seventeenth century, appeared the incomparable songbird, known to her admiring contemporaries as "the tenth muse"—Sor Juana Inés de la Cruz, the remarkable nun and poet who assembled in her convent one of the finest mathematical libraries of the time. But Sor Juana could not escape the pressures of her environment. Rebuked by the bishop of Puebla for her worldly interests, she ultimately gave up her books and scientific interests and devoted the remainder of her brief life to religious devotion and charitable works.

Colonial art drew its principal inspiration from Spanish sources, but, especially in the sixteenth century, Indian influence was sometimes visible in design and ornamentation. Quito in Ecuador and Mexico City were among the chief centers of artistic activity. The first school of fine arts in the New World was established in Mexico City in 1779 under royal auspices. As might be expected, religious motifs dominated painting and sculpture. In architecture the colonies followed Spanish examples, with the severe classical style of the sixteenth century giving way in the seventeenth to the highly ornamented baroque and in

the eighteenth century to a style that was even more ornate.

The intellectual atmosphere of the Spanish colonies was not conducive to scientific inquiry or achievement. As late as 1773, the Colombian botanist Mutis was charged with heresy for giving lectures in Bogotá on the Copernican system. The prosecutor of the Inquisition asserted that Mutis was "perhaps the only man in Latin America to uphold Copernicus." In the last decades of the eighteenth century, however, the growing volume of economic and intellectual contacts with Europe and the patronage and protection of enlightened governors created more favorable conditions for scientific activity. Science made its greatest strides in the wealthy province of New Spain, where the expansion of the mining industry stimulated interest in geology, chemistry, mathematics, and metallurgy. In Mexico City there arose a school of mines, a botanical garden, and an academy of fine arts. The Mexican scientific renaissance produced a galaxy of brilliant figures that included Antonio de León y Gama, an astronomer of whose writings Humboldt commented that they displayed "a great precision of ideas and accuracy of observation"; Antonio de Alzate, whose *Gaceta de Literatura* brought to creole youth the knowledge of Europe's scientific advances and who championed the intelligence and capacity of the Indian; and Joaquín Velázquez Cárdenas y León, astronomer, geographer, and mathematician, whose services to his country included the founding of the school of mines. These men combined Enlightenment enthusiasm for rationalism, empiricism, and progress with a strict Catholic orthodoxy; Alzate, for example, vehemently denounced in his *Gaceta* the "infidelity" and skepticism of Europe's philosophes.

Spain itself, now under the rule of the enlightened Bourbon kings, contributed to the intellectual renovation of the colonies. A major liberalizing influence, in both Spain and its colonies, was exerted by the early eighteenth-century friar Benito Feijóo, whose numerous essays waged war on folly and superstition of every kind. Feijóo helped to naturalize the Enlightenment in the Spanish-speaking world by his lucid exposition of the ideas of Bacon, Newton, and Descartes. Spanish and foreign scientific expeditions to Spanish America, authorized and sometimes financed by the crown, also stimulated the growth of scientific thought and introduced the colonists to such distinguished representatives of European science as the Frenchman La Condamine and the German Alexander von Humboldt.

Among the clergy, the Jesuits were most skillful and resourceful in the effort to reconcile church dogma with the ideas of the Enlightenment, in bridging the old and the new. In Mexico, Jesuit writers like Andrés de Guevara, Pedro José Marquez, and Francisco Javier Clavigero praised and taught the doctrines of Bacon, Descartes, and Newton. These Jesuits exalted physics above metaphysics and the experimental method over abstract reasoning and speculation, but all of them combined these beliefs with undeviating loyalty to the teachings of the church. Thus, the expulsion of the Jesuits from Spanish America removed from the scene the ablest, most subtle defenders of the traditional Catholic world view. In their Italian exile—for it was in Italy that most of the Jesuit exiles settled—some of them occupied their leisure time writing books designed to make known to the world the history and geography of their American homelands. The most important of these works by Jesuit exiles was the *History of Ancient Mexico* (1780–1781) of Francisco Clavigero, the best work of its kind written to date and an excellent illustration of the characteristic Jesuit blend of Catholic orthodoxy with the critical, rationalist approach of the Enlightenment.

Despite their frequent and sincere professions of loyalty to the crown, the writings of colonial intellectuals revealed a sensitivity to social and political abuses, a discontent with economic backwardness, and a dawning sense of nationality that contained potential dangers for the Spanish regime. Colonial newspapers and journals played a significant part in the development of a critical and reformist spirit among the educated creoles of Spanish America. Subjected to an op-

Sor Juana Inés de la Cruz, sometimes called the greatest Spanish-American poet of the colonial period, entered a convent when she was eighteen years old and died at the age of forty-four. Sor Juana wrote both secular and religious poetry, but it is her love poems for which she was most admired. (Bradley Smith Collection/Laurie Platt Winfrey, Inc.)

pressive censorship by church and state and beset by chronic financial difficulties, they generally had short and precarious lives. More important than the routine news items they carried were the articles on scientific, economic, and social problems they housed and the ideas of social utility, progress, and the conquest of nature they vigorously announced.

The circulation and influence of forbidden books among educated colonials steadily increased in the closing decades of the eighteenth century and the first years of the nineteenth. It

136 would nevertheless be incorrect to conclude, as some writers have done, that the Inquisition became a toothless tiger in the eighteenth century and that radical ideas could be advocated with almost total impunity. It is true that the influence of the Inquisition weakened under the Bourbons, especially Charles III, because of the growth of French influence. But the censorship was never totally relaxed, the Inquisition continued vigilant, and with every turn of the diplomatic wheel that drew Spain and France apart the inquisitorial screws were tightened. Thus, the outbreak of the French Revolution brought a wave of repression against advocates of radical ideas in Mexico, culminating in a major *auto-da-fé* (public sentencing) in Mexico City at which long prison sentences and other severe penalties were handed out. How powerless these repressions were to check the movement of new thought is illustrated by the writings of the fathers of Spanish-American independence. Their works reveal a thorough knowledge of the ideas of Locke, Montesquieu, Raynal, and other important figures of the Enlightenment.

Creole Nationalism

The incipient creole nationalism, however, built on other foundations than the ideas of the European Enlightenment, which were alien and suspect to the masses. Increasingly conscious of themselves as a class and of their respective provinces as their *patrias* (fatherlands), creole intellectuals of the eighteenth century assembled an imposing body of data designed to refute the attacks of such eminent European writers as Comte Georges de Buffon and Cornelius de Pauw, who proclaimed the inherent inferiority of the New World and its inhabitants.

In the largest sense, the creole patria was all America. As early as 1696, the Mexican Franciscan Agustín de Vetancurt claimed that the New World was superior to the Old in natural beauty and resources. New Spain and Peru, he wrote in florid prose, were two breasts from which the whole world drew sustenance, drinking blood changed into the milk of gold and silver. In a change of imagery, he compared America to a beautiful woman adorned with pearls, emeralds, sapphires, chrysolites, and topazes, drawn from the jewel boxes of her rich mines.

In the prologue to his *History of Ancient Mexico,* Clavigero stated that his aim was "to restore the truth to its splendor, truth obscured by an incredible multitude of writers on America." The epic, heroic character that Clavigero gave the history of ancient Mexico reflected the creole search for origins, for a classical antiquity other than the European, to which the peninsulars could lay better claim. The annals of the Toltecs and the Aztecs, he insisted, offered as many examples of valor, patriotism, wisdom, and virtue as the histories of Greece and Rome. Mexican antiquity displayed such models of just and benevolent rule as the wise Chichimec king Xolotl and philosopher-kings such as Nezahualcoyotl and Nezahualpilli. In this way, Clavigero provided the nascent Mexican nationality with a suitably dignified and heroic past. The Chilean Jesuit Juan Ignacio Molina developed similar themes in his *History of Chile* (1782).

The creole effort to develop a collective self-consciousness also found expression in religious thought and symbolism. In his *Quetzalcoatl and Guadalupe: The Formation of Mexican National Consciousness* (1976), Jacques Lafaye has shown how creole intellectuals exploited two powerful myths in the attempt to achieve Mexican spiritual autonomy and even superiority vis-à-vis Spain. One was the myth that the Virgin Mary appeared in 1531 on the hill of Tepeyac, near Mexico City, to an Indian called Juan Diego and through him commanded the bishop of Mexico to build a church there. The proof demanded by the bishop came in the form of winter roses from Tepeyac, enfolded in Juan Diego's cloak, which was miraculously painted with the image of the Virgin. From the seventeenth century, the *indita,* the brown-faced Indian Virgin (as opposed to the Virgin of Los Remedios, who had allegedly aided Cortés) was venerated throughout Mexico as the Virgin of Guadalupe. Under her banner, in fact,

Miguel Hidalgo in 1810 was to lead the Indian and mestizo masses in a great revolt against Spanish rule.

The other great myth was that of Quetzalcóatl, the Toltec redeemer-king and god. Successive colonial writers had suggested that Quetzalcóatl was none other than the Christian apostle St. Thomas. On December 12, 1794, the creole Dominican Servando Teresa de Mier arose in his pulpit in the town of Guadalupe to proclaim that Quetzalcóatl was in fact St. Thomas, who long centuries before had come with four disciples to preach the Gospel in the New World. In this the Apostle had succeeded, and at the time of the Conquest, Christianity—somewhat altered, to be sure—reigned in Mexico. If Mier was right, America owed nothing to Spain, not even her Christianity. Spanish officials, quickly recognizing the revolutionary implications of Mier's sermon, arrested him and exiled him to Spain.

The episode illustrates the devious channels through which creole nationalism moved to achieve its ends. One of those ends was creole hegemony over the Indian and mixed-blood masses, based on their awareness of their common patria and their collective adherence to such national cults as that of the Virgin of Guadalupe in Mexico. In the 1780s, however, the accumulated wrath of those people broke out in a series of explosions that threatened the very existence of the colonial social and political order. In this crisis the creole upper class showed that their aristocratic patria did not really include the Indians, mestizos, and blacks among its sons, that their rhetorical sympathy for the dead Indians of Moctezuma's and Atahualpa's time did not extend to the living Indians of their own time.

Colonial Society in Transition, 1750–1810: An Overview

An estimate by the late historian Charles Gibson put the population of Spanish America toward the end of the colonial period at about 17,000,000 people. Gibson supposed that of this total some 7,500,000 were Indians; about 3,200,000, whites; perhaps 750,000, blacks; and the remaining 5,500,000, castas. Those figures point to a continuing steady revival of the Indian population from the low point of its decline in the early seventeenth century, a more rapid increase of the European population, and an even faster increase of the castas.

In the late colonial period the racial categories used to describe and rank the groups composing the colonial population in terms of their "honor" or lack of "honor" became increasingly ambiguous. One reason was the growing mobility of the colonial population, resulting in a more rapid pace of Hispanicization and racial mixture. The laws forbidding Indians to reside in Spanish towns and whites and mixed-bloods to live in Indian towns were now generally disregarded. Large numbers of Indians seeking escape from tribute and repartimiento burdens migrated to the Spanish cities and mining camps, where they learned to speak Spanish, wore European clothes, and adopted other Spanish ways. The many Spaniards and mestizos who settled in Indian communities contributed to the process of race mixture and Hispanicization. Indians who lived in villages remote from the main areas of Spanish economic activity were less likely to be influenced by the presence of Spaniards and mestizos and therefore remained more "Indian." For a variety of reasons connected with the area's history, geography, and economic patterns, the Indian communities in the viceroyalty of Peru seem to have resisted acculturation more tenaciously than those of New Spain. But those Indians who left their pueblos and became assimilated to the white population in dress and language and who achieved even a modest level of prosperity increasingly came to be regarded legally "Spaniards," that is, creoles. The same was true of Hispanicized mestizos and, less frequently perhaps, blacks and mulattos. An individual's race, in short, now tended to be defined not by his color but by such traits as occupation, dress, speech, and how he perceived himself.

The economic advance of the late Bourbon era, featured by the rapid growth of commercial

138

agriculture, mining, and domestic and foreign trade, created opportunities for some fortunate lower-class individuals and contributed to the declining significance of racial labels. A growing number of wealthy mestizo and mulatto families sought to rise in the social scale by marrying their sons and daughters to children of the white elite. Charles III's policy on interracial marriage reflected the dilemmas of this reformer-king, who wished to promote the rise of a progressive middle class but feared to undermine the foundations of the old aristocratic order. Charles, who removed the stigma attached to artisan labor by decreeing that it was no bar to nobility, also issued decrees that empowered colonial parents to refuse consent to interracial marriages of their children that threatened the family's "honor." As interpreted by high colonial courts, however, these decrees as a rule only sanctioned such parental refusal when the parties to a proposed marriage were unequal in wealth, meaning, as previously noted, that a wealthy mulatto was a suitable marriage partner for a member of the white elite. The last Bourbon kings also promoted social mobility by permitting *pardos* (free blacks and mulattos), despised for their slave origin, to buy legal whiteness through the purchase of dispensations (*cédulas de gracias al sacar*) that freed them from the status of "infamous." The motives for this liberal policy were not altogether fiscal. The policy, says John Lynch, "was also perhaps part of the economic program of the metropolis and an aspect of its attack on aristocratic power and independence. To increase social mobility would be to reinforce the white elite by an economically motivated and ambitious class; this would simultaneously subvert aristocratic ideals of honor and status and enhance entrepreneurial values."

It would be an error to suppose that these concessions to a small number of wealthy mixed-bloods reflected a crumbling of the caste system and the ideology on which it was based. The very eagerness of mulattos and mestizos to achieve whiteness by purchase of the dispensations mentioned above, the protest of elite groups like the cabildo of Caracas against the more liberal Bour-

bon racial policy as promoting "the amalgamation of whites and pardos," and the readiness of some parents to litigate against their children to prevent their marriage to dark-skinned individuals testify to the continuing hold of racial prejudice and stereotypes on the colonial mentality.

The partial penetration of elite society, even on its highest levels, by individuals having some traces of Indian or Negro blood, did not alter the rigidity of the class structure, the sharp class distinctions, the vast gulf separating the rich and the poor. Humboldt spoke of "that monstrous inequality of rights and wealth" which characterized late colonial Mexico. But the late colonial period saw some change in the economic base of the elite and some shifts in the relative weight of its various sectors. If the seventeenth century was the golden age of the large landowners, the eighteenth century, especially its last decades, saw their ascendancy challenged by the growing wealth and political and social influence of the export-import merchant class, most of whose members were of Spanish immigrant origin. The merchants provided the capital needed by the mining industry and absorbed much of its profits. They also financed the purchase of the posts of corregidors, officials who monopolized trade with the Indian communities in collusion with the merchants. In order to provide a hedge against commercial losses—not just to secure the prestige identified with landownership—wealthy merchants acquired estates, establishing hacienda complexes producing a variety of crops and situated to supply the major markets. They further diversified by acquiring flour mills, obrajes, and establishing themselves as major retailers, not only in the cities but in the countryside. The wealthiest married into rich and powerful creole extended families, forming an Establishment whose offspring had preference in appointments to important and prestigious positions in the colonial government and church.

The second half of the eighteenth century saw a new wave of immigration from the peninsula. The presence of these newcomers, often of humble origins, who competed with the American-born Spaniards for limited employment opportunities, sharpened the traditional creole resentment of gachupines or chapetones (tenderfoot). Although, according to Humboldt, "the lowest, least educated and uncultivated European believes himself superior to the white born in the New World," most of the new arrivals failed to find the high-status and well-paid employments they expected. The 1753 and 1811 census reports for Mexico City listed some Spaniards working as unskilled laborers and house servants and still others as jobless. The *Diario de México* often carried advertisements by jobless Spanish immigrants willing to accept any kind of low-level supervisory post. Two observant Spanish officials, Jorge Juan and Antonio de Ulloa, who visited the city of Cartagena in New Granada about 1750, found that there the whites, whether creoles or Europeans, disdained any trade below that of commerce. "But it being impossible for all to succeed, great numbers not being able to secure sufficient credit, they become poor and miserable from their aversion to the trades they follow in Europe, and instead of the riches which they flattered themselves with possessing in the Indies, they experience the most complicated wretchedness."

The Revolt of the Masses

A traditional view portrayed the Indian as the more or less passive object of Spanish rule or of an acculturation process. In recent decades, deeper, more careful study of the Indian response to Spanish rule has revealed that the Indians were not mere "passive victims of Spanish colonization" but activists who from the first resisted Spanish rule with a variety of strategies and thereby were able in some degree to modify the colonial environment and shape their own lives and futures. These strategies included revolts, flight, riots, sabotage, and sometimes even using their masters' legal codes for purposes of defense and offense.

Flight, under conditions of intense Spanish competition for Indian labor, effectively evaded Spanish pressures. Jeffrey Cole points out, for example, that Indians' abandonment of pueblos subject to the mita in order to work as yanaconas on farms, ranches, and other enterprises in exempted areas "was their most effective means of opposing the mita, the demands of their curacas and corregidores, and other obligations."[5] Indians also skillfully used Spanish legal codes for purposes of "defense, redress, and even offense." A recent study of the Peruvian province of Huamanga shows that the Indians lightened the burdens of the mita through the defensive strategy of "engaging in aggressive, persistent, often shrewd use of Spanish juridical institutions to lower legal quotas, delay delivery of specific corvées and tributes, disrupt production, and the like."[6] In Mexico there were countless riots—*tumultos*—in the eighteenth century. Indians let Spanish authority know that it could not take them for granted and must heed their complaints.

Revolt was the highest, most dramatic form of resistance to Spanish rule by the Indians and other oppressed groups. Numerous Indian and black slave revolts punctuated the colonial period of Spanish-American history. Before Spanish rule had been firmly established, the Indians rose against their new masters in many regions. In Mexico the Mixton war raged from 1540 to 1542. The Maya of Yucatán staged a great uprising in 1546. A descendant of the Inca kings, Manco II, led a nationwide revolt in 1536 against the Spanish conquerors of Peru. In Chile the indomitable Araucanians began a struggle for independence that continued into the late nineteenth century. In the jungles and mountains of the West Indies, Central America, and northern South America, groups of runaway black slaves established communities that successfully resisted Spanish efforts to destroy them. The revolutionary wave

[5] Jeffrey Cole, *The Potosí Mita, 1573–1701, Compulsory Indian Labor in the Andes* (Stanford, Calif.: Stanford University Press, 1985), p. 125.

[6] Steve Stern, *Peru's Indian Peoples and the Challenge of Spanish Conquest: Huamanga to 1640* (Madison: University of Wisconsin Press, 1983), p. 192.

subsided in the seventeenth century but peaked again in the eighteenth when new burdens were imposed on the common people.

The Bourbon reforms helped to enrich colonial landowners, merchants, and mine owners, beautified their cities, and broadened the intellectual horizons of upper-class youths, but the multitude did not share in these benefits. On the contrary, Bourbon efforts to increase the royal revenues by the creation of governmental monopolies and privileged companies and the imposition of new taxes actually made more acute the misery of the lower classes. This circumstance helps to explain the popular character of the revolts of 1780–1781, as distinct from the creole wars of independence of the next generation. With rare exceptions, the privileged creole group either supported the Spaniards against the native uprisings or joined the revolutionary movements under pressure, only to desert them at a later time.

Revolt in Peru

In the eighteenth century, Spanish pressures and demands on the Peruvian Indians increased considerably. A major mechanism for the extraction of surplus from the natives was the previously mentioned repartimiento de mercancías, the mandatory purchase of goods from the corregidor by the Indians of his district. The system functioned as follows: a Lima merchant advanced the sum of money needed by a corregidor to buy his post from the crown. The merchant also outfitted the corregidor with the stock of goods that he would "distribute," that is, force the Indians of his district to buy, sometimes for six or eight times their fair market price. In the Cuzco region typical repartimiento goods were mules and textiles, but sometimes these goods included items for which the Indians had no possible use. The Indians had to pay for their purchases within an allotted time or else go to prison, forcing many to leave their villages in order to obtain the needed cash by work in mines, obrajes, and haciendas. The system thus served to erode the traditional peasant economy and promoted two ob-

jectives of the state, the merchants, and other ruling class groups: the expansion of both the internal market for goods and the labor market.

The repartimiento de mercancías was among the most hateful of the exactions to which the Indians were subjected. A recent study finds that it figured as a cause in the great majority of Indian revolts in Peru in the eighteenth century.

In the same period the burdens imposed on the Indians by the mining mita increased. Determined to return the output of Potosí silver to its former high levels, the crown and the mine owners made innovations that greatly intensified the exploitation of Indian labor. The ore quotas that the *mitayos* (drafted workers) were required to produce were doubled between 1740 and 1790 from about fifteen loads per day to thirty, forcing the mitayos to work longer for the same wages and compelling their wives and children to assist them in meeting the quotas. In the same period the wages of both mitayos and mingas (free workers) were reduced. These innovations produced the desired revival of Potosí, with a doubling of silver production, but at a heavy price in Indian health and living standards.

Coupled with increases in alcabalas (sales taxes), the continuing abuses of the repartimiento de mercancías and the mita caused intense discontent. A critical point was reached when visitador José de Areche, sent out by Charles III in 1777 to reform conditions in the colony, tightened up the collection of tribute and sales taxes and broadened the tributary category to include all mestizos. As a result the contribution of the Indians was increased by one million pesos annually. These measures not only caused great hardships to the commoners but created greater difficulties for the native curacas, or chiefs, who were responsible for meeting tribute quotas. Areche himself foretold the storm to come when he wrote: "The lack of righteous judges, the mita of the Indians, and provincial commerce have made a corpse of this America. Corregidores are interested only in themselves. . . . How near everything is to ruin if these terrible abuses are not corrected, for they have been going on a long time."

The discontent of the Indian masses with their intolerable conditions inspired messianic dreams and expectations of a speedy return of the Inca and the Inca empire. The popular imagination transformed this Inca empire into an ideal state, free from hunger and injustice, and free from the presence of oppressive colonial officials and exploitative mines, haciendas, and obrajes. This utopian vision of a restored Inca empire played a part in causing the great revolt of 1780–1781 and determining its direction.

That revolt had its forerunners; between 1730 and 1780 there were 128 rebellions, large and small, in the Andean area. From 1742 to 1755, a native leader called Juan Santos, "the invincible," waged partisan warfare against the Spaniards from his base in the eastern slopes of the Andes. The memory of his exploits was still alive when the revolt of José Gabriel Condorcanqui began. A well-educated, wealthy mestizo descendant of the Inca kings who was strongly influenced by accounts of the Inca splendor in the *Royal Commentaries* of Garcilaso de la Vega, he had made repeated, fruitless efforts to obtain relief for his people through legal channels. In November 1780 he raised the standard of revolt by ambushing the hated corregidor Antonio de Arriaga near the town of Tinta and putting him to death after a summary trial. At this time he also took the name of the last head of the neo-Inca state and became Tupac Amaru II. His actions were preceded by an uprising led by the Catari brothers in the territory of present-day Bolivia. By the first months of 1781, the southern highlands of the viceroyalty of Peru were aflame with revolt. Although the various revolutionary movements lacked a unified direction, the rebel leaders generally recognized Tupac Amaru as their chief and continued to invoke his name even after his death.

In the first stage of the revolt, Tupac Amaru did not make his objectives entirely clear. In some public statements he proclaimed his loyalty to the Spanish king and church, limiting his demands to the abolition of the mita, the repartimiento, the alcabala, and other taxes; the suppression of the corregidors; and the appointment of Indian governors for the provinces. But it is difficult to believe that the well-educated Tupac Amaru, who had had years of experience in dealing with Spanish officialdom, seriously believed that he could obtain sweeping reforms from the crown by negotiation, especially after his execution of the corregidor Arriaga. His protestations of loyalty were soon contradicted by certain documents in which he styled himself king of Peru, by the war of fire and blood that he urged against peninsular Spaniards (excepting only the clergy), and by the government that he established for the territory under his control.

More plausible is the view that his professions of loyalty to Spain represented a mask by which he could utilize the still strong faith of many Indians in the mythical benevolence of the Spanish king, attract creole supporters of reform to his cause, and perhaps soften his punishment in case of defeat.

José Gabriel Condorcanqui, an educated and wealthy mestizo, took the name of the last Inca and led the great Peruvian revolt against Spain. Like his predecessor, Tupac Amaru II was defeated, captured, and executed. (The Granger Collection, N. Y.)

For Tupac Amaru, who had been educated in a Spanish colegio and had thoroughly absorbed the values of Spanish culture, the objective of the revolt was the establishment of an independent Peruvian state that would be essentially European in its political and social organization. His program called for complete independence from Spain, expulsion of peninsular Spaniards, and the abolition of the offices of viceroy, audiencia, and corregidor. The Inca empire would be restored, with himself as king, assisted by a nobility formed from other descendants of the Cuzco noble clans. Caste distinctions would disappear, and creoles, on whose support Tupac Amaru heavily counted, would live in harmony with Indians, blacks, and mestizos. The Catholic church would remain the state church and be supported by tithes. Tupac Amaru's economic program called for suppression of the mita, the repartimiento de mercancías, customshouses and sales taxes, and for elimination of great estates and servitude, but would permit small and medium-sized landholdings and encourage trade. Tupac Amaru's plan, in short, called for an anticolonial, national revolution that would create a unified people and a modern state of European type that could promote economic development.

But the Indian peasantry who responded to his call for revolt had a different conception of its meaning and goal. In an atmosphere of messianic excitement they came to view it as a *pachacuti,* a great cataclysm or "overthrow" that would bring a total inversion of the existing social order and a return to an idealized Inca empire where the humble *runa* or peasant would not be last but first. In their desire to avenge the cruelties of the Conquest and two and a half centuries of brutal exploitation they sacked haciendas and killed their owners without troubling to ascertain whether they were creoles or Europeans; a Spaniard was one who had a white skin and wore European dress. As the revolt spread, the old pagan religion emerged from the underground where it had hidden and flourished for centuries. Tupac Amaru, who sought to maintain good relations with the Catholic church, always went about accompanied by two priests and hoped for support

by Bishop Moscoco of Cuzco. But his peasant followers sacked the vestments and ornaments of churches and attacked and killed priests, hanging a number of friars during the siege of Cuzco. In December 1780 Tupac Amaru entered one Indian village and summoned its inhabitants, who greeted him with the words: "You are our God and we ask that there be no priests to pester us." He replied that he could not allow this, for it would mean that there would be no one to attend them "in the moment of death."

These opposed conceptions of the meaning and objectives of the revolt held by Tupac Amaru and his peasant followers spelled defeat for Tupac Amaru's strategy of forming a common proindependence front of all social and racial groups except the peninsular Spaniards. The spontaneous, uncontrollable violence of the peasant rebels ended what little chance existed of attracting the support of the creoles, reformist clergy like Bishop Moscoso, and many Indian nobles. At least twenty Indian caciques, jealous of Tupac Amaru or fearful of losing their privileged status, led their subjects into the Spanish camp. Although the principal base of the revolt was ayllus (free peasant communities), the Spaniards were able to mobilize large numbers of yanaconas who helped to break the siege of Cuzco and suppress the revolt.

Tactical errors contributing to the revolt's defeat included failure to attack Cuzco (the ancient Inca capital) and capitalize on the political and psychological significance of its capture before the arrival of Spanish reinforcements. Poor communications between the rebel forces and the vastly superior arms and organization of the royalist armies contributed to the same result. Despite some initial successes, the rebel leader soon suffered a complete rout. Tupac Amaru, members of his family, and his leading captains were captured and put to death, some with ferocious cruelty. In the territory of present-day Bolivia the insurrection continued two years longer, reaching its high point in two prolonged sieges of La Paz (March-October 1781).

The last Inca revolt was not entirely in vain, however. Among the reforms hastily instituted by the crown were abolition of the repartimiento de mercancías, a lightening of mita burdens, the replacement of the hated corregidors by the system of intendants, and the establishment of an audiencia, or high court, in Cuzco—another of Tupac Amaru's goals before the revolt. As a result of these and other reforms under the able viceroy Teodoro de Croix, there was at least a temporary improvement in the condition of the Peruvian Indians.

Insurrection in New Granada (1781)

The revolt of the Comuneros in New Granada, like that in Peru, had its origin in intolerable economic conditions. Unlike the Peruvian upheaval, however, it was more clearly limited in its aims to the redress of grievances. Increases in the alcabala and a whole series of new taxes, including one on tobacco and a poll tax, provoked an uprising in Socorro, an important agricultural and manufacturing center in the north. The disturbances soon spread to other communities. The reformist spirit of the revolt was reflected in the insurgent slogan: *viva el rey y muera el mal gobierno!* (Long live the king, down with the evil government!)

In view of its organization and its effort to form a common front of all colonial groups with grievances against Spanish authority (excepting the black slaves), the revolt of the Comuneros marked an advance over the rather chaotic course of events to the south. A *común* (central committee), elected in the town of Socorro by thousands of peasants and artisans from adjacent towns, directed the insurrection. Each of the towns in revolt also had its común and a captain chosen by popular election.

Under the command of hesitant or unwilling creole leaders, a multitude of Indian and mestizo peasants and artisans marched on the capital of Bogotá, capturing or putting to flight the small forces sent from the capital. Playing for time until reinforcements could arrive from the coast, the royal audiencia dispatched a commission headed by the archbishop to negotiate with the Comuneros. The popular character of the movement and the unity of oppressed groups that it represented were reflected in the terms that the rebel delegates presented to the Spanish commissioners and that the latter signed and later repudiated: these terms included reduction of Indian and mestizo tribute and sales taxes, return to the Indians of land usurped from them, abolition of the new tax on tobacco, and preference for creoles over Europeans in the filling of official posts.

An agreement reached on June 4, 1781 satisfied virtually all the demands of the rebels and was sanctified by the archbishop in a special religious service. Secretly, however, the Spanish commissioners signed another document declaring the agreement void because it was obtained by force. The jubilant insurgents scattered and returned to their homes. Only José Antonio Galán, a young mestizo peasant leader, maintained his small force intact and sought to keep the revolt alive.

Having achieved their objective of disbanding the rebel army, the Spanish officials prepared to crush the insurrection completely. The viceroy Manuel Antonio Flores openly repudiated the agreement with the Comuneros. Following a pastoral visit to the disaffected region by the archbishop, who combined seductive promises of reform with threats of eternal damnation for confirmed rebels, Spanish troops brought up from the coast moved into the region and took large numbers of prisoners. The creole leaders of the revolt hastened to atone for their political sins by collaborating with the royalists. Galán, who had vainly urged a new march on Bogotá, was seized by a renegade leader and handed over to the Spaniards, who put him to death by hanging on January 30, 1782. The revolt of the Comuneros had ended.

Chapter 7

Colonial Brazil

Brazil's existence was unknown in Europe when the Treaty of Tordesillas (1494) between Spain and Portugal, fixing the dividing line between the overseas possessions of the two powers 370 leagues west of the Cape Verde Islands, assigned a large stretch of the coastline of South America to the Portuguese zone of exploration and settlement. (See map on page 70.) In 1500, Pedro Álvares Cabral sailed with a large fleet to follow up Vasco da Gama's great voyage to India. He was, according to one explanation, driven by a storm farther west than he had intended and therefore made landfall on the Brazilian coast on April 22. Some historians speculate that he purposely changed course to investigate reports of land to the west or to verify a previous discovery. Whatever the reason for his westward course, Cabral promptly claimed the land for his country and sent a ship to report his discovery to the king.

The Beginning of Colonial Brazil

Portugal's limited resources, already committed to the exploitation of the wealth of Africa and the Far East, made it impossible to undertake a full-scale colonization of Brazil. But Portugal did not entirely neglect its new possession. Royal expeditions established the presence of a valuable dyewood, called brazilwood, that grew abundantly on the coast between the present states of Pernambuco and São Paulo. Merchant capitalists soon obtained concessions to engage in the brazilwood trade and established a scattering of trading posts where European trinkets and other goods were exchanged with the Indians for brazil logs and other exotic commodities. A small

ATLANTIC OCEAN

Negro R.

Solimões R.

GRÃO PARÁ

Amazonas R.

R.

Ilha
Marajó

Belem

São Luis
Maranhão

MARANHÃO

Fortaleza

RIO
GRANDE DO
NORTE

Natal

CEARÁ

PIAUÍ

PARAÍBA

Olinda

PERNAMBUCO

Recife

Xingu R.

Araguaia R.

São Francisco R.

ALAGOAS

SERGIPE

BAHIA

GOIÁS

Salvador

MATO GROSSO

Cuiabá R.

Pôrto Seguro

Santa Cruz

MINAS GERAIS

Vila Rica do
Ouro Preto

ESPÍRITO SANTO

Paraná R.

Tietê R.

SÃO PAULO

RIO DE JANEIRO

São Paulo

Rio de Janeiro

Paraguay R.

PARANÁ

São Vicente

Santos

SANTA CATARINA

Ilha Santa Catarina

Paraná R.

Uruguay R.

Treaty boundary 1777

RIO GRANDE DO SUL

Colônia do Sacramento

0   600 miles

0   600 kilometers

COLONIAL BRAZIL

146   trickle of settlers began—some castaways, others *degredados* (criminals exiled from Portugal to distant parts of the empire). These exiles were often well received by the local Indians and lived to sire a large number of mixed-bloods who gave valuable assistance to Portuguese colonization. Meanwhile, French merchant ships, also drawn by the lure of brazilwood, began to appear on the Brazilian coast. Alarmed by the presence of these interlopers, King João III sent in 1530 an expedition under Martim Affonso de Sousa to drive away the intruders and to establish permanent settlements in Brazil. In 1532 the first Portuguese town in Brazil, named São Vicente, was founded near the present port of Santos.

The Captaincy System

The limited resources of the Portuguese crown, combined with its heavy commitments in the spice-rich East, forced the king to assign to private individuals the major responsibility for the colonization of Brazil. This responsibility took the form of the captaincy system, already used by Portugal in Madeira, the Azores, and the Cape Verde Islands. The Brazilian coastline was divided into fifteen parallel strips extending inland to the uncertain line of Tordesillas. These strips were granted as hereditary captaincies to a dozen individuals, each of whom agreed to colonize, develop, and defend his captaincy or captaincies at his own expense. The captaincy system represented a curious fusion of feudal and commercial elements. The grantee or donatory was not only a vassal owing allegiance to his lord the king, but a businessman who hoped to derive large profits from his own estates and from taxes obtained from the colonists to whom he had given land. This fusion of feudal and commercial elements characterized the entire Portuguese colonial enterprise in Brazil from the first.

Few of the captaincies proved successful from either the economic or political point of view, since few donatories possessed the combination of investment capital and administrative ability required to attract settlers and defend their captaincies against Indian attacks and foreign intruders. One of the most successful was Duarte Coelho, a veteran of the India enterprise who was granted the captaincy of Pernambuco. His heavy investment in the colony paid off so well that by 1575 his son was the richest man in Brazil, collecting large amounts in quitrents (rents paid in lieu of feudal services) from the fifty sugar mills of the province and himself exporting more than fifty shiploads of sugar a year.

By the mid-sixteenth century, sugar had replaced brazilwood as the foundation of the Brazilian economy. Favored by its soil and climate, the northeast (the provinces of Pernambuco and Bahia) became the seat of a sugar cane civilization characterized by three features: the *fazenda* (large estate), monoculture, and slave labor. There soon arose a class of large landholders whose extensive plantations and wealth marked them off from their less affluent neighbors. Only the largest planters could afford to erect the *engenhos* (mills) needed to process the sugar before export. Small farmers had to bring their sugar to the millowner for grinding, paying one-fourth to one-third of the harvest for the privilege. Since Europe's apparently insatiable demand for sugar yielded quick and large profits, planters had no incentive to diversify crops, and food agriculture was largely limited to small farms. Although the basic techniques of sugar making remained relatively unchanged from the late sixteenth to the late eighteenth centuries, the reputation of the Brazilian sugar industry for being traditional and backward appears unjustified. In the seventeenth century the Brazilian system was considered a model, and other powers sought to copy it. Not until the mid-eighteenth century, when declining demand and prices for Brazilian sugar produced a crisis, and Brazil's Caribbean rivals developed some new techniques, did that reputation for backwardness arise, and even then, according to historian Stuart Schwartz, "the charge was undeserved."

Portugal's Indian Policy

The problem of labor was first met by raids on Indian villages, the raiders returning with trains of captives who were sold to planters and other employers of labor. These aggressions were the primary cause of the chronic warfare between the Indians and the Portuguese. But Indian labor was unsatisfactory from an economic point of view, since the natives, lacking any tradition of organized work of the kind required by plantation agriculture, worked poorly and offered many forms of resistance, ranging from attempts at escape to suicide.

As a result, after 1550, planters turned increasingly to the use of black slave labor imported from Africa. But the supply of black slaves was often cut off or sharply reduced by the activity of Dutch pirates and other foreign foes, and Brazilian slave hunters continued to find a market for their wares throughout the colonial period. The most celebrated slave hunters were the *bandeirantes* (from the word *bandeira* meaning "banner" or "military company") from the upland settlement of São Paulo. Unable to compete in sugar production with the more favorably situated plantation areas of the northeast, these men, who were themselves part Indian in most cases, made slave raiding in the interior their principal occupation. The eternal hope of finding gold or silver in the mysterious interior gave added incentive to their expeditions. As the Indians near the coast dwindled in numbers or fled before the invaders, the bandeirantes pushed even deeper south and west, expanding the frontiers of Brazil in the process.

The Brazilian Indians did not accept the loss of land and liberty without a struggle, but their resistance was handicapped by the fatal tendency of tribes to war against each other, a situation that the Portuguese utilized for their own advantage. Forced to retreat into the interior by the superior arms and organization of the whites, the natives often returned to make destructive forays on isolated Portuguese communities. As late as the first part of the nineteenth century, stretches of the Brazilian shore were made uninhabitable by the raids of Indians who lurked in the forests and mountains back of the coast.

But the unequal struggle at last ended here, as in the Spanish colonies, in the total defeat of the natives. Overwork, loss of the will to live, and the ravages of European diseases to which the Indians had no acquired immunity caused very heavy loss of life among the enslaved Indians. Punitive expeditions against tribes that resisted enslavement or gave some other pretext for sanctions also caused depopulation. The Jesuit father Antônio Vieira, whose denunciations of Portuguese cruelty recall the accusations of Las Casas about the Spanish, claimed that Portuguese mistreatment of Indians had caused the loss of more than 2 million lives in Amazonia in forty years. A distinguished English historian, Charles R. Boxer, considers this claim exaggerated but concedes that the Portuguese "often exterminated whole tribes in a singularly barbarous way."[1]

Almost the only voices raised in protest against the enslavement and mistreatment of Indians were those of the Jesuit missionaries. The first fathers, led by Manoel da Nóbrega, came in 1549 with the captain general Tomé de Sousa. Four years later, another celebrated missionary, José de Anchieta, arrived in Brazil. Far to the south, on the plains of Piratininga, Nóbrega and Anchieta established a colegio or school for Portuguese, mixed-blood, and Indian children that became a model institution of its kind. Around this settlement gradually arose the town of São Paulo, an important point of departure into the interior for "adventurers in search of gold and missionaries in search of souls."

The Jesuits followed a program for the settlement of their Indian converts in *aldeias* (villages) where they lived under the care of the priests, completely segregated from the harmful influence of the white colonists. This program provoked many clashes with the slave hunters and the planters, who had very different ends in view. In an angry protest to the *Mesa da Consciência,* a royal council entrusted with responsibility for the religious affairs of the colony, the planters sought to turn the tables on the Jesuits by claiming that the Indians in the Jesuit villages were

---

[1] Charles R. Boxer, *The Golden Age of Brazil, 1695–1750* (Berkeley: University of California Press, 1962), p. 278.

"true slaves, who labored as such not only in the colegios but on the so-called Indian lands, which in the end became the estates and sugar mills of the Jesuit fathers."

The clash of interests between the planters and slave hunters, on the one hand, and the Jesuit missionaries, on the other, reached a climax about the middle of the seventeenth century, an era of great activity on the part of the bandeirantes of São Paulo. In various parts of Brazil, the landowners rose in revolt, expelled the Jesuits, and defied royal edicts proclaiming the freedom of the Indians. In 1653 the Jesuit Antônio Vieira, a priest of extraordinary oratorical and literary powers, arrived in Brazil with full authority from the king to settle the Indian question as he saw fit. During Lent, Vieira preached a famous sermon to the people of Maranhão, in which he denounced Indian slavery in terms comparable to those used by Father Montesinos on Santo Domingo in 1511. The force of Vieira's tremendous blast was somewhat weakened by his suggestion that Indian slavery should be continued under certain conditions and by the well-known fact that the Jesuit order itself had both Indian and black slaves. Yet there can be no doubt that the condition of the Indians in the Jesuit mission villages was superior to that of the Indian slaves in the Portuguese towns and plantations. A stronger argument against Jesuit practices is the fact that the system of segregation, however benevolent in intent, represented an arbitrary and mechanical imposition of alien cultural patterns on the Indian population and that it hindered rather than facilitated true social integration of the Indian.

The crown, generally sympathetic to the Jesuit position but under strong pressure from the planter class, pursued for two centuries a policy of compromise that satisfied neither Jesuits nor planters. A decisive turn came during the reform ministry of the marquis de Pombal (1750–1777), who expelled the Jesuits from Portugal and Brazil and secularized their missions. His legislation, forbidding Indian raids and enslavement, accepted the Jesuit thesis of Indian freedom; he also accepted the need for preparing the natives for civilized life and even the principle of concen-

trating the Indians in communities under the care of administrators responsible for their education and welfare. But his policy did not segregate the Indians from the Portuguese community; it made them available for use as paid workers by the colonists and actually encouraged contact and mingling between the two races, including interracial marriage. In the meantime, the growth of the African slave trade, also encouraged by Pombal, diminished the demand for Indian labor and thus brought a greater measure of peace to the Indians. Whether Pombal's reform legislation significantly improved the material condition of the Indian population is doubtful, but it contributed to the absorption of the Indians into the colonial population and ultimately into the Brazilian nation. The decisive factor here was race mixture, which increased as a result of the passing of the Jesuit temporal power.

The French and Dutch Challenges

The dyewood, the sugar, and the tobacco of Brazil early attracted the attention of foreign powers. The French were the first to challenge Portuguese control of the colony. With the aid of Indian allies, they made sporadic efforts to entrench themselves on the coast, and in 1555 founded Rio de Janeiro as the capital of what they called Antarctic France. One cultural by-product of French contact with the Indians was the creation of a French image of the Brazilian Indian as a "noble savage," immortalized by the sixteenth-century French philosopher Montaigne in his essay "On Cannibals." But the French offensive in Brazil was weakened by Catholic-Huguenot strife at home, and in 1567 the Portuguese commander Mem de Sá ousted the French and occupied the settlement of Rio de Janeiro.

A more serious threat to Portuguese sovereignty over Brazil was posed by the Dutch, whose West India Company seized and occupied for a quarter of a century (1630–1654) the richest sugar-growing portions of the Brazilian coast. Under the administration of Prince Maurice of Nassau (1637–1644), Dutch Brazil, with its capital at Recife, became the site of brilliant scientific and artistic activity. The Portuguese struggle against the Dutch became an incipient struggle for independence, uniting elements of all races from various parts of Brazil. These motley forces won victories over the Dutch at the first and second battles of Guararapes (1648–1649). Weakened by tenacious Brazilian resistance and a simultaneous war with England, the Dutch withdrew from Pernambuco in 1654. But they took with them the lessons they had learned in the production of sugar and tobacco, and their capital, and transferred both to the West Indies. Soon the plantations and refineries of Barbados and other Caribbean islands gave serious competition to Brazilian sugar in the world market, with a resulting fall of prices. By the last decade of the seventeenth century, the Brazilian sugar industry had entered a long period of stagnation.

The Mineral Cycle, the Cattle Industry, and the Commercial System

In this time of gloom, news of the discovery of gold in the southwestern region later known as Minas Gerais reached the coast in 1695. This discovery opened a new economic cycle, led to the first effective settlement of the interior, and initiated a major shift in Brazil's center of economic and political gravity from north to south. Large numbers of colonists from Bahia, Pernambuco, and Rio de Janeiro, accompanied by their slaves and servants, swarmed into the mining area. Their exodus from the older regions caused an acute shortage of field hands that continued until the gold boom had run its course by the middle of the eighteenth century. The crown tried to stem the exodus by legislation and by policing the trails that led to the mining area, but its efforts were in vain. For two decades (1700–1720), it had no success in asserting royal authority and collecting the royal fifth in the gold fields. Violence between rival groups, especially pioneers from São Paulo and European-born newcomers, reached the scale of civil war in 1708. The mutual weakening of the two sides as a result of these struggles finally enabled the crown to restore order.

St. Peter Claver was a Spanish Jesuit whose ministry was mainly with black slaves in what is present-day Colombia. Declaring himself "the slave of the slaves," Claver boarded slave ships as soon as they docked in the Cartegena harbor, where he tended the aged, the children, the sick, and the dying. (Mansell Collection)

In 1710 a new captaincy of "São Paulo and the Mines of Gold" was established; in 1720 it was divided into "São Paulo" and "Minas Gerais." In 1729, wild excitement was caused by the discovery that certain stones found in the area, hitherto thought to be crystals, were in reality diamonds; many adventurers with their slaves turned from gold to diamond washing. The great increase in the supply of diamonds to Europe upset the market, causing a serious fall in price. As a result, the Portuguese government instituted a regime of drastic control over the *Diamantina* (Diamond District) to limit mining and prevent smuggling and thus maintain prices; this regime effectively isolated the district from the outside world.

Like its predecessor, the mineral cycle was marked by rapid and superficial exploitation of the new sources of wealth, followed by an equally swift decline. By 1750 the river gold washings of Minas Gerais were nearly exhausted. The Diamond District also suffered a progressive exhaustion of deposits. By 1809 the English traveler John Mawe could describe the gold-mining center of Villa Rica as a town that "scarcely retains a shadow of its former splendor."

Yet the mineral cycle left a permanent mark on the Brazilian landscape in the form of new centers of settlement in the southwest, not only in Minas Gerais but in the future provinces of Goias and Matto Grosso, Brazil's Far West, which was penetrated by pioneers in search of gold. If the mining camps became deserted, the new towns survived, although with diminished vitality. The decline of the mining industry also spurred efforts to promote the agricultural and pastoral wealth of the region. The shift of the center of economic and political gravity southward from Pernambuco and Bahia to Minas Gerais and Rio de Janeiro was formally recognized in 1763, when Rio de Janeiro became the seat of the viceregal capital.

As the provinces of Minas Gerais and Goias sank into decay, the northeast experienced a partial revival based on increasing European demand for sugar, cotton, and other semitropical products. Between 1750 and 1800, Brazilian cotton production made significant progress but then declined as rapidly as a result of competition from the more efficient cotton growers of the United States. The beginnings of the coffee industry, future giant of the Brazilian economy, also date from the late colonial period.

Cattle raising also made its contribution to the advance of the Brazilian frontier and the growing importance of the south. The intensive agriculture of the coast and the concentration of population in coastal cities like Bahia and Pernambuco created a demand for fresh meat that gave an initial impulse to cattle raising. Since the expansion of plantation agriculture in the coastal zone did not leave enough land for grazing, the cattle industry inevitably had to move inland.

By the second half of the seventeenth century, the penetration of the distant São Francisco Valley from Bahia and Pernambuco was well under way. Powerful cattlemen, with their herds of cattle, their *vaqueiros* (cowboys), and their slaves, entered the *sertão* (backcountry), drove out the Indians, and established fortified ranches and villages for their retainers. Such occupation was legitimized before or after the fact by the official grant of a huge tract of land, a virtual feudal domain, to the cattle baron in question, whose word became law on his estate. The landowner's cattle provided meat for the coastal cities and mining camps, draft animals for the plantations, and hides for export to Europe.

The cattle industry later expanded into the extreme southern region of Rio Grande do Sul, which was colonized by the government in the interests of defense against Spanish expansionist designs. Here too vast land grants were made. The counterpart of the vaqueiro in the south was the *gaucho.* Like the vaqueiro, the gaucho was an expert horseman, but he reflected the blend of cultures in the Río de la Plata in his speech, a mixture of Portuguese, Spanish, and Indian dialects; in his dress, the loose, baggy trousers of the Argentine cowboy; and in his chief implement, the *bolas,* balls of stone attached to a rawhide rope, a loan from the pampas Indians, which was used for entangling and bringing down animals.

Portugal, like Spain (with which it was united during the so-called Babylonian Captivity, 1580–1640), pursued a mercantilist commercial policy, though not as consistently or rigorously. During the period of Spanish domination, the commerce of Brazil was firmly restricted to Portuguese nationals and ships. The Dutch, who had been the principal carriers of Brazilian sugar and tobacco to European markets, responded with extensive smuggling and a direct attack on the richest sugar-growing area of Brazil.

Following the successful Portuguese revolt against Spain, a most favorable trade treaty was made with England, Portugal's protector and ally. By this treaty, British merchants were permitted to trade between Portuguese and Brazilian ports.

But English ships frequently neglected the formality of touching at Lisbon and plied a direct contraband trade with the colony. Since Portuguese industry was incapable of supplying the colonists with the required quantity and quality of manufactured goods, a large proportion of the outward-bound cargoes consisted of foreign textiles and other products, of which England provided the lion's share. Thus, Portugal, mistress of Brazil, itself became a colony of Dutch and English merchants with offices in Lisbon.

In the eighteenth century, during the reign of Dom José I (1750–1777), his able prime minister, the marquis de Pombal, launched an administrative and economic reform of the Portuguese Empire that bears comparison with the Bourbon reforms in Spain and Spanish America that were taking place at the same time. Pombal's design

The gaucho, often a product of racial mixture, was a fearless nomadic horseman. The gaucho wore long, full, riding pantaloons that fell in accordion pleats to his ankle, where they fit tightly over the tops of the boots. (Library of Congress)

152 was to nationalize Portuguese-Brazilian trade by creating a Portuguese merchant class with enough capital to compete with British merchants and a national industry whose production could dislodge English goods from the Brazilian market. The program required an active state intervention in the imperial economy through the creation of a Board of Trade, which subsidized merchant-financiers with lucrative concessions in Portugal and Brazil; the formation of companies that were granted monopolies over trade with particular regions of Brazil and were expected to develop the economies of those regions; and the institution of a policy of import substitution through state assistance to old and new industries. Despite mistakes, failures, and a partial retreat from Pombal's program after he was forced out of office in 1777, the Pombaline reform achieved at least partial success in its effort to reconquer Brazilian markets for Portugal. Between 1796 and 1802, 30 percent of all the goods shipped to Brazil consisted of Portuguese manufactures, especially cotton cloth. But the flight of the Portuguese royal family from Lisbon to Brazil in 1808 as a result of Napoleon's invasion of Portugal, followed two years later by the signing of a treaty with England that gave the British all the trade privileges they requested, effectively "dismantled the protective edifice so painfully put together since 1750." Britain once again enjoyed a virtual monopoly of trade with Brazil.

Government and Church

The donatory system of government first established in Brazil by the Portuguese crown soon proved unsatisfactory. There was a glaring contradiction between the vast powers granted to the donatories and the authority of the monarch; moreover, few donatories were able to cope with the tasks of defense and colonization for which they had been made responsible. The result was a governmental reform. In 1549, Tomé de Sousa was sent out as governor general to head a central colonial administration for Brazil. Bahia, situated about midway between the flourishing settlements of Pernambuco and São Vicente, became his capital. Gradually, the hereditary rights and privileges of the donatories were revoked, as they were replaced by governors appointed by the king. As the colony expanded, new captaincies were created. In 1763, as previously noted, the governor of Rio de Janeiro replaced his colleague at Bahia as head of the colonial administration, with the title of viceroy. In practice, however, his authority over the other governors was negligible.

The Administrators and Their Deficiencies

The government of Portuguese Brazil broadly resembled that of the Spanish colonies in its spirit, structure, and vices. One notable difference, however, was the much smaller scale of the Portuguese administration. The differing economies of the two empires help to explain this divergence. The Spanish Indies had a relatively diversified economy that served local and regional, as well as overseas, markets and a large Indian population that was an important source of labor and royal tribute. Combined with a Spanish population that numbered 300,000 in 1600 (when only 30,000 Portuguese lived in Brazil), these conditions created an economic base for the rise of hundreds of towns and the need for a numerous officialdom charged with the regulation of Indian labor, the collection of Indian tribute, and many other fiscal and administrative duties. In Portuguese America, on the other hand, the establishment of an elaborate bureaucracy was rendered unnecessary by several factors: the overwhelming importance of exports, especially of sugar, which could be taxed when it was unloaded in Lisbon; the economic and social dominance of the plantation, which made for a weak development of urban life; and the minor role of the Indian population as a source of labor and royal revenue.

During the "Babylonian Captivity," the colonial policies of Spain and Portugal were aligned by the creation in 1604 of the *Conselho de India,* whose functions resembled those of the Spanish Council of the Indies. In 1736, the functions of the conselho were assumed by a newly created ministry of *Marinha e Ultramar* (Marine and Overseas). Under the king, this body framed laws for Brazil, appointed governors, and supervised their conduct. The governor, captain general, or viceroy combined in himself military, administrative, and even some judicial duties. His power tended to be absolute but was tempered by certain factors: the constant intervention of the home government, which bound him with precise, strict, and detailed instructions; the counterweights of other authorities, especially the *relações* (high courts), which were both administrative and judicial bodies; and the existence of special administrative organs, such as the intendancies created in the gold and diamond districts, which were completely independent of the governor. Thus in Brazil, as in the Spanish colonies, there functioned a system of checks and balances that reflected above all the distrust felt by the home government for its agents. Other factors that tended to diminish the authority of the governor were the vastness of the country, the scattered population, the lack of social stability, and the existence of enormous landholdings in which the feudal power of the great planters and cattle barons was virtually unchallenged.

The most important institution of local government was the *Senado de Câmara* (municipal council). The influence of this body varied with the size of the city. Whether elected by a restricted property-owning electorate or chosen by the crown, its membership represented the ruling class of merchants, planters, and professional men. Elections were often marked by struggles for control by rival factions, planters and creoles on one side, merchants and peninsulars on the other. The authority of the câmara extended over its entire *comarca* (district), which often was very large. But its power was limited by the frequent intervention of the *ouvidor,* who usually combined his judicial functions with the administrative duties of corregedor. Generally speaking, the greater the size and wealth of the city,

and the farther it was from the viceregal capital, the greater its powers.

Both the crown and the municipal councils levied numerous taxes, whose collection was usually farmed out to private collectors. In return for making a fixed payment to the treasury, these men collected the taxes for the crown and could keep the surplus once the set quota had been met. The system, of course, encouraged fraud and extortion of every kind. Another crippling burden on the population was tithes, which came to 10 percent of the total product, originally payable in kind but later only in cash. Tithes, writes the Brazilian historian Caio Prado Júnior, "ran neck and neck with conscription as one of the great scourges inflicted on the population by the colonial administration."[2]

The besetting vices of Spanish colonial administration—inefficiency, bureaucratic attitudes, slowness, and corruption—were equally prominent in the Portuguese colonial system. Justice was not only costly but incredibly slow and complicated. Cases brought before lower courts ascended the ladder of the higher tribunals: ouvidor, relação, and on up to the crown Board of Appeals, taking as long as ten to fifteen years for resolution.

Over vast areas of the colony, however, administration and courts were virtually nonexistent. Away from the few large towns, local government often meant the rule of great landowners, who joined to their personal influence the authority of office, for it was from their ranks that the royal governors invariably appointed the *capitães móres* (district militia officers). Armed with unlimited power to enlist, command, arrest, and punish, the capitão mor became a popular symbol of despotism and oppression. Sometimes these men used the local militia as feudal levies for war against a rival family; boundary questions and questions of honor were often settled by duels or pitched battles between retainers of rival clans. The feudalism that still dominates

[2] Caio Prado Júnior, *The Colonial Background of Modern Brazil* (Berkeley: University of California Press, 1967), p. 377.

154   much of the Brazilian backcountry may be traced back to these colonial origins.

Corruption pervaded the administrative apparatus from top to bottom. The miserably paid officials prostituted their trusts in innumerable ways: embezzlement, graft, and bribery were well-nigh universal. The Jesuit Antônio Vieira referred to this universal corruption when he conjugated the verb *rapio* (I steal) in all its inflections in his sermon on the "Good Thief."

Some improvement, at least on the higher levels of administration, took place under the auspices of the extremely able and energetic marquis de Pombal. The same tendency toward centralization that characterized Bourbon colonial policy appeared in Portuguese policy in this period. Pombal abolished the remaining hereditary captaincies, restricted the special privileges of the municipalities, and increased the power of the viceroy. In a mercantilist spirit, he sought to promote the economic advance of Brazil with a view to promoting the reconstruction of Portugal, whose condition was truly forlorn.

Typical of the enlightened viceroys of the Pombaline period was the marquis de Lavradio (1769–1779), whose achievements included the transfer of coffee from Pará into São Paulo, in whose fertile red soil it was to flourish mightily. How little changed, however, the administration of Brazil was by the Pombaline reform is suggested by Lavradio's letter of instructions to his successor, in which he gloomily observed that

> as the salaries of these magistrates [*the judges*] are small . . . they seek to multiply their emoluments by litigation and discord, which they foment, and not only keep the people unquiet, but put them to heavy expenses, and divert them from their occupations, with the end of promoting their own vile interest and that of their subalterns, who are the principal concocters of these disorders.[3]

During the twelve years that he had governed in Brazil, wrote the viceroy, he had never found one useful establishment instituted by any of these magistrates.

The Church and the State

In Brazil, as in the Spanish colonies, church and state were intimately united. By comparison with the Spanish monarchs, however, the Portuguese kings seemed almost niggardly in their dealings with the church. But their control over its affairs, exercised through the *padroado*—the ecclesiastical patronage granted by the pope to the Portuguese king in his realm and overseas possessions—was as absolute. The king exercised his power through a special board, the *Mesa da Consciência e Ordens* (Board of Conscience and Orders). Rome, however, long maintained a strong indirect influence through the agency of the Jesuits, who were very influential in the Portuguese court until they were expelled from Portugal and Brazil in 1759.

With some honorable exceptions, notably that of the entire Jesuit order, the tone of clerical morality and conduct in Brazil was deplorably low. The clergy were often criticized for their extortionate fees and for the negligence they displayed in the performance of their spiritual duties. Occasionally, priests combined those duties with more mundane activities. Many were planters; others carried on a variety of businesses. One high-ranking crown official summed up his impressions of the clergy in the statement "All they want is money, and they care not a jot for their good name."

Yet the church and the clergy made their own contributions to the life of colonial Brazil. The clergy provided such educational and humanitarian establishments as existed in the colony. From its ranks—which were open to talent and even admitted individuals of mixed blood despite the formal requirement of a special dispensation—came most of the few distinguished names in Brazilian colonial science, learning, and literature. Among them, Jesuit writers again occupy a prominent place. We must mention Manoel da

[3] E. Bradford Burns, ed., *A Documentary History of Brazil* (New York: Alfred A. Knopf, 1966), p. 144.

Nóbrega and José de Anchieta for their lucid, informative letters and their studies of the Tupi Indian language; Antônio Vieira for his powerful sermons; Fernão Cardim for his *Treatise on the Land and People of Brazil,* first published in 1925; and the important *Culture and Opulence of Brazil* (1711) by the author who signed himself André João Antonil (João Antônio Andreoni). The chronicler and planter Gabriel Soares de Sousa contributed a detailed account of Brazilian geography, Indians, and natural resources in his *A Description of Brazil* (1587), and in the late colonial period José da Rocha Pitta published the first history of Brazil, *History of Portuguese America* (1730). But the cultural poverty of colonial Brazil is suggested by the fact that throughout the colonial period there was not a single university or even a printing press.

Masters and Slaves

Race mixture played a decisive role in the formation of the Brazilian people. The scarcity of white women in the colony, the freedom of the Portuguese from puritanical attitudes, and the despotic power of the great planters over their Indian and black slave women all gave impetus to miscegenation. Of the three possible race combinations—white-black, white-Indian, black-Indian—the first was the most common. The immense majority of these unions were outside wedlock. In 1755 the marquis de Pombal, pursuing the goals of population growth and strengthening of Brazil's borders, issued an order encouraging marriages between Portuguese and Indians and proclaiming the descendants of such union eligible to positions of honor and dignity, but this favor was not extended to white-black unions.

Color, Class, and Slavery

In principle, color lines were strictly drawn. A "pure" white wife or husband, for example, was indispensable to a member of the upper class. But the enormous number of mixed unions outside wedlock and the resulting large progeny,

some of whom, at least, were regarded with affection by white fathers and provided with some education and property, inevitably led to blurring of color lines and a fairly frequent phenomenon of "passing." There was a tendency to classify individuals racially, if their color was not too dark, on the basis of social and economic position rather than on their physical appearance. The English traveler Henry Koster alludes to this "polite fiction" in his anecdote concerning a certain great personage, a capitão mor, whom Koster suspected of being a mulatto. In response to his question, his servant replied, "He was, but is not now." Asked to explain, the servant continued, "Can a capitão mor be a mulatto man?"

Slavery played as important a role in the social organization of Brazil as race mixture did in its ethnic make-up. The social consequences of the system were entirely negative. Slavery corrupted both master and slave, fostered harmful attitudes with respect to the dignity of labor, and distorted the economic development of Brazil. The tendency to identify labor with slavery sharply limited the number of socially acceptable occupations in which whites or free mixed-bloods could engage. This gave rise to a populous class of vagrants, beggars, "poor whites," and other degraded or disorderly elements who would not or could not compete with slaves in agriculture and industry. Inevitably, given the almost total absence of incentive to work on the part of the slave, the level of efficiency and productivity of his or her labor was very low.

Much historical writing has fostered the idea that Brazilian slavery was mild by comparison with slavery in other colonies. In part, this tradition owes its popularity to the writings of the Brazilian sociologist Gilberto Freyre, who emphasized the patriarchal relations existing between masters and slaves in the sugar plantation society of the northeast. But the slaves described by Freyre were usually house slaves who occupied a privileged position. Their situation was very different from that of the great majority of slaves, who worked on the sugar and tobacco plantations of Bahia and Pernambuco. During harvest time and when the mills were grinding the cane, says Charles Boxer, the slaves sometimes worked round the clock and often at least from dawn to dusk. In the off season, the hours were not so long. But "discipline was maintained with a severity that often degenerated into sadistic cruelty where the infliction of corporal punishment was concerned." A royal dispatch of 1700 denounced the barbarity with which owners of both sexes treated their slaves and singled out for special condemnation the practice of women owners who forced their female slaves to engage in prostitution.[4]

Obviously, the treatment of slaves varied considerably with the temperament of the individual slave owner. Although the crown provided slaves with legal means of redress, there is little evidence that these were effective in relieving their plight. The church, represented on the plantation by a chaplain paid and housed by the landowner, probably exerted little influence on the problem. A very low rate of reproduction among slaves and frequent suicides speak volumes concerning their condition. Many slaves ran away and formed *quilombos* (settlements of fugitive slaves in the bush). The most famous of these was the so-called republic of Palmares, founded in 1603 in the interior of the northeastern captaincy of Alagoas. A self-sufficient African kingdom with several thousand inhabitants who lived in ten villages spread over a 90-mile territory, Palmares was exceptional among quilombos in its size, complex organization, and ability to survive repeated expeditions sent against it by colonial authorities. Not until 1694 did a Paulista army destroy it after a two-year siege. But the quilombos continued to alarm planters and authorities; as late as 1760 they complained of the threat posed by quilombos around Bahia.

Slavery played a decisive role in the economic life of colonial Brazil and placed its stamp on all social relations. In addition to masters and slaves, however, there existed a large free peasant population of varied racial make-up who

lived on estates and in villages and hamlets scattered throughout the Brazilian countryside. Some were small landowners, often possessing a few slaves of their own, who brought their sugar cane for processing or sale to the *senhor de engenho* (sugar-mill owner). Their economic inferiority made their independence precarious, and their land and slaves tended to pass into the hands of the great planters in a process of concentration of landownership and growing social stratification. The majority, however, were *lavradores, moradores, foreiros* (tenant farmers or sharecroppers), who owed labor and allegiance to a great landowner in return for the privilege of farming a parcel of land. Other free peasants were squatters who in the seventeenth and eighteenth centuries pushed out of the coastal zone to settle in the backcountry and were regarded as intruders by the cattle barons and other great landowners who laid claim to those lands.

Other free commoners were the artisans, including many black or mulatto freedmen, who served the needs of the urban population. An important group of salaried workers—overseers, mechanics, coopers, and the like—supplied the special skills required by the sugar industry.

Large Estates and Colonial Towns

The nucleus of Brazilian social as well as economic organization was the large estate, or fazenda, which usually rested on a base of black slavery. The large estate centered about the *Casa Grande* (Big House) and constituted a patriarchal community that included the owner and his family, his chaplain and overseers, his slaves, his *obrigados* (sharecroppers), and his *agregados* (retainers)—free men of low social status who received the landowner's protection and assistance in return for a variety of services.

In this self-contained world, an intricate web of relations arose between the master and his slaves and white or mixed-blood subordinates. No doubt, long contact sometimes tended to mellow and humanize these relationships and added to mere commercial relationship a variety of emotional ties. The protective role of the master

---

[4] Boxer, *The Golden Age of Brazil,* pp. 8, 173.

found expression in the relationship of *compadrio* (godfathership), in which the master became sponsor or godfather of a baptized child or a bridal pair whose marriage he witnessed. The system implied relations of mutual aid and a paternalistic interest in the welfare of the landowner's people. But it by no means excluded intense exploitation of those people or the display of the most ferocious cruelty if they should cross him or dispute his absolute power.

In the sugar-growing northeast the great planters became a distinct aristocratic class, possessed of family traditions and pride in their name and blood. In the cattle-raising regions of the sertão and the south, the small number of slaves, the self-reliant character of the vaqueiro or gaucho, and the greater freedom of movement of workers gave society a somewhat more democratic tone. Everywhere, however, says the Brazilian historian Caio Prado Júnior, "the existence of pronounced social distinctions and the absolute and patriarchal domination of the owner and master were elements invariably associated with all the colony's large landed estates."[5]

By contrast with the decisive importance of the fazenda, most colonial towns were mere appendages of the countryside, dominated politically and socially by the rural magnates. Even in the few large cities like Bahia and Rio de Janeiro, the dominant social group was composed of *fazendeiros* and sugar-mill owners. These men often left the supervision of their estates to majordomos and overseers, preferring the pleasures and bustle of the cities to the dreary routines of the countryside. But in the city lived other social groups that disputed or shared power with the great landowners: high officials of the colonial administration; dignitaries of the church; wealthy professional men, especially lawyers; and the large merchants, almost exclusively peninsulars, who monopolized the export-import trade and financed the industry of the planters.

The social position of the merchant was not very high, because of the medieval prejudice against commerce brought over from Portugal (a prejudice that did not prevent the highest officials from engaging in trade, albeit discreetly), but nothing barred the merchants from membership on the municipal councils. The conflict between native-born landowners and European-born merchants, aggravated by nationalistic resentment against upstart immigrants, sometimes broke out into armed struggle. An illustration is the petty War of the Mascates (1710–1711) between Olinda, provincial capital of Pernambuco, which was dominated by the sugar planters, and its neighboring seaport of Recife, which was controlled by the merchants.

This struggle between *mazombos* (Brazilian-born whites) and *reinóis* (peninsulars) foreshadowed the later rise of a broader Brazilian nationalism and the first projects of Brazilian independence. In the late eighteenth century, Minas Gerais, the most urbanized Brazilian region, had the most diversified economy. It became a seat of much unrest as a result of official efforts to reinforce the area's dependency on Portuguese exporters, collect large amounts of delinquent taxes, and impose a new head tax. A conspiracy to revolt and establish a republic on the American model was hatched in 1788–1789 by a group of dissidents, most of whom were highly placed members of the colonial elite. The only leading conspirator who was not a member of the aristocracy was José da Silva Xavier, a military officer of low rank who practiced the part-time profession of "Toothpuller," whence the name of *Tiradentes* by which he is known in Brazilian history. An enthusiast for the American Revolution, Silva Xavier apparently possessed copies of the Declaration of Independence and American state constitutions. When the conspiracy was discovered, all the principal conspirators were condemned to death, but the sentences were commuted to exile for all but the plebeian Silva Xavier. His barbarous execution, which he faced with great courage, made him a martyr as well as a precursor of Brazilian independence.

[5] Prado, *The Colonial Background of Modern Brazil,* p. 339.

Chapter 8

The Independence of Latin America

The Bourbon reforms, combined with the up-surge of the European economy in the eighteenth century, brought material prosperity and less tangible benefits to many upper-class creoles of Spanish America. Enlightened viceroys and intendants introduced improvements and refinements that made life in colonial cities more healthful and attractive. Educational reforms, the influx of new books and ideas, and increased opportunities to travel and study in Europe widened the intellectual horizons of creole youth.

These gains, however, did not strengthen creole feelings of loyalty to the mother country. Instead, they enlarged their aspirations and sharpened their sense of grievance. The growing wealth of some sections of the creole elite made more galling its virtual exclusion from important posts in administration and the church. Meanwhile, the swelling production of creole haciendas, plantations, and ranches pressed against the trade barriers maintained by Spanish mercantilism. The intendant of Caracas, José Abalos, warned that "if His Majesty does not grant them [the creoles] the freedom of trade which they desire, then he cannot count on their loyalty." At the same time, Bourbon policy denied American manufacturers the protection they needed against crippling European competition.

Background of the Wars of Independence

Creoles and Peninsular Spaniards

The conflict of interest between Spain and its colonies was most sharply expressed in the cleavage between the creoles and the peninsular Spaniards. This quarrel was constantly renewed by the arrival of more Spaniards. In the late eighteenth century, a typical immigrant was a poor but hardworking and thrifty Basque or Navarrese who became an apprentice to a peninsular merchant, often a relative. In the course of time, as his merits won recognition, the immigrant might receive a daughter of the house in marriage and eventually succeed to the ownership of the business. One of the merchant's own creole sons might be given a landed estate; other creole sons might enter the church or the law, both overcrowded professions.

Thus, although there was some elite creole presence in both foreign and domestic trade, peninsular Spaniards continued to dominate the lucrative export-import trade and provincial trade. Spanish-born merchants, organized in powerful consulados, or merchant guilds, also played a key role in financing mining and the repartimiento business carried on among the Indians by Spanish officials. Not unnaturally, some upper-class creoles, excluded from mercantile activity and responsible posts in the government and church, developed the aristocratic manners and idle, spendthrift ways with which the peninsulars reproached them. Many other creoles of the middling sort, vegetating in ill-paid Indian curacies and minor government jobs, bitterly resented the institutionalized discrimination that barred their way to advancement.

As a result, although some wealthy and powerful creoles maintained excellent relations with their peninsular counterparts, fusing their economic interests through marriage and forming a single colonial Establishment, creoles and peninsulars tended to become mutually hostile castes. The peninsulars sometimes justified their privileged position by charging the creoles with innate indolence and incapacity, qualities that some Spanish writers, following the Comte Georges de Buffon and Cornelius de Pauw, attributed to the noxious effects of the American climate and soil; the creoles retorted by describing the Europeans as mean and grasping parvenus. So intense was the hatred between many members of these groups that a Spanish bishop in New Spain, Joseph Joaquín Granados, protested

against the feeling of some young creoles that "if they could empty their veins of the Spanish part of their blood, they would gladly do so." This cleavage inevitably fostered the growth of creole nationalism; Humboldt, who traveled in Spanish America in the twilight years of the colony, reports a common saying: "I am not a Spaniard, I am an American."

The entrance of Enlightenment ideas into Latin America certainly contributed to the growth of creole discontent, but the relative weight of various influences is uncertain. Bourbon Spain itself contributed to the creole awakening by the many-sided effort of reforming officials to improve the quality of colonial life. Typical of this group was the intendant Juan Antonio Riaño, who introduced to the Mexican city of Guanajuato, the capital of his province, a taste for the French language and literature; he was also responsible "for the development of interest in drawing and music, and for the cultivation of mathematics, physics, and chemistry in the school that had been formerly maintained by the Jesuits."[1]

Many educated creoles read the forbidden writings of Raynal, Montesquieu, Voltaire, Rousseau, and other radical philosophes, but another, innocuous-seeming agency for the spread of Enlightenment ideas in Latin America consisted of scientific texts, based on the theories of Descartes, Leibnitz, and Newton, which circulated freely in the colonies. By 1800, through all these channels, the creole elite had become familiar with the most advanced thought of contemporary Europe.

The American Revolution contributed to the growth of "dangerous ideas" in the colonies. Spain was well aware of the ideological as well as political threat the United States posed to its empire. Spain had reluctantly joined its ally France in war against England during the American Revolution, but it kept the rebels at arm's length, refused to recognize American independence, and in the peace negotiations tried unsuccessfully to

[1] Lucas Alamán, *Historia de Mejico,* 5 vols. (Mexico, 1849–1852), 1:76.

coop up the United States within the Allegheny Mountains. After 1783, a growing number of United States ships touched legally or illegally at Spanish-American ports. Together with "Yankee notions," these vessels sometimes introduced such subversive documents as the writings of Thomas Paine and Thomas Jefferson.

The French Revolution probably exerted a greater influence on the creole mind. Recalled the Argentine revolutionary Manuel Belgrano,

Since I was in Spain in 1789, and the French Revolution was then causing a change in ideas, especially among the men of letters with whom I associated, the ideals of liberty, equality, security, and property took a firm hold on me, and I saw only tyrants in those who would restrain a man, wherever he might be, from enjoying the rights with which God and Nature had endowed him.[2]

Another cultivated creole, the Colombian Antonio Nariño, incurred Spanish wrath in 1794 by translating and printing on his own press the French Declaration of the Rights of Man of 1789. Sentenced to prison in Africa for ten years, Nariño lived to become leader and patriarch of the independence movement in Colombia and to witness its triumph.

But the French Revolution soon took a radical turn, and the creole aristocracy became disenchanted with it as a model. Scattered conspiracies in some Spanish colonies and Brazil owed their inspiration to the French example, but they were invariably the work of a few radicals, drawing their support almost exclusively from lower-class elements. The most important result directly attributable to the French Revolution was the slave revolt in the French part of Haiti under talented black and mulatto leaders: Toussaint L'Ouverture, Jean Jacques Dessalines, Henri Christophe, and Alexandre Pétion. By January 1, 1804, Toussaint's lieutenant, General Dessalines, could proclaim the independence of the new state of Haiti. Black revolutionaries had established the first liberated territory in Latin America. But their achievement dampened rather than aroused support for independence among the creole elite of other colonies. Thus, fear that secession from Spain might touch off a slave revolt helped to keep the planter class of neighboring Cuba loyal to Spain during and after the Latin American wars of independence.

Despite the existence of small conspiratorial groups, organized in secret societies, with correspondents in Europe as well as America, the movement for independence might have long remained puny and ineffectual. As late as 1806, when the precursor of revolution, Francisco de Miranda, landed on the coast of his native Venezuela with a force of some two hundred foreign volunteers, his call for revolution evoked no response, and he had to make a hasty retreat. Creole timidity and political inexperience and the apathy of the people might have long postponed the coming of independence if external developments had not hastened its arrival. The revolution that Miranda and other forerunners could not set in motion came as a result of decisions by European powers with very different ends in view.

The Causes of Revolution

Among the causes of the revolutionary crisis that matured from 1808 to 1810, the decline of Spain under the inept Charles IV was certainly a major one. The European wars unleashed by the French Revolution glaringly revealed the failure of the Bourbon reforms to correct the structural defects in Spanish economic and social life. In 1793, Spain joined a coalition of England and other states in war against the French republic. The struggle went badly for Spain, and in 1795 the royal favorite and chief minister, Manuel de Godoy, signed the Peace of Basel. The next year, Spain became France's ally. English sea power promptly drove Spanish shipping from the Atlantic, virtually cutting off communication between Spain and its colonies. Hard necessity compelled Spain to permit neutral ships, sailing from Span-

[2] Richardo Levene, ed., *Los sucesos de mayo contados por sus actores* (Buenos Aires, 1928), p. 60.

ish for foreign ports, to trade with its overseas subjects. United States merchants and ship-owners were the principal beneficiaries of this departure from the old, restrictive system.

Godoy's disastrous policy of war with England had other results. An English naval officer, Sir Home Popham, undertook on his own initiative to make an attack on Buenos Aires. His fleet sailed from the Cape of Good Hope for La Plata in April 1806 with a regiment of soldiers on board. In its wake followed a great number of English merchant ships eager to pour a mass of goods through a breach in the Spanish colonial system. A swift victory followed the landing of the British troops. The viceroy, the Marquis of Sobremonte, fled from the capital at the ap-proach of the enemy. The English soldiers en-tered Buenos Aires, meeting only token resis-tance. Hoping to obtain the support of the population, the English commander issued a proclamation guaranteeing the right of private property, free trade, and freedom of religion. But the English had mistaken the temper of the *por-teños,* as the inhabitants of Buenos Aires were called. Creoles and peninsulars joined to expel their unwanted liberators. A volunteer army, se-cretly organized, attacked and routed the occu-pation troops, capturing the English general and twelve hundred of his men. To an English officer who tempted him with ideas of independence un-der a British protectorate, the creole Manuel Bel-grano replied: "Either our old master or none at all."

The British government, meanwhile, had sent strong reinforcements to La Plata. This second invasion force was met with a murderous hail of fire as it tried to advance through the narrow streets of Buenos Aires and was beaten back with heavy losses. Impressed by the tenacity of the de-fense, the British commander gave up the strug-gle and agreed to evacuate both Buenos Aires and the previously captured town of Montevideo. This defeat of a veteran British army by a peo-ple's militia spearheaded by the legion of *patri-cios* (creoles) was a large step down the road to-ward Argentine independence. The creoles of

Buenos Aires, having tasted power, would not willingly relinquish it again.

In Europe, Spain's distresses now reached a climax. Napoleon, at the helm of France, gradu-ally reduced Spain to a helpless satellite. In 1807, angered by Portugal's refusal to cooperate with his Continental System by closing its ports to English shipping, Napoleon obtained from Charles IV permission to invade Portugal through Spain. French troops swept across the peninsula; as they approached Lisbon, the Portuguese royal family and court escaped to Brazil in a fleet un-der British convoy. A hundred thousand French troops continued to occupy Spanish towns. Pop-ular resentment at their presence, and at the pro-French policies of the royal favorite Godoy, broke out in stormy riots that compelled Charles IV to abdicate in favor of his son Ferdinand. Napoleon now intervened and offered his services as a me-diator in the dispute between father and son. Foolishly, the trusting pair accepted Napoleon's invitation to confer with him in the French city of Bayonne. There Napoleon forced both to abdi-cate in favor of his brother Joseph, his candidate for the Spanish throne. Napoleon then sum-moned a congress of Spanish grandees, which meekly approved his dictate.

The Spanish people had yet to say their word. On May 2, 1808, an insurrection against French occupation troops began in Madrid and spread like wildfire throughout the country. The insur-gents established local governing juntas in the regions under their control. Later, a central junta assumed direction of the resistance movement in the name of the captive Ferdinand VII. This junta promptly made peace with England. When the Spanish armies fought the superbly trained French troops in conventional battles in the field, they usually suffered defeat, but guerrilla warfare pinned down large French forces and made Napoleon's control of conquered territory ex-tremely precarious.

By early 1810, however, French victory seemed inevitable, for French armies had overrun Anda-lusia and were threatening Cádiz, the last city in Spanish hands. The central junta now dissolved itself and appointed a regency to rule Spain; this body in turn yielded its power to a national Cortes, or parliament, which met in Cádiz from 1810 to 1814 under the protection of English naval guns. Since most of the delegates actually came from Cádiz, whose liberal, cosmopolitan atmosphere was hardly typical of Spain, their views were much more liberal than those of the Spanish people as a whole. The constitution the Cortes approved in 1812 provided for a limited monarchy, promised freedom of speech and assembly, and abolished the Inquisition. But the Cortes made few concessions to the Spanish American colonies. It invited Spanish American delegates to join its deliberations but made clear that the system of peninsular domination and commercial monopoly would remain essentially intact.

In Spanish America, creole leaders, anticipating the imminent collapse of Spain, considered how they might turn this dramatic rush of events to their own advantage. Those events had transformed the idea of self-rule or total independence, until lately a remote prospect, into a realistic goal. Confident that the armies of the invincible Napoleon would crush all opposition, some creole leaders prepared to take power into their hands with the pretext of loyalty to the "beloved Ferdinand." They could justify their action by the example of the Spanish regional juntas formed to govern in the name of the captive king. The confusion caused among Spanish officials by the coming of rival emissaries who proclaimed both Ferdinand and Joseph Bonaparte the legitimate king of Spain also played into creole hands.

In the spring of 1810, with the fall of Cádiz apparently imminent, the creole leaders moved into action. Charging viceroys and other royal officials with doubtful loyalty to Ferdinand, they organized popular demonstrations in Caracas, Buenos Aires, Santiago, and Bogotá that compelled those authorities to surrender control to local juntas dominated by creoles. But creole hopes of a peaceful transition to independence were doomed to failure. Their claims of loyalty did not deceive the groups truly loyal to Spain, and fighting broke out between patriots and royalists.

The Liberation of South America

The Latin American struggle for independence suggests comparison with the American Revolution. Some obvious parallels exist between the two upheavals. Both sought to throw off the rule of a mother country whose mercantilist system hindered the further development of a rapidly growing colonial economy. Both were led by well-educated elites who drew their slogans and ideas from the ideological arsenal of the Enlightenment. Both were civil wars in which large elements of the population sided with the mother country. Both owed their final success in part to foreign assistance (although the North American rebels received far more help from their French ally than came to Latin America from outside sources).

The differences between the two revolutions are no less impressive, however. Unlike the American Revolution, the Latin American struggle for independence did not have a unified direction or strategy. This lack was due not only to vast distances and other geographical obstacles to unity but to the economic and cultural isolation of the various Latin American regions from each other. Moreover, the Latin American movement for independence lacked the strong popular base provided by the more democratic and fluid society of the English colonies. The creole elite, itself part of an exploitative white minority, feared the oppressed Indians, blacks, and half-castes, and as a rule sought to keep their intervention in the struggle to a minimum. This lack of unity of regions and classes helps to explain why Latin America had to struggle so long against a power like Spain, weak and beset by many internal and external problems.

The struggle for independence had four main centers. In Spanish South America there were two principal theaters of military operations, one in the north, another in the south. One stream of liberation flowed southward from Venezuela; another ran northward from Argentina. In Peru, last Spanish bastion on the continent, these two currents joined. Brazil achieved its own swift and relatively peaceful separation from Portugal. Finally, Mexico had to travel a very difficult, devious road before gaining its independence.

Simón Bolívar, the Liberator

Simón Bolívar is the symbol and hero of the liberation struggle in northern South America. Born in Caracas, Venezuela, in 1783, he came from an aristocratic creole family rich in land, slaves, and mines. His intellectual formation was greatly influenced by his reading of the rationalist, materialist classics of the Enlightenment. Travel in various European countries between 1803 and 1807 further widened his intellectual horizons. He returned to Caracas and soon became involved in conspiratorial activity directed at the overthrow of the Spanish regime.

In April 1810, the creole party in Caracas organized a demonstration that forced the abdication of the captain general. A creole-dominated junta that pledged to defend the rights of the captive Ferdinand took power, but its assurances of loyalty deceived neither local Spaniards nor the Regency Council in Cádiz. A considerable number of wealthy creoles of the planter class also opposed independence, and when it triumphed many emigrated to Cuba or Puerto Rico. The patriots were also divided over what policy to follow; some, like Bolívar, favored an immediate declaration of independence, while others preferred to postpone the issue.

Perhaps to get Bolívar out of the way, the junta sent him to England to solicit British aid. He had no success in this mission but convinced the veteran revolutionary Francisco de Miranda to return to Venezuela and take command of the patriot army. In 1811 a Venezuelan congress proclaimed the country's independence and framed a republican constitution that abolished Indian tribute and special privileges (fueros) but retained black slavery, made Catholicism the state religion, and limited the rights of full citizenship to property owners. This last provision excluded the free pardo (black and mulatto) population.

Fighting had already broken out between patriots and royalists. In addition to peninsulars, the troops sent from Puerto Rico by the Regency Council, and a section of the creole aristocracy, the royalist cause had the support of some free blacks and mulattos, angered by the republic's denial of full citizenship to them. In many areas, the black slaves took advantage of the chaotic situation to rise in revolt, impartially killing creole and peninsular Spanish hacendados. But the majority of the population remained neutral, fleeing from their villages at the approach of royal or republican conscription officers; if conscripted, they often deserted when they could or changed sides if prospects seemed better.

On the patriot side, differences arose between the commander-in-chief, Miranda, and his young officers, especially Bolívar, who were angered by Miranda's military conservatism and indecisiveness. Amid these disputes came the earthquake of March 26, 1812, which caused great loss of life and property in Caracas and other patriot territories but spared the regions under Spanish control. The royalist clergy proclaimed this disaster a divine retribution against the rebels. A series of military defeats completed the discomfiture of the revolutionary cause.

With his forces disintegrating, Miranda attempted to negotiate a treaty with the royalist commander and then tried to flee the country, taking with him part of the republic's treasury. He may have intended to continue working for independence, but the circumstances made it appear as if he wished to save his own skin. Bolívar and some of his comrades, regarding Miranda's act as a form of treachery, seized him before he could embark and turned him over to the Spaniards. He died in a Spanish prison four years later. Bolívar, saved from the Spanish reaction by the influence of a friend of his family, received a safe conduct to leave the country.

Bolívar departed for New Granada (present-day Colombia), which was still partially under patriot control. Here, as in Venezuela, creole leaders squabbled over forms of government. Two months after his arrival, Bolívar issued a

Manifesto to the Citizens of New Granada in which he called for unity, condemned the federalist system as impractical under war conditions, and urged the liberation of Venezuela as necessary for Colombian security. Given command of a small detachment of troops to clear the Magdalena River of enemy troops, he employed a strategy that featured swift movement, aggressive tactics, and the advancement of soldiers for merit without regard to social background or color.

A victory at Cúcuta gained Bolívar the rank of general in the Colombian army and approval of his plan for the liberation of Venezuela. In a forced march of three months, he led five hundred men through Venezuela's Andean region toward Caracas. In Venezuela the Spaniards had unleashed a campaign of terror against all patriots. At Trujillo, midway in his advance on Caracas, Bolívar proclaimed a counterterror, a war to the death against all Spaniards. As Bolívar approached the capital, the Spanish forces withdrew. He entered Caracas in triumph and received from the city council the title of liberator; soon afterward the grateful congress of the restored republic voted to grant him dictatorial powers.

Bolívar's success was short-lived, for developments abroad and at home worked against him. The fall of Napoleon in 1814 brought Ferdinand VII to the Spanish throne, released Spanish troops for use in Spanish America, and gave an important lift to the royal cause. Meanwhile, the republic's policies alienated large sectors of the lower classes. The creole aristocrats stubbornly refused to grant freedom to their slaves. As a result, the slaves continued their struggle, independent of Spaniards and creoles, and republican forces had to be diverted for punitive expeditions into areas of slave revolt.

The *llaneros* (cowboys) of the Venezuelan *llanos* (plains) also turned against the republic as a result of agrarian edicts that attempted to end the hunting or rounding up of cattle in the llanos without written permission from the owner of the land in question. These edicts also sought to transform the llaneros into semiservile peons by forcing them to carry an identity card and belong to a ranch. These attacks on their customary rights and freedom angered the llaneros. Under the leadership of the formidable José Tomás Boves, a mass of cowboys, armed with the dreaded lance, invaded the highlands and swept down on Caracas, crushing all resistance. In July 1814, Bolívar hastily abandoned the city and retreated toward Colombia with the remains of his army. Although Boves died in battle in late 1814, he had destroyed the Venezuelan "second republic."

Bolívar reached Cartagena in September to find that Colombia was on the verge of chaos. Despite the imminent threat of a Spanish invasion, the provinces quarreled with each other and defied the authority of the weak central government. Having determined that the situation was hopeless, Bolívar left in May 1815 for the British island of Jamaica. Meanwhile, a strong Spanish army under General Pablo Morillo had landed in Venezuela, completed the reconquest of the colony, and then sailed to lay siege to Cartagena. Cut off by land and sea, the city surrendered in December, and the rest of Colombia was pacified within a few months. Of all the provinces of Spanish America, only Argentina remained in revolt. Had Ferdinand made the concession (as one of his generals urged him to do) of granting legal equality with whites to the mixed-bloods who supported his cause, the Spanish Empire in America might have survived much longer. But the reactionary Ferdinand would make no concessions.

Bolívar still had an unshakable faith in the inevitable triumph of independence. From Jamaica he sent a famous letter in which he affirmed that faith and offered a remarkable analysis of the situation and prospects of Spanish America. He scoffed at the ability of Spain, that "aged serpent," to maintain Spanish America forever in subjection.

Can that nation carry on the exclusive commerce of one-half the world when it lacks manufactures, agricultural products, crafts and sciences, and even a policy? Assume that this mad venture were successful, and further assume that pacification ensued, would not the sons of the Americans today, together with the sons of the conquistadors twenty years hence, conceive the same patriotic designs that are now being fought for?

Bolívar also looked into the political future of the continent. Monarchy, he argued, was foreign to the genius of Latin America; only a republican regime would be accepted by its peoples. A single government for the region was impracticable, divided as it was by "climatic differences, geographic diversity, conflicting interests, and dissimilar characteristics." Bolívar boldly forecast the destiny of the different regions, taking account of their economic and social structures. Chile, for example, seemed to him to have a democratic future; Peru, on the other hand, was fated to suffer dictatorship because it contained "two factors that clash with every just and liberal principle: gold and slaves."[3]

From Jamaica, Bolívar went to Haiti, where he received a sympathetic hearing and the offer of some material support from the mulatto president Alexandre Pétion, who asked in return for the freedom of the slaves in the territory that Bolívar should liberate. In March 1816, Bolívar and a small band of followers landed on the island of Margarita off the Venezuelan coast. Two attempts to gain a foothold on the mainland were easily beaten back, and soon Bolívar was back in the West Indies. Reflecting on his failures, he concluded that the effort to invade the well-fortified western coast of Venezuela was a mistake and decided to establish a base in the Orinoco River valley, distant from the centers of Spanish power. Roving patriot bands still operated in this region, and Bolívar hoped to win the allegiance of the llaneros, who were becoming disillusioned with their Spanish allies. In September 1816, Bolívar sailed from Haiti for the Orinoco River delta, which he ascended until he reached the small town of Angostura (modern Ciudad Bolívar), which he made his headquarters.

The tide of war now began to flow in Bolívar's favor. The patriot guerrilla bands accepted his leadership; even more important, he gained the support of the principal llanero chieftain, José Antonio Páez. European developments also favored Bolívar. The end of the Napoleonic wars idled a large number of British soldiers; many of these veterans came to Venezuela, forming a British Legion that distinguished itself in battle by its valor. English merchants made loans that enabled Bolívar to secure men and arms for the coming campaign. Helpful too was the mulish attitude of Ferdinand VII, whose refusal to consider making any concessions to the colonists caused the English government to lose patience and regard with more friendly eyes the prospect of Spanish-American independence.

On the eve of the decisive campaign of 1819, Bolívar summoned to Angostura a makeshift congress that vested him with dictatorial powers. To this congress he presented a project for a constitution for Venezuela in which he urged the abolition of slavery and the distribution of land to revolutionary soldiers. But the proposed constitution also had some nondemocratic features. They included a president with virtually royal powers, a hereditary senate, and restriction of the suffrage and officeholding to the propertied and educated elite. The congress disregarded Bolívar's reform proposals but elected him president of the republic and adopted a constitution embodying many of his ideas.

The war, however, still had to be won. Bolívar's bold strategy for the liberation of Venezuela and Colombia envisaged striking a heavy blow at Spanish forces from a completely unexpected direction. While llanero cavalry under Páez distracted and pinned down the main body of Spanish troops in northern Venezuela with swift raids, Bolívar advanced with an army of some twenty-five hundred men along the winding Orinoco and Arauco rivers, across the plains, and then up the towering Colombian Andes until he reached the plateau where lay Bogotá, capital of New Granada. On the field of Boyacá the patriot army surprised and defeated the royalists in a short, sharp battle that netted sixteen hundred prisoners and

[3] *Selected Writings of Bolívar*, compiled by Vicente Lecuna and edited by Harold A. Bierck, Jr., 2 vols. (New York: Colonial Press, 1951), 1:103–122.

considerable supplies. Bogotá lay defenseless, and Bolívar entered the capital to the cheers of its people, who had suffered greatly under Spanish rule.

Leaving his aide, Francisco Santander, to organize a government, Bolívar hurried off to Angostura to prepare the liberation of Venezuela. Then thrilling news arrived from Spain; on January 1, 1820, a regiment awaiting embarkation for South America had mutinied, starting a revolt that forced Ferdinand to restore the liberal constitution of 1812 and give up his plans for the reconquest of the colonies. This news caused joy among the patriots, gloom and desertions among the Venezuelan royalists. In July 1821, the troops of Bolívar and Páez crushed the last important Spanish force in Venezuela at Carabobo. Save for some coastal towns and forts still held by beleaguered royalists, Venezuela was free.

Bolívar had already turned his attention southward. The independence of Spanish America remained precarious as long as the Spaniards held the immense mountain bastion of the central Andes. While Bolívar prepared a major offensive from Bogotá against Quito, he sent his able young lieutenant, Antonio José Sucre, by sea from Colombia's Pacific coast to seize the port of Guayaquil. Before Sucre even arrived, the creole party in Guayaquil revolted, proclaimed independence, and placed the port under Bolívar's protection. With his forces swelled by reinforcements sent by the Argentine general José de San Martín, Sucre advanced into the Ecuadoran highlands and defeated a Spanish army on the slopes of Mount Pichincha, near Quito. Bolívar, meanwhile, advancing southward from Bogotá along the Cauca River valley, encountered stiff royalist resistance, but this crumbled on news of Sucre's victory at Pichincha. The provinces composing the former viceroyalty of New Granada— the future republics of Venezuela, Colombia, Ecuador, and Panama—were now free from Spanish control. They were temporarily united into a large state named Colombia or Gran Colombia, established at the initiative of Bolívar by the union of New Granada and Venezuela in 1821.

The Southern Liberation Movement and San Martín

The time had come for the movement of liberation led by Bolívar to merge with that flowing northward from Argentina. Ever since the defeat of the British invasions of 1806–1807, the creole party, although nominally loyal to Spain, had effectively controlled Buenos Aires. The hero of the invasions and the temporary viceroy, Santiago Liniers, cooperated fully with the creole leaders. A new viceroy, sent by the Seville junta to replace Liniers, joined with the viceroy at Lima to crush abortive creole revolts in Upper Peru (Bolivia). But in Buenos Aires he walked softly, for he recognized the superior power of the creoles. Under their pressure he issued a decree permitting free trade with allied and neutral nations, a measure bitterly opposed by representatives of the Cádiz monopoly. But this concession could not save the Spanish regime. Revolution was in the air, and the creole leaders waited only, in the words of one of their number, for the figs to be ripe.

In May 1810, when word came that French troops had entered Seville and threatened Cádiz, the secret patriot society organized a demonstration that forced the viceroy to summon an open town meeting to decide the future government of the colony. This first Argentine congress voted to depose the viceroy and establish a junta to govern in the name of Ferdinand. The junta promptly attempted to consolidate its control of the vast viceroyalty. The interior provinces were subdued after sharp fighting. Montevideo, across the Río de la Plata on the Eastern Shore (modern Uruguay), remained in Spanish hands until 1814, when it fell to an Argentine siege. The junta met even more tenacious resistance from the gauchos of the Uruguayan pampa, led by José Gervasio Artigas, who demanded Uruguayan autonomy in a loose federal connection with Buenos Aires. The porteños (inhabitants of Buenos Aires) would have nothing to do with Artigas's gaucho democracy, and a new struggle began. It ended when Artigas, caught between the fire of Buenos Aires and that of Portuguese forces claiming Uruguay for Brazil, had to flee to Paraguay. Uruguay did not achieve independence until 1828.

The creole aristocracy in another portion of the old viceroyalty of La Plata, Paraguay, also suspected the designs of the Buenos Aires junta and defeated a porteño force sent to liberate Asunción. This done, the creole party in Asunción rose up, deposed Spanish officials, and proclaimed the independence of Paraguay. A key figure in this uprising was the remarkable Dr. José Rodríguez de Francia, soon to become his country's first president and dictator.

Efforts by the Buenos Aires junta to liberate the mountainous northern province of Upper Peru also failed. Two thrusts by a patriot army into this area were defeated and the invaders rolled back. The steep terrain, long lines of communication, and the apathy of the Bolivian Indians contributed to these defeats.

The Buenos Aires government also had serious internal problems. A dispute broke out between liberal supporters of the fiery Mariano Moreno, secretary of the junta and champion of social reform, and a conservative faction led by the great landowner Cornelio Saavedra. This dispute foreshadowed the liberal-conservative cleavage that dominated the first decades of Argentine history after independence. In 1813 a national assembly gave the country the name of the United Provinces of La Plata and enacted such reforms as the abolition of mita, encomienda, titles of nobility, and the Inquisition. A declaration of independence, however, was delayed until 1816.

Also 1816 was the year in which the military genius of José de San Martín broke the long-standing military stalemate. San Martín, born in 1778 in what is now northeastern Argentina, was a colonel in the Spanish army with twenty years of service behind him when revolution broke out in Buenos Aires. He promptly sailed for La Plata to offer his sword to the patriot junta. He was soon raised to the command of the army of Upper Peru, which was recuperating in Tucumán after a sound defeat at royalist hands. Perceiving that a frontal attack on the Spanish position in Upper Peru was doomed to failure, San Martín offered a plan for total victory that gained the support of the director of the United Provinces, Juan Martín de Pueyrredón. San Martín proposed a march over the Andes to liberate Chile, where a Spanish reaction had toppled the revolutionary regime established by Bernardo O'Higgins and other patriot leaders in 1810. This done, the united forces of La Plata and Chile would descend on Peru from the sea.

To mask his plans from Spanish eyes and gain time for a large organizational effort, San Martín obtained an appointment as governor of the province of Cuyo, whose capital, Mendoza, lay at the eastern end of a strategic pass leading across the Andes to Chile. He spent two years recruiting, training, and equipping his Army of the Andes. Like Bolívar, he used the promise of freedom to secure black and mulatto volunteers, and later declared they were his best soldiers. Chilean refugees fleeing the Spanish reaction in their country also joined his forces.

San Martín, methodical and thorough, demanded of the Buenos Aires government arms, munitions, food, and equipment of every kind. The director Pueyrredón ended one letter to San Martín on a note of humorous desperation:

I am sending the world, the flesh, and the devil! I don't know how I shall get out of the scrape I'm in to pay for all this, unless I declare bankruptcy, cancel my accounts with everyone, and clear out to join you, so that you can give me some of the dried beef I'm sending you. Damn it, don't ask me for anything else unless you want to hear that they found me in the morning dangling from a beam in the Fort!

In January 1817, the army began the crossing of the Andes. Its march over the frozen Andean passes equaled in difficulty Bolívar's scaling of the Colombian sierra. Twenty-one days later, the army issued onto Chilean soil. A decisive defeat of the Spanish army at Chacabuco in February opened the gates of Santiago to San Martín. He won another victory at Maipú (1818), in a battle that ended the threat to Chile's independence. Rejecting Chilean invitations to become supreme ruler of the republic, a post assumed by O'Higgins, San Martín began to prepare the attack by sea on Lima, fifteen hundred miles away.

The execution of his plan required the creation of a navy. He secured a number of ships in England and the United States and engaged a competent though eccentric naval officer, Thomas, Lord Cochrane, to organize the patriot navy. In August 1820, the expedition sailed for Peru in a fleet made up of seven ships of war and eighteen transports. San Martín landed his army about a hundred miles south of Lima but delayed moving on the Peruvian capital. He hoped to obtain its surrender by economic blockade, propaganda, and direct negotiation with the Spanish officials. The desire of the Lima aristocracy, creole and peninsular, to avoid an armed struggle that might unleash an Indian and slave revolt worked in favor of San Martín's strategy. In June 1821, the Spanish army evacuated Lima and retreated toward the Andes. San Martín entered the capital and in a festive atmosphere proclaimed the independence of Peru.

But his victory was far from complete. He had to deal with counterrevolutionary plots and the resistance of Lima's corrupt elite to his program of social reform, which included the end of Indian tribute and the grant of freedom to the children of slaves. San Martín's assumption of supreme military and civil power in August 1821 added to the factional opposition. Meanwhile, a large Spanish army maneuvered in front of Lima, challenging San Martín to a battle he dared not join with his much smaller force. Disheartened by the atmosphere of intrigue and hostility that surrounded him, San Martín became convinced that only monarchy could bring stability to Spanish America and sent a secret mission to Europe to search for a prince for the throne of Peru.

Such was the background of San Martín's departure for Guayaquil, where he met in conference with Bolívar on July 26 and 27, 1822. The agenda of the meeting included several points. One concerned the future of Guayaquil. San Martín claimed the port city for Peru; Bolívar, however, had already annexed it to Gran Colombia, confronting San Martín with a fait accompli. An-

other topic was the political future of all Spanish America. San Martín favored monarchy as the solution for the emergent chaos of the new states; Bolívar believed in a governmental system that would be republican in form, oligarchical in content. But the critical question before the two men was how to complete the liberation of the continent by defeating the Spanish forces in Peru.

San Martín's abrupt retirement from public life after the conference, the reluctance of the two liberators to discuss what was said there, and the meager authentic documentary record of the proceedings have surrounded the meeting with an atmosphere of mystery and produced two opposed and partisan interpretations. A view favored by Argentine historians holds that San Martín came to Guayaquil in search of military aid but was rebuffed by Bolívar, who was unwilling to share with a rival the glory of bringing the struggle for independence to an end; San Martín then magnanimously decided to leave Peru and allow Bolívar to complete the work he had begun. Venezuelan historians, on the other hand, argue that San Martín came to Guayaquil primarily in order to recover Guayaquil for Peru. The historians deny that San Martín asked Bolívar for more troops and insist that he left Peru for personal reasons having nothing to do with the conference.

Both interpretations tend to diminish the stature and sense of realism of the two liberators. San Martín was no martyr, nor was Bolívar an ambitious schemer who sacrificed San Martín to his passion for power and glory. San Martín must have understood that Bolívar alone combined the military, political, and psychological assets needed to liquidate the factional hornet's nest in Peru and gain final victory over the powerful Spanish army in the sierra. Given the situation in Lima, San Martín's presence there could only hinder the performance of those tasks. In this light, the decision of Bolívar to assume sole direction of the war and of San Martín to withdraw reflected a realistic appraisal of the Peruvian problem and the solution it required.

San Martín returned to Lima to find that in his absence his enemies had rallied and struck at him by driving his reforming chief minister, Bernardo Monteagudo, out of the country. San Martín made no effort to reassert his power. In September 1822, before the first Peruvian congress, he announced his resignation as protector and his impending departure. He returned to Buenos Aires by way of Chile, where the government of his friend O'Higgins was on the verge of collapse. In Buenos Aires the people seemed to have forgotten his existence. Accompanied by his daughter, he sailed for Europe at the end of 1823. He died in France in 1850 in virtual obscurity. His transfiguration into an Argentine national hero began a quarter-century later.

San Martín's departure left Lima and the territory under its control in serious danger of reconquest by the strong Spanish army in the sierra. Bolívar made no move to rescue the squabbling factions in Lima from their predicament; he allowed the situation to deteriorate until May 1823, when the Peruvian congress called on him for help. Then he sent Sucre with only a few thousand men, for he wanted to bring the Lima politicians to their knees. The scare produced by a brief reoccupation of the capital by the Spanish army prepared the creole leaders to accept Bolívar's absolute rule.

Bolívar arrived in Peru in September 1823. He required almost a year to achieve political stability and to weld the army he brought with him and the different national units under his command into a united force. After a month of difficult ascent of the sierra, in an altitude so high that Bolívar and most of his men suffered from mountain sickness, cavalry elements of the patriot and royalist armies clashed near the lake of Junín, and the Spaniards suffered defeat (August 6, 1824). The royalist commander, José de Canterac, retreated toward Cuzco. Leaving Sucre in command, Bolívar returned to Lima to gather reinforcements. To Sucre fell the glory of defeating the Spanish army in the last major engagement of the war, at Ayacucho (December 9, 1824). Only scattered resistance at some points in the highlands and on the coast remained to be mopped up. The work of continental liberation was achieved.

The Achievement of Brazilian Independence

In contrast to the political anarchy, economic dislocation, and military destruction in Spanish America, the drive toward independence of Brazil proceeded as a relatively bloodless transition between 1808 and 1822. The idea of Brazilian independence first arose in the late eighteenth century as a Brazilian reaction to the Portuguese policy of tightening political and economic control over the colony in the interests of the mother country. The first significant conspiracy against Portuguese rule, we recall, was organized in 1788–1789 in Minas Gerais, where rigid governmental control over the production and prices of gold and diamonds, as well as heavy taxes, caused much discontent, and where there existed a group of intellectuals educated in Europe and familiar with the ideas of the Enlightenment. But this conspiracy never went beyond the stage of discussion and was easily discovered and crushed. Other conspiracies in Río de Janeiro (1794), Bahia (1798), and Pernambuco (1801), and a brief revolt in Pernambuco (1817), reflected the influence of republican ideas over sections of the elite and even the lower strata of urban society. All proved abortive or were soon crushed. The stagnation of Brazilian life and the fear of slave owners that resistance to Portugal might spark slave insurrections effectively inhibited the spirit of revolt. Were it not for an accident of European history, the independence of Brazil might have long been delayed.

The French invasion of Portugal (1807), followed by the flight of the Portuguese court to Rio de Janeiro, brought large benefits to Brazil. Indeed, the transfer of the court in effect signified achievement of Brazilian independence. The Portuguese prince regent João opened Brazil's ports to the trade of friendly nations, permitted the rise of local industries, and founded a Bank of Brazil. In 1815 he elevated Brazil to the legal status of a kingdom co-equal with Portugal. In one sense, however, Brazil's new status signified the substitution of one dependence for another. Freed from Portuguese control, Brazil came under the economic domination of England, which obtained major tariff concessions and other privileges by the Strangford Treaty of 1810. One result was an influx of cheap machine-made goods that swamped the handicrafts industry of the country.

Brazilian elites took satisfaction in Brazil's new role and the growth of educational, cultural, and economic opportunities for their class. But this feeling was mixed with resentment at the thousands of Portuguese courtiers and hangers-on who came with the court and who competed with Brazilians for jobs and favors. Portuguese merchants in Brazil, for their part, were bitter over the passing of the Lisbon monopoly. Thus, the change in the status of Brazil sharpened the conflict between mazombos and reinóis.

The event that precipitated the break with the mother country was the revolution of 1820 in Portugal. The Portuguese revolutionists framed a liberal constitution for the kingdom, but they were conservative or reactionary in relation to Brazil. They demanded the immediate return of Dom João to Lisbon, an end to the system of dual monarchy that he had devised, and the restoration of the Portuguese commercial monopoly. Timid and vacillating, Dom João did not know which way to turn. Under the pressure of his courtiers, who hungered to return to Portugal and their lost estates, he finally approved the new constitution and sailed for Portugal. He left behind him, however, his son and heir, Dom Pedro, as regent of Brazil, and in a private letter advised him, in the event the Brazilians should demand independence, to assume leadership of the movement and set the crown of Brazil on his head. Pedro received the same advice from José Bonifácio de Andrada, a Brazilian scientist whose stay in Portugal had completely disillusioned him about the Portuguese capacity for colonial reform.

Soon it became clear that the Portuguese Côrtes intended to set the clock back by abrogating all the liberties and concessions won by Brazil since 1808. One of its decrees insisted on the immediate return of Dom Pedro from Brazil in order that he might complete his political education. The pace of events moved more rapidly

in 1822. On January 9, Dom Pedro, urged on by José Bonifácio de Andrada and other Brazilian advisers who perceived a golden opportunity to make an orderly transition to independence without the intervention of the masses, refused an order from the Côrtes to return to Portugal and issued his famous *fico* ("I remain"). On September 7, regarded by all Brazilians as Independence Day, he issued the even more celebrated Cry of Ipiranga, "Independence or Death!" In December 1822, having overcome slight resistance by Portuguese troops, Dom Pedro was formally proclaimed constitutional emperor of Brazil.

Mexico's Road to Independence

In New Spain, as in other colonies, the crisis of the Bourbon monarchy in 1808–1810 encouraged some creole leaders to strike a blow for self-rule or total independence under "the mask of Ferdinand." But in Mexico the movement for independence took an unexpected turn. Here the masses, instead of remaining aloof, joined the struggle and for a time managed to convert it from a private quarrel between two elites into an incipient social revolution.

In July 1808 news of Napoleon's capture of Charles IV and Ferdinand VI and his invasion of Spain reached Mexico City and provoked intense debates and maneuvers among Mexican elites to take advantage of these dramatic events. Faced with the prospect of an imminent collapse of Spain, creoles and peninsulars alike prepared to seize power and ensure that their group would control New Spain, whatever the outcome of the Spanish crisis. The creoles moved first. The Mexico City cabildo, a creole stronghold, called on the viceroy to summon an assembly to be chosen by the creole-dominated cabildos. This assembly, composed of representatives of various elite groups, would govern Mexico until Ferdinand VII, whose forced abdication was null and void, regained his throne. The viceroy, José de Iturrigaray, supported such a call noting that Spain was in "a state of anarchy."

The conservative landed elite that sponsored the movement for a colonial assembly, it must be stressed, desired autonomy or home rule within the Spanish empire, not independence. They had no intention of taking up arms in a struggle that might bring a dangerous intervention of the exploited classes and thus endanger their own personal and economic survival. The reforms that the chief creole ideologist, Fray Melchor de Talamantes, recommended to the proposed assembly suggested the limits of creole elite ambitions: abolition of the Inquisition and the ecclesiastical fuero (the clergy's privilege of exemption from civil courts), free trade, and measures to promote the reform of mining, agriculture, and industry.

The creole movement for home rule and free trade, however, posed a threat to the peninsular merchants whose prosperity depended on the continuance of the existing closed commercial system with Seville as its center. On the night of September 15, 1808, the merchants struck back. The wealthy peninsular merchant Gabriel de Yermo led the consulado's militia in a preemptive coup, ousting Viceroy Iturrigaray and arresting leading creole supporters of autonomy. A series of transient peninsular-dominated regimes then held power until a new viceroy, Francisco Javier de Venegas, arrived from Spain in September 1810.

The leaders of the creole aristocracy, mindful of its large property interests, did not respond to the peninsular counteroffensive. The leadership of the movement for creole control of Mexico's destinies now passed to a group consisting predominantly of "marginal elites"—upper-class individuals of relatively modest economic and social standing—in the Bajío, a geographic region roughly corresponding to the intendency of Querétaro.

The special economic and social conditions of this region help to explain its decisive role in the first stage of the Mexican struggle for independence. It was the most modern of Mexican regions in its agrarian and industrial structure. There were few Indian communities of the traditional type; the bulk of its population, Indians, free blacks, and castas (mixed-bloods), were partially Europeanized urban workers, miners, and peons or tenants of various types. Agriculture was dominated by large commercial irrigated estates producing wheat and other products for the upper classes; maize, the diet of the masses, was chiefly grown on marginal land by impoverished tenants. There was an important textile industry, which had experienced a shift from large obrajes using slaves and other coerced labor to a putting-out system in which merchant-financiers provided artisan families with cotton and wool, which they turned into cloth on their own looms, "forcing growing numbers of artisan families to exploit themselves by working long hours for little compensation." Mining was the most profitable and capital-intensive industry of the region; in some good years the largest mine at Guanajuato, the Valenciana, netted its owners over 1,000,000 pesos in profits.

The quasi-capitalist structure of the Bajío's economy, based largely on free wage labor, promoted a growth of workers' class consciousness and militancy. The mineworkers at Guanajuato, for example, resisted attempts to end their partidos (shares of the ores they mined over a given quota) by methods that included a production slowdown; the employers responded by calling in the militia to force resumption of full production. The Bajío's labor force experienced a decline of wage and living standards and employment opportunities in the last decades of the eighteenth century. These losses were a result of conditions over which they had no control: rapid population growth that enabled landowners to drive down wages or replace permanent workers by seasonal laborers; competition for domestic textiles from cheap industrially produced imports; and the rising cost of aging mines. These factors caused deep insecurity and resentment. Then in 1808 and 1809 drought and famine again struck the Bajío, aggravating all the existing tensions and grievances. As in the earlier drought and famine in 1785, the great landowners profited from the misery of the poor by holding their reserves of grain off the market until prices reached their peak. "These were hard times," says John Tutino,

"—except for profiteering landed elites." It was against this background of profound social unrest and a grave subsistence crisis that the struggle for Mexican independence began. The Bajío was its storm center, and the Bajío's peasantry and working class formed its spearhead.

In 1810 a creole plot for revolt was taking shape in the important political and industrial center of Querétaro. Only two of the conspirators belonged to the highest circle of the creole regional elite, and efforts to draw other prominent creoles into the scheme were rebuffed. The majority were "marginal elites"—struggling landowners, a grocer, an estate administrator, a parish priest. From the first the conspirators seem to have planned to mobilize the Indian and mixed-blood proletariat, probably because they doubted their ability to win over the majority of their class. If the motive of most of the plotters was the hope of raising troops, Miguel Hidalgo y Costilla, a priest in the town of Dolores and onetime rector of the colegio of San Nicolás at Valladolid, was inspired by a genuine sympathy with the natives. The scholarly Hidalgo had already called the attention of Spanish authorities to himself by his freethinking ideas; he was also known for his scientific interests and his efforts to develop new industries in his parish.

Informed that their plot had been denounced to Spanish officials, the conspirators held an urgent council and decided to launch their revolt although arrangements were not complete. On Sunday, September 16, 1810, Hidalgo called on the people of his parish, assembled for Mass, to rise against their Spanish rulers. Here, as elsewhere in Spanish America, the "mask of Ferdinand" came into play; Hidalgo claimed to be leading an insurrection in support of a beloved king treacherously captured and deposed by godless Frenchmen. In less than two weeks the insurgent leaders had assembled thousands of rebels and began a march on the industrial and mining center of Guanajuato. On the march Hidalgo secured a banner bearing the image of the Virgin of Guadalupe and proclaimed her the patron of his movement, thus appealing to the religious devotion of his followers. All along the route the established elites held back from joining the revolt. They watched with dismay as the rebels looted stores and took the crops provided by the bountiful harvest of 1810, after two years of drought and famine. The capture of Guanajuato on September 28 was accomplished with the aid of several thousand mineworkers, who joined in storming the massive municipal granary in which Spanish officials, militia, and local elites attempted to hold out. It was followed by the killing of hundreds of Spaniards in the granary and the city. The massacre and sack of Guanajuato was a turning point in the rebellion, for it brought into the open the conflict between the basic objective of Hidalgo and his allies—creole domination of an autonomous or independent Mexico—and the thirst for revenge and social justice of their lower-class followers. Learning of the events at Guanajuato, the great majority of the creole elite recoiled in horror before the elemental violence of a movement that Hidalgo was unable to control.

After his first victories, Hidalgo issued decrees abolishing slavery and tribute—the yearly head tax paid by Indians and mulattos. Three months later, from his headquarters at Guadalajara, in his first and only reference to the land problem, he ordered that the Indian communal lands in the vicinity of the city that had been rented to Spaniards be returned to the Indians; it was his wish that "only the Indians in their respective pueblos should enjoy the use of those lands." Moderate though they were, these reforms gave the Mexican revolution a popular character absent from the movement for independence in South America, but further alienated many creoles who may have desired autonomy or independence—but not social revolution. On the other hand, these reforms did not go far enough to redress the fundamental grievances of Hidalgo's peasant and working-class followers in regions like the Bajío and Jalisco: landlessness, starvation wages and high rents, lack of tenant security, and the monopoly of grain by profiteering landowners. John Tutino calls attention to the dilemma of Hidalgo and his creole allies. "Hidalgo and his allies among the rebel leaders were only marginal

AÑO DE 1834

Miguel Hidalgo's leadership in the struggle for independence and his martyrdom in that struggle assured him an early place in the pantheon of Mexico's national heroes. In this allegorical painting of 1843, he crowns Mexico and assists in breaking its Spanish chains. (Instituto Nacional de Antropología e Historia)

elites, but they retained elite perspectives. They would not propose changes that might threaten the established structure of Mexico's economy and society." In the absence of a clearly defined program of structural social and economic reform, Hidalgo's followers vented their rage at an intolerable situation by killing Spaniards and plundering the properties of creoles and peninsulars alike.

Hidalgo proved unable to weld his rebel horde into a disciplined army or to capitalize on his early victories. Having defeated a royalist army near Mexico City, he camped outside the city for three days and then, after his demand for its surrender was rejected, inexplicably withdrew from the almost defenseless capital without attacking. It has been suggested that he feared a repetition of the atrocities that followed earlier victories or that he believed that he could not hold the great city without the support of the local population. The peasantry of the central highlands, who still possessed communal lands that satisfied their minimal needs and supplemented their meager crops by wage labor on large haciendas, did not rally to Hidalgo's cause. With his army melting away through desertions, Hidalgo retreated toward the Bajío. Driven out of Guanajuato by royalist forces, Hidalgo and other rebel leaders fled northward, hoping to establish new bases for their movement in Coahuila and Texas. Less than one year after his revolt had begun, Hidalgo was captured as he fled toward the United States border, condemned as a heretic and subversive by an inquisitorial court, and executed by a firing squad.

The defeat and death of Hidalgo did not end the insurrection he had begun. The fires of revolt continued to smolder over vast areas of Mexico. New leaders arose who learned from the failure of Hidalgo's tactics. Many, abandoning the effort to defeat the royalist forces with their superior arms and training in conventional warfare developed a flexible and mobile guerrilla style of fighting. The Spaniards themselves had effectively employed guerrilla warfare—a war of swift movement by small units that strike and flee—in their struggle against Napoleon, taking advantage of a familiar terrain and the support of rural populations to foil pursuit and repression. The new Mexican rebel strategy was not to win a quick victory but to exhaust the enemy and undermine his social and economic base by pillaging the stores and haciendas of his elite allies, disrupting trade, and creating war weariness and hostility toward an increasingly arbitrary colonial regime.

Following Hidalgo's death, a mestizo priest, José María Morelos, assumed supreme command of the revolutionary movement. Morelos had ministered to poor congregations in the hot, humid Pacific lowlands of Michoacán before offering his services to Hidalgo, who asked him to organize insurrection in that area. Economic and social conditions in the coastal lowlands region bore some resemblance to those of the Bajío; its principal industries, sugar, cotton, and indigo,

were in decline as a result of competition from regions closer to highland markets and from imported cloth. As a result the position of estate tenants and laborers had become increasingly dependent and insecure. The material conditions of Indian villagers had also deteriorated as a result of the renting of community lands by village leaders to outsiders, a practice that left many families without the minimal land needed for subsistence.

The discontent generated by these conditions provided Morelos and his insurgent movement with a mass base in the coastal lowlands. Morelos was sensitive to the problems and needs of the area's rural folk. Like Hidalgo, he ordered an end to slavery and tribute. He also ended the rental of Indian community lands and abolished the community treasuries (*cajas de comunidad*), whose funds were often misused by village notables or drained off by royal officials; henceforth, the villagers were to keep the proceeds of their labor. Morelos also extended Hidalgo's program of social reform by prohibiting all forced labor and forbidding the use of all racial terms except gachupines, applied to the hated peninsular Spaniards. There seems little doubt that in principle Morelos favored a radical land reform. In a "plan" found among his papers, he proposed the division of all haciendas greater than two leagues into smaller plots, denounced a situation in which "a single individual owns vast extents of uncultivated land and enslaves thousands of people who must work the land as *gañanes* [peons] or slaves," and proclaimed the social benefits of the small landholding. Some of Morelos' supporters were members of the secret society known as the Guadalupes. Mostly composed of middle-class professionals from Mexico City, the Guadalupes urged the breakup of the haciendas as a means of weakening elite landed power. But Morelos' freedom of action was restrained by his links with the creole landowning elite, some of whom were his lieutenants and whose property he promised to respect.

A brilliant guerrilla leader who substituted strict discipline, training, and centralized direction for the loose methods of Hidalgo, Morelos, having established a firm base in the Pacific low-lands, advanced toward the strategic central highlands and the capital. His thrust into the rich sugar-producing area (modern Morelos) just south of Mexico City failed to gain sufficient support from the local Indian communities, which retained substantial landholdings, and he was forced to retreat southward into the rugged mountainous region of Oaxaca. His military efforts were hampered by differences with fractious civilian allies and by his decision to establish a representative government at a time when his military situation was turning precarious. In the fall of 1813 a congress which he had convened at Chilpancingo declared Mexico's independence, enacted Morelos' social reforms, and vested him with supreme military and executive power. But in the months that followed, the tide of war turned against the insurgent cause, in part because of tactical mistakes by Morelos that involved abandonment of fluid guerrilla warfare in favor of fixed position warfare, illustrated by his prolonged siege of the fortress of Acapulco. In late 1813 Morelos suffered several defeats at the hands of royalist forces directed by the able and aggressive viceroy Felix Calleja.

The defeat of Napoleon and the return of the ferociously reactionary Ferdinand VII to the throne of Spain in 1814 released thousands of soldiers who could be sent overseas to suppress the Spanish American revolts. The congress of Chilpancingo, put to flight, became a wandering body whose squabbling and need for protection diverted Morelos' attention from the all-important military problem. Hoping to revitalize the rebel cause and gain creole elite support by offering an alternative to Ferdinand's brutal despotism, the congress met at Apatzingan and drafted a liberal constitution (October 1814) that provided for a republican frame of government and included an article proclaiming the equality of citizens before the law and freedom of speech and the press. In the course of the year 1815, unrelenting royalist pressure forced the congress to flee from place to place. In November, fighting a rearguard action that enabled the congress to escape, Morelos was captured by a royalist force

and brought to the capital. Like Hidalgo, he was found guilty by an Inquisition court of heresy and treason; he was shot by a firing squad on December 22, 1815.

The great guerrilla leader had died, but the revolutionary movement, although fragmented, continued. Indeed, the struggle between numerous insurgent bands and the Spanish counterinsurgency reached new heights of virulence between 1815 and 1820. Avoiding the mistakes of Hidalgo and even Morelos, the rebel leaders shunned pitched battles and made no effort to capture large population centers. Instead, they conducted a fluid warfare in which small units attacked loyalist haciendas that they sacked and destroyed, disrupted or levied tolls on trade, severed communications, and controlled large stretches of the countryside. They fled when pursued by counterinsurgent forces and reappeared when the overextended Spanish troops has departed. The destructive effects of a hopeless war on the economy, the heavy taxes imposed on all inhabitants by regional commanders and local juntas for the support of that war, and the harsh treatment meted out not only to insurgents but to high-ranking creoles who favored compromise and autonomy, alienated even the most loyal elements of the creole elite.

These elements, as well as many conservative Spaniards, sought a way out of the impasse that would avoid radical social change under a republican regime of the kind proposed by Morelos. A way out seemed to appear in 1820 when a liberal revolt in Spain forced Ferdinand VII to accept the constitution of 1812. Mexican deputies elected to the Spanish Cortes or parliament proposed a solution that would have retained ties with Spain but granted New Spain and the other American "kingdoms" autonomy within the empire. The Spanish majority in the Cortes rejected the proposal and sealed the doom of the empire.

The radical reforms adopted by the Cortes in 1820, including the abolition of the ecclesiastical and military fueros, antagonized conservative landlords, clergy, army officers, and merchants, whether creole or peninsular. Fearing the loss of privileges, they schemed to separate Mexico from the mother country and to establish independence under conservative auspices. Their instrument was the creole officer Agustín de Iturbide, who had waged implacable war against the insurgents. Iturbide offered peace and reconciliation to the principal rebel leader, Vicente Guerrero. His plan combined independence, monarchy, the supremacy of the Roman Catholic church, and the civil equality of creoles and peninsulars. Guerrero was a sincere liberal and republican, Iturbide an unprincipled opportunist who dreamed of placing a crown on his own head. For the moment, however, Iturbide's program offered advantages to both sides, and Guerrero reluctantly accepted it. The united forces of Iturbide and Guerrero swiftly overcame scattered loyalist resistance. On September 28, 1821, Iturbide proclaimed Mexican independence, and eight months later an elected congress summoned by Iturbide confirmed him as Agustín I, emperor of Mexico.

Despite its tinsel splendor, Iturbide's empire had no popular base. Within a few months, Agustín I had to abdicate, with a warning never to return. Hoping for a comeback, Iturbide returned from England in 1824 and landed on the coast with a small party. He was promptly captured by troops of the new republican regime and shot.

Latin American Independence: A Reckoning

After more than a decade of war, accompanied by immense loss of life and property, most of Latin America had won its political independence. The revolutions were accompanied or quickly followed by a number of social changes. Independence brought the death of the Inquisi-

tion, the end of legal discrimination on the basis of race, and the abolition of titles of nobility in most lands. It also gave an impetus to the abolition of slavery, to the founding of public schools, and to similar reforms. All these changes, however, were marginal; independence left intact the existing economic and social structures. This was natural, for the creole elite that headed the movement had no intention of transforming the existing order. They sought to replace the peninsulars in the seats of power and to open their ports to the commerce of the world but desired no change of labor and land systems. Indeed, their interests as producers of raw materials and foodstuffs for sale in the markets of Europe and North America required the maintenance of the system of great estates worked by a semiservile native proletariat. No agrarian reform accompanied independence. The haciendas abandoned by or confiscated from loyalists usually fell into the hands of the creole aristocracy. Some land also passed into the possession of mestizo or mulatto officers, who were assimilated into the creole elite and as a rule promptly forgot the groups from which they had come.

Instead of broadening the base of landownership in Latin America, the revolutions actually helped to narrow it. The liberal, individualist ideology of the revolutionary governments undermined Indian communal land tenure in some cases by requiring the division of community lands among its members. This process facilitated the usurpation of Indian land by creole landlords and hastened the transformation of the Indian peasantry into a class of peons or serfs on white haciendas (see Chapters 9 and 10). Since no structural economic change took place, aristocratic values continued to dominate Latin American society, despite an elaborate façade of republican constitutions and law codes.

Part 2

Latin America in the Nineteenth Century

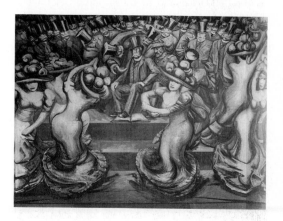

After winning their independence, the new Latin American states began a long, uphill struggle to achieve economic and political stability. They faced immense obstacles, for independence, as previously noted, was not accompanied by economic and social changes that could spur rapid progress—for example, no redistribution of land and income in favor of the lower classes took place. The large estate, generally operated with primitive methods and slave or peon labor, continued to dominate economic life. Far from diminishing, the influence of the landed aristocracy actually increased as a result of the leading military role it played in the wars of independence and of the passing of Spanish authority.

Economic life stagnated, for the anticipated large-scale influx of foreign capital did not materialize, and the European demand for Latin American staples remained far below expectations. Free trade brought increased commercial activity to the coasts, but this increase was offset by the near destruction of some local craft industries by cheap, factory-made European goods. The sluggish pace of economic activity and the relative absence of interregional trade and true national markets encouraged local self-sufficiency, isolation, political instability, and even chaos.

As a result of these adverse factors, the period from about 1820 to about 1870 was for many Latin American countries an age of violence, of alternate dictatorship and revolution. Its symbol was the *caudillo* (strong man), whose power was always based on force, no matter what kind of constitution the country had. Usually, the caudillo ruled with the aid of a coalition of lesser caudillos, each supreme in his region. Whatever their methods, the caudillos generally displayed some regard for republican ideology and institutions. Political parties, bearing such labels as "conservative" and "liberal," "unitarian" and "federalist," were active in most of the new states. Conservatism drew most of its support from the great landowners and their urban allies. Liberalism typically attracted provincial landowners, professional men, and other groups that had en-

joyed little power in the past and were dissatisfied with the existing order. As a rule, conservatives sought to retain many of the social arrangements of the colonial era and favored a highly centralized government. Liberals, often inspired by the example of the United States, usually advocated a federal form of government, guarantees of individual rights, lay control of education, and an end to special privileges for the clergy and military. Neither party displayed much interest in the problems of the Indian peasantry and other lower-class groups.

Beginning in about 1870, the accelerating tempo of the Industrial Revolution in Europe stimulated a more rapid change in the Latin American economy and politics. European capital flowed into the area, creating the facilities needed to expand and modernize production and trade. The pace and degree of economic progress of the various countries were very uneven, and depended largely on their geographic position and natural resources.

Extreme one-sidedness was a feature of the new economic order. One or two products became the basis of each country's prosperity, making it highly vulnerable to fluctuations in the world demand and the price of these commodities. Meanwhile, other sectors of the economy remained stagnant or even declined through diversion of labor and land to other industries.

The late nineteenth-century expansion had two other characteristics: in the main, it took place within the framework of the hacienda system of land tenure and labor, and it was accompanied by a steady growth of foreign control over the natural and man-made resources of the region. Thus, by 1900 a new structure of dependency, or colonialism, had arisen, called neo-colonialism, with Great Britain and later the United States replacing Spain and Portugal as the dominant power in the area.

The new economic order demanded peace and continuity in government, and after 1870 political conditions in Latin America did, in fact, grow more stable. Old party lines dissolved as conservatives adopted the positivist dogma of science and progress, while liberals abandoned their concern with constitutional methods and civil liberties in favor of an interest in material prosperity. A new type of "progressive" caudillo—Porfirio Díaz in Mexico, Rafael Núñez in Colombia, Antonio Guzmán Blanco in Venezuela—symbolized the politics of acquisition. The cycle of dictatorship and revolution continued in many lands, but the revolutions became less frequent and less devastating.

These are some major trends in the political and economic history of Latin America in the period extending from about 1820 to 1900. Naturally, these trends were accompanied by other changes in the Latin American way of life and culture, notably the development of a powerful literature that often sought not only to mirror Latin American society but to change it. In Part 2, we shall present short histories of four leading Latin American countries—Mexico, Argentina, Chile, and Brazil—in the nineteenth century. All four contain themes and problems common to the area in that period, but each displays variations that reflect the specific backgrounds of the different states.

Chapter 9

Dictators and Revolutions

Independence did not bring Latin America the ordered freedom and prosperity that the liberators had hoped for. In most of the new states, decades of civil strife followed the passing of Spanish and Portuguese rule. Bolívar reflected the disillusionment of many patriot leaders when he wrote in 1829: "There is no good faith in America, nor among the nations of America. Treaties are scraps of paper; constitutions, printed matter; elections, battles; freedom, anarchy; and life, a torment." The contrast between Latin American stagnation and disorder and the meteoric advance of the former English colonies—the United States—intensified the pessimism and self-doubt of some Latin American leaders and intellectuals.

The Fruits of Independence

Frustration of the great hopes with which the struggle for liberation began was inevitable, for independence was not accompanied by economic and social changes that could shatter the colonial mold. Aside from the passing of the Spanish and Portuguese trade monopolies, the colonial economic and social structures remained intact. The hacienda, fazenda, or estancia, employing archaic techniques and a labor force of peons or slaves, continued to dominate agriculture; no significant class of small farmers arose to challenge the economic and political might of the great landowners. Indeed, the revolutions strengthened the power of the landed aristocracy by removing the agencies of Spanish rule—viceroys, audiencias, intendants—and by weakening the ingrained habits of obedience to a central authority. In contrast, all other colonial elites—the merchant class, weakened by the expulsion or emigration of many loyalist merchants; the mine owners, ruined by wartime destruction or confiscation of their properties; and the church hierarchy, often in disgrace for having sided with Spain—emerged from the conflict with diminished weight.

To their other sources of influence the landed aristocracy added the prestige of a military elite crowned with the laurels of victory, for many revolutionary officers had arisen from its ranks. The militarization of the new states as a result of years of destructive warfare and postwar instability assured a large political role for this officer group. Standing armies that often consumed more than half of the national budgets arose. Not content with the role of guardians of order and national security, the military became arbiters of political disputes, as a rule intervening in favor of the conservative landowning interests and the urban elites with whom the great landowners were closely linked.

Economic Stagnation

Revolutionary leaders had expected that a vast expansion of foreign trade, which would aid economic recovery, would follow the passing of Spanish commercial monopoly. In fact, some countries, favored by their natural resources or geographic position, soon recovered from the revolutionary crisis and scored modest to large economic advances; they included Brazil (coffee and sugar), Argentina (hides), and Chile (metals and hides). But others, such as Mexico, Bolivia, and Peru, whose mining economies had suffered shattering blows, failed to recover colonial levels of production.

Several factors accounted for the economic stagnation that plagued many of the new states in the first half of the nineteenth century. Independence was not accompanied by a redistribution of land and income that might have stimulated a growth of internal markets and productive forces. The anticipated large-scale influx of foreign capital did not materialize, partly because political disorder discouraged foreign investment, partly because Europe and the United States, then financing their own industrial revolutions, had as yet little capital to export. Exports of Latin American staples also remained below expectations, for Europe still viewed Latin America primarily as an outlet for manufactured goods, especially English textiles. The resulting flood of cheap, factory-made European products damaged local craft industries and drained the new states of their stocks of gold and silver, creating a chronic balance-of-trade problem. The British conquest of the Latin American markets further weakened the local merchant class, which was unable to compete with its English rivals. By mid-century the wealthiest and most prestigious merchant houses, from Mexico City to Buenos Aires and Valparaíso, bore English names. Iberian merchants, however, continued to dominate the urban and provincial retail trade in many areas.

In their totality, these developments retarded the development of native capitalism and capitalist relations and reinforced the dominant role of the hacienda in the economic and political life of the new states. The deepening stagnation of the interior of these nations, which was aggravated by lack of roads and by natural obstacles to communication (such as jungles and mountains), intensified tendencies toward regionalism and the domination of regions by caudillos great and small, who were usually local large landowners.[1] The sluggish tempo of economic activity encouraged these caudillos to employ their private followings of peons and retainers as pawns in the game of politics and revolution on a national scale. Indeed, politics and revolution became in some countries a form of economic activity that compensated for the lack of other opportunities,

---

[1] The term *caudillo* is commonly applied to politico-military leaders who held power on the national and regional level in Latin America before more or less stable parliamentary government became the norm in the area beginning about 1870. Military ability and charisma are qualities often associated with caudillos, who came in many guises, but not all possessed the same qualities. Since the semifeudal conditions that gave rise to the caudillo still survive in parts of Latin America, it can be said that caudillos and *caudillismo* still exist.

since the victors, having gained control of the all-important customhouse (which collected duties on imports and exports) and other official sources of revenue, could reward themselves and their followers with government jobs, contracts, grants of public land, and other favors.

Politics: The Conservative and Liberal Programs

The political systems of the new states made large formal concessions to the liberal bourgeois ideology of the nineteenth century. With the exception of Brazil, all the new states adopted the republican form of government (Mexico had two brief intervals of imperial rule) and paid their respects to the formulas of parliamentary and representative government. Their constitutions provided for presidents, congresses, and courts; often they contained elaborate safeguards of individual rights.

These façades of modernity, however, poorly concealed the dictatorial or oligarchical reality beneath. Typically, the chief executive was a caudillo whose power rested on force, no matter what the constitutional form; usually, he ruled with the support of a coalition of lesser caudillos, each more or less supreme in his own domain. The supposed independence of the judicial and legislative branches was a fiction. As a rule, elections were exercises in futility. Since the party in power generally counted the votes, the opposition had no alternative but revolt.

Literacy and property qualifications disfranchised most Indians and mixed-bloods; where they had the right to vote, the *patrón* (master) often herded them to the polls to vote for him or his candidates. Whether liberal or conservative, all sections of the ruling class agreed on keeping the peasantry, gauchos, and other "lower orders" on the margins of political life, on preventing their emergence as groups with collective philosophies and goals. The very privileges that the new creole constitutions and law codes granted the Indians—equality before the law, the "right" to divide and dispose of their communal lands—

weakened the solidarity of the native people and their ability to resist the competitive individualism of the creole world. However, especially gifted, ambitious, and fortunate members of these marginal groups were sometimes co-opted into the creole elite and provided some of its most distinguished leaders; two examples are the Zapotec Indian Benito Juárez in Mexico and the mestizo president Andrés Santa Cruz in Bolivia.

At first glance, the political history of Latin America in the first half-century after independence, with its dreary alternation of dictatorship and revolt, seems pointless and trivial. But the political struggles of this period were more than disputes over spoils between sections of a small upper class. Genuine social and ideological cleavages helped to produce those struggles and the bitterness with which they were fought. Such labels as "conservative" and "liberal," "unitarian" and "federalist," assigned by the various parties to themselves or each other, were more than masks in a pageant, although opportunism contributed to the ease with which some leaders assumed and discarded these labels.

Generally speaking, conservatism reflected the interests of the traditional holders of power and privilege, men who had a stake in maintaining the existing order. Hence, the great landowners, the upper clergy, the higher ranks of the military and the civil bureaucracy, and monopolistic merchant groups tended to be conservatives. Liberalism, in contrast, appealed to those groups that in colonial times had little or no access to the main structures of economic and political power and were naturally eager to alter the existing order. Thus, liberalism drew much support from provincial landowners, lawyers and other professional men (the groups most receptive to new ideas), shopkeepers, and artisans; it also appealed to ambitious, aspiring Indians and mixed-bloods. But regional conflicts and clan or family loyalties often cut across the lines of social and occupational cleavage, complicating the political picture.

Liberals wanted to break up the hierarchical social structure inherited from the colonial period. They had a vision of their countries remade into dynamic middle-class states on the model of the United States or England. Inspired by the success of the United States, they usually favored a federal form of government, guarantees of individual rights, lay control of education, and an end to a special legal status for the clergy and military. In their modernizing zeal, liberals sometimes called for abolition of entails (which restricted the right to inherit property to a particular descendant or descendants of the owner), dissolution of convents, confiscation of church wealth, and abolition of slavery. The federalism of the liberals had a special appeal for secondary regions of the new states, eager to develop their resources and free themselves from domination by capitals and wealthy primary regions.

Conservatives typically upheld a strong centralized government, the religious and educational monopoly of the Roman Catholic church, and the special privileges (fueros) of the clergy and military. They distrusted such radical novelties as freedom of speech and the press and religious toleration. Conservatives, in short, sought to salvage as much of the colonial social order as was compatible with the new republican system. Indeed, some conservative leaders ultimately despaired of that system and dreamed of implanting monarchy in their countries.

Neither conservatives nor liberals displayed much interest in the problems of the Indian, black, and mixed-blood masses that formed the majority of people in most Latin American countries. Liberals, impatient with the supposed backwardness of the Indians, regarded their communalism as an impediment to the development of a capitalist spirit of enterprise and initiated legislation providing for the division of communal lands—a policy that favored land grabbing at the expense of Indian villages. Despite their theoretical preference for small landholdings and a rural middle class, liberals recoiled from any program of radical land reform. Conservatives, for their part, correctly regarded the great estate as the very foundation of their power. As traditionalists, however, the conservatives sometimes claimed to continue the Spanish paternalist policy toward the Indians and enjoyed some support among the natives, who tended to be suspicious of all innovations.

This summary of the conservative and liberal programs for Latin America in the first half-century after independence inevitably overlooks variations from the theoretical liberal and conservative norms—variations that reflected the specific conditions and problems of the different states. An examination of the history of four leading Latin American countries in this period, Mexico, Argentina, Chile, and Brazil, reveals not only certain common themes but a rich diversity of political experience.

Mexico

The struggle for Mexican independence, begun by the radical priests Hidalgo and Morelos, was completed by the creole officer Agustín de Iturbide, who headed a coalition of creole and peninsular conservatives terrified at the prospect of being governed by the liberal Spanish constitution of 1812, which was reestablished in 1820. Independence, achieved under such conservative auspices, meant that Mexico's economic and social patterns underwent little change. The great hacienda continued to dominate the countryside in many areas. Although Indian villages managed to retain substantial community lands until after mid-century and even improved their economic and political position somewhat with the passing of Spanish centralized authority, the trend toward usurpation of Indian lands grew stronger as a result of the lapse of Spanish protective legislation. Peons and tenants on the haciendas often suffered from debt servitude, miserable wages, oppressive rents, and excessive religious fees. At the constitutional convention of 1856–1857, the liberal Ponciano Arriaga declared:

With some honorable exceptions, the rich landowners of Mexico . . . resemble the feudal lords of the Middle Ages. On his seigneurial lands, with more or less formalities, the landowner makes and executes laws, administers justice and exercises civil power, imposes taxes and fines, has his

184

own jails and irons, metes out punishments and tortures, monopolizes commerce, and forbids the conduct without his permission of any business but that of the estate.[2]

The church continued to wield diminished but still considerable economic and spiritual power. An anonymous contemporary writer reflected the disillusionment of the lower classes with the fruits of independence: "Independence is only a name. Previously they ruled us from Spain, now from here. It is always the same priest on a different mule. But as for work, food, and clothing, there is no difference."

The Mexican Economy

The ravages of war had left mine shafts flooded, haciendas deserted, the economy stagnant. The end of the Spanish commercial monopoly, however, brought a large increase in the volume of foreign trade; the number of ships entering Mexican ports jumped from 148 in 1823 to 639 in 1826. But exports did not keep pace with imports, leaving a trade deficit that had to be covered by exporting precious metals. The drain of gold and silver aggravated the problems of the new government, which inherited a bankrupt treasury and had to support a swollen bureaucracy and an officer class ready to revolt against any government that suggested a cut in their numbers or pay. The exodus of Spanish merchants and their capital added to the economic problems of the new state.

Foreign loans appeared to be the only way out of the crisis. In 1824–1825, English bankers made loans to Mexico amounting to 32 million pesos, guaranteed by Mexican customs revenues. Of this amount the Mexicans received only a little more than 11 million pesos, as the bankers, Barclay and Company, went bankrupt before all the money due to Mexico from the loan proceeds was paid. By 1843 unpaid interest and principal had

raised the nation's foreign debt to more than 54 million pesos. This mounting foreign debt not only created crushing interest burdens but threatened Mexico's independence and territorial integrity, for behind foreign capitalists stood governments that might threaten intervention in case of default.

Foreign investments, mainly from Britain, however, made possible a partial recovery of the decisive mining sector. Old mines, abandoned and flooded during the wars, were reopened, but the available capital proved inadequate, the technical problems of reconstruction were greater than anticipated, and production remained on a relatively low level.

An ambitious effort to revive and modernize Mexican industry also got under way, spurred by the founding in 1830 of the *Banco de Avío,* which provided governmental assistance to industry. Manufacturing, paced by textiles, made some limited progress in the three decades after independence. Leading industrial centers included Mexico City, Puebla, Guadalajara, Durango, and Veracruz. But shortages of capital, lack of a consistent policy of protection for domestic industry, and a socioeconomic structure that sharply limited the internal market hampered the growth of Mexican factory capitalism. By 1843 the Banco de Avío had to close its doors for lack of funds. The Mexican economy, therefore, continued to be based on mining and agriculture. Mexico's principal exports were precious metals, especially silver, and such agricultural products as tobacco, coffee, vanilla, cochineal, and henequen (a plant fiber used in rope and twine). Imports consisted primarily of manufactured goods that Mexican industry could not supply.

Politics: Liberals versus Conservatives

A liberal-conservative cleavage dominated Mexican political life in the half-century after independence. That conflict was latent from the moment that the "liberator" Iturbide, the former scourge of insurgents, rode into Mexico City on September 27, 1821, flanked on either side by two

[2] Francisco Zarco, *Historia del congreso estraordinario constituyente de 1856 y 1857,* 2 vols. (México, 1857), 1:555.

MEXICO
1821

San Antonio

Rio Grande

GULF OF MEXICO

Mexico City

Veracruz

BR. HONDURAS

Guatemala

UNITED PROVINCES OF
CENTRAL AMERICA
1823-1839

ATLANTIC OCEAN

BAHAMA IS.
(Br.)

PUERTO RICO
(Sp.)

CUBA
(Sp.)

HAITI
1804

CARIBBEAN SEA

TRINIDAD
(Br.)

Panama

Caracas

Bogotá

GRAN COLOMBIA
1819-1830

Quito

GALAPAGOS IS.

BR. GUIANA

DUTCH GUIANA

FR. GUIANA

Indefinite Boundary

PERU
1821

Lima

EMPIRE OF BRAZIL
1822

Bahia

BOLIVIA
1825

Sucre

PACIFIC OCEAN

PARAGUAY
1813

Asunción

Rio de Janeiro

CHILE
1817

Santiago

UNITED
PROVINCES
OF
LA PLATA
1816

URUGUAY
1828

Montevideo

Buenos Aires

0   500   1000 Miles

0   500   1000 Kilometers

LATIN AMERICA IN 1830

186 insurgent generals, Vicente Guerrero and Guadalupe Victoria, firm republicans and liberals. The fall of Iturbide in 1823 cleared the way for the establishment of a republic. But it soon became apparent that the republicans were divided into liberals and conservatives, federalists and centralists.

The constitution of 1824 represented a compromise between liberal and conservative interests. It appeased regional economic interests, which were fearful of a too-powerful central government, by creating nineteen states that possessed taxing power; their legislatures, each casting one vote, chose the president and vice president for four-year terms. The national legislature was made bicameral, with an upper house (Senate) and a lower house (Chamber of Deputies). By assuring the creation of local civil bureaucracies, the federalist structure also satisfied the demand of provincial middle classes for greater access to political activity and office. But the constitution had a conservative tinge as well: although the church lost its monopoly of education, Catholicism was proclaimed the official religion, and the fueros of the church and the army were specifically confirmed.

A hero of the war of independence, the liberal general Guadalupe Victoria, was elected first president under the new constitution. Anxious to preserve unity, Victoria brought the conservative Lucas Alamán into his cabinet. But this era of good feeling was very short-lived; by 1825, Alamán was forced out of the government. The liberal-conservative cleavage now assumed the form of a rivalry between two Masonic lodges, the York Rite lodge, founded by the American minister Joel Roberts Poinsett, and the Scottish Rite lodge, sponsored by the British chargé d'affaires Henry Ward. Their rivalry reflected the Anglo-American competition for economic and political influence in Mexico. The old mining and landowning aristocracy, which looked to Great Britain for leadership and assistance in the economic and political reconstruction of Mexico on a sound conservative basis, formed a pro-British faction; the liberals and federalists, who regarded the United States as a model for their own reform program, formed a pro-American *Yorkino* faction.

The fate of the thousands of Spaniards, including many wealthy merchants who remained in Mexico after the fall of the colonial regime, soon became a major political issue. Spain's continued occupation of the fortress of Veracruz until 1825, its refusal (until 1836) to recognize Mexican independence, and the discovery of plots against independence in which Spaniards were implicated created much anti-Spanish feeling. But conservative leaders like Alamán strongly opposed ouster of the Spaniards as being harmful to the economy and to the Mexican upper class, threatened by the ambitions of upstart middle-class politicians. Nonetheless, in 1827 the liberal Yorkinos pushed through Congress a decree of expulsion against the Spaniards. Although not fully enforced, the decree hastened the transformation of the conservative and liberal factions into political parties.

The Conservative party represented the old landed and mining aristocracy, the clerical and military hierarchy, monopolistic merchants, and some manufacturers. Its intellectual spokesman and organizer was Lucas Alamán, statesman, champion of industry, and author of a brilliant history of Mexico from the conservative point of view. The Liberal party represented a creole and mestizo middle class—provincial landowners, professional men, artisans, the lower ranks of the clergy and military—determined to end special privileges and the concentration of political and economic power in the upper class. A priest-economist, José María Luis Mora, presented the liberal position with great force and lucidity. But the Liberal party was divided; its right wing, the *moderados,* wanted to proceed slowly and sometimes joined the conservatives; its left wing, the *puros,* advocated sweeping antifeudal, anticlerical reforms.

The election of 1828 produced the first political crisis of the republic. The conservatives united behind Manuel Gómez Pedraza, a leader of the moderados; the puro candidate was Vicente Guerrero, a hero of the war for independence whose popularity should have assured his election. But Gómez Pedraza was secretary of war, and army pressure on the state legislatures produced a vote of ten to nine for him and the conservative vice-presidential candidate, Anastasio Bustamante. Liberal indignation was great, and General Antonio López de Santa Anna, who had overthrown Iturbide and saw another opportunity to make political capital by assuming the role of liberator, rose in revolt against Gómez Pedraza. By January 1829, the liberals had triumphed and Congress declared Guerrero president of the republic. Hoping to promote unity, Guerrero asked Bustamante to remain as vice president—a serious error, as events proved.

An honest but uneducated man who doubted his own ability to govern, a mestizo scorned by the aristocratic creole society of the capital, Guerrero lasted barely one year in office. He coped successfully with a Spanish effort to reconquer Mexico (1829), but was overthrown the next year by an army revolt organized by Bustamante. For two years, a conservative dictatorship dominated by Lucas Alamán used the army to remove liberal governors and legislatures in the states, suppress newspapers, and jail, shoot, or exile puro leaders. The climax of this reign of terror was the execution of the veteran revolutionary Guerrero by a firing squad in 1831.

Growing unrest informed Santa Anna that the political pendulum was swinging toward the liberals, and in 1832 this careerist, a true conservative at heart, led a revolt against Bustamante. Province after province joined the revolt, and by the end of the year Bustamante had been forced into exile. Following congressional elections in March 1833, a new liberal government, dominated by the puros, was formed. Santa Anna, still posing as a liberal, was elected president, and Valentín Gómez Farías, a physician who remained a pillar of the liberal cause for a quarter-century, was chosen vice president. But Santa Anna would not assume responsibility for carrying out the liberal program; pleading ill health, he retired to his hacienda on the Veracruz coast and turned over to Gómez Farías his office.

The year 1833 was a high-water mark of liberal achievement. Aided by José María Luis Mora, his minister of education, Gómez Farías pushed through Congress a series of radical reforms: abolition of the special privileges and immunities of the army and church (meaning that officers and priests would now be subject to the jurisdiction of civil courts), abolition of tithes, secularization of the clerical University of Mexico, creation of a department of public instruction, reduction of the army, and creation of a civilian militia. These measures were accompanied by a program of internal improvements designed to increase the prosperity of the interior by linking it to the capital and the coasts. In their use of the central government to promote education and national economic development, the liberals showed that they were not doctrinaire adherents of laissez faire.

The liberal program inevitably provoked clerical and conservative resistance. Army officers began to organize revolts; priests proclaimed from their pulpits that the great cholera epidemic of 1833 was a sign of divine displeasure with the works of the impious liberals. Santa Anna waited until the time was ripe. Then, in April 1834, he placed himself at the head of the conservative rebellion, occupied the capital, and sent Gómez Farías and Mora into exile. Resuming the presidency, he summoned a hand-picked reactionary congress that repealed the reform laws of 1833 and suspended the constitution of 1824. Under the new conservative constitution of 1836, the states were reduced to departments completely dominated by the central government, upperclass control of politics was assured through high property and income qualifications for holding office, and the fueros of the church and army were restored.

Santa Anna and the conservatives ruled Mexico for the greater part of two decades, 1834 to 1854. Politically and economically, the conservative rule subordinated the interests of the regions and the country as a whole to a wealthy, densely populated central core linking Mexico City, Puebla, and Veracruz. Its centralist trend was reflected in the tariff act of 1837, which restored the alcabala, or sales tax system, inland customhouses, and the government tobacco monopoly, insuring the continuous flow of revenues to Mexico City.

War and Territorial Losses

Conservative neglect and abuse of outlying or border areas like northern Mexico and Yucatán contributed to the loss of Texas and almost led to the loss of Yucatán. Santa Anna's destruction of provincial autonomy enabled American colonists in Texas, led by Sam Houston, to pose as patriotic federalists in revolt against Santa Anna's tyranny. Santa Anna's incompetent generalship contributed to the defeat of his miserable Indian and mestizo conscripts at the battle of San Jacinto (1837), which secured the de facto independence of Texas. In Yucatán, the Caste or Social War of 1839 combined elements of a regional war against conservative centralism and an Indian war against feudal landlords. For almost a decade, Yucatán remained outside Mexico.

After the definitive loss of Texas through annexation by the United States in 1845 came the greater disaster of the Mexican War (1846–1848). Its immediate cause was a dispute between Mexico and the United States over the boundary of Texas, but the decisive factor was the determination of the Polk administration to acquire not only Texas but California and New Mexico. The war ended in catastrophic Mexican defeat, basically due to U.S. superiority in resources, military training, and leadership, but the irresponsible, selfish attitudes of the Mexican aristocracy and church contributed to the debacle.

In 1846, after conservative generals had suffered a series of reverses, a liberal revolt returned the puros to power and re-established the constitution of 1824. Led by Gómez Farías, the puros had a plan for winning the war that produced a curious replay of the events of 1834. The plan called for recalling Santa Anna—still regarded as the best of Mexico's generals—from the exile to which his own conservatives had

consigned him. Having been allowed by the Americans to slip through their blockade and re-enter Mexico, Santa Anna was named president and commander in chief of the Mexican armies.

Gómez Farías, meanwhile, undertook to finance the war by seizure of church property. This proposal horrified the clergy and their aristocratic supporters. Some aristocratic militia regiments in the capital, mobilized to fight the Americans, decided it was more urgent to save the church from the puros and rose in revolt against Gómez Farías. At the critical moment, Santa Anna repeated his betrayal of 1834. Returning to the capital, he ousted Gómez Farías, installed the moderado General Pedro María de Anaya as president, then turned to meet the advance of General Winfield Scott from Veracruz. Despite the tenacious resistance of a volunteer army at the approaches to the capital, the American invaders entered Mexico City in September 1847.

Mexican armies had been beaten in the field, but guerrilla warfare, joined with the ravages of disease, was taking a heavy toll of American lives; continued resistance and refusal to admit defeat might have secured a better peace for Mexico. In some regions of the country, peasant revolts broke out that combined demands for division of large haciendas among the peasantry and other reforms with calls for a continued resistance to the invaders. But the aristocratic creoles—some of whom favored a total take-over of Mexico by the United States—and their clerical allies feared the consequences of partisan warfare to their wealth and privileges and hastened to make peace. "The Mexican government," says Leticia Reina, "preferred coming to terms with the United States rather than endanger the interests of the ruling class." While Santa Anna fled to a new exile in Jamaica, a moderado government, formed at Querétaro, opened negotiations with the Americans. By the treaty of Guadalupe Hidalgo (1848), Mexico ceded Texas, California, and New Mexico to the United States; in return, Mexico received $15 million and the cancellation of certain claims against it.

La Reforma, Civil War, and the French Intervention

A succession of moderado administrations, mildly conservative but reasonably honest and efficient, struggled with the myriad problems of postwar Mexico. Meanwhile, the disasters suffered by Mexico under conservative rule had created a widespread revulsion against conservative policies and stimulated a revival of puro liberalism. In 1846, during the war, liberal administrations had come to power in the states of Oaxaca and Michoacán. In Michoacán the new governor was Melchor Ocampo, a scholar and scientist profoundly influenced by Rousseau and French utopian socialist thought, who was described by Justo Sierra as a "man of thought and action, agriculturalist, naturalist, economist, a public man from love of the public good, with no other ambition than that of doing something for his country." In Oaxaca a Zapotec Indian, Benito Juárez, became governor. Aided by a philanthropic creole, Juárez had worked his way through law school and established a law office in the city of Oaxaca. As governor, he gained a reputation for honesty, efficiency, and the democratic simplicity of his manners.

Ocampo and Juárez were two leaders of a renovated liberalism that ushered in the movement called *La Reforma.* Like the older liberalism of the 1830s, the Reforma sought to destroy feudal vestiges and implant capitalism in Mexico. Its ideology, however, was more spirited than the aristocratic, intellectual liberalism of Mora; and its puro left wing included a small number of figures, such as Ponciano Arriaga and Ignacio Ramírez, who rose above the general level of liberal ideology by their attacks on the latifundio, defense of labor and women's rights, and other advanced ideas.

The revived liberal ferment, with its demand for the abolition of fueros and secularization of church property, inspired alarm among the reactionary forces. They feared that the moderado regime of Mariano Arista, who became president in 1850, did not offer adequate insurance against radical change. In January 1853, a coalition of high clergy, generals, and great creole landowners, headed by the aged Alamán, organized a successful revolt against Arista and named Santa Anna, then living in Venezuela, dictator for one year. On his arrival in Mexico City on April 20, Santa Anna was formally proclaimed president.

For Alamán, the old dictator was merely a stopgap for an imported foreign prince. Alamán died on June 2, 1853, and with him died what intelligence and integrity remained in the conservative camp. Free from Alamán's restraining influence, Santa Anna returned to his familiar ways of graft and plunder, looting the public treasury for his own benefit and that of his sycophants. In December he had himself proclaimed perpetual dictator, with the title of His Most Supreme Highness.

Santa Anna's return to power, accompanied by a terrorist campaign against all dissenters, spurred a gathering of opposition forces, including many disgruntled moderados and conservatives. In early 1854, the old liberal caudillo from the state of Guerrero, Juan Álvarez, and the moderado general Ignacio Comonfort issued a call for revolt, the Plan of Ayutla, demanding the end of the dictatorship and the election of a convention to draft a new constitution. Within a year, Santa Anna's regime began to disintegrate, and in August 1855, seeing the handwriting on the wall, he went into exile for the last time. Some days later, a puro-dominated provisional government took office in Mexico City. The seventy-five-year-old Juan Álvarez was named provisional president; to his cabinet he named Benito Juárez as minister of justice and Miguel Lerdo de Tejada as minister of the treasury.

One of Juárez's first official acts was to issue a decree, the *Ley Juárez,* proclaiming the right of the state to limit the clerical and military fueros to matters of internal discipline. The decree raised a storm of conservative wrath, and Comonfort, now minister of war, himself disapproved of the measure. By December, moderado and conservative pressure, wielded through Comonfort, brought a shift to the right in the cabinet.

190   Melchor Ocampo, the most radical of the puros, was forced out, and a few days later Álvarez himself resigned, turning over the presidency to Comonfort, who proposed to steer a cautious middle course that he hoped would satisfy both liberals and conservatives.

The *Ley Lerdo* (Lerdo Law) of June 1856, drafted by Comonfort's minister of the treasury, Miguel Lerdo de Tejada, was poorly designed to achieve such a reconciliation, for it struck a heavy blow at the material base of the church's power, its landed wealth. The law barred the church from holding land not used for religious purposes and compelled the sale of all such property to tenants, with the rent considered to be 6 percent of the sale value of the property. Real estate not being rented was to be auctioned to the highest bidder, with payment of a large sales tax to the government.

The intent of the law was to create a rural middle class, but since it made no provision for division of the church estates, the bulk of the land passed into the hands of great landowners, merchants, and capitalists, both Mexican and foreign. What was worse, the law barred Indian villages from owning land and ordered that such land be sold in the same manner as church property, excepting only land and buildings used exclusively for the "public use" of the inhabitants and for communal pastures (*ejidos*). As a result, land-grabbers descended on the Indian villages, "denounced" their land to the local courts, and proceeded to buy it at auction for paltry sums. The law provided that the Indian owners should have the first opportunity to buy, but few Indians could pay the minimum purchase price. When the Indians responded with protests and revolts, Lerdo explained in a circular that the intent of his law was that Indian community lands should be divided among the natives, not sold to others. But he insisted that "the continued existence of the Indian communities ought not to be tolerated . . . , and this is exactly one of the goals of the law." He was also adamant on the right of those who rented Indian lands to buy them if they chose to do so. As a result, during the summer and fall of 1856 many Indian pueblos lost crop and pasturelands from which they had derived revenues vitally needed to defray the cost of their religious ceremonies and other communal expenses. Indian resistance and the liberals' need to attract popular support during their struggle with the conservative counterrevolution and French interventionists in the decade 1857–1867 seem to have slowed enforcement of the Lerdo Law as it applied to Indian villages, but the long-range tendency of liberal agrarian policy was to compel division of communal lands, facilitating their acquisition by hacendados and even small and middle-sized farmers. The result was a simultaneous strengthening of the latifundio and some increase in the size of the rural middle class.[3]

While the provisional government was causing consternation among conservatives with the Ley Juárez and the Ley Lerdo, a constitutional convention dominated by moderate liberals had been completing its work. The constitution of 1857 proclaimed freedom of speech, press, and assembly; limited fueros; forbade ecclesiastical and civil corporations to own land; and proclaimed the sanctity of private property. It restored the federalist structure of 1824, with the same division of Mexico into states, but replaced the bicameral national legislature with a single house and eliminated the office of vice president (the chief justice of the Supreme Court should succeed if the office of president became vacant). An effort by the puro minority to incorporate freedom of religion in the constitution failed; the resulting compromise neither mentioned toleration nor explicitly adopted Catholicism as the official faith.

---

[3] In 1863, in order to finance the struggle against the French intervention, the liberal Juárez issued a decree that authorized the sale of *tierras baldías* (vacant lands) to which there was no valid title. Since the Indians often lacked titles that were regarded as valid, their lands were exposed to "denunciation" and purchase from the state by land-grabbing landlords and speculators. In four years, Juárez issued titles to nearly 4.5 million acres of land, further stimulating the spoliation of Indian lands and the growth of peonage.

A few voices were raised against the land monopoly, peonage, and the immense inequalities of wealth. "We proclaim ideas and forget realities," complained the radical delegate Ponciano Arriaga. "How can a hungry, naked, miserable people practice popular government? How can we condemn slavery in words, while the lot of most of our fellow citizens is more grievous than that of the black slaves of Cuba or the United States?" Despite his caustic attack on the land monopoly, Arriaga offered a relatively moderate solution: the state should seize and auction off large uncultivated estates. The conservative opposition promptly branded Arriaga's project "communist"; the moderate majority in the convention passed over it in silence.

Having completed its work, the convention disbanded and elections followed for the first Congress and president and the members of the Supreme Court. Comonfort, who had already expressed unhappiness with the constitution, was elected president, and Juárez chief justice of the Supreme Court.

Since the new constitution incorporated the Lerdo Law and the Juárez Law, the church now openly entered the political struggle by excommunicating all public officials who took the required oath of loyalty. Counterrevolution had been gathering its forces for months and found an instrument in the vacillating president Comonfort. In December 1857, General Félix Zuloaga "pronounced" in favor of a Comonfort dictatorship, occupied the capital, and arrested Juárez. Pressed by the reactionaries to repeal the Juárez and Lerdo laws, Comonfort refused and finally found the strength to break with his reactionary supporters. He released Juárez, declared the constitution re-established, and himself went into exile, unmolested by the victorious rebels. Meanwhile, the liberals in the provinces had raised an army; proclaiming that Comonfort had violated the constitution and ceased to be president, they declared Juárez president of Mexico. For their part, the conservatives, in control of Mexico City, Puebla, and other major cities, declared the constitution void and the Juárez and Lerdo laws repealed.

Benito Juárez. (Courtesy of the Organization of American States)

The tremendous Three Years' War (1857–1860) had begun. In regional terms, the war pitted the rich central area, dominated by the conservatives, against the liberal south, north, and Veracruz. Controlling extensive regions and enjoying the support of a clear majority of the population, the liberals nevertheless suffered serious defeats in the first stage of the war. The main reason was that most of the permanent army had gone over to the conservatives, while the liberals had to create their own armed forces. The liberal armies, composed of elements of the national guard and guerrilla bands, were at the outset inevitably inferior in discipline and equipment to the conservative troops, which won almost all the pitched battles. In March 1858, conservative troops occupied the important mining center of Guanajuato and approached Querétaro, the seat of Juárez's government. He was forced to move his headquarters, first to Guadalajara and later to Veracruz, which remained the liberal capital until the end of the war.

As the struggle progressed, both sides found themselves in serious financial difficulties. The conservatives, however, had the advantage of generous support from the church. In July 1859, Juárez struck back at the clergy with reform laws that nationalized without compensation all ecclesiastical property except church buildings; the laws also suppressed all monasteries, established freedom of religion, and separated church and state. The reform laws were designed to encourage peasant proprietorship by dividing church estates into small farms, but this goal proved illusory; thanks to the Ley Lerdo, wealthy purchasers had already acquired much of the church land.

By the middle of 1860, the tide of war had turned in favor of the liberals. In August 1860, the best conservative general, Miguel Miramón, was routed at Silao. In October, Guadalajara fell to the liberals. And by the beginning of January 1861, Juárez had re-entered the capital, and the conservative leaders had fled the country. The war was effectively over, although conservative bands in the provinces continued to make devastating raids.

Beaten in the field, the reactionaries looked for help abroad. The conservative governments of England, France, and Spain had no love for the Mexican liberals and their leader Juárez. Moreover, there were ample pretexts for intervention, for both sides had seized or destroyed foreign property without compensation, and foreign bondholders were clamoring for payments from an empty Mexican treasury. The three European powers demanded compensation for damages to their nationals and payment of just debts. Juárez vainly pleaded poverty and noted the dubious nature of some of the claims.

In October 1861, the three powers agreed on a joint intervention in Mexico, and in January 1862, they sent occupation forces to Veracruz. England and Spain, having received assurances of future satisfaction of their claims, soon withdrew, but

the French government rejected all Mexican offers, and its troops remained. Napoleon III wanted more than payment of debts. A group of Mexican conservative exiles had convinced the ambitious emperor that the Mexican people would welcome a French army of liberation and the establishment of a monarchy. Napoleon had visions of a French-protected Mexican Empire that would yield him great political and economic advantages. It remained only to find a suitable unemployed prince, and one was found in the person of Archduke Ferdinand Maximilian of Hapsburg, brother of Austrian Emperor Franz Josef.

To prepare the ground for the arrival of the new ruler of Mexico, the French army advanced from Veracruz into the interior toward Puebla. At Puebla, instead of being received as liberators, the interventionists met determined resistance on the part of a poorly armed Mexican garrison and were thrown back with heavy losses. The date—May 5, 1862—is still celebrated as a Mexican national holiday. Reinforced by the arrival of thirty thousand fresh troops, General Elie-Frédéric Forey again besieged Puebla in March 1863, and by May 17 the starving garrison had been forced to surrender. The fall of Puebla and the loss of its garrison of some thirty thousand men left Juárez without an adequate force to defend the capital, and at the end of May his government and the remnants of his army abandoned it and retreated northward. On June 10, the French entered the city to the rejoicing of the clergy; by the end of the year the interventionists had occupied Querétaro, Monterrey, San Luis Potosí, and Saltillo. But the invaders had secure control only of the cities; republican guerrilla detachments controlled most of the national territory.

Meanwhile, in October 1863, a delegation of conservative exiles called on Maximilian to offer him a Mexican crown. As a condition of acceptance, the prince insisted that the Mexican people be consulted, and the French authorities obligingly staged a plebiscite that supposedly gave an overwhelming vote in favor of Maximilian. In April 1864, he accepted the Mexican throne and presently departed with his wife Carlota for their new home.

The conservative conspirators had counted on Maximilian to help them recover their lost wealth and privileges, but the emperor, mindful of realities, would not consent to their demands; the purchase of church lands by native and foreign landlords and capitalists had created new interests that Maximilian refused to antagonize. Confident of conservative support, Maximilian even wooed moderate liberals and won the support of such intellectual lights as the historians José Fernando Ramírez and Manuel Orozco y Berra. These scholars were impressed by Maximilian's good will and they cherished the illusion of a stable and prosperous Mexico ruled by an enlightened monarch.

But the hopes of both conservatives and misguided liberals were built on quicksand. The victories of Maximilian's generals could not destroy the fluid and elusive liberal resistance, firmly grounded in popular hatred for the invaders and aided by Mexico's geography (a rugged terrain with vast, thinly populated territories and few roads). A turning point in the war came in the spring of 1865 in the United States, with the Union triumph over the Confederacy. American demands that the French evacuate Mexico, a region regarded by Secretary of State William Seward as a U.S. zone of economic and political influence, grew more insistent, and American troops were massed along the Rio Grande. Facing serious domestic and diplomatic problems at home, Napoleon decided to cut his losses and liquidate the Mexican adventure.

Marshal Achille François Bazaine, preparing to embark with the remaining French troops, urged Maximilian to abdicate and leave Mexico, but his conservative advisers, who still believed that defeat could be avoided, prevailed on him to stay. With liberal armies converging on Querétaro, the same die-hard conservatives persuaded Maximilian to go there and assume supreme command. Together with the imperialist generals Miguel Miramón and Tomás Mejía, he was captured on May 14, 1867. After a trial by court-martial, all three were found guilty of treason, sentenced to death, and executed by a *Juarista* firing squad.

Postwar Attempts at Reconstruction and the Death of *La Reforma*

Juárez, symbol of the successful Mexican resistance to a foreign usurper, resumed his office of president in August 1867. His government inherited a devastated country. Agriculture and industry were in ruins; as late as 1873, the value of Mexican exports was below the level of 1810. To reduce the state's financial burdens and end the danger of military control, Juárez dismissed two-thirds of the army, an act that produced discontent and uprisings that his generals managed to suppress.

Juárez devoted a considerable part of the state's limited resources to the development of a public school system, especially on the elementary level; by 1874 there were about eight thousand schools with some three hundred and fifty thousand pupils. One of the few material achievements of his administration was the construction of an important railroad line running from Veracruz through Puebla to Mexico City, completed after his death in 1872.

In his agrarian policy, Juárez continued the liberal program of seeking to implant capitalism in the countryside, at the expense not of the hacienda but of the Indian communities. Indeed, the period of the "Restored Republic" (1868–1876) saw an intensified effort by the federal government to implement the Lerdo Law by compelling dissolution and partition of Indian communal lands, opening the way for a new wave of frauds and seizures by neighboring hacendados and other land-grabbers. The result was a series of nationwide peasant revolts, the most serious occurring in the state of Hidalgo (1869–1870). Proclaiming the rebels to be "communists," the hacendados, aided by state and federal authorities, restored order by the traditional violent methods. A few liberals raised their voices in protest, but were ignored; one was Ignacio Ramírez, who condemned the usurpations and

194 frauds practiced by the hacendados with the complicity of corrupt judges and officials and called for suspension of the law. On the other hand, the period saw the first legislative efforts to improve labor conditions and the formation in the cities of numerous trade unions whose leaders combined liberal and trade unionist principles.

Re-elected president in 1871, Juárez was able to put down a revolt by a hero of the wars of the Reforma, General Porfirio Díaz, who charged Juárez with attempting to become a dictator. But Juárez died the next year of a heart attack and was succeeded as acting president by the chief justice of the Supreme Court, Sebastián Lerdo de Tejada. Lerdo scheduled new elections for October 1872, ran against, and easily defeated Díaz, but in turn faced a growing movement of opposition that accused him of violations of republican legality. When Lerdo announced in 1876 that he intended to seek re-election, Díaz again rose in revolt. Aided by a group of Texas capitalists with strong links to New York banks, who financed and armed his rebellion, he defeated troops loyal to Lerdo and sent him into flight.

Díaz had seized power in the name of the ideals of the Reforma. In fact, the year 1876 marked the death of the Reforma and the idealistic principles of natural law that formed its theoretical base. The age of Díaz continued the efforts of the Reforma to construct a bourgeois society, but with new men, new methods, and a new ideology. The libertarian creed to which Juárez subscribed, no matter how often he deviated from it, was replaced by the ideology of positivism as propounded by its French founder, Auguste Comte— ideology that ranked order and progress above freedom.

The Reforma had paved the way for this change by transforming the Mexican bourgeoisie from a revolutionary class into a ruling class that was more predatory and acquisitive than the old creole aristocracy. The remnants of that aristocracy speedily adapted to the ways of the new ruling class and merged with it. The interests of the old and the new rich required political stability, a docile labor force, internal improvements, and a political and economic climate favorable to foreign investments. The mission of the "honorable tyranny" of Porfirio Díaz was to achieve those ends.

Argentina

In 1816 delegates to the congress of Tucumán proclaimed the independence of the United Provinces of the Río de la Plata. "Disunited," however, would have better described the political condition of the area of La Plata, for the creole seizure of power in Buenos Aires in 1810 brought in its train a dissolution of the vast viceroyalty of the Río de la Plata.

The Liberation of Paraguay, Uruguay, and Upper Peru

Paraguay, having repelled efforts by the junta of Buenos Aires to "liberate" it, declared its own independence and fell under the dictatorial rule of the creole lawyer José Gaspar Rodríguez de Francia, who effectively sealed it off from its neighbors. Francia had his reasons for the system of isolation: the rulers of Buenos Aires controlled Paraguay's river outlets to the sea, and isolation and self-sufficiency were the alternatives to submission and payment of tribute to Buenos Aires. Francia did permit a limited licensed trade with the outside world by way of Brazil, chiefly to satisfy military needs.

Francia's state-controlled economy brought certain benefits: the planned diversification of agriculture, which reduced production of such export crops as yerba maté, tobacco, and sugar, insured a plentiful supply of foodstuffs and the well-being of the Indian and mestizo masses. An interesting feature of Francia's system was the establishment of state farms or ranches—called *estancias de la patria*—that successfully specialized in the raising of livestock and ended Paraguay's dependence on livestock imports from the Argentine province of Entre Ríos. The principal sufferers under Francia's dictatorship were Spaniards, many of whom he expelled or penalized in various ways, and creole aristocrats, who were kept under perpetual surveillance and subjected to severe repression.

Uruguay, then known as the Banda Oriental, was led toward independence by the gaucho chieftain José Gervasio Artigas, who resisted the efforts of the junta of Buenos Aires to dominate the area. In 1815 the junta abandoned these efforts, evacuated Montevideo, and turned it over to Artigas. No ordinary caudillo, Artigas not only defended Uruguayan nationality but sought to achieve social reform. In 1815 he issued a plan for distributing royalist lands to the landless, with preference shown to blacks, Indians, zambos, and poor whites. But he was not given the opportunity to implement this radical program. In 1817 a powerful Brazilian army invaded Uruguay and soon had a secure grip on the Banda Oriental. Artigas had to flee across the Paraná River into Paraguay. He received asylum from Francia but was never allowed to leave again; he died in Paraguay thirty years later.

Soon Uruguay again became a battlefield when a small group of Uruguayan exiles, supported by Buenos Aires, crossed over the estuary in 1825 and launched a general revolt against Brazilian domination. Brazil retaliated by declaring war against the United Provinces. The three-sided military conflict ended in a stalemate. Uruguay finally achieved independence in 1828 through the mediation of Great Britain, which was unwilling to see Uruguay fall under the control of either of its more powerful neighbors.

Upper Peru, the mountainous northern corner of the old viceroyalty of La Plata, also escaped the grasp of Buenos Aires after 1810. Three expeditions were sent into the high country, won initial victories, then were rolled back by Spanish counteroffensives. Logistical problems, the apathy of the Indian population, and the hostility of the creole aristocracy, which remained loyal to Spain until it became clear that the royalist cause was doomed, contributed to the patriot defeats. Not until 1825 was Upper Peru liberated by General Antonio José de Sucre, Bolívar's lieutenant.

Renamed Bolivia in honor of the liberator, it began its independent life the next year under a complicated, totally impractical constitution drafted by Bolívar himself.

The Struggle for Progress and National Unity

Even among the provinces that had joined at Tucumán to form the United Provinces of La Plata, discord grew and threatened the dissolution of the new state. The efforts of the wealthy port and province of Buenos Aires to impose its hegemony over the interior met with tenacious resistance. The end of the Spanish trade monopoly brought large gains to Buenos Aires and lesser gains to the littoral provinces of Santa Fe, Entre Ríos, and Corrientes; their exports of meat and hides increased, and the value of their lands rose. But the wine and textile industries of the interior, which had been protected by the colonial monopoly, suffered from the competition of cheaper and superior European wares imported through the port of Buenos Aires.

The interests of the interior provinces required a measure of autonomy or even independence in order to protect their primitive industries, but Buenos Aires preferred a single free-trade zone under a government dominated by the port city. This was one cause of the conflict between Argentine *federales* (federalists) and *unitarios* (unitarians). By 1820 the federalist solution had triumphed; the United Provinces had in effect dissolved into a number of independent republics, with the interior provinces ruled by caudillos, each representing the local ruling class and having a gaucho army behind him.

A new start toward unity came with the appointment in 1821 of Bernardino Rivadavia as chief minister under Martín Rodríguez, governor of the province of Buenos Aires. An ardent liberal, strongly influenced by the English philosopher Jeremy Bentham, Rivadavia launched an ambitious program of educational, social, and economic reform. He promoted primary education, founded the University of Buenos Aires, abolished the ecclesiastical fuero and the tithe, and suppressed some monasteries. Rivadavia envisioned a balanced development of industry and agriculture, with a large role assigned to British investment and colonization. But the obstacles in the way of industrialization proved too great, and little came of efforts in this direction. The greatest progress was made in cattle raising, which expanded rapidly southward into former Indian territory.

In 1822, hoping to raise revenue and increase production, Rivadavia introduced the system of emphyteusis, a program of distribution of public lands through long-term leases at fixed rentals. Some writers have seen in this system an effort at agrarian reform, but there were no limits on the size of grants, and the measure actually contributed to the growth of latifundia. The lure of large profits in livestock raising induced many native and foreign merchants, politicians, and members of the military to join the rush for land. The net result was the creation not of a small-farmer class but of a new and more powerful *estanciero* class that was the enemy of Rivadavia's progressive ideals.

Rivadavia's planning went beyond the province of Buenos Aires; he had a vision of a unified Argentina under a strong central government that would promote the rounded economic development of the whole national territory. In 1825 a constituent congress met in Buenos Aires at Rivadavia's call to draft a constitution for the United Provinces of the Río de la Plata. Rivadavia, who was elected president of the new state, made a dramatic proposal to federalize the city and port of Buenos Aires. The former capital of the province would henceforth belong to the whole nation, with the revenues of its customhouse to be used to advance the general welfare.

Rivadavia's proposal reflected his nationalism and the need to mobilize national resources for a war with Brazil (1825–1828) over Uruguay. Congress approved Rivadavia's project, but the federalist caudillos of the interior, fearing that the rise of a strong national government would mean the end of their power, refused to ratify the constitution and even withdrew their delegates from the congress. In Buenos Aires a similar stand was taken by the powerful estancieros, who had no intention of surrendering the privileges of their province and regarded Rivadavia's program of social and economic reform as a costly folly.

Defeated on the issue of the constitution, Rivadavia suffered a further loss of prestige when his agent signed a peace treaty with Brazil recognizing Uruguay as a province of the Brazilian Empire. Rivadavia rejected the treaty, but popular anger at the agreement combined with opposition to his domestic program had sealed his political doom. In July 1827, he resigned the presidency and went into exile. The liberal program for achieving national unity had failed.

After an interval of factional struggles, the federalism espoused by the landed oligarchy of Buenos Aires triumphed in the person of Juan Manuel Rosas, who became governor of the province in 1829. Under his influence there was forged (1831) a federal pact under which Buenos Aires assumed representation for the other provinces in foreign affairs but left them free to run their own affairs in all other respects. Federalism, as defined by Rosas, meant that Buenos Aires retained the revenues of its customhouse for its exclusive use and controlled trade on the Río de la Plata system for the benefit of its merchants. A network of personal alliances between Rosas and provincial caudillos, backed by use of force against recalcitrant leaders, insured for him a large measure of control over the interior.

Rosas' long reign saw a total reversal of Rivadavia's progressive policies. For Rosas and the ruling class of estancieros, virtually the only economic concern was the export of hides and salted meat and the import of foreign goods. The dictator also showed some favor to wheat farming, which he protected by tariff laws, but he neglected artisans and machine industry. Rosas himself was a great estanciero and owner of a saladero (salting plant) that enjoyed a monopoly on the curing of meat and hides. He vigorously pressed the conquest of Indian territory, bringing much new land under the control of the province of Buenos Aires; this land was sold for low prices to estancieros, and Rivadavia's policy of retaining ownership of land by the state was abandoned. Rosas also discarded Rivadavia's policy of promoting immigration and education. Rosas handed over what schools remained to the Jesuits, who were recalled from exile in 1836 (ultimately, Rosas found the order too independent and expelled it).

By degrees, the press and all other potential dissidents were cowed or destroyed. To enforce the dictator's will there arose a secret organization known as the *Mazorca* (ear of corn—a reference to the close unity of its members). In collaboration with the police, this terrorist organization beat up or even murdered Rosas' opponents. The masthead of the official journal and all official papers carried the slogan "Death to the savage, filthy unitarians!" Even horses had to display the red ribbon that was the federalist symbol. Those opponents who did not knuckle under and escaped death fled by the thousands to Montevideo, Chile, Brazil, or other places of refuge.

Under Rosas, the merchants of the city and the estancieros of the province of Buenos Aires enjoyed a measure of prosperity, although an Anglo-French blockade of the estuary of La Plata from 1845 to 1848, caused by Rosas' mistreatment of English and French nationals and his efforts to subvert Uruguayan independence, resulted in severe losses to both groups. But this prosperity bore no proportion to the possibilities of economic growth; technical backwardness marked all aspects of livestock raising and agriculture, and port facilities were totally inadequate.

Meanwhile, the littoral provinces, which had experienced some advance of livestock raising and agriculture, became increasingly aware that Rosas' brand of federalism was harmful to their interests and that free navigation of the river system of La Plata was necessary to assure their prosperity. In 1852 the anti-Rosas forces formed a coalition that united the liberal émigrés with the caudillo Justo José de Urquiza of Entre Ríos, who was joined by the great majority of the pro-

vincial caudillos, and Brazil and Uruguay. At Monte Caseros, their combined forces defeated Rosas' army and sent him fleeing to an English exile.

Victory over Rosas did not end the dispute between Buenos Aires and the other provinces, between federalism and unitarianism. Only the slower process of economic change would forge the desired unity. A rift soon arose between the liberal exiles who assumed leadership in Buenos Aires and the caudillo Urquiza of Entre Ríos, who was backed by his victorious army. Urquiza, who still sported the red ribbon of federalism, proposed a loose union of the provinces, with all of them sharing the revenues of the Buenos Aires customhouse. But the leaders of Buenos Aires feared the loss of their economic and political predominance to Urquiza, whom they wrongly considered a caudillo of the Rosas type; in fact, Urquiza was a sincere convert to the gospel of modernity and progress.

Within the province of Buenos Aires, opinions were divided. Some favored entry into a new confederation but with very precise guarantees of the interests of their province; others argued for total separation from the other thirteen provinces. After Urquiza had unsuccessfully attempted to make Buenos Aires accept unification by armed force, the two sides agreed to a peaceful separation. As a result, delegates from Buenos Aires were absent from the constitutional convention that met at Santa Fe in Entre Ríos in 1852.

The constitution of 1853 reflected the influence of the ideas of the journalist Juan Bautista Alberdi on the delegates. His forcefully written pamphlet, *Bases and Points of Departure for the Political Organization of the Argentine Republic,* offered the United States as a model for Argentina. The new constitution strongly resembled that of the United States in certain respects. The former United Provinces became a federal republic, presided over by a president with significant power who served a six-year term without the possibility of immediate re-election. Legislative functions were vested in a bicameral legislature, a senate and a house of representatives. The

Catholic religion was proclaimed the official religion of the nation, but freedom of worship for non-Catholics was assured. The states were empowered to elect governors and legislatures and frame their own constitutions, but the federal government had the right of intervention—including armed intervention—to insure respect for the provisions of the constitution. General Urquiza was elected the first president of the Argentine Republic.

The liberal leaders of Buenos Aires, joined by the conservative estancieros who had been Rosas' firmest supporters, refused to accept the constitution of 1853, for they feared the creation of a state they did not control. As a result, two Argentinas arose: the Argentine Confederation, headed by Urquiza, and the province of Buenos Aires. For five years, the two states maintained their separate existence. In Paraná, capital of the confederation, Urquiza struggled to repress gaucho revolts, stimulate economic development, and foster education and immigration. Modest advances were made, but the tempo of growth lagged far behind that of the wealthy city and province of Buenos Aires, which prospered on the base of a steadily increasing trade with Europe in hides, tallow, salted beef, and wool.

Hoping to increase the confederation's scanty revenues, Urquiza began a tariff war with Buenos Aires, levying surcharges on goods landed at the Paraná River port of Rosario if duties had been paid on them at Buenos Aires. Buenos Aires responded with sanctions against ships sailing to Rosario and threatened to close commerce on the Paraná altogether. In 1859 war between the two Argentine states broke out. Defeated at the battle of Cepeda, Bartolomé Mitre, the commander of the Buenos Aires forces, accepted a compromise whereby Buenos Aires would join the confederation after a constitutional reform that protected its special interests. But the peace was short-lived; war broke out again in the presidency of Santiago Derqui, Urquiza's successor and personal rival. In the decisive battle of Pavón (1861), in which Mitre, now governor of the provinces of Buenos Aires, commanded the Buenos

Aires army, the forces of the confederation, led by Urquiza, suffered defeat.

The military and economic superiority of Buenos Aires, the need of the other provinces to use its port, and an awareness on all sides of the urgent need to achieve national unity dictated a compromise. At a congress representing all the provinces, held at Buenos Aires in 1862, it was agreed over the opposition of a die-hard group of Buenos Aires federalists that the city should be the provisional capital of both the Argentine Republic and the province and that the Buenos Aires customhouse should be nationalized, with the proviso that for a period of five years the revenues of the province would not fall below the 1859 level. In conformity with decisions of the congress, elections to choose the first president of a united Argentina were held the same year, and Bartolomé Mitre—distinguished historian, poet, soldier, and statesman—was elected president for a six-year term.

Mitre's term of office saw continued economic progress and consolidation of national unity. The customhouse was nationalized, as had been promised, and plans were made for the federalization of the capital. The construction of railways and telegraph lines that would forge closer links between Buenos Aires and the interior had begun, and European immigrants arrived in growing numbers. Some advances were made in the establishment of a public school system. But great problems remained. The shadow of the provincial caudillo continued to fall on the Argentine Republic; in the north, a revolt by one of Rosas' old allies had to be put down by armed force. The most difficult problem Mitre had to deal with, however, was the long, exhausting Paraguayan War (1865–1870).

The Paraguayan War

On the death of the dictator Francia in 1840, power in Paraguay was assumed by a triumvirate in which Carlos Antonio López soon emerged as the dominant figure. In essence, López continued Francia's dictatorial system but gave it a thin disguise of constitutional, representative government. Since he had inherited a stable, prosperous state, López could afford to rule in a less repressive fashion than his predecessor. More flexible than Francia, too, with a better understanding of the outside world, López made a successful effort to end Paraguay's diplomatic and commercial isolation. After the fall of Rosas, a stubborn enemy of Paraguayan independence, López obtained Argentine recognition of his country's independence, and the Paraná was at last opened to Paraguayan trade. López also established diplomatic relations with a series of countries, including England, France, and the United States. A special diplomatic mission to Europe, headed by his son, Francisco Solano López, also made important economic and cultural contacts, placing orders for ship construction, and inviting specialists to work in Paraguay.

The end of the policy of isolation was accompanied by a major expansion of the Paraguayan economy. Although agriculture (especially the production of such export crops as tobacco and yerba maté) continued to be the principal economic activity, López assigned great importance to the development of industry. One of his proudest achievements in this field was the construction of an iron foundry, the most modern enterprise of its type in Latin America. Transportation was improved with the building of roads and canals, the creation of a fleet of merchant ships, and the construction of a short railroad line.

Continuing Francia's policy, López enlarged the role of the state sector in the national economy. In 1848 he transferred to state ownership forest lands producing yerba maté and other commercial wood products and much arable land. The lucrative export trade in yerba maté and some other products became a government monopoly, and the number of state-owned ranches rose to sixty-four. López promoted education as well as economic growth; by the time of his death, Paraguay had 435 elementary schools with some 25,000 pupils, and a larger proportion of literate inhabitants than any other Latin American country.

At the same time, López took advantage of his position to concentrate ownership of land and various commercial enterprises in his own hands and those of his children, relatives, and associates; thus, there arose a bourgeoisie that profited by its close connection with the state apparatus, which enabled it to promote its own interests. The number of large private estates, however, was small; the private agricultural sector was dominated by small or medium-sized farms cultivated by owners or tenants, sometimes aided by a few hired laborers. By contrast with the situation in other Latin American countries, peonage and debt servitude were rare (slavery had been put in the way of extinction by a gradual manumission law in 1842). The relative absence of peonage and feudal survivals contributed to a rapid growth of Paraguayan capitalism and the well-being of its predominantly Indian and mestizo population. When López died in 1862, Paraguay was one of the most progressive and prosperous states in South America.

His son, Francisco Solano, whom López designated his heir apparent when his death approached, succeeded his father as dictator. The younger López inherited a tradition of border disputes with Brazil that erupted into open war when Brazil sent an army into Uruguay in 1864 to insure the victory of a pro-Brazilian faction in that country's civil strife. López could not be indifferent to this action, which threatened the delicate balance of power in the basin of La Plata. López also feared that Brazilian control over Uruguay would end unrestricted Paraguayan access to the port of Montevideo, which would make Paraguayan trade dependent entirely on the good will of Buenos Aires.

When the Brazilian government disregarded his protests, López sent an army to invade the Brazilian province of Mato Grosso, but this foray into virtually empty territory had no military significance, and he soon withdrew his troops. Hoping to strike a more effective blow at Brazil, López requested President Mitre's permission in January 1865 to cross Argentine territory (the state of Corrientes) en route to Uruguay. López regarded Mitre's refusal as an unfriendly act. In March 1865, the Paraguayan congress declared war on Argentina, and Paraguayan troops occupied the town of Corrientes. On May 1, 1865, Brazil, Argentina, and the Brazilian-sponsored Flores regime in Uruguay concluded a Triple Alliance against Paraguay; a separate secret treaty between Brazil and Argentina provided for the partition of more than half of Paraguay's territory between them. Mitre was named commander in chief of the allied forces. Paraguay thus faced a coalition that included the two largest states in South America, with an immense superiority in manpower and other resources.

Yet the war dragged on for five years, for at its outset Paraguay possessed an army of some 70,000 well-armed and disciplined soldiers that outnumbered the combined forces of its foes. Expelled from the territory that had overrun in Argentina and Brazil, the Paraguayan troops stubbornly defended themselves against the allied forces that crossed the Paraná into Paraguay in mid-April 1866. In August 1868, Fort Humaitá was stormed by Brazilian troops under Marshal Luis Alves de Lima Caxias, at the cost of two thousand men. In January 1869, the allies occupied Asunción. Retreating northward, López attempted to organize a new defense against overwhelming numerical odds. The end came on March 1, 1870. With a few followers, López made his last stand at a point near the Brazilian border. López was slain by a Brazilian soldier. With his death, effective Paraguayan resistance ended.

For Paraguay the war's consequences were tragic. Perhaps as many as 20 percent of the prewar population of some 300,000 perished as a result of military action, famine, disease, and a devastating Brazilian occupation. The peace treaty assigned much Paraguayan territory to the victors and burdened Paraguay with extremely heavy reparations. Brazil, the occupying power, installed a puppet regime composed of former López generals, who began a radical reconstruction of the Paraguayan economy and state. The essence of the new policy was to liquidate the progressive changes made under the Francia and

López regimes. Most of the state-owned lands were sold to land speculators and foreign businessmen at bargain prices, with no restriction on the size of holdings. Tenants who could not present the necessary documents were ejected even though they and their forebears had cultivated the land for decades. By the early 1890s, the state-owned lands were almost gone. Foreign penetration of the economy through loans, concessions, and land purchases soon deprived Paraguay of its economic as well as its political independence.

The Paraguayan War caused increased taxes and other hardships; for these reasons, it was unpopular in Argentina. The burdens of the war revived the dying spirit of provincial separatism and compelled Mitre to leave the front to direct the suppression of revolts in different provinces. By 1867 these domestic difficulties had virtually taken Argentina out of the war; when it ended, however, Argentina obtained its share of Paraguayan reparations and territorial concessions (Formosa, Chaco, and Misiones).

Progress and Development Under Sarmiento

At the close of his presidential term, Mitre returned to civilian life. He was succeeded by Domingo Faustino Sarmiento (1868–1874), a gifted essayist, sociologist, and statesman, former Argentine minister to the United States, and an enthusiast for its institutions. Like Mitre, Sarmiento worked for Argentine unity and economic and social progress.

After the Paraguayan War, a flood of technological change began to sweep over Argentina. Railways penetrated the interior, extending the stock-raising and farming area. The gradual introduction of barbed-wire fencing and alfalfa ranges made possible a dramatic improvement in the quality of livestock. In 1876 the arrival of an experimental shipload of chilled carcasses from France prepared the way for the triumph of frozen over salted meat, which led to a vast expansion of European demand for Argentine beef. Labor was needed to exploit the rapidly expanding pasturelands and farmlands; during Sarmiento's administration alone, some three hundred thousand immigrants poured into the country. But Sarmiento taught that it was not enough to build railroads and expand acreage; it was necessary to change people's minds. Believing in the need for an educated citizenry in a democratic republic, he labored to expand and improve the public school system; to this end he introduced to Argentina teacher-training institutions of the kind his friend Horace Mann had founded in the United States.

When Sarmiento left office, Argentina presented the appearance of a rapidly developing, prosperous state. But there were clouds in the generally bright Argentine sky. The growth of exports and the rise in land values did not benefit the forlorn gauchos, aliens in a land over which they had once freely roamed, or the majority of European immigrants. Little was done to provide these newcomers with homesteads. Immigrants who wished to farm usually found the price of land out of reach; as a result, many preferred to remain in Buenos Aires or other cities of the littoral, where they began to form an urban middle class largely devoted to trade. Meanwhile, foreign economic influence grew as a result of increasing dependence on foreign—chiefly British—capital to finance the construction of railways, telegraph lines, gasworks, and other needed facilities. The growing concentration of landownership reinforced the colonial land tenure pattern; the tightening British control of markets and the country's economic infrastructure reinforced the colonial pattern of dependence on a foreign metropolis, with London replacing Seville as commercial center. But Mitre, Sarmiento, and other builders of the new Argentina were dazzled by their success in nation-building and by a climate of prosperity they believed permanent. These men did not suspect the extent of the problems that were in the making nor did they anticipate what problems future generations of Argentines would have to attempt to solve.

Chile

The victories of José de San Martín's Army of the Andes over royalist forces at Chacabuco and Maipú in 1817 and 1818 gave Chile its definitive independence. From 1818 until 1823, Bernardo O'Higgins, a hero of the struggle for Chilean liberation and a true son of the Enlightenment, ruled the country with the title of supreme director. O'Higgins energetically pushed a program of reform designed to weaken the landed aristocracy and the church and promote a rapid development of the Chilean economy along capitalist lines. His abolition of titles of nobility and entails angered the great landowners of the fertile Central Valley between the Andes and the Pacific; his expulsion of the royalist bishop of Santiago and his restrictions on the number of religious processions and the veneration of images infuriated the church. The opposition to O'Higgins was joined by dissident liberals who resented his sometimes heavy-handed rule. In 1823 O'Higgins resigned and went into exile in Lima. There followed seven turbulent years, with presidents and constitutions rising and falling.

Portales and Economic Growth

In Chile, as in other Latin American countries, the political and armed struggle gradually assumed the form of a conflict between conservatives, who usually were also centralists, and liberals, who were generally federalists. The conservative-centralists were the party of the great landowners of the Central Valley and the wealthy merchants of Santiago; the liberal-federalists spoke for the landowners, merchants, and artisans of the northern and southern provinces, who were resentful of political and economic domination by the wealthy central area. The victory of the conservative General Joaquín Prieto over the liberal General Ramón Freire in the decisive battle of Lircay (1830) brought to power a government headed by Prieto as president but dominated by one of his cabinet ministers, Diego Portales.

From 1830 until his death in 1837, Portales, who never held an elective office, placed the enduring stamp of his ideas on Chilean politics and society. A businessman of aristocratic origins, owner of a successful import house, he faithfully served the interests of an oligarchy of great landlords and merchants that dominated the Chilean scene for decades. Although Portales expressed atheist views in private, he supported the authority of the church as an instrument for keeping the lower classes in order. He understood the importance of trade, industry, and mining and promoted their interests. Assisted by his able finance minister, Manuel Rengifo, Portales continued the work of O'Higgins, removing remaining obstacles to internal trade. He introduced income and property taxes to increase the state's revenues and trimmed government spending by dismissing unnecessary employees. Agriculture was protected by high tariffs on agricultural imports. Port facilities were improved, measures were taken to strengthen the Chilean merchant marine, and in 1835 a steamship line began to connect the Chilean ports. Under the fostering care of the conservative regime and in response to a growing European demand for Chilean silver, copper, and hides, the national economy made steady progress in the 1830s.

Measures designed to stimulate economic growth were accompanied by others that fortified the social and political power of the oligarchy. In order to tighten the bond between the conservative government and the church, Portales restored the privileges the church had lost under liberal rule and normalized the troubled relations between Chile and the papacy.

In 1833 a conservative-dominated assembly adopted a constitution that further consolidated the power of the oligarchy. Elections were made indirect, with the suffrage limited to men of twenty-five years or over who could satisfy literacy and property qualifications. Still higher property qualifications were required of members of the lower and upper houses. The constitution restored entails, insuring perpetuation of the latifundio. Catholicism was declared the state religion, and the church was given control over marriage. The president enjoyed an absolute veto over congressional legislation, appointed all high officials, and could proclaim a state of siege. The process of amending the constitution was made so difficult as to be virtually impossible. Since the president controlled the electoral machinery, the outcome of elections was a foregone conclusion. In 1836, Prieto was re-elected president for a second five-year term.

Realizing the futility of legal opposition to the conservative dictatorship, many liberals boycotted the election and later took to arms. This revolt, led by General Freire, was quickly crushed, and Freire was exiled to Australia. The Freire revolt had been organized in Peru, and this fact added to the tensions created by a tariff war between Peru and Chile. Relations between the two countries deteriorated further in 1836 as a result of the formation of a Peruvian-Bolivian confederation under the auspices of the ambitious Bolivian president, Andrés Santa Cruz. Portales saw in this union a threat to Chile's northern borders and obtained a congressional declaration of war on Peru in November 1836. The war lasted three years; it ended with a Chilean victory and dissolution of the confederation. Meanwhile, however, Portales had caused much resentment at home by his highhanded use of the extraordinary powers vested in him in wartime to arrest and jail all critics of the war. In June 1837, mutinous troops seized Portales and killed him before loyal troops could gain his release.

Recovery Under Bulnes

In 1841, Prieto was succeeded in the presidency by General Manuel Bulnes, who was re-elected to a second five-year term in 1846. Victorious at home and abroad, the conservative leadership decided it could relax the strict discipline of the Portales period. Chile's economic life quickly recovered from the strains caused by the war of 1836–1839 and began a renewed advance. Commerce, mining, and agriculture prospered as never before. The Crimean War and the gold rushes to California and Australia of the 1850s created large new markets for Chilean wheat, stimulating a considerable expansion of the cultivated area. In 1840 a North American, William Wheelright, established a steamship line to operate on the Chilean coasts, using coal from newly developed hard coal mines. Wheelright also founded a company that in 1852 completed Chile's first railroad line, providing an outlet to the sea for the production of the mining district of Copiapó. The major Santiago-Valparaíso line, begun in 1852, was not completed until 1863. Foreign—especially British—capital began to penetrate the Chilean economy; it dominated foreign trade and had a large interest in mining and railroads, but national capitalists constituted an important, vigorous group and displayed much initiative in the formation of joint stock companies and banks.

The great landowners were the principal beneficiaries of this economic upsurge; their lands appreciated in value without any effort on their part. Some great landowners invested their money in railroads, mining, and trade. But the essential conservatism of the landed aristocracy and the urge to preserve a semifeudal control over its peons discouraged the transformation of the great landowners into capitalist farmers. A pattern of small landholdings arose in southern Chile, to which German as well as Chilean colonists came in increasing numbers in the 1840s and 1850s. The rich Central Valley, still dominated by the latifundio, reflected inefficient techniques and reliance on the labor of *inquilinos*—tenants who also had to work the master's fields. Thus, alongside an emerging capitalist sector based on mining, trade, banking, intensive agriculture, and some industry, there existed a semifeudal sector based on the latifundio, peonage, and an aristocracy that hindered the development of Chilean capitalism.

Yet Chile at this period presented a more progressive aspect than most other Latin American states. President Bulnes continued the law-and-order system initiated by Portales but tempered its authoritarian rigor. His minister of justice and

instruction, Manuel Montt, established a system of public instruction that included the humanities and technical subjects. In 1842 the University of Chile was founded. Its first rector was the distinguished Venezuelan poet, scholar, and educator Andrés Bello, who helped to train a whole generation of Chilean intellectuals.

One of Bello's disciples was José Victorino Lastarria, historian, sociologist, and a deputy of the Liberal party, which he helped to revive. Dissatisfied with the modest concessions to modernity of the new conservatives, liberals like Lastarria wanted to accelerate the rate of change. They demanded radical revision of the constitution of 1833 and an end to oligarchical rule.

To the left of Lastarria stood the firebrand Francisco Bilbao, author of a scorching attack on the church and the Hispanic heritage, "The Nature of Chilean Society" (1844). Later, he spent several years in France and was profoundly influenced by utopian socialist and radical republican thought. He returned to Chile in 1850 to found, with Santiago Arcos, the Society of Equality, which advocated these advanced ideas. The society carried on an intensive antigovernmental campaign and within a few months had a membership of four thousand.

Montt's Moderate Reforms

The Society of Equality was founded on the eve of the election of 1850, for which President Bulnes had designated Manuel Montt his heir. Despite Montt's progressive educational policies and patronship of the arts and letters, liberals identified him with the repressive system of Portales and the constitution of 1833. Liberals like Lastarria and radical democrats like Bilbao proclaimed the impending election a fraud and demanded constitutional reforms. The government responded by proclaiming a state of siege and suppressing the Society of Equality. Regarding these acts as a prelude to an attempt to liquidate the opposition, groups of liberals in Santiago and La Serena rose in revolts that were quickly crushed. Lastarria was exiled; Bilbao and Arcos fled to Argentina. The conservatives easily elected their candidate; like his predecessor, he served two terms (1851–1861). In the wake of the election, however, the liberals again rose in a large-scale revolt that Montt crushed with a heavy loss of life. Montt had triumphed but immediately took steps to resolve the crisis by granting amnesty to the insurgents; he went on to make concessions to the spirit of the times with two important reforms: the abolition of entails and the tithe.

The abolition of entails, which was designed to encourage the breakup of landed estates among the children of the great landowners, affected a dwindling number of great aristocratic clans. Its effects were less drastic than the anguished cries of the affected parties suggested, for the divided estates were almost invariably acquired by other latifundists, and the condition of the inquilinos who worked the land remained the same. The elimination of the tithe, and Montt's refusal to allow the return of the Jesuits, greatly angered the reactionary clergy. Responding to their attacks, Montt promulgated a new civil code in 1857 that placed education under state control, gave the state jurisdiction over the clergy, and granted non-Catholics the right of civil marriage.

The abolition of entails and the tithe represented a compromise between liberals and conservatives, between the new bourgeoisie and the great landowners. In the process, the bourgeoisie gained little, and the landowners lost almost nothing; the chief loser was the church. Montt's reforms alienated the most reactionary elements of the Conservative party; in Congress these elements combined into a conservative-clerical bloc that formed the right-wing opposition to the government. On the other hand, his reforms gained Montt the support of moderate liberals while he retained the loyalty of the majority of moderate conservatives. In the 1850s, this coalition of moderate liberals and conservatives took the name of the National party. Its motto was the typically positivist slogan "Freedom in Order."

The radical liberals, however, continued to demand the repeal of the constitution of 1833. A leading spokesman for the left wing of the Liberal party was the brilliant historian Benjamín Vicuña Mackenna, who founded a newspaper in 1858 in which he hammered away at the need for drastic political and social change. The government shut the newspaper down and Vicuña Mackenna was exiled.

In the last years of his second term, President Montt faced severe economic and political problems. The depression of 1857 caused a sharp fall in the price of copper and reduced Australian and Californian demand for Chilean wheat. The economic decline fed the fires of political discontent. Montt had designated his energetic and influential cabinet minister, Antonio Varas, to succeed him in 1861. But the radical liberals disliked Varas for his stern suppression of dissidents, while clerical conservatives associated him with Montt's attacks on the church's privileges. Agitation against Varas's candidacy erupted into armed revolt in several Chilean cities in January 1859. Montt managed to quell the revolt, but his political position had been seriously weakened. Hoping to avoid new storms, Montt allowed Varas to withdraw his candidacy and supported a new candidate, José Joaquín Pérez, who was acceptable to moderate liberals and many conservatives. He easily won election as the candidate of the National party but formed a coalition government composed of Nationals, conservatives, and liberals. He served the customary two terms (1861–1871).

By 1861 the depression had lifted, and another boom began, creating new fortunes and bringing large shifts of regional influence. A growing stream of settlers, including many Germans, flowed into southern Chile, founding cities and transforming woodlands into farms.

But Chile's true center of economic gravity became the desert north, rich in copper, nitrates, and guano; the last two, in particular, were objects of Europe's insatiable demand for fertilizers. The major nitrate deposits, however, lay in the Bolivian province of Antofagasta and the Peruvian province of Tarapacá. Chilean capital, supplemented by English and German capital, began to pour into these regions and soon dominated the Peruvian and Bolivian nitrate industries. In the north there arose an aggressive mining capitalist class that demanded a place in the sun for itself and its region. A rich mine owner, Pedro León Gallo, abandoned the liberals to form a new party, called Radical, that fought more militantly than the liberals for constitutional changes, religious toleration, and an end to repressive policies. Under Pérez, liberals and Radicals combined to secure reforms that included toleration for non-Catholics, a curtailment of presidential powers, and a ban on immediate presidential re-election.

Liberal Control

The transition of Chile's political life to liberal control, begun under Montt, was completed in 1871 with the election of the first liberal president, Federico Errázuriz Zañartú. Between 1873 and 1875, a coalition of liberals and Radicals pushed through Congress a series of constitutional reforms: reduction of senatorial terms from nine to six years; direct election of senators; and freedom of speech, press, and assembly. These victories for enlightenment also represented a victory of new capitalist groups over the old merchant-landowner oligarchy that traced its beginnings back to colonial times. By 1880, of the fifty-nine Chilean personal fortunes of over 1 million pesos, only twenty-four were of colonial origin and only twenty had made their fortunes in agriculture; the rest belonged to coal, nitrate, copper, and silver interests or to merchants whose wealth had been formed only in the nineteenth century. Arnold Bauer has observed that the more interesting point is "not that only twenty made their fortune in agriculture, but that the remaining thirty-nine—designated as miners, bankers, and capitalists—subsequently invested their earnings in rural estates. This would be comparable to Andrew Carnegie sinking his steel income into Scarlett O'Hara's plantation." Bauer's comment points to the "powerful social model" that the Chilean agrarian oligarchy continued to

exert. For the rest, the victories of the new bourgeoisie brought no relief to the Chilean masses, the migrant laborers and tenant farmers on the haciendas, and the young working class in Chile's mines and factories.

Brazil

Dom Pedro, Emperor

Brazil took its first major step toward independence in 1808, when the Portuguese crown and court, fleeing before a French invasion of Portugal, arrived in Rio de Janeiro to make it the new capital of the Portuguese Empire. Full national sovereignty came in 1822, when Dom Pedro, who ruled Brazil as regent for his father, João VI, rejected a demand that he return to Portugal and issued the famous Cry of Ipiranga: "Independence or Death!" Dom Pedro acted with the advice and support of the Brazilian aristocracy, determined to preserve the autonomy Brazil had enjoyed since 1808. It was equally determined to make a transition to independence without the violence that marked the Spanish-American movement of liberation. The Brazilian aristocracy had its wish; Brazil made a transition to independence with comparatively little disruption and bloodshed. But separation from Portugal with a minimum of internal dislocation meant that independent Brazil retained not only monarchy and slavery but such other colonial features as the large landed estate and monoculture; a wasteful, inefficient agricultural system; a highly stratified society; and a free population that was 90 percent illiterate and prejudiced against manual labor.

Dom Pedro had promised to give his subjects a constitution, but the constituent assembly that he summoned in 1823 drafted a document that seemed to the emperor to place excessive limits on his power. He responded by dissolving the assembly and assigning to a hand-picked commission the making of a new constitution, which he approved and promulgated by imperial proclamation. This constitution, under which Brazil was governed until the fall of the monarchy in 1889, concentrated great power in the hands of the monarch. In addition to a Council of State, it provided for a two-chamber parliament, a lifetime Senate whose members were chosen by the emperor, and a Chamber of Deputies elected by voters who met property and income requirements. The emperor had the right to appoint and dismiss ministers and summon or dissolve parliament at will. He also appointed the provincial governors or presidents.

Resentment over Dom Pedro's high-handed dissolution of the constituent assembly and the highly centralist character of the constitution of 1824 was particularly strong in Pernambuco, a center of republican and federalist ferment. Here in 1824 a group of rebels, led by the merchant Manoel de Carvalho, proclaimed the creation of a Confederation of the Equator that would unite the six northern provinces under a republican government. A few leaders voiced antislavery sentiments, but nothing was done to abolish slavery, which deprived the movement of the potential support of a large slave population. Within a year, imperial troops had smashed the revolt, and fifteen of its leaders were executed.

Dom Pedro had won a victory but resentment of his autocratic tendencies continued to smolder, and his popularity steadily waned. The emperor's foreign policies contributed to this growing discontent. In 1826, in return for recognition of Brazilian independence and a trade agreement, Dom Pedro signed a treaty with Great Britain that obligated Brazil to end the slave traffic by 1830. Despite this ban and the efforts of British warships to intercept and seize the slave ships, the trade continued with the full knowledge and approval of the Brazilian government. But British policing practices caused the price of slaves to rise sharply. The prospering coffee growers of Rio de Janeiro, São Paulo, and Minas Gerais could afford to pay high prices for slaves, but the cotton and sugar growers of the depressed north could not compete with them for workers and blamed Dom Pedro for their difficulties.

Another source of discontent was the costly and fruitless war with Argentina (1825–1828)

over the Banda Oriental (Uruguay), which the Brazilians called the Cisplatine Province. The war was supported by the ranchers of Rio Grande do Sul, who coveted the rich pasturelands of Uruguay, but it aroused much opposition elsewhere. When it ended in a compromise that guaranteed the independence of Uruguay, its outcome was regarded as a humiliating defeat for Brazil, and Dom Pedro suffered a further loss of prestige. Two other causes of the emperor's growing unpopularity were the favoritism he showed to the corrupt Portuguese courtiers of his entourage and his continued involvement in Portuguese politics, especially his effort in upholding the claims of his daughter Maria to the Portuguese throne.

News of the July Revolution of 1830 in France, a revolution that toppled an unpopular, autocratic king, produced rejoicing and violent demonstrations in Brazilian cities. *Exaltados* (radical liberals) placed themselves at the head of the movement of revolt and called for the abolition of the monarchy and the establishment of a federal republic. In the face of the growing crisis, Don Pedro vacillated; first he made concessions to anti-Portuguese sentiment by appointing a new cabinet of Brazilian-born ministers, then he dissolved it and named a new cabinet that included the most hated figures in his Brazilian entourage. In April 1831, mass demonstrations in the capital were joined by the local garrison. A delegation of city magistrates demanded that he reinstate the former ministry; Dom Pedro refused. The next day, April 7, he abdicated in favor of his five-year-old son Pedro, and two weeks later he sailed for Portugal, never to return.

Regency, Revolt, and a Boy Emperor

The revolution had been the work of radical liberals who viewed Dom Pedro's downfall as the first step toward the establishment of a federal republic, but its fruits were garnered by more moderate men. In effect, the radicals had played the game of the monarchist liberals who guided the movement of secession from Portugal and later lost influence at court as a result of Dom

Pedro's shift to the right. Dom Pedro's departure was a victory for these moderates, and they hastened to restore their ascendancy over the central government and prevent the revolution from getting out of hand.

As a first step, parliament appointed a three-man regency composed of moderate liberals to govern for the child emperor until he reached the age of eighteen. Another measure created a national guard, recruited from the propertied classes, to repress urban mobs and slave revolts. Simultaneously, the new government began work on a project of constitutional reform designed to appease the strong federalist sentiment. After a three-year debate, parliament approved the Additional Act of 1834, which gave the provinces elective legislative assemblies with broad powers, including control over local budgets and taxes. This provision assured the great landowners of a large measure of control over their regions. The Council of State, identified with Dom Pedro's reactionary rule, was abolished. But centralism was not abandoned, for the national government continued to appoint provincial governors with a partial veto over the acts of the provincial assemblies. Centralism was even strengthened by the replacement of the three-man regency with a single regent. To this post parliament named the moderate liberal Diogo Antônio Feijó.

Almost immediately, Feijó had to struggle against a rash of revolts, most numerous in the northern provinces, whose economy suffered from a loss of markets for their staple crops, sugar and cotton. None occurred in the central southern zone (the provinces of Rio de Janeiro, São Paulo, and Minas Gerais), whose coffee economy prospered and whose planter aristocracy had secure control of the central government. These revolts had a variety of local causes. Some were elemental, popular revolts; such was the so-called *cabanagem* (from the word *cabana,* "cabin") of Pará, which originated in the grievances of small tradesmen, farmers, and lower-class elements against the rich Portuguese merchants who monopolized local trade. Others, like the republican and separatist revolt in Bahia

Dom Pedro II. (Courtesy of the Organization of American States)

(1837–1838), reflected the frustrations of the planter aristocracy of this once-prosperous area over its loss of economic and political power.

Most serious of all was the revolt that broke out in 1835 in the province of Rio Grande do Sul. Although it was dubbed the *Revolução Farroupilha* (Revolution of the Ragamuffins) in contemptuous reference to its supposed lower-class origins, the movement was led by cattle barons who maintained a more or less patriarchal sway over the gauchos who formed the rank-and-file of the rebel armies. An intense regionalism, resentment over taxes and unpopular governors imposed by the central government, and the strength of republican sentiment were major factors in producing the revolt of Rio Grande. The presence of considerable numbers of Italian exiles such as Giuseppe Garibaldi, ardent republicans and antislavery men, gave a special radical tinge to the revolt in Rio Grande. In September 1835, the rebels captured the provincial capital of Pôrto Alegre; one year later they proclaimed Rio Grande an independent republic. For almost a decade, two states—one a republic, the other an empire—existed on Brazilian territory.

The secession of Rio Grande and the inability of imperial troops to quell the revolt further weakened the position of Feijó, whose authoritarian temper and disregard for parliamentary majorities in the choice of ministers had caused much discontent. By now the political struggle had begun to assume an organized form, with the emergence of a Liberal party composed chiefly of moderate liberals who favored concessions to federalism, and a Conservative party, which preferred to strengthen the central government. However, on such essential issues as the monarchy, slavery, and the maintenance of the status quo in general, liberals and conservatives saw eye to eye.

In September 1837, Feijó resigned and was succeeded as regent by the conservative Pedro de Araújo Lima. Like his predecessor, Araújo Lima concentrated his efforts on putting down the Rio Grande rebellion and other regional revolts in the north. The Rio Grande experiment in republican government and its offer of freedom to all slaves who joined the republic's armed forces posed an especially serious threat to monarchy and slavery. Among both liberals and conservatives, the idea gained favor of calling the young Pedro to rule before his legal majority in order to strengthen the central government in its war against subversive and separatist movements. By the beginning of 1840, the project had won virtual acceptance, liberals and conservatives differing only with respect to timing and other details. On July 22, in what was in effect a parliamentary coup d'état the two chambers of parliament proclaimed the fourteen-year-old Dom Pedro emperor; he was formally crowned a year later, in July 1841.

In March 1841, after forcing a short-lived liberal ministry to resign, the emperor called the conservatives to power. The new government proceeded to dismantle the federalist reforms in the Additional Act of 1834. The powers of the provincial assemblies were sharply curtailed; locally elected judges were stripped of their judicial and police powers, which were vested in a new national police; and the Council of State was restored. Having consolidated their position, the conservatives decided to change the balance of forces in the new Chamber of Deputies, where the liberals had won a majority and, charging corruption in the elections, persuaded the emperor to dissolve it.

The liberals of São Paulo and Minas Gerais responded with a revolt (1842) that had little popular support, for it was dictated solely by the desire for the spoils of office. Troops led by the conservative leader Baron Caxias swiftly crushed the uprising. But the emperor treated the vanquished rebels leniently; indeed, a short time later he called on the liberals to form a new ministry. Once returned to power, the liberals made no effort to repeal the conservative revisions of the constitution and made use of the broad police powers vested in the central government for their own ends.

With the unity of the ruling class restored, the government undertook to settle scores with the rebels of Rio Grande. As a result of internal squabbles and the cessation of aid from friendly Uruguay when that country was invaded by Rosas' troops in February 1843, the situation of the republic became extremely difficult. Meanwhile, Baron Caxias advanced with large forces against the rebels and wrested town after town from their troops. Facing defeat, the republican leaders accepted an offer from Rio de Janeiro to negotiate a peace, which was signed in February 1845. The peace treaty extended amnesty to all rebels but annulled all laws of the republican regime. The cattle barons won certain concessions, including the right to nominate their candidate for the post of provincial governor and retention of their military titles.

The last large-scale revolt in the series that shook Brazil in the 1830s and 1840s was the uprising of 1848 in Pernambuco. Centered in the city of Recife, its causes included hostility toward the Portuguese merchants who monopolized local trade, the appointment of an unpopular governor by the conservative government, and hatred for the greatest landowners of the region, the powerful Cavalcanti family. The rebel program called for the removal from Recife of all Portuguese merchants, expansion of provincial autonomy, work for the unemployed, and division of the Cavalcanti lands. Even this radical program, however, contained no reference to the abolition of slavery. The movement collapsed after the capture of Recife by imperial troops in 1849. Many captured leaders were condemned to prison for life, but all were amnestied in 1852.

The Game of Politics and the Crisis of Slavery

By 1850, Brazil was at peace. The emperor presided over a pseudo-parliamentary regime that in reality was a royal dictatorship exercised in the interests of a tiny ruling class. He paid his respects to parliamentary forms by alternately appointing conservative and liberal prime ministers at will; if the new ministry did not command a majority in parliament, one was obtained by holding rigged elections. Since the ruling class was united on essential issues, the only thing at stake in party struggles was the spoils of office. An admirer of Dom Pedro, Joaquim Nabuco, described the operation of the system in his book *O abolicionismo:*

The president of the council lives at the mercy of the crown, from which he derives his power; even the appearance of power is his only when he is regarded as the emperor's lieutenant and is believed to have in his pocket the decree of dissolution—that is, the right to elect a chamber made up of his own henchmen. Below him are the ministers, who live by the favor of the president of the council; farther down still, on the third plane, are found the deputies, at the mercy of the ministers. The representative system, then, is a graft of parliamentary forms on a patriarchal government, and senators and deputies only take their roles seriously in this parody of democracy because of the personal advantage they derive therefrom. Suppress the subsidies, force them to stop using their positions for personal and family ends, and no one who had anything else to do would waste his time in such shadow boxing.[4]

The surface stability of Brazilian political life in the decades after 1850 rested on the prosperity created by a growing demand and good prices for Brazilian coffee. As the sugar-growing northeast and its plantation society continued to decline because of exhausted soil, archaic techniques, and competition from foreign sugars, the coffee-growing zone of Rio de Janeiro, São Paulo, and Minas Gerais gained new importance.

The crisis of the northeast grew more acute as a result of English pressure on Brazil to enforce the Anglo-Brazilian treaty banning the importation of slaves into Brazil after November 7, 1831. Before 1850 this treaty was never effectively enforced; more than fifty thousand slaves a year were brought to Brazil during the 1840s. In 1849 and 1850, however, the British government instructed its warships to enter Brazilian territorial waters if necessary to seize and destroy Brazilian slave ships. Under British pressure, the Brazilian parliament passed the Queiroz anti-slave-trade law, which was effectively enforced. By the middle 1850s, the importation of slaves had virtually ended.

The ending of the slave trade had major consequences. Because of the high mortality among slaves due to poor food, harsh working conditions, and other negative factors, the slave population could not be maintained by natural reproduction, and the eventual doom of the slave system was assured. The passing of the slave trade created a serious labor shortage, with a large flow of slaves from the north to the south because of the coffee planters' greater capacity to compete for slave labor. This movement aggravated the imbalance between the prosperous

[4] Quoted in Benjamin Keen, ed., *Latin American Civilization: The National Era,* vol. 2 (Boston: Houghton Mifflin, 1974), p. 159.

south central zone and the declining north. The end of the slave trade had another important result: large sums formerly expended for the purchase of slaves were now channeled to other uses, partly into coffee agriculture, partly into the building of an infrastructure for the emerging national economy. The first telegraph lines in Brazil were established in 1852; the first railroad line was begun in 1854. In these years, a pioneer of Brazilian capitalism, Irineu Evangelista de Sousa, later the Baron Maúa, laid the foundations of a veritable industrial and banking empire.

By the 1860s, a growing number of Brazilians had become convinced that slavery brought serious discredit to Brazil and must be ended. The abolition of slavery in the United States as a result of the Civil War, which left Brazil and the Spanish colonies of Cuba and Puerto Rico the only slaveholding areas in the Western Hemisphere, sharpened sensitivity to the problem. The Paraguayan War also promoted the cause of emancipation. In an effort to fill the gaps caused by heavy losses at the front, a decree was issued granting freedom to government-owned slaves who agreed to join the army, and some private slave owners followed the official example. Criticism of slavery was increasingly joined with criticism of the emperor, censured for his cautious posture on slavery. The antislavery movement began to merge with the nascent republican movement. In 1869 the left wing of the Liberal party, organized in a Reform Club, issued a manifesto demanding restrictions on the powers of the emperor and the grant of freedom to the newborn children of slaves. The crisis of slavery was fast becoming a crisis of the Brazilian Empire.

Chapter 10

The Triumph
of Neocolonialism

Beginning about 1870, the quickening tempo of the Industrial Revolution in Europe stimulated a more rapid pace of change in the Latin American economy and politics. Responding to a mounting demand for raw materials and foodstuffs, Latin American producers increased their output of those commodities. The growing trade with Europe helped to stabilize political conditions in Latin America, for the new economic system demanded peace and continuity in government.

Encouraged by the increased stability, European capital flowed into Latin America, creating railroads, docks, processing plants, and other facilities needed to expand and modernize production and trade. Latin America became integrated into an international economic system in which it exchanged raw materials and foodstuffs for the factory-made goods of Europe and North America. Gradual adoption of free-trade policies by many Latin American countries, which marked the abandonment of efforts to create a native factory capitalism, hastened the area's integration into this international division of labor.

The New Colonialism

The new economic system fastened a new dependency on Latin America, with Great Britain and later the United States replacing Spain and Portugal in the dominant role; it may, therefore, be called "neocolonial." Despite its built-in flaws and local breakdowns, the neocolonial order displayed a certain stability until 1914. By disrupting the markets for Latin America's exports and making it difficult to import the manufactured goods that Latin America required, World War I marked the beginning of a general crisis the area has not yet overcome.

Although the period from 1870 to 1914 saw a rapid overall growth of the Latin American economy, the pace and degree of progress were uneven, with some countries (like Bolivia and Paraguay) joining the advance much later than others. A marked feature of the neocolonial order was its one-sidedness (monoculture). One or a few primary products became the basis of each country's prosperity, making it highly vulnerable to fluctuations in the world demand and price of these products. Thus, Argentina and Uruguay depended on wheat and meat; Brazil on coffee, sugar, and briefly on rubber; Chile on copper and nitrates; Honduras on bananas; Cuba on sugar.

In each country, the modern export sector became an enclave largely isolated from the rest of the economy; this enclave actually accentuated the backwardness of other sectors by draining off their labor and capital. The export-oriented nature of the modern sector was reflected in the pattern of the national railway systems, which as a rule were not designed to integrate each country's regions but to satisfy the traffic needs of the export industries. In addition, the modern export sector often rested on extremely precarious foundations. Rapid, feverish growth, punctuated by slumps that sometimes ended in a total collapse, formed part of the neocolonial pattern; such meteoric rise and fall is the story of Peruvian guano, Chilean nitrates, and Brazilian rubber.

Expansion of the Hacienda System

The neocolonial order evolved within the framework of the traditional system of land tenure and labor relations. Indeed, it led to an expansion of the hacienda system on a scale far greater than the colonial period had known. As the growing European demand for Latin American products raised the value of land, the great landowners in country after country launched assaults on the surviving Indian community lands. In Mexico the Reforma laid the legal basis for this attack in

the 1850s and 1860s; it reached its climax in the era of Porfirio Díaz.

Seizure of church lands by liberal governments also contributed to the growth of the latifundio. Mexico again offered a model, with its Lerdo Law and the Juárez anticlerical decrees. Following the Mexican example, Colombian liberal governments confiscated church lands in the 1860s, the liberal dictator Antonio Guzmán Blanco seized many church estates in Venezuela in the 1870s, and Ecuadoran liberals expropriated church lands in 1895.

Expansion of the public domain through railway construction and Indian wars also contributed to the growth of great landed estates. Lands taken from the church or wrested from Indian tribes were usually sold to buyers in vast tracts at nominal prices. Concentration of land, reducing the cultivable area available to Indian and mestizo small landowners, was accompanied by a parallel growth of the *minifundio*—an uneconomical small plot worked with primitive techniques.

The seizure of Indian community lands to use immediately or to hold for a speculative rise in value provided great landowners with another advantage by giving them control of the local labor force at a time of increasing demand for labor. Expropriated Indians rarely became true wage earners paid wholly in cash, for such workers were too expensive and independent in spirit. A more widespread labor system was debt peonage, in which workers were paid wholly or in part with vouchers redeemable at the *tienda de raya* (company store), whose inflated prices and often devious bookkeeping created a debt that was passed on from father to son. The courts enforced the obligation of peons to remain on the estate until they had liquidated their debts. Peons who protested low wages or the more intensive style of work demanded by the new order were brought to their senses by the landowner's armed retainers or by local police or military authorities.

In some countries, the period saw a revival of the colonial repartimiento system of draft labor for Indians. In Guatemala, this system—here called *mandamiento*—required able-bodied Indians to work for a specified number of days on haciendas. It was the liberal President Justo Rufino Barrios who issued instructions to local magistrates to see to it "that any Indian who seeks to evade his duty is punished to the full extent of the law, that the farmers are fully protected and that each Indian is forced to do a full day's work while in service."

Slavery survived in some places well beyond mid-century—for example, in Peru until 1855, in Cuba until 1886, in Brazil until 1888. Closely akin to slavery was the system of bondage, under which some ninety thousand Chinese coolies were imported into Peru between 1849 and 1875 to work on the guano islands and in railway construction. The term *slavery* also applies to the system under which political deportees and captured Indian rebels were sent by Mexican authorities to labor in unspeakable conditions on the coffee, tobacco, and henequen plantations of southern Mexico.

More modern systems of agricultural labor and farm tenantry arose only in such regions as southern Brazil and Argentina, whose critical labor shortage required the offer of greater incentives to the millions of European immigrants who poured into those countries between 1870 and 1910.

Labor conditions were little better in the mining industry and in the factories that arose in some countries after 1890. Typical conditions were a workday of twelve to fourteen hours, miserable wages frequently paid in vouchers redeemable only at the company store, and arbitrary, abusive treatment by employers and foremen. Latin American law codes usually prohibited strikes and other organized efforts to improve working conditions, and police and the armed forces were commonly employed to break strikes, sometimes with heavy loss of life.

Foreign Control of Resources

The rise of the neocolonial order was accompanied by a steady growth of foreign corporate control over the natural and man-made resources of the continent. The process went through stages; in 1870 foreign investment was still largely concentrated in trade, shipping, railways, public utilities, and government loans. At that date, British capital enjoyed an undisputed hegemony in the Latin American investment field. By 1914 foreign corporate ownership had expanded to include most of the mining industry and had deeply penetrated real estate, ranching, plantation agriculture, and manufacturing. By that date, too, Great Britain's rivals had effectively challenged its domination in Latin America. Of these rivals, the most spectacular advance was made by the United States, whose Latin American investments had risen from a negligible amount in 1870 to over $1.6 billion by the end of 1914 (still well below the nearly $5 billion investment of Great Britain).

Foreign economic penetration went hand in hand with a growth of political influence and even armed intervention. The youthful U.S. imperialism proved to be the most aggressive of all. In the years after 1898, a combination of "dollar diplomacy" and armed intervention transformed the Caribbean into an "American lake" and reduced Cuba, the Dominican Republic, and several Central American states to the status of dependencies and protectorates of the United States.

The Politics of Acquisition

The new economy demanded a new politics. Conservatives and liberals, fascinated by the atmosphere of prosperity created by the export boom, the rise in land values, the flood of foreign loans, and the growth of government revenues, put aside their ideological differences and joined in the pursuit of wealth. The positivist slogan, "Order and Progress," now became the watchword of Latin America's ruling classes. The social Darwinist idea of the struggle for survival of the fittest and Herbert Spencer's doctrine of "inferior races," frequently used to support claims of the inherent inferiority of the Indian, mestizo, and mulatto masses, also entered the upper-class ideological arsenal.

214

The growing domination of national economies by the export sectors and the development of a consensus between the old landed aristocracy and more capitalist-oriented groups caused political issues like the federalist-centralist conflict and the liberal-conservative cleavage to lose much of their meaning; in some countries, the old party lines dissolved or became extremely tenuous. A new type of "progressive" caudillo—Porfirio Díaz in Mexico, Rafael Núñez in Colombia, Justo Rufino Barrios in Guatemala, Antonio Guzmán Blanco in Venezuela—symbolized the politics of acquisition.

As the century drew to a close, dissatisfied urban middle-class, immigrant, and entrepreneurial groups in some countries combined to form parties, called Radical or Democratic, that challenged the traditional domination of politics by the creole aristocracy. They demanded political, social, and educational reforms that would give more weight to the new middle sectors. But these middle sectors—manufacturers, shopkeepers, professionals, and the like—were in large part a creation of the neocolonial order, depended on it for their livelihood, and as a rule did not question its viability. The small socialist, anarchist, and syndicalist groups that arose in various Latin American countries in the 1890s challenged both capitalism and neocolonialism, but the full significance of these movements lay in the future.

The trends just described lend a certain unity to the history of Mexico, Argentina, Chile, and Brazil in the period from 1870 to 1914. Each country's history, however, presents significant variations on the common theme—variations that reflect that country's specific historical background and conditions.

Mexican Politics and Economy

Dictatorship Under Díaz

General Porfirio Díaz seized power in 1876 from President Lerdo de Tejada with the support of disgruntled regional caudillos and military personnel, liberals angered by the political manipulations of the entrenched Lerdo machine, and Indian and mestizo small landholders who believed that Díaz would put an end to land seizures. Having installed himself as president, Díaz paid his respects to the principle of no re-election by allowing a trusted crony, General Manuel González, to succeed him in 1880. However, he returned to the presidential palace in 1884 and continued to occupy it through successive re-elections until his resignation and flight from Mexico in 1911. He got rid of the now-inconvenient issue of no re-election by having the constitution amended in 1887 and 1890 to permit his indefinite re-election; in 1904 he obtained an extension of the president's term from four to six years. Thus, Díaz, who had seized power in the name of republican legality, erected one of the longest personal dictatorships in Latin American history.

The construction of the dictatorship, however, was a gradual process. During his first presidential term, Díaz permitted reasonably fair elections, Congress and the judiciary enjoyed a certain independence, and the press, including a vocal radical labor press, was free. The outlines of Díaz's economic and social policies, however, soon became clear. Confronted with an empty treasury, facing pressures from above and below, Díaz decided in favor of the great landowners, moneylenders, and foreign capitalists, whose assistance could insure his political survival. In return, he assured these groups of protection for their property and other interests. Díaz, who had once proclaimed that in the age-old struggle between the people and the haciendas he was on the side of the people, now sent troops to suppress peasant resistance to land seizures. Before taking power, Díaz had denounced Lerdo for his generous concessions to British capitalists; by 1880, Díaz had granted even more lavish subsidies for railway construction to North American companies. Economic development had become for Díaz the great object, the key to the solution of his own problems and those of the nation.

Economic development required political stability; accordingly, Díaz promoted a policy of conciliation that consisted of offering an olive branch and a share of spoils to all influential op-

Beginning in the 1920s, with considerable support from the state, there arose in Mexico a school of socially conscious artists who sought to enlighten the masses about their bitter past and the promise of the revolutionary present. One of the greatest of these artists was David Alfaro Siqueiros, whose painting depicts with satire the former President Porfirio Díaz, who tramples on the Constitution of 1857 as he diverts his wealthy followers with dancing girls. (Reproduccion autorizada por el Instituto Nacional de Bellas Artes y Literatura/Collection Museo Nacional de Historia, I.N.A.H.-S.E.P.)

ponents, no matter what their political past or persuasion—*Lerdistas,* Juaristas, conservatives, clericals, anticlericals. A dog with a bone in its mouth, Díaz cynically observed, neither kills nor steals. In effect, Díaz invited all sections of the upper class and some members of the middle class, including prominent intellectuals and journalists, to join the great Mexican barbecue, from which only the poor and humble were barred. An important instrument of Díaz's law-and-order policy was a force of mounted police, the *rurales,* distinguished by their picturesque dress. The former bandits and vagrants who had composed a good part of this force were gradually replaced by artisan and peasant recruits, who had been dislocated by the large social changes that took place during the *Porfiriato.* Aside from chasing unrepentant bandits, the major function of the rurales was to suppress peasant unrest and break strikes.

There was another side to the policy of conciliation, however, a side described by the formula *pan o palo* (bread or the club). Opponents who refused Díaz's bribes—political offices, monopolies, and the like—suffered swift reprisal. Dissidents were beaten up, murdered, or arrested and sent to the damp underground dungeons of San Juan de Ulúa or the grim Belén prison, a sort of Mexican Bastille. Designed to hold two hundred prisoners, Belén commonly held four to five thousand inmates. One prominent journalist, Filomeno Mata, was jailed thirty-four times.

By such means, Díaz virtually eliminated all effective opposition by the end of his second term (1884–1888). The constitution of 1857 and the liberties it guaranteed existed only on paper. Elections to Congress, in theory the highest organ of government, were a farce; Díaz simply circulated a list of his candidates to local officials, who certified their election. The dictator contemptuously called Congress his *caballada,* his stable of horses. The state governors were appointed by Díaz, usually from the ranks of local great landlords or his generals. In return for their loyalty, he gave them a free hand to enrich themselves and terrorize the local population. Under them were district heads called *jefes políticos,* petty tyrants appointed by the governors with the approval of Díaz; below them were municipal presidents who ran the local administrative units. One feature of the Díaz era was a mushrooming of the administrative and coercive apparatus; government costs during this period soared by 900 percent.

The army, as indispensable to Díaz as it had been to Santa Anna, naturally enjoyed special favor. Higher officers were well paid and enjoyed many opportunities for enrichment at the expense of the regions in which they were quartered. The Díaz army, however, was pathetically inadequate for purposes of national defense. Generals and other high officers were appointed not for their ability but for their loyalty to the dictator. Discipline, morale, and training were extremely poor. A considerable part of the rank-and-file were recruited from the dregs of society; the remainder were young Indian conscripts. These soldiers, often used for brutal repression of strikes and agrarian unrest, were themselves harshly treated and miserably paid—the wage of ranks below sergeant was fifty cents a month.

The church became another pillar of the dictatorship. Early in his second term, Díaz reached an accommodation with the hierarchy. The church agreed to support Díaz; in return he allowed the anticlerical Reforma laws to fall into disuse. In disregard of those laws, monasteries and nunneries were restored, church schools established, and wealth again began to accumulate in the hands of the church. Faithful to its bargain, the church turned a deaf ear to the complaints of the lower classes and taught complete submission to the authorities. As in colonial times, many priests were utterly venal and corrupt. Only in the closing years of the dictatorship did the church, sensing the coming storm, begin to advocate modest social reforms.

The Díaz policy of conciliation was directed at prominent intellectuals as well as more wealthy and powerful figures. A group of such intellectuals, professional men, and businessmen made up a closely knit clique of Díaz's advisers. Known as *Científicos,* they got their name from their insistence on "scientific" administration of the state and were especially influential after 1892. About fifteen men made up the controlling nucleus of the group. Their leader was Díaz's all-powerful father-in-law, Manuel Romero Rubio, and, after his death in 1895, the new minister of finance, José Yves Limantour.

For the Científicos, the economic movement was everything. Most Científicos accepted the thesis of the inherent inferiority of the Indian and mestizo population and the consequent necessity for relying on the native white elite and on foreigners and their capital to lead Mexico out of its backwardness. In the words of the journalist Francisco G. Cosmes, "the Indian has only the passive force of inferior races, is incapable of actively pursuing the goal of civilization."

But there were differences of opinion within the group. The most distinguished intellectual among the Científicos was the old-time liberal Justo Sierra, a biographer of Juárez who wistfully clung to his libertarian ideas, yet served Díaz, believing that he was preparing Mexico to be free. By contrast with such racists as Francisco Bulnes and José Yves Limantour, Sierra rejected the notion of Indians' racial inferiority and argued that education could correct their seeming dullness and apathy.

Some members of the Díaz establishment even harbored doubts about Díaz's policies and methods. Troubled by the immobility of the regime, fearing revolution, some Científicos urged a variety of reforms, including an end to re-election and the introduction of a multiparty system. But their advice was not heeded and, being practical men, most resigned themselves to the more profitable task of enriching themselves.

Thanks to the devoted efforts of educators like Justo Sierra, the Díaz era saw some advances in public education. In 1887, Sierra secured the adoption of a federal law making primary education obligatory. Despite the law, however, it appears that on the average only one out of three children between the ages of six and twelve were enrolled. The vast majority of these children probably went only through the first year and remained functionally illiterate. The principal beneficiaries of the educational progress under Díaz were the sons of the rich: for every student enrolled in the primary schools in 1910, the state spent about 7 pesos; for every student in the college preparatory schools, it spent nearly 100 pesos.

In the last analysis, however, apologists for the dictatorship rested their case on the "economic miracle" that Díaz had allegedly worked in Mexico. A survey of the Mexican economy in 1910 reveals how modest that miracle was.

Concentration of Landownership

At the opening of the twentieth century, Mexico was still predominantly an agrarian country; 77 percent of its population of 15 million still lived on the land. The laws of the Reforma had already given impetus to the concentration of landownership, and under Díaz this trend was greatly accelerated. There is some evidence of a link between the rapid advance of railway construction, which increased the possibilities of production for export and therefore stimulated a rise in land values, and the growth of land-grabbing in the Díaz period.

A major piece of land legislation was a law of 1883 that provided for the survey of so-called vacant public lands, *tierras baldías.* The law authorized real estate companies to survey such lands and retain one-third of the surveyed area; the remainder was sold for low fixed prices in vast tracts, usually to Díaz's favorites and their foreign associates. The 1883 law required the surveying companies and purchasers to settle at least one person for each five hundred acres surveyed, but a second law (1894) removed this obligation and deleted the clause restricting the amount of land that one individual could purchase.

The 1883 and 1894 laws opened the way for vast territorial acquisitions. One individual alone obtained nearly 12 million acres in Baja California and other northern states. But the land companies were not satisfied with the acquisition of true vacant lands. The law of 1894 declared that a parcel of land to which a legal title could not be produced might be declared vacant land, opening the door to expropriation of Indian villages and other small landholders whose forebears had tilled their lands from times immemorial but who could not produce the required titles. If the victims offered armed resistance, troops were sent against them, and the vanquished rebels were sold like slaves to labor on henequen plantations in Yucatán or sugar plantations in Cuba. This was the fate of the Yaqui Indians of the northwest, defeated after a long, valiant struggle.

Another instrument of land seizure was an 1890 law designed to give effect to older Reforma laws requiring the distribution of Indian village lands among the villagers. The law created enormous confusion. In many cases, land speculators and hacendados cajoled the illiterate Indians into selling their titles for paltry sums. Hacendados also used other means, such as cutting off a village's water supply or simply brute force, to achieve their predatory ends. By 1910 the process of land expropriation was largely complete. More than 90 percent of the Indian villages of the central plateau, the most densely populated region of the country, had lost their communal lands. Only the most tenacious resistance enabled villages that still held their lands to survive the assault of the great landowners. Landless peons and their families made up 9.5 million of a rural population of 12 million.

As a rule, the new owners did not use the land seized from Indian villages or small landholders more efficiently. Hacendados let much of the usurped land lie idle. They waited for a speculative rise in value or for an American buyer. By keeping land out of production, they helped to keep the price of maize and other staples artificially high. The technical level of hacienda agriculture was generally extremely low, with little use of irrigation, machinery, and commercial fertilizer, although some new landowning groups— such as northern cattle raisers and cotton growers, the coffee and rubber growers of Chiapas, and the henequen producers of Yucatán—employed more modern equipment and techniques.

The production of foodstuffs stagnated, barely keeping pace during most of the period with the growth of population, and per capita production of such basic staples as maize and beans actually declined toward the end of the century. This decline culminated in three years of bad harvests, 1907–1910, due principally to drought. As a result, the importation of maize and other foodstuffs from the United States steadily increased in the last years of the Díaz regime. Despite the growth of pastoral industry, per capita consumption of milk and cheese barely kept pace with the growth of population, for a considerable proportion of the cattle sold was destined for the export market.

The only food products whose increase exceeded the growth of population were alcoholic beverages. Some idea of the increase in their consumption is given by the fact that the number of bars in Mexico City rose from 51 in 1864 to 1,400 in 1900. At the end of the century, the Mexican death rate from alcoholism—a common response to intolerable conditions of life and labor—was estimated to be six times that of France. Meanwhile, inflation, rampant during the last part of the Díaz regime, greatly raised the cost of the staples on which the mass of the population depended. Without a corresponding increase in wages, the situation of agricultural and industrial laborers deteriorated sharply.

The Economic Advance

While food production for the domestic market declined, production of food and industrial raw materials for the foreign market experienced a vigorous growth. By 1910, Mexico had become the largest producer of henequen, source of a fiber in great demand in the world market. Mexican export production became increasingly geared to the needs of the United States, which was the principal market for sugar, bananas, rubber, and tobacco produced on plantations that were largely foreign-owned. American companies dominated the mining industry, whose output of copper, gold, lead, and zinc, rose sharply after 1890. A spectacular late development was shown by the oil industry, which was controlled by American and British interests; by 1911, Mexico was third among the world's oil producers. French and Spanish capitalists virtually monopolized the textile industry and other consumer goods industries that had a relatively rapid growth after 1890. Operating behind the protection of tariff walls that excluded foreign competition in cheap goods, they compelled the masses to pay high prices for articles of inferior quality.

Foreign control of key sectors of the economy and the fawning attitude of the Díaz regime toward foreigners gave rise to a popular saying: "Mexico, mother of foreigners and stepmother of Mexicans." The ruling clique of Científicos justified this favoritism by citing the need for a rapid development of Mexico's natural resources and the creation of a strong country capable of defending its political independence and territorial integrity.

Thanks to an influx of foreign capital, some quickening and modernization of economic life did take place under Díaz. The volume of foreign trade greatly increased, a modern banking system arose, and the country acquired a relatively dense network of railways. But these successes were achieved at a very heavy price: a brutal dictatorship, the pauperization of the mass of the population, the stagnation of food agriculture, the strengthening of the inefficient latifundio, and the survival of many feudal or semifeudal vestiges in Mexican economic and social life.

Labor, Agrarian, and Middle-Class Unrest

The survival of feudal vestiges was especially glaring in the area of labor relations. There was some variation in labor conditions from region to region. In 1910 forced labor and outright slavery, as well as older forms of debt peonage, were characteristic of the south (the states of Yucatán, Tabasco, Chiapas, and parts of Oaxaca and Veracruz). The rubber, coffee, tobacco, henequen, and sugar plantations of this region depended heavily on the forced labor of political deportees, captured Indian rebels, and contract workers kidnaped or lured to work in the tropics by a variety of devices.

In central Mexico, where a massive expropriation of Indian village lands had created a large landless Indian proletariat, tenantry, sharecropping, and the use of migratory labor had increased, and living standards had declined. The large labor surplus of this area diminished the need for hacendados to tie their workers to their estates with debt peonage. In the north the proximity of the United States, with its higher wage scales, and the competition of hacendados with mine owners for labor made wages and sharecropping arrangements somewhat more favorable and weakened debt peonage. In all parts of

the country, however, the life of agricultural workers was filled with hardships and abuses of every kind.

Labor conditions in mines and factories were little better than in the countryside. Workers in textile mills labored twelve to fifteen hours daily for a wage ranging from eleven cents for unskilled women and children to seventy-five cents for highly skilled workers. Employers found ways of reducing even these meager wages. Wages were discounted for alleged "carelessness" in the use of tools or machines or for "defective goods"; workers were usually paid wholly or in part with vouchers good only in company stores, whose prices were higher than in other stores. Federal and state laws banned trade unions and strikes. Scores of workers, both men and women, were shot down by troops who broke the great textile strike in the Orizaba (Veracruz) area in 1907, and scores were killed or wounded in putting down the strike at the American-owned Consolidated Copper Company mine at Cananea (Sonora) in 1906. Despite such repressions, the trade union movement continued to grow in the last years of the Díaz era, and socialist, anarchist, and syndicalist ideas began to influence the still small working class.

The growing wave of strikes and agrarian unrest in the last, decadent phase of the Díaz era indicated an increasingly rebellious mood among ever broader sections of the Mexican people. Alienation spread among teachers, lawyers, journalists, and other professionals, whose opportunities for advancement were sharply limited by the monolithic control of economic, political, and social life by the Científicos, their foreign allies, and regional oligarchies. In the United States in 1905 a group of middle-class intellectuals, headed by the Flores Magón brothers, organized the Liberal party, which called for the overthrow of Díaz and advanced a platform whose economic and social provisions anticipated many articles of the constitution of 1917.

Even members of the ruling class began to join the chorus of criticism. These upper-class dissidents included liberal hacendados of a more

Striking workers at the Rio Blanco textile works in Mexico in 1909; the business was controlled by French capital. Troops broke up the strike and much blood was shed. (Brown Brothers)

bourgeois type and national capitalists who resented the competitive advantages enjoyed by foreign companies in Mexico. They also feared that the static, reactionary Díaz policies could provoke the masses to overthrow the capitalist system itself. Fearing revolution, these upper-class critics urged Díaz to end his personal rule, shake up the regime, and institute the reforms needed to preserve the existing economic and social order. When their appeals fell on deaf ears, some of these bourgeois reformers reluctantly prepared to take the road of revolution. Typical of these men was the wealthy hacendado and businessman Francisco Madero, soon to become the Apostle of the Mexican Revolution.

The simultaneous advent of an economic recession and a food crisis sharpened this growing discontent. The depression of 1906–1907, which spread from the United States to Mexico, caused a wave of bankruptcies, layoffs, and wage cuts. At the same time the crop failures of 1907–1910 provoked a dramatic rise in the price of staples like maize and beans. By 1910, Mexico's internal conflicts had reached an explosive stage. The workers' strikes, the agrarian unrest, the agitation of middle-class reformers, the disaffection of some great landowners and capitalists all reflected the disintegration of the dictatorship's social base. Despite its superficial stability and posh splendor, the house of Díaz was rotten from top to bottom. Events proved that only a slight push was needed to send it toppling to the ground.

Argentinian Politics and Economy

In the presidential contest of 1874, Nicolás Avellaneda, a lawyer from Tucumán who had the support of Domingo Sarmiento and powerful provincial bosses, defeated former president Bartolomé Mitre. Mitre, who believed that Buenos Aires must retain control of the republic if it were to stay on a progressive course, promptly organized a revolt. He was defeated and captured but was soon released and continued to enjoy for many years the position of Argentina's most honored elder statesman.

Avellaneda, however, did not represent provincial backwardness and caudillismo. A cultured liberal and a disciple of Sarmiento, in whose cabinet he had held office, he continued his predecessor's work of promoting education, immigration, and domestic tranquillity. In 1876 he inaugurated railroad service between Buenos Aires and his native city of Tucumán. The new line forged stronger economic and political links between the port city and the remote northwest, contributing to the end of the long quarrel between Buenos Aires and the interior.

Consolidation of the State

One more sharp confrontation, however, proved necessary before the quarrel between Buenos Aires and the interior could be finally laid to rest. For almost two decades, Buenos Aires had been both capital of the province of the same name and provisional capital of the republic. In 1880, Carlos Tejedor, governor of the province of Buenos Aires and a fanatical champion of the city's predominance, became a candidate for the presidency against another *Tucumano,* Julio Roca. Roca was Avellaneda's secretary of war and protégé and was supported by a powerful group of provincial politicians known as the Córdoba

League. Tejedor and his supporters responded to Roca's election with a new revolt that government and provincial forces soon crushed.

The victors proceeded to carry out the long-standing pledge to federalize Buenos Aires, which became the capital of the nation, while the provincial capital was moved to the city of La Plata. The interior seemed to have triumphed over Buenos Aires, but that apparent victory was an illusion; the provincial lawyers and politicians who carried the day in 1880 had absorbed the commercial and cultural values of the great city and wished not to diminish but to share in its power. Far from losing influence, Buenos Aires steadily gained in wealth and power until it achieved an overwhelming ascendancy over the rest of the country.

The federalization of Buenos Aires completed the consolidation of the Argentine state. Simultaneously, however, a certain decline appeared in the quality of Argentina's political leadership. The great architects of Argentine national unity—Mitre, Alberdi, Sarmiento—had ardently promoted material progress, which they regarded as the key to the solution of all other problems, but their ultimate goal was a democratic society based on access to land and education for the broad masses. That is why they had sponsored—unsuccessfully—homestead legislation and promoted public education, believing, in the words of Sarmiento, that education would "make the poor gaucho a useful man." Austere idealists, they took pride in their personal integrity; their harshest critics never charged Mitre or Sarmiento with using their high offices to advance their personal fortunes.

With President Roca, a new generation of leaders came to the fore, closely identified with and often recruited from the ruling class of great landowners and wealthy merchants. The "generation of 1880," or the oligarchy, as it was also called, shared the faith of Alberdi and Sarmiento in economic development and the value of the North American and European models, but that faith was now deeply tinged with cynicism, egotism, and a profound distrust for the popular classes. These autocratic liberals prized order and progress above freedom. They regarded the gauchos, the Indians, and the mass of illiterate European immigrants flooding Argentina unfit to exercise civic functions. Asked to define universal suffrage, a leading oligarch, Eduardo Wilde, replied, "It is the triumph of universal ignorance."

The new rulers identified the national interest with the interest of the great landowners, wealthy merchants, and foreign capitalists. Regarding the apparatus of state as their personal property or as the property of their class, they used their official connections to enrich themselves. Although they maintained the forms of parliamentary government, they were determined not to let power slip from their hands and organized what came to be called the *unicato* (one-party rule), exercised by the National Autonomist party, which they formed. Extreme concentration of power in the executive branch and systematic use of fraud, violence, and bribery were basic features of the system.

There are some obvious political and ideological affinities between Argentina's rulers in the period from 1880 to 1910 and Mexico's ruling clique of Científicos in the same period, but also some important differences. Whereas the Díaz government favored the church, Argentine governments displayed a moderate anticlericalism, as indicated by a law of 1884 that barred the church from taking part in public education. This official anticlericalism could have been a tactical maneuver designed to win for the oligarchy a progressive reputation and allay middle-class discontent with its other policies; it may also have reflected the influence of the strong English colony, interested for its own reasons in the secularization of Argentine life. Argentine governments also seem to have made greater efforts than the Díaz regime in the field of public education. By 1914 the Argentine illiteracy rate had been reduced from more than two-thirds in 1869 to a little over one-third (but this improvement was largely concentrated on the coast and in the cities). Finally, the Argentine oligarchy had a better record than the Mexican dictatorship with respect to civil liberties, although suppression of the press, jailings, and even torture of radical dissidents were far from unknown.

Economic Boom and Inflation

The ominous new trends of the oligarchy emerged in the administration of President Julio Roca (1880–1886) and flowered exuberantly under his political heir and brother-in-law, Miguel Juárez Celman (1886–1890). Roca presided over the beginnings of a great boom that appeared to justify all the optimism of the oligarchy. As secretary of war under Avellaneda, Roca had led a military expedition—the so-called Conquest of the Desert—southward against the pampa Indians in 1879–1880. This conquest added vast new areas to the province of Buenos Aires and to the national public domain. The campaign created a last opportunity for implementing a democratic land policy directed toward the creation of an Argentine small farmer class. Instead, the Roca administration sold off the area in huge tracts for nominal prices to army officers, politicians, and foreign capitalists. The aging Sarmiento, who had seen the defeat of his own effort to acquire and distribute to settlers public land suitable for farming, lamented: "Soon there will not remain a palm of land for distribution to our immigrants."

Coming at a time of steadily mounting European demand for Argentine meat and wheat, the Conquest of the Desert triggered an orgy of land speculation that drove land prices ever higher and caused a prodigious expansion of cattle raising and agriculture. This expansion took place under the sign of the latifundio. Few of the millions of Italian and Spanish immigrants who entered Argentina in this period realized the common dream of becoming independent small landowners.

Some foreign agricultural colonies were founded in the provinces of Santa Fe and Entre Ríos in the 1870s and 1880s. By the mid-1890s, with wheat prices declining and land prices rising, there was a shift from small-scale farming to extensive tenant farming. This was true even in Santa Fe, the heartland of the foreign colonies.

Soaring land prices and the traditional unwilling-ness of the estancieros to sell land forced the ma-jority of would-be independent farmers to be-come ranch hands, sharecroppers, or tenant farmers. As sharecroppers or tenants, their hold on the land was very precarious; leases were usually limited to one, two, or three years. The immigrant broke the virgin soil, replaced the tough pampa grass with the alfalfa pasturage needed to fatten cattle, and produced the first wheat harvests but then had to move on, leaving the landowner in possession of all improve-ments.

As a result, the great majority of new arrivals either remained in Buenos Aires or, having spent some years in the countryside, returned with their small savings to the city, where the rise of meat-salting and meat-packing plants, railroads, public utilities, and many small factories created a growing demand for labor. True, the immigrant workers received very low wages, worked long hours, and crowded with their families into one-room apartments in wretched slums. But in the city barrio they lived among their own people, free from the loneliness of the pampa and the ar-bitrary rule of great landowners, and had some opportunity of rising in the economic and social scale. As a result, the population of Buenos Aires shot up from 500,000 in 1889 to 1,244,000 in 1909. There arose a growing imbalance between the great city and its hinterland, which held the greater portion of the wealth, population, and culture of the nation, and the interior—particu-larly the northwest—which was impoverished, stagnant, and thinly peopled. Argentina, to use a familiar metaphor, became a giant head set on a dwarf body.

Foreign capital and management played a de-cisive role in the expansion of the Argentine economy in this period. The creole elite obtained vast profits from the rise in the price of their land and the increasing volume of exports but showed little interest in plowing those gains into industry or the construction of the infrastructure required by the export economy, preferring a lavish and leisurely lifestyle over entrepreneurial activity.

Just as they left to English and Irish managers the task of tending their estates, so they left to Eng-lish capital the financing of meat-packing plants, railroads, public utilities, and docks and other fa-cilities. As a result, most of these resources re-mained in British hands. Typical of the oligar-chy's policy of surrender to foreign interests was the decision of Congress in 1889 to sell the state-owned Ferrocarril Oeste, the most profitable and best-run railroad in Argentina, to a British com-pany. Service on a growing foreign debt claimed an ever larger portion of the government's re-ceipts.

Meanwhile, imports of iron, coal, machinery, and consumer goods grew much faster than ex-ports. Combined with the unfavorable price ratio of raw materials to finished goods, the result was an unfavorable balance of trade and a steady drain of gold. New loans with burdensome terms brought temporary relief but aggravated the long-range problem. Under President Miguel Juárez Celman, the disappearance of gold and the government's determination to keep the boom going at all costs led to the issue of great quan-tities of unbacked paper currency and a massive inflation.

The great landowners did not mind, for they were paid for their exports in French francs and English pounds, which they could convert into cheap Argentine pesos for the payment of local costs; besides, inflation caused the price of their lands to rise. The sacrificial victims of the infla-tion were the urban middle class and the work-ers, whose income declined in real value.

The Formation of the Radical Party

In 1889–1890, just as the boom was turning into a depression, the accumulated resentment of the urban middle class and some alienated sectors of the elite over the catastrophic inflation, one-party rule, and official corruption produced a protest movement that took the name *Unión Cív-ica* (Civic Union). Although the new organization had a middle-class base, its leadership united such disparate elements as urban politicians like

Leandro Além, its first president, who was at odds with the Roca–Juárez Celman machine; new landowners and descendants of old aristocratic families who felt excluded from office and access to patronage by the same clique; and Catholics outraged by the government's anticlerical legislation. Aside from the demand for effective suffrage, the only thing uniting these heterogeneous elements was a common determination to overthrow the government.

The birth of the new party at a mass meeting in Buenos Aires in 1890 coincided with a financial storm: the stock market collapsed, bankruptcies multiplied, and in April the cabinet resigned. Encouraged by this last development, and counting on support from the army, the leaders of the Unión Cívica planned a revolt against Juárez Celman in July. Three days of sharp fighting ended in defeat for the rebels.

The oligarchy now showed its ability to maneuver and divide its enemies. Juárez Celman was forced to resign with an abject confession of his errors; his place was taken by his vice president, Carlos Pellegrini (1890–1892), who moved to appease disgruntled elements of the elite by revising the system of distribution of jobs. Bartolomé Mitre, among other aristocratic dissidents, took the bait and reached an accommodation with the oligarchy that provided for an electoral accord between the National party and his followers. Simultaneously, Pellegrini took steps to improve economic conditions by a policy of retrenchment that reduced inflation, stabilized the peso, and revived Argentine credit abroad. Thanks to these measures and a gradual recovery from the depression, popular discontent began to subside.

The defection of Mitre and other aristocratic leaders of the Unión Cívica isolated Leandro Além and other dissidents who were excluded from Pellegrini's peacemaking scheme. Denouncing the accord between Mitre and Pellegrini as a sellout, Além and his nephew, Hipólito Yrigoyen, formed a new party committed to a "radical" democracy—the *Unión Cívica Radical.* The party named Bernardo de Yrigoyen as its presidential

candidate in 1892 but, knowing that rigged elections made his victory impossible, they also prepared for another revolt—a move that Pellegrini effectively squelched by deporting Além and other Radical leaders until after the election of Luis Sáenz Peña (1892–1895).

On his return from exile, Além organized a new revolt, which began in July 1893. The rebels briefly seized Santa Fe and some other towns, but after two and a half months of fighting, the revolt collapsed for lack of significant popular support. Depressed by his failures and the intrigues of his nephew to seize control of the Radical party, Além committed suicide in 1896.

Between 1896 and 1910, the Radical party, now led by Yrigoyen, proved unable to achieve political reform by peaceful or revolutionary means. The reunited oligarchy continued to win election after election by the traditional methods. The architect of the system of corruption and nepotism, Julio Roca, was re-elected president in 1898 and was succeeded by another oligarch, Manuel Quintana, in 1904; on Quintana's death in 1906, Vice President José Figueroa Alcorta served out the rest of his term. A Radical revolt in 1905 proved to be another dismal fiasco.

In Yrigoyen, however, the Radicals possessed a charismatic personality and a masterful organizer who refused to admit defeat. Yrigoyen was a one-time police superintendent in Buenos Aires, a former minor politician who had maneuvered among various factions in the official party, using his political connections to acquire a considerable wealth, which he invested in land and cattle. As a Radical caudillo, Yrigoyen surrounded himself with an aura of mystery, lived in an ostentatiously modest manner, avoided making speeches, and cultivated a literary style that cloaked the poverty of his thought with turgid rhetoric. "Abstention," refusal to participate in rigged elections, and "Revolutionary Intransigence," the determination to resort to revolution until free elections were achieved, were the party's basic slogans.

The vagueness of the Radical program was dictated by the party's need to appeal to very diverse elements and by its wholehearted acceptance of the economic status quo. The Radical party represented the bourgeoisie, but it was a dependent bourgeoisie that did not champion industrialization, economic diversification, or nationalization of foreign-owned industries. Far from attacking the neocolonial order, the Radical party proposed to strengthen it by promoting cooperation between the landed aristocracy and the urban sectors, which were challenging the creole elite's monopoly of political power. In all respects, it was much more conservative than the contemporaneous reformist movement of José Batlle y Ordóñez in Uruguay.[1]

The Radical party went into eclipse after the debacles of 1890 and 1893, but gradually revived after 1900, due in part to Yrigoyen's charismatic personality and organizing talent. The most important factor, however, was the steady growth of an urban and rural middle class largely composed of sons of immigrants. The domination of the export sector, which limited the growth of industry and opportunities for entrepreneurial activity, focused middle-class ambitions more and more on government employment and the professions—two fields dominated by the creole elite. Signs of growing unrest and frustration in the middle class included a series of student strikes in the universities, caused by efforts of creole governing boards to restrict enrollment of students of immigrant descent.

Electoral Reform and the Growth of the Labor Movement

Meanwhile, a section of the oligarchy, headed by Carlos Pellegrini, had begun to advocate electoral reform. These aristocratic reformers argued that the existing situation created a permanent state of tension and instability; they feared that sooner or later the Radical efforts at revolution would succeed. It would be much better, they believed, to make the concessions demanded by the Radicals, open up the political system, and thereby gain for the ruling party—now generally called Conservative—the popular support and legitimacy it needed to remain in power. Moreover, the conservative reformers were aware of a new threat from the left—from the labor movement and especially its vanguard, the socialists, anarchists, and syndicalists—and hoped to make an alliance with the bourgeoisie against the revolutionary working class.

Pellegrini converted President Figueroa Alcorta to his viewpoint, and Figueroa's disciple and political heir, Roque Sáenz Peña, took office as president in 1910 with a promise that he would satisfy the Radical demands. At his urging, Congress passed a series of measures known collectively as the Sáenz Peña Law (1912). The new law established universal and secret male suffrage for citizens when they reached the age of eighteen. This measure, conceding the Radicals' basic demands, compelled them to abandon their revolutionary posture and operate as a regular party through legal channels. In 1912, having abandoned "Abstention," the Radicals made large gains in congressional and local elections, foreshadowing the victory of Hipólito Yrigoyen in the presidential election of 1916.

The Sáenz Peña Law, "an act of calculated retreat by the ruling class," in the words of David Rock, opened the way for a dependent bourgeoisie to share power and the spoils of office with

---

[1] Under the leadership of José Batlle y Ordóñez (1856–1929), president of Uruguay from 1903 to 1907 and again from 1911 to 1915, Uruguay adopted an advanced program of social reform that made it "the chief laboratory for social experimentation in the Americas and a focal point of world interest." The program included the establishment of the eight-hour day, old-age pensions, minimum wages, and accident insurance; abolition of capital punishment, separation of church and state, education for women, and recognition of divorce; and a system of state capitalism that gradually brought under public ownership banks, railroads, electric systems, telephone and telegraph companies, street railways, and meat-packing plants. Batlle supported labor in its strikes against foreign-owned enterprises. But his advanced welfare legislation was effective only in the port city of Montevideo. Batlle made no effort to challenge the land monopoly of the great estancieros or to apply his social legislation to their peons.

226

the landed aristocracy. The principal political vehicle for working-class aspirations was the Socialist party, founded in 1894 as a split-off from the Unión Cívica Radical by the Buenos Aires physician and intellectual Juan B. Justo, who led the party until his death in 1928.

Despite its professed Marxism, the party's socialism was of the parliamentary reformist kind, appealing chiefly to highly skilled native-born workers and the lower middle class. The majority of workers, foreign-born noncitizens who still dreamed of returning someday to their homelands, remained aloof from electoral politics but readily joined trade union organizations. Here the Socialist party competed for influence with the anarchists and syndicalists, who in turn competed with each other for leadership of trade unions and strikes. Between 1902 and 1910 wage scales and working conditions deteriorated as surplus immigrant labor accumulated in Buenos Aires; a series of great strikes was broken by the government with brutal repression and the deportation of so-called "foreign agitators." Despite these defeats and the negative consequences of discord among socialists, anarchists, and syndicalists, the labor movement continued to grow and struggle, winning such initial victories as the ten-hour workday and the establishment of Sunday as a compulsory day of rest.

Chilean Politics and Economy

Nitrates and War

In 1876 the official Liberal candidate for the presidency, Aníbal Pinto, defeated two rivals, both distinguished historians—Miguel Luis Amunátegui and Benjamín Vicuña Mackenna. From his predecessor, the new president inherited a severe economic crisis (1874–1879). Wheat and copper prices dropped, exports declined, and unemployment grew. The principal offset to these unfavorable developments was the continued growth of nitrate exports from the Atacama Desert as a result of a doubling of nitrate production between 1865 and 1875. But nitrates, the foundation of Chilean material progress, also became the cause of a major war with dramatic consequences for Chile and her two foes, Bolivia and Peru.

The nitrate deposits exploited by the Anglo-Chilean companies lay, it will be recalled, in territories belonging to Bolivia (the province of Antofagasta) and Peru (the province of Tarapacá). In 1866 a treaty between Chile and Bolivia defined their boundary in the Atacama Desert as the twenty-fourth parallel, gave Chilean and Bolivian interests equal rights to exploit the territory between the twenty-third and twenty-fifth parallels, and guaranteed each government half of the tax revenues obtained from the export of minerals from the whole area. Anglo-Chilean capital soon poured into the region, developing a highly efficient mining-industrial complex. By a second treaty of 1874, Chile's northern border with Bolivia was left at the twenty-fourth parallel. Chile relinquished her rights to a share of the taxes from exports north of that boundary but received in return a twenty-five-year guarantee against increase of taxes on Chilean enterprises operating in the Bolivian province of Antofagasta.

Chile had no boundary dispute with Peru, but aggressive Chilean mining interests, aided by British capital, soon extended their operations from Antofagasta into the Peruvian province of Tarapacá. By 1875, Chilean enterprises in Peruvian nitrate fields employed more than ten thousand workers, engineers, and supervisory personnel. At this point, the Peruvian government, on the brink of bankruptcy as a result of a very expensive program of public works, huge European loans, and the depletion of the guano deposits on which it had counted to service those loans, decided to expropriate the foreign companies in Tarapacá and establish a state monopoly over the production and sale of nitrates. Meanwhile, Peru and Bolivia had negotiated a secret treaty in 1874 providing for a military alliance in the event either power went to war with Chile.

Ejected from Tarapacá, the Anglo-Chilean capitalists intensified their exploitation of the nitrate deposits in Antofagasta. In 1878, Bolivia, counting on her military alliance with Peru, challenged Chile by imposing higher taxes on nitrate exports from Antofagasta, in violation of the treaty of 1874. When the Chilean companies operating in Antofagasta refused to pay the new taxes, the Bolivian government threatened them with confiscation. The agreement of 1874 provided for arbitration of disputes, but the Bolivians twice rejected Chilean offers to submit the dispute to arbitration.

In February 1879, despite Chilean warnings that expropriation of Chilean enterprises would void the treaty of 1874, the Bolivian government ordered the confiscation carried out. On February 14, the day set for the seizure and sale of the Chilean properties, Chilean troops occupied the port of Antofagasta, encountering no resistance, and proceeded to extend Chilean control over the whole province. Totally unprepared for war, Peru made a vain effort to mediate between Chile and Bolivia. Chile, however, having learned of the secret Peruvian-Bolivian alliance, charged Peru with intolerable duplicity and declared war on both Peru and Bolivia on April 5, 1879.

In this war, called the War of the Pacific, Chile faced enemies whose combined population was more than twice its own; one of these powers, Peru, also possessed a respectable naval force. But Chile enjoyed major advantages. By contrast with its neighbors, it possessed a stable central government, a people with a strong sense of national identity, and a disciplined, well-trained army and navy. Although small, the navy included two modern ironclads with revolving turrets and heavy firing power. Chile also enjoyed the advantage of being closer to the theater of operations, since Bolivian troops had to come over the Andes, while the Peruvian army had to cross the Atacama Desert.

All three powers had serious economic problems, but Chile's situation was not as catastrophic as that of its foes. Equally important, Chile had the support of powerful English capitalist interests, who knew that the future of the massive English investment in Chile depended in large part on the outcome of the war. The prospect of Chilean acquisition of the valuable nitrate areas of Antofagasta and Tarapacá naturally pleased the British capitalists. British capital was also invested in Bolivia and Peru, but whereas the Chilean government had maintained service on its debt, Bolivia and Peru had suspended payment on their English loans. Besides, the Peruvian nationalization of the nitrate industry in Tarapacá had seriously injured British interests.

The decisive battle of the war took place on the sea on October 8, 1879, when the two Chilean ironclads, recently acquired from England, forced the surrender of the Peruvian ship *Huáscar,* which had done great damage to Chilean coastal traffic, and severed communications between Santiago and the Chilean forces operating in the Atacama Desert. Having command of the sea, the Chilean forces resumed operations in the Atacama, and in a short time overran the Peruvian provinces of Tarapacá, Tacna, and Arica. By the middle of 1880, Bolivia had effectively been knocked out of the war. In January 1881, a thirty-thousand-man Chilean army under the command of General Manuel Baquedano overcame tenacious Peruvian resistance and occupied the enemy capital of Lima. Meanwhile, the Chilean navy had sunk the last Peruvian warship, the *Atahualpa.* Although scattered fighting between Chilean occupation forces and Peruvian guerrillas continued for over two years, Chile had clearly won the war.

By the Treaty of Ancón (October 20, 1883), Peru ceded the province of Tarapacá to Chile in perpetuity. Tacna and Arica would be Chilean for ten years, after which a plebiscite would decide their ultimate fate. But the plebiscite was never held, and Chile continued to administer the two territories until 1929, when Peru recovered Tacna and Arica went to Chile. An armistice signed in April 1884 by Bolivia and Chile assigned the former Bolivian province of Antofagasta to Chile, but for many years no Bolivian government would sign a formal treaty acknowledging that loss. Meanwhile, Chile remained in de facto possession of the port and province of Antofagasta. Finally, in 1904, Bolivia signed a treaty in which Chile agreed to pay an indemnity and to build a railroad connecting the Bolivian capital of La Paz with the port of Arica. That railroad was completed in 1913.

Aftermath of the War of the Pacific

Chile took advantage of the continued mobilization of its armed forces during the negotiations with Peru to settle scores with the Araucanian Indians, whose struggle in defense of their land against encroaching whites had continued since colonial times. After two years of resistance against very unequal odds, the Araucanians were forced to admit defeat and sign a treaty (1883) that resettled the Indians on reservations but permitted them to retain their tribal government and laws. The Araucanian campaign of 1880–1882, which extended the Chilean frontier to the south into a region of mountain and forest, sparked a brisk movement of land speculation and colonization in that area.

From the War of the Pacific, which shattered Peru economically and psychologically and left Bolivia more isolated than before from the outside world, Chile emerged the strongest nation on the west coast, in control of vast deposits of nitrates and copper, the mainstays of its economy. But the greater part of these riches would soon pass into foreign hands. In 1881 the Chilean government made an important decision: it decided to return the nitrate properties of Tarapacá to private ownership, that is, to the holders of the certificates issued by the Peruvian government as compensation for the nationalized properties.

During the war, uncertainty as to how Chile would dispose of those properties had caused the Peruvian certificates to depreciate until they fell to a fraction of their face worth. Speculators, mostly British, had bought up large quantities of these depreciated certificates. In 1878, British capital controlled some 13 percent of the nitrate industry of Tarapacá; by 1890, its share had risen to at least 70 percent. British penetration of the nitrate areas proceeded not only through formation of companies for direct exploitation of nitrate deposits but through the establishment of banks that financed entrepreneurial activity in the nitrate area and the creation of railways and

other companies more or less closely linked to the central nitrate industry. An English railway company with a monopoly of transport in Tarapacá, the Nitrate Railways Company, controlled by John Thomas North, paid dividends of up to 20 and 25 percent, compared with earnings of from 7 to 14 percent for other railway companies in South America.

The Chilean national bourgeoisie, which had pioneered in the establishment of the mining-industrial-railway complex in the Atacama, offered little resistance to the foreign take-over. Lack of strong support from the state, the relative financial weakness of the Chilean bourgeoisie, and the cozy and profitable relationships maintained throughout the nineteenth century between the Chilean elite and British interests facilitated the rapid transfer of Chilean nitrate and railway properties into British hands and the transformation of the Chilean bourgeoisie into a dependent bourgeoisie content with a share in the profits of British companies.

The presidential election of 1881 pitted a conservative military hero of the War of the Pacific, General Manuel Baquedano, against the candidate of a liberal coalition, Domingo Santa María, who won handily. The religious issue, one of the few still separating the new bourgeoisie from the landed aristocracy, dominated his administration (1881–1886). A dispute with the Vatican over its refusal to approve the government's nomination of an archbishop of liberal views led to the expulsion of the apostolic delegate, followed by congressional passage of a series of religious reforms: civil marriage, civil registration of births and deaths, and lay control of some cemeteries. However, the church continued to own extensive properties and receive subsidies from the state. More radical proposals to divorce church and state failed to win approval. In 1884 an electoral reform was adopted; the property qualification for voting was replaced with a literacy test. Since the great majority of Chilean males were illiterate *rotos* (seasonal farm workers) and inquilinos, this change did not materially add to the number of voters; as late as 1915, out of a population of about 3.5 million, only 150,000 persons voted.

The official liberal candidate for president in the election of 1886, José Manuel Balmaceda, had a distinguished record of public service as a diplomat and cabinet minister. As minister of the interior in Santa María's cabinet, he had piloted through Congress the religious reforms just described. Balmaceda took office with a well-defined program of state-directed economic modernization. By the 1880s, factory capitalism had taken root in Chile. The Chilean Society for Industrial Development, which campaigned for state assistance to industrialization in the form of tariffs, subsidies, and other preferential treatment, was founded in 1883. In addition to consumer goods industries—flour mills, breweries, leather factories, furniture factories, and the like—there existed foundries and metal-working enterprises that served the mining industry, railways, and agriculture. Balmaceda proposed to consolidate and expand this native industrial capitalism.

Balmaceda's Nationalistic Policies

Balmaceda came to office when government revenues were at an all-time high (they had risen from about 15 million pesos a year before the War of the Pacific to about 45 million pesos in 1887). The chief source of this government income was the export duty on nitrates. Knowing that the proceeds from this source would taper off as the nitrate deposits diminished, Balmaceda wisely planned to employ those funds for the development of an economic infrastructure that would remain when the nitrate was gone. Hence, public works figured prominently in his program. In 1887 he created a new ministry of industry and public works, which expended large sums on extending and improving the telegraphic and railway systems and on the construction of bridges, roads, and docks. Balmaceda also generously endowed public education, needed to provide skilled workers for Chilean industry. During his presidency, the total enrollment in Chilean schools rose in four years from some 79,000 in 1886 to over 150,000 in 1890. He also favored raising the wages of workers but was inconsistent in his labor policy; yielding to strong pressure from foreign and domestic employers, he sent troops to crush a number of strikes.

Central to Balmaceda's program was his determination to "Chileanize" the nitrate industry. In his inaugural address to Congress, he declared that his government would consider what measures it should take "to nationalize industries which are, at present, chiefly of benefit to foreigners," a clear reference to the nitrate industry. Later, Balmaceda's strategy shifted; he encouraged the entrance of Chilean private capital into nitrate production and exportation to prevent the formation of a foreign-dominated nitrate cartel whose interest in restricting output clashed with the government's interest in maintaining a high level of production in order to collect more export taxes. In November 1888, he scolded the Chilean elite for their lack of entrepreneurial spirit:

Why does the credit and the capital which are brought into play in all kinds of speculations in our great cities hold back and leave the foreigner to establish banks at Iquique and abandon to strangers the exploiting of the nitrate works of Tarapacá? . . . The foreigner exploits these riches and takes the profit of native wealth to give to other lands and unknown people the treasures of our soil, our own property and the riches we require. [2]

Balmaceda waged a determined struggle to end the monopoly of the British-owned Nitrate Railways Company, whose prohibitive freight charges reduced production and export of nitrates. His nationalistic policies inevitably provoked the hostility of English nitrate "kings" like North who had close links with the Chilean elite and employed prominent liberal politicians as their legal advisers.

But Balmaceda had many domestic as well as foreign foes. The clericals remembered his leading role in the religious reforms and noted his

[2] Harold Blakemore, *British Nitrates and Chilean Politics, 1886–1896: Balmaceda and North* (London, 1974), p. 80.

230

plans to further curb the powers of the church. The landed aristocracy resented his public works program because it drew labor from agriculture and pushed up rural wages. The banks, whose uncontrolled emission of notes had fed an inflation whose sole beneficiaries were mortgaged landlords and exporters who received payment in foreign currencies, were angered by his proposal to establish a national bank with a monopoly of note issue. The entire oligarchy, liberals as well as conservatives, opposed his use of the central government as an instrument of progressive economic and social change.

Meanwhile, the government's economic problems multiplied, adding to Balmaceda's political difficulties by narrowing his mass base. By 1890 foreign demand for copper and nitrates had weakened. Prices in an overstocked world market fell, and English nitrate interests responded to the crisis by forming a cartel to reduce production. Reduced production and export of nitrates and copper sharply diminished the flow of export duties into the treasury and caused growing unemployment and wage cuts even as inflation cut into the value of wages. The result was a series of great strikes in Valparaíso and the nitrate zone in 1890. Despite his sympathy with the workers' demands and unwillingness to use force against them, Balmaceda, under pressure from domestic and foreign employers, sent troops to crush the strikes. These repressive measures insured much working-class apathy or even hostility toward the president in the eventual confrontation with his foes.

Indeed, Balmaceda had few firm allies at his side when that crisis came. The industrial capitalist group whose growth he had ardently promoted was still weak. The mining interests, increasingly integrated with or dominated by English capital, joined the bankers, the clericals, and the landed aristocracy in opposition to his nationalist program of economic development and independence.

Since the elections of 1888, Balmaceda had lacked a reliable parliamentary majority, a condition that made for a growing deadlock between president and Congress. In October 1890, Balmaceda dismissed a cabinet imposed upon him by the congressional majority and appointed one acceptable to himself. Instead of summoning Congress, which was dominated by a coalition of anti-Balmaceda forces, to pass the budget for 1891, the president simply announced that the 1890 budget would continue in force for the next year. In effect, Balmaceda abolished the system of parliamentary government and returned to the traditional system of presidential rule established by the constitution of 1833. His rash act, made without any serious effort to mobilize popular forces, played into the hands of his enemies, who were already preparing for civil war.

On January 7, 1891, congressional leaders proclaimed a revolt against the president in the name of legality and the constitution. The navy, then as now led by officers of aristocratic descent, promptly went over to the rebels, while most army units remained loyal to the president. A junta headed by fleet captain Jorge Montt assumed direction of the revolt. With navy support, the congressionalists seized the ports and customhouses in the north and established their capital at Iquique, the chief port of Tarapacá.

English-owned enterprises actively aided the rebels. Indeed, by the admission of the British minister at Santiago, "our naval officers and the British community of Valparaíso and all along the coast rendered material assistance to the opposition and committed many breaches of neutrality." Many nitrate workers, alienated by Balmaceda's repression of their strike, remained neutral or even joined the rebel army, organized by a German army officer, General Emil Korner. Having gained control of the north and its vast revenues, the congressionalist forces moved south. Victories over Balmaceda's army in the battles of Concón and Placilla opened the way for capture of Valparaíso and Santiago, forcing the president to seek refuge in the Argentine embassy. On September 19, 1891, the day on which his legal term of office came to an end, Balmaceda put a bullet through his head.

The death of Chile's first anti-imperialist president restored the reign of the oligarchy, a coalition of landowners, bankers, merchants, and mining interests closely linked to English capital. A new era began, the era of the so-called Parliamentary Republic. Taught by experience, the oligarchy now preferred to rule through a Congress divided into various factions rather than through a strong executive. Such decentralization of government favored the interests of the rural aristocracy and its allies. A new law of 1892, vesting local governments with the right to supervise elections both for local and national offices, reinforced the power of the landowners, priests, and political bosses who had fought Balmaceda's progressive policies. The presidents of this period, beginning with Jorge Montt (1891–1896), were little more than puppets pulled by strings in the hands of congressional leaders. Corruption, cynicism, and factional intrigue characterized the political life of the Parliamentary Republic. Members of Congress, who received no salaries, paid large sums to secure election, which gave them access to the ample opportunities for graft on the national level.

The Parliamentary Republic, Foreign Economic Domination, and the Growth of the Working Class

The era of the Parliamentary Republic was accompanied by a growing subordination of the Chilean economy to foreign capital, which was reflected in a steady increase in the foreign debt and foreign ownership of the nation's resources. English investments in Chile amounted to 24 million pounds in 1890; they rose to 64 million pounds in 1913. Of this total, 34.6 million pounds formed part of the Chilean public debt. In the same period, North American and German capital began to challenge the British hegemony in Chile. England continued to be Chile's principal trade partner, but United States and German trade with Chile grew at a faster rate. German instructors also acquired a strong influence in the Chilean army, and the flow of German immigrants into southern Chile continued, resulting in the formation of compact colonies dominated by a Pan-German ideology.

The revival of the Chilean economy from the depression of the early 1890s brought an increase of nitrate, copper, and agricultural exports and further enriched the ruling classes, but it left inquilinos, miners, and factory workers as desperately poor as before. Meanwhile, the working class grew from 120,000 to 250,000 between 1890 and 1900, and the doctrines of trade unionism, socialism, and anarchism achieved growing popularity in its ranks.

Luis Emilio Recabarren (1876–1924), the father of Chilean socialism and communism, played a decisive role in the social and political awakening of the Chilean proletariat. In 1906, Recabarren was elected to Congress from a mining area but was not allowed to take his seat because he refused to take his oath of office on the Bible. In 1909, he organized the Workers Federation of Chile, the first national trade union movement. Three years later, he led the founding of the Socialist party, a revolutionary Marxist movement, and became its first secretary.

The growing self-consciousness and militancy of the Chilean working class found expression in a mounting wave of strikes. Between 1911 and 1920, almost three hundred strikes, involving more than 300,000 workers, took place. Many were crushed with traditional brutal methods that left hundreds and thousands of workers dead.

Brazilian Politics and Economy

The Antislavery Movement

From the close of the Paraguayan War (1870), the slavery question surged forward, becoming the dominant issue in Brazilian political life. Dom Pedro, personally opposed to slavery, was caught in a crossfire between a growing number of liberal leaders, intellectuals, and urban middle-class groups who demanded emancipation and slave owners determined to postpone the inevitable as long as possible. In 1870, Spain freed all the newborn and aged slaves of Cuba and Puerto

232

Rico, leaving Brazil the only nation in the Americas to retain slavery in its original colonial form. Yielding to pressure, a conservative ministry pushed through parliament the Rio Branco Law in 1871. This measure freed all newborn children of slaves but obligated the masters to care for them until they reached the age of eight. At that time, owners could either release the children to the government in return for an indemnity or retain them as laborers until they reached the age of twenty-one. The law also freed all slaves belonging to the state or crown and created a fund to be used for the manumission of slaves.

The Rio Branco Law was a tactical retreat designed to put off a final solution of the slavery problem. The imperial government applied the law with ponderous slowness, the compensation fund was never large enough to buy the freedom of many slaves, and few slave owners came forward to redeem slave children for money. At late as 1884, only 113 had been freed by this means. Given the option of exploiting the labor of these children until they reached the age of twenty-one or exchanging them for government bonds, the great majority of slave owners chose the first course. Regarding them as temporary property, masters often worked these "free" children very hard; even after they reached the age of twenty-one, tradition and lack of education tended to keep them in a condition of semibondage. In effect, the Rio Branco Law gave an indefinite stay of execution to Brazilian slavery.

Abolitionist leaders denounced the law as a sham and illusion and advanced ever more vigorously the demand for total and immediate emancipation. From 1880 on, the antislavery movement developed great momentum. Concentrated in the cities, it drew strength from the process of economic, social, and intellectual modernization under way there. To the new urban groups, slavery was an anachronism, glaringly incompatible with modernization. Among the slave owners themselves, divisions of opinion appeared. In the north, where slavery had long been dying as a result of the sale of the best slaves south and where many of those who remained were aged or dying, a growing number of planters

converted to the use of free labor, drawing on the pool of freedmen made available by the Rio Branco Law and the *sertanejos* (inhabitants of the interior), poor whites and mixed-bloods who lived on the fringes of the plantation economy. Another factor in the decline of the slave population of the northeast was the great drought of 1877–1879, which caused many of the region's wealthier folk to abandon the area. Some sold their slaves before departing for Rio; others brought slaves with them. In states like Amazonas and Ceará, where black slaves were few and most of the work was done by Indians and mixed-bloods, the move to emancipation was relatively easy; in 1884 both of these states declared the end of slavery within their borders. By contrast, the coffee planters of Rio de Janeiro, São Paulo, and Minas Gerais, joined by northern planters who trafficked in slaves, selling them to the coffee zone, offered the most tenacious resistance to the advance of abolition.

The abolitionist movement produced leaders of remarkable intellectual and moral stature. One was Joaquim Nabuco, son of a distinguished liberal statesman of the empire, whose eloquent dissection and indictment of slavery, *O abolicionismo,* had a profound impact on its readers. Another was a mulatto journalist, José do Patrocinio, a master propagandist noted for his fiery, biting style. Another mulatto, André Rebouças, an engineer and teacher whose intellectual gifts won him the respect and friendship of the emperor, was a leading organizer of the movement. For Nabuco and his comrades-in-arms, the antislavery struggle was the major front in a larger struggle for the transformation of Brazilian society. Abolition, they hoped, would pave the way for the attainment of other goals: land reform, public education, and political democracy.

Yielding to mounting pressure, parliament adopted another measure on September 28, 1885, that liberated all slaves when they reached the age of sixty but required them to continue to serve their masters for three years and forbade them to leave their place of residence for five years. These conditions, added to the fact that few slaves lived beyond the age of sixty-five, im-

Slaves drying coffee on a plantation in Terreiros, in the state of Rio de Janeiro, about 1882. (Courtesy, Hack Hoffenburg)

plied little change in the status of the vast majority of slaves. The imperial government also promised to purchase the freedom of the remaining slaves in fourteen years—a promise that few took seriously, in the light of experience with the Rio Branco Law. Convinced that the new law was another tactical maneuver, the abolitionists spurned all compromise solutions and demanded immediate, unconditional emancipation.

By the middle 1880s, the antislavery movement had assumed massive proportions and a more militant character. Large numbers of slaves began to vote for freedom with their feet; they were aided by abolitionists who organized an under-ground railway that ran from São Paulo to Ceará, where slavery had ended. Efforts to secure the return of fugitive slaves encountered growing resistance. Army officers, organized in a *Club Militar,* protested against the use of the army for the pursuit of fugitive slaves.

In February 1887, São Paulo liberated all slaves in the city with funds raised by popular subscription. Many slave owners, seeing the handwriting on the wall, liberated their slaves on condition that they remain at work for some time longer. By the end of 1887, even the die-hard coffee planters of São Paulo were ready to adjust to new conditions by offering to pay wages to their slaves and improve their working and living conditions; they also increased efforts to induce European immigrants to come to São Paulo. These efforts were highly successful; the flow of immigrants into São Paulo rose from 6,600 in 1885 to over 32,000 in 1887 and to 90,000 in 1888. As a result, coffee production reached record levels. With its labor problem solved, São Paulo was ready to abandon its resistance and even join the abolitionist crusade.

When parliament met on May 3, 1888, to deliberate again on the slavery question, the institution was in its last throes. By overwhelming majorities, both houses of parliament approved a measure whose laconic text read: "Article 1. From the date of this law slavery is declared abolished in Brazil. Article 2. All contrary provisions are revoked." Princess Isabel, ruling as regent for Dom Pedro, who was in Europe for medical treatment, signed the bill on May 13. Contrary to a traditional interpretation, however, the decision of May 1888 was not the climax of a gradual process of slavery's decline and the peaceful acceptance of the inevitable by the slave owners. The total slave population dropped sharply only after 1885, as a result of abolitionist agitation, mass flights of slaves, armed clashes, and other upheavals that appeared to many conservatives to threaten anarchy. In effect, abolition had come not through reform but by revolution.

The aftermath of abolition refuted the dire predictions of its foes. Freed from the burdens of slavery, Brazil made more economic progress in a few years than it had during the almost seven decades of imperial rule. For the former slaves, however, little had changed. The abolitionist demand for the grant of land to the freedmen was forgotten. Relationships between former masters and slaves in many places remained largely unchanged; tradition and the economic and political power of the fazendeiros gave them almost absolute control over their former slaves. Denied land and education, victims of prejudices inherited from the days of slavery, the freedmen were assigned the hardest, most poorly paid jobs. Fazendeiros replaced freedmen with immigrants in the coffee plantations; in the cities, black artisans lost their jobs to immigrants.

The Fall of the Monarchy

Abolition dragged down slavery's sister institution—the monarchy. The empire had long rested on the support of the planter class, especially the northern planters, who saw in the empire a guarantee of the survival of slavery. Before 1888, the Republican party had its principal base among the coffee interests, who resented the favor shown by the imperial government to the sugar planters and wished to achieve a political power corresponding to their economic power. Now, angered by abolition and embittered by the failure of the crown to indemnify them for their lost slaves, those planters who had not previously shifted to the use of free labor joined the Republican movement. The monarchy that had served the interest of the regional elites for the previous sixty-seven years had lost its reasons for existence.

Republicanism and a closely allied ideology, positivism, also made many converts in the officer class, disgruntled by what it regarded as neglect and mistreatment of the armed forces by the imperial government. Many of the younger officers came from the new urban middle class or, if of aristocratic descent, were discontented with the ways of their fathers. Positivism, it has been said, became "the gospel of the military academy," where it was brilliantly expounded by a popular young professor of mathematics, Benjamin Constant Botelho de Magalhães, a devoted disciple of Auguste Comte, the doctrine's founder. The positivist doctrine, with its stress on science, its ideal of a dictatorial republic, and its distrust of the masses, fitted the needs of urban middle-class groups, progressive officers, and businessmen-fazendeiros who wanted modernization but without drastic changes in land tenure and class relations.

In June 1889, the liberal ministry headed by the Viscount of Ouro Prêto made a last effort to save the monarchy by proposing a reform program that included extension of the suffrage, autonomy for the provinces, and land reform. It was too late. On November 15, a military revolt organized and headed by Benjamin Constant and Marshal Floriano Peixoto overthrew the government and proclaimed a republic with Marshal Deodoro da Fonseca as provisional chief of state. Like the revolution that gave Brazil its independence, the republican revolution came from above; the coup d'état encountered little resistance but also inspired little enthusiasm. Although the provisional government included some sincere reformers like Ruy Barbosa, a champion of public education and civil liberties, the radical wing of the abolitionist movement was excluded. Power was firmly held by representatives of the business and landed elites and the military.

The new rulers promptly promulgated a series of reforms. On November 15, 1889, the same day that Brazil was proclaimed a republic, a decree ended corporal punishment in the army; on November 19, a literacy test replaced property qualifications for voting (since property and literacy usually went together, this measure did not significantly enlarge the electorate); and in January 1891, successive decrees separated church and state and established civil marriage.

The New Republic

In November 1891, two years after the revolt, a constituent assembly met in Rio de Janeiro to draft a constitution for the new republic. The draft offered for approval by the assembly provided for a federal, presidential form of government with the customary three branches—legislative, executive, and judicial. The principal debate was between the partisans of greater autonomy for the states and those who feared the divisive results of an extreme federalism. The coffee interests, which dominated the wealthy south central region, sought to strengthen their position at the expense of the central power. The bourgeois groups, represented in the convention

chiefly by lawyers, favored a strong central government that could promote industry, aid the creation of a national market, and offer protection from British competition.

The result was a compromise tilted in favor of federalism. The twenty provinces in effect became self-governing states with popularly elected governors, the exclusive right to tax exports (a profitable privilege for wealthy states like São Paulo and Minas Gerais), and the right to maintain militias. The national government was given control over the tariff and the income from import duties, while the president obtained very large powers: he designated his cabinet ministers and other high officers, he could declare a state of siege, and he could intervene in the states with the federal armed forces in the event of a threat to their political institutions. The constitution proclaimed the sanctity of private property and guaranteed freedom of the press, speech, and assembly.

If these freedoms had some relevance in the cities and hinterlands touched by the movement of modernization, they lacked meaning over the greater part of the national territory. The fazendeiros, former slave owners, virtually monopolized the nation's chief wealth, its land. The land monopoly gave them absolute control over the rural population. Feudal and semifeudal forms of land tenure, accompanied by the obligation of personal and military service on the part of tenants, survived in the backlands, especially in the northeast. Powerful *coronéis* (colonels) maintained armies of *jagunços* (full-time private soldiers) and waged war against each other.[3] Banditry flourished in the interior, the bandits sometimes hiring themselves out to the coronéis, sometimes operating on their own, and occasionally gaining the reputation of modern Robin Hoods.

---

[3] The title *coronel* was often honorary and did not necessarily indicate a military command or landownership; especially after 1870, a coronel might be simply a political boss or even an influential lawyer or priest.

In this medieval atmosphere of constant insecurity and social disintegration, there arose messianic movements that reflected the aspirations of the oppressed sertanejos for peace and justice. One of the most important of such movements arose in the interior of Bahia, where the principal activity was cattle raising. In this area appeared a messiah called Antônio Conselheiro (Anthony the Counselor), who established a settlement at the abandoned cattle ranch of Canudos. Rejecting private property, Antônio required all who joined his sacred company to give up their goods, but he promised a future of prosperity in his messianic kingdom through the sharing of the treasure of the "lost Sebastian" (the Portuguese king who had disappeared in Africa in 1478 but would return as a redeemer) or through division of the property of hostile landowners.

Despite its religious coloration, the existence of such a focus of social and political unrest was intolerable to the fazendeiros and the state authorities. When the sertanejos easily defeated state forces sent against them in 1896, the governor called on the federal government for aid. Four campaigns, the last a large-scale operation directed by the minister of war in person, were required to break the epic resistance of the men of Canudos. A Brazilian literary masterpiece, *Os sertões* (Rebellion in the Backlands) by Euclides da Cunha (1856–1909), immortalized the heroism of the defenders and the crimes of the victors. It also revealed to the urban elite another and unfamiliar side of Brazilian reality.

The Economic Revolution

An enormous historical gulf separated the bleak sertão—in which the tragedy of Canudos was played out—from the cities, the scene of a mushrooming growth of banks, stock exchanges, and corporations. With the economic revolution came a revolution in manners. In Rio de Janeiro, writes Pedro Calmon,

barons with recently acquired titles jostled each other in the corridors of the Stock Exchange or in

the Rua da Alfandega, buying and selling stocks; the tilburies [light two-wheeled carriages] that filled the length of São Francisco Street were taken by a multitude of millionaires of recent vintage—commercial agents, bustling lawyers, promoters of all kinds, politicians of the new generation, the men of the day.[4]

A few more years and even the physical appearance of some of Brazil's great urban centers would change. These changes were most marked in the federal capital of Rio de Janeiro, which was made into a beautiful and healthful city between 1902 and 1906 through the initiative and efforts of Prefect Pereira Passos, who mercilessly demolished the narrow old streets to permit the construction of broad, modern avenues, and the distinguished scientist Oswaldo Cruz, who waged a victorious struggle to conquer the endemic malaria and yellow fever by filling in swamps and installing adequate water and sewerage systems.

The economic policies of the new republican regime reflected pressures from different quarters: from the planter class, from urban capitalists, from the military. Many planters, left in a difficult position by the abolition of slavery, required subsidies and credits to enable them to convert to the new wage system. The emerging industrial bourgeoisie, convinced that Brazil must develop an industrial base in order to emerge from backwardness, asked for protective tariffs, the construction of an economic infrastructure, and policies favorable to capital formation. Within the provisional government, these aspirations had a fervent supporter in the minister of finance, Ruy Barbosa, who believed that the factory was the crucible in which an "intelligent and independent democracy" would be forged in Brazil. Finally, the army, whose decisive role in the establishment of the republic had given it great prestige and influence, called for increased appropriations for the armed services.

---

[4] Quoted in Benjamin Keen, ed., *Latin American Civilization: The National Era,* vol. 2 (Boston: Houghton Mifflin, 1974), p. 313.

Their demands far exceeded the revenue available to the federal and state governments.

The federal government solved this problem by resorting to the printing press and allowing private banks to issue notes backed by little more than faith in the future of Brazil. In two years, the volume of paper money in circulation doubled, and the foreign exchange value of the Brazilian monetary unit, the *milréis,* plummeted disastrously. Since objective economic conditions (the small internal market and the lack of an adequate technological base, among other factors) limited the real potential for Brazilian growth, much of the newly created capital was used for highly speculative purposes, including the creation of fictitious companies.

The great boom collapsed in 1891, bringing ruin to many investors and unemployment to workers even as inflation continued to cut into the real value of their wages. Disputes over methods of coping with the crisis contributed to a clash between President Deodoro da Fonseca and Congress when it assembled for its first session in November 1891. When da Fonseca attempted to dissolve Congress and assume dictatorial power, the army and navy turned against him. Faced with a threat from the navy to bombard Rio, the president resigned and was succeeded by his vice president, Marshal Floriano Peixoto.

Under Peixoto, the urban middle-class sector gained even greater influence in the government, and inflation continued unchecked, to the dismay of the planters. The rapid fall in the price of coffee expressed in foreign hard currency brought a decline of real income from exports and a rise in the cost of many imported items to almost prohibitive levels. This hurt the planters but stimulated the growth of Brazilian manufactures: the number of such enterprises almost doubled between 1890 and 1895. The discontent of the "outs" sparked a new revolt with strong aristocratic and monarchical overtones in 1893. The movement began in Rio Grande do Sul and was soon joined by the navy, a stronghold of aristocratic prejudice and influence. Peixoto's firm re-fusal to bow to threats of a naval bombardment of the capital brought a collapse of the fleet revolt and allowed the governments to launch an offensive south against the rebels of Rio Grande; by August 1895, the last insurgents had surrendered.

Peixoto's victory, which won him the name of "consolidator of the republic," was largely due to the loyalty and financial and military support of the state of São Paulo. But this support came at a price; the coffee planters were resolved to end the ascendancy of the urban middle classes, whose policies of rapid industrialization they distrusted and held responsible for the inflation and political instability that had plagued the first years of the republic. In 1893 the old planter oligarchies, whose divisions had temporarily enabled the middle classes to gain the upper hand in coalition with the military, reunited to form the Federal Republican party, with a program of support for federalism and fiscal responsibility. Since they controlled the electoral machinery, they easily elected Prudente de Morais president in 1894. Morais, the first civilian president of Brazil (1894–1898), initiated an era marked by the domination of the coffee interests and the relegation of urban capitalist groups to a secondary role in political life.

Morais' successor, Manuel Ferraz de Campos Sales (1898–1902), continued and expanded his program of giving primacy to agriculture. Campos Sales fully endorsed the system of the international economic division of labor as it applied to Brazil. "It is time," he proclaimed, "that we take the correct road; to that end we must strive to export all that we can produce better than other countries, and import all that other countries can produce better than we." This formula meant the abandonment of the goal of independent economic development—in other words, the acceptance of neocolonialism. Determined to halt inflation, Campos Sales drastically reduced expenditures on public works, increased taxes, and made every effort to redeem the paper money in order to improve Brazil's international credit and secure new loans, which were vital to the coffee interests.

Coffee was king. Around the monarch were grouped his obedient barons: rubber, cacao, cotton, sugar. Whereas in the period from 1880 to 1889, Brazil produced only 56 percent of the world's coffee output, in the period from 1900 to 1904, it accounted for 76 percent of the total production. Its closest competitor, rubber, supplied only 28 percent of Brazil's exports in 1901. Sugar, once the ruler of the Brazilian economy, now accounted for barely 5 percent of the nation's exports. Minas Gerais and especially São Paulo became the primary coffee regions, while Rio de Janeiro declined in importance. Enjoying immense advantages—the famous rich, porous *terra roxa* (red soil), an abundance of immigrant labor, and closeness to the major port of Santos—the *Paulistas* harvested 60 percent of the national coffee production.

Coffee was king, but from the closing years of the nineteenth century its reign was a troubled one. The classic symptoms of overproduction—falling prices and unsalable stocks—had appeared as early as 1896. The problem arose from a vast increase in plantings of coffee trees (from 220 to 520 million between 1890 and 1900). Foreign competition and speculative activity on the part of middlemen added to the difficulties of the planters. These middlemen (usually agents of foreign banks and merchant houses) bought when the coffee harvest flowed into the ports, forcing prices down, and formed reserves that they doled out in periods of shortage, when prices were high.

Responding to the planters' clamor for help, the government of São Paulo took the first step for the "defense" of coffee in 1902, forbidding new coffee plantings for five years. Other steps soon proved necessary. Faced with a bumper crop in 1906, São Paulo launched a coffee price-support scheme to protect the state's economic lifeblood. With financing from British, French, German, and North American banks, and the eventual collaboration of the federal government, São Paulo purchased several million bags of coffee and held them off the market in an effort to maintain profitable price levels. Purchases continued into 1907; from that date until World War I the stocks were gradually sold off with little market disruption. The operation's principal gainers were the foreign merchants and bankers who, since they controlled the Coffee Commission formed to liquidate the purchased stocks, gradually disposed of them with a large margin of profit. The problem, temporarily exorcised, was presently to return in even more acute form.

The valorization scheme, which favored the coffee-raising states at the expense of the rest, reflected the coffee planters' political domination. Under President Campos Sales, this ascendancy was institutionalized by the so-called *política dos governadores* (politics of the governors). Its essence was a formula that gave the two richest and most populous states (São Paulo and Minas Gerais) a virtual monopoly of federal politics and the choice of presidents. Thus, the first three civilian presidents from 1894 to 1906 came from São Paulo; the next two, from 1906 to 1910, came from Minas Gerais and Rio de Janeiro, respectively.

In return, the oligarchies of the other states were given almost total freedom of action within their jurisdictions, the central government intervening as a rule only when it suited the local oligarchy's interest. Informal discussions among the state governors determined the choice of president, with his election a foregone conclusion. No official candidate for president lost an election before 1930. In 1910 the distinguished statesman and orator Ruy Barbosa ran for president on a platform of democratic reform and antimilitarism against the official candidate, Hermes da Fonseca, a conservative military man. Barbosa was beaten by almost two to one; out of a population of 22 million, about 360,000 voted. Similar reciprocal arrangements existed on the state level between the governors and the coronéis, urban or rural bosses who rounded up the local vote to elect the governors and were rewarded with a free hand in their respective domains.

Despite the official bias in favor of agriculture, industry continued to grow in the period from 1904 to 1914. By 1908, Brazil could boast of more than three thousand industrial enterprises. Foreign firms dominated the fields of banking, public works, utilities, transportation, and the export and import trade. Manufacturing, on the other hand, was carried on almost exclusively by native Brazilians and permanent immigrants. This national industry was concentrated in the four states of São Paulo, Minas Gerais, Rio de Janeiro, and Rio Grande do Sul. Heavy industry did not exist; over half of the enterprises were textile mills and food-processing plants. Many of these "enterprises" were small workshops employing a few artisans or operated with an archaic technology, and Brazilians in the market economy continued to import most quality products. The quantitative and qualitative development of industry was hampered by the semifeudal conditions prevailing in the countryside, by the extreme poverty of the masses, which sharply limited the internal market, by the lack of a skilled, literate labor force (as late as 1910, Brazil had an enrollment of only 566,000 pupils out of a population of 22 million, and the great majority received less than two years of formal instruction), and by the hostility of most fazendeiros and foreign interests to industry.

Together with industry there arose a working class destined to play a significant role in the life of the country. The Brazilian proletariat was partly recruited from sharecroppers and minifundio peasants fleeing to the cities to escape dismal poverty and the tyranny of coronéis, but above all it was composed of the flood of European immigrants, who arrived at a rate of 100,000 to 150,000 each year. Working and living conditions of the working class were often intolerable. Child labor was common, for children could be legally employed from the age of twelve. The workday ranged from nine hours for some skilled workers to more than sixteen hours for various categories of unskilled workers. Wages were pitifully low and often paid in vouchers redeemable at the company store. There was a total absence of legislation to protect workers against the hazards of unemployment, old age, or industrial accidents.

Among the European immigrants were many militants with socialist, syndicalist, or social-democratic backgrounds who helped to organize the Brazilian labor movement and gave it a radical political orientation. National and religious divisions among workers, widespread illiteracy, and quarrels between socialists and anarcho-syndicalists hampered the rise of a trade union movement and a labor party.

But trade unions grew rapidly after 1900 in response to unsatisfactory working conditions, with immigrant workers often providing the leadership. In 1906 the first national labor congress, representing the majority of the country's trade unions, met and began a struggle for the eight-hour workday. One result of the congress was the formation of the first national trade union organization, the Brazilian Labor Confederation, which conducted a number of strikes. Repression was the typical answer of the authorities and employers to labor's demands. Police conducted periodic roundups of labor leaders. Immigrants were deported, while native-born leaders were imprisoned or sent to forced labor on a railroad under construction in distant Mato Grosso. The phrase "the social question is a question for the police" was often used to sum up the labor policy of the Brazilian state.

Chapter 11

Society and Culture in the Nineteenth Century

Independence left much of the colonial social structure intact. This fact was very apparent to liberal leaders of the postindependence era. "The war against Spain," declared the Colombian liberal Ramón Mercado in 1853, "was not a revolution. . . . Independence only scratched the surface of the social problem, without changing its essential nature." A modern historian, Charles C. Griffin, comes to much the same conclusion. "Only the beginnings of a basic transformation took place," he writes, "and there were many ways in which colonial attitudes and institutions carried over into the life of republican Spanish America."

How New Was the New Society?

We should not minimize, however, the extent and importance of the changes that did take place. Independence produced, if not a major social upheaval, at least a minor one. It opened wide fissures within the elite, dividing aristocratic supporters of the old social order from modernizers who wanted a more democratic, bourgeois order. Their struggle is an integral aspect of the first half-century after the end of Spanish and Portuguese rule. Independence also enabled such formerly submerged groups as artisans and gauchos to enter the political arena, although in subordinate roles, and even allowed a few to climb into the ranks of the elite. The opening of Latin American ports to foreign goods also established a relatively free market in ideas, at least in the capitals and other cities. With almost no time lag, such new European doctrines as utopian socialism, romanticism, and positivism entered Latin

America and were applied to the solution of the continent's problems. These new winds of doctrine, blowing through what had lately been dusty colonial corridors, contributed to the area's intellectual renovation and promoted further social change.

The Passing of the Society of Castes

Verbally, at least, the new republican constitutions established the equality of all men before the law, destroying the legal foundations of colonial caste society. Since little change in property relations took place, however, the ethnic and social lines of division remained essentially the same. Wealth, power, and prestige continued to be concentrated in the hands of a ruling class that was mainly white, although in some countries, such as Venezuela, it became more or less heavily tinged with individuals of darker skin who had managed to climb the social ladder through their prowess in war or politics.

The Indians

Of all the groups composing the old society of castes, the status of the Indians changed least of all. The Mexican historian Carlos María Bustamante was one of the few creole leaders who recognized that independence had not freed the Indians from their yoke. "They still drag the same chains," he wrote, "although they are flattered with the name of freemen." Even Indian tribute and forced labor, abolished during or after the wars of independence, soon reappeared in many countries under other names. What was worse, Indian communal landholding, social organization, and culture, which Spanish law and policy had to some extent protected in colonial times, came under increasing attack, especially from liberals who believed that Indian communal traditions constituted as much of an obstacle to progress as the Spanish system of castes and special privileges.

Until about 1870, however, large, compact Indian populations continued to live under the traditional communal landholding system in Mexico, Central America, and the Andean region. Then, the rapid growth of the export economy, the coming of the railroads, and the resulting rise in land values and demand for labor caused white and mestizo landowners and landowner-dominated governments to launch a massive assault on Indian lands. The expropriation of Indian lands was accompanied, as noted in Chapter 10, by a growth of Indian peonage and tenantry. Employers used a variety of devices, ranging from debt servitude to outright coercion, to attach laborers to their estates. In some areas, there arose a type of Indian serfdom that closely resembled the classic European model. In the Andean region, for example, Indian tenants, in addition to working the master's land, had to render personal service in his household, sometimes at the hacienda, sometimes in the city. During his term of domestic service, the Indian serf could be given or sold to the master's friends. This and other forms of serfdom survived well into the twentieth century.

The master class, aided by the clergy and local magistrates, sought to reinforce the economic subjection of the Indian with psychological subjection. There evolved a pattern of relations and role-playing that assigned to the patrón the role of a benevolent figure who assured his peons or tenants of a livelihood and protected them in all emergencies in return for their absolute obedience. In countries with Indian populations or peasants descended from Indians, the relations between master and peon often included an elaborate ritual that required the Indian to request permission to speak to the patrón, to appear before him with head uncovered and bowed, and to seek his approval for all major personal decisions, including marriage.

But these relationships and attitudes of submission and servility, more characteristic of resident peons, were not accepted by all Indians. In the Andean area, Mexico, and elsewhere during the second half of the nineteenth century,

242 the surviving Indian landowning communities fought stubbornly to prevent the absorption of their lands by advancing haciendas and to halt the process by which the Indians became landless laborers. They fought with all the means at their disposal, including armed revolts as a last resort. Such revolts occurred in Mexico in the 1860s and 1870s and were called "communist" by the landowners and government officials who crushed the Indians with their superior military force.

The greater freedom of movement that came with independence, the progressive disappearance of Indian communities, and the growth of the hacienda, in which Indians mingled with mestizos, strengthened a trend toward Indian acculturation that had begun in the late colonial period. This acculturation was reflected in a growth of Indian bilingualism: Indians increasingly used Spanish in dealing with whites, reserving their native languages for use among themselves. To the limited extent that the public school entered Indian regions, it contributed to the adoption of Spanish as a second language or, in the case of the rare Indian whose talents and good fortunes elevated him into the ranks of the white and mestizo elite, sometimes led to total abandonment of his native tongue. The Mexican historian Eduardo Ruíz recalled that as a child he spoke only Tarascan but had forgotten it during his twelve years of study at the colegio. "I did not want to remember, I must confess, because I was ashamed of being thought to be an Indian." Some acculturation also occurred in dress, with frequent abandonment of picturesque regional styles in favor of a quasi-European style, sometimes enforced by legislation and fines. Over much of Mexico, for example, the white trousers and shirt of coarse cotton cloth and the broad-brimmed hat became almost an Indian "uniform."

Yet pressures toward Indian acculturation or assimilation failed to achieve the integration into white society that well-meaning liberals had hoped to secure through education, the growth of Indian wants, and the Indian's entrance into the modern world of industry and trade. At the end of the nineteenth century, the processes of acculturation had not significantly reduced the size of the Indian sector in the five countries with the largest native populations: Mexico, Guatemala, Ecuador, Peru, and Bolivia. There were various reasons for this. The economic stagnation and political troubles of the first postrevolutionary decades tended to reinforce the isolation and cultural separateness of Indian communities. When the Latin American economies revived as a result of the expansion of the export sector, this revival was achieved largely at the expense of the Indians and served mainly to accentuate their poverty and backwardness. Their economic marginality, their almost total exclusion from the political process, the intense exploitation to which they were subjected by white and mestizo landowners, priests, and officials, and the barriers of distrust and hatred that separated them from the white world prevented any thoroughgoing acculturation, much less integration.

Indian communities made such concessions to the pressures for assimilation as were necessary but preserved their traditional housing, diet, social organization, and religion—which combined pagan and Christian features. In some regions, the pre-Conquest cults and rituals, including occasional human sacrifice, survived. The existence in a number of countries of large Indian populations, intensely exploited and branded as inferior by the ruling social Darwinist ideology, constituted a major obstacle to the formation of a national consciousness in those lands. With good reason, the pioneer Mexican anthropologist Manuel Gamio wrote in 1916 that Mexico did not constitute a nation in the European sense but was composed of numerous small nations, differing in speech, economy, social organization, and psychology.

A Question of Color

The wars for independence, by throwing "careers open to talents," enabled a few Indians and a larger number of mixed-bloods of humble origins to rise high in the military, political, and social scale. The liberal caudillos Vicente Guerrero and Juan Álvarez in Mexico and such talented leaders as Juan José Flores of Ecuador, Andrés Santa Cruz of Bolivia, and Ramón Castilla of Peru illustrate the ascent of the mixed-bloods.

The rise of these mestizo or mulatto leaders inspired fears in some members of the creole elite, beginning with Bolívar, who gloomily predicted a race war that would also be a struggle between haves and have-nots. Bolívar revealed his obsessive race prejudice in his description of the valiant and generous Mexican patriot Vicente Guerrero as the "vile abortion of a savage Indian and a fierce African." These fears proved groundless; although some mixed-blood leaders, like Guerrero and Álvarez, remained to one degree or another loyal to the humble masses from which they had sprung, the majority were soon co-opted by the creole aristocracy and firmly defended its interests.

On the other hand, creole politicians of the postrevolutionary era had to take account of the new political weight of the mixed-blood middle and lower classes, especially the artisan groups. The mixed-bloods were exploited politically by white elites who promised to satisfy the aspirations of the masses—promises they failed to fulfill. This happened in Bogotá, where Colombian liberals courted the artisans in their struggle against conservatives, and in Buenos Aires, where Rosas demagogically identified himself with the gauchos and urban artisans—who were mixed-bloods in the great majority—against the aristocratic liberal *unitarios.*

After mid-century, the growing influence of European racist ideologies, especially Spencerian biological determinism, led to a heightened sensitivity to color. From Mexico to Chile, members of the white elite and even the middle class claimed to be superior to Indians and mixed-bloods. A dark skin increasingly became an obstacle to social advancement. Typical of the rampant pseudoscientific racism by the turn of the century is the remark of the Argentine Carlos Bunge, son of a German immigrant, that mestizos and mulattos were "impure, atavistically anti-

Christian; they are like the two heads of a fabulous hydra that surrounds, constricts, and strangles with its giant spiral a beautiful, pale virgin, Spanish America."

Even before the revolutions, black slavery had declined in various parts of Latin America. This occurred in part because of economic developments that made slavery unprofitable and favored manumission or commutation of slavery to tenantry. An even more significant reason, perhaps, was the frequent flight of slaves to remote jungles and mountains, where they formed self-governing communities. In Venezuela, in about 1800, it was estimated that alongside some eighty-seven thousand slaves there were twenty-four thousand fugitive slaves.

The wars of independence gave a major stimulus to emancipation. Patriot commanders like Bolívar and San Martín and royalist officers often offered slaves freedom in return for military service, and black slaves sometimes formed a majority of the fighting forces on both sides. About a third of San Martín's army in the campaign of the Andes was black. Moreover, the confusion and disorder produced by the fighting often led to a collapse of plantation discipline, easing the flight of slaves and making their recovery difficult if not impossible.

After independence, slavery further declined, partly because of its patent incompatibility with the libertarian ideals proclaimed by the new states but even more as a result of the hostile attitude of Great Britain, which had abolished the slave trade in all its possessions in 1807 and henceforth brought pressure for similar action by all countries still trading in slaves: we have seen that British pressure on Brazil contributed to the crisis of Brazilian slavery and its ultimate demise.

Emancipation came most easily and quickly in countries where slaves were a negligible element in the labor force; thus, Chile, Mexico, and the Federation of Central America (1823–1839) abolished slavery between 1823 and 1829. In other countries, the slave owners fought a tenacious rear-guard action. In Venezuela a very gradual manumission law was adopted in 1821, but not

244

until 1854 was slavery finally abolished. Slavery was abolished in Peru in 1855 by Ramón Castilla. The Spanish Cortes decreed the end of slavery in Puerto Rico in 1873 and in Cuba in 1880, but in Cuba the institution continued in a disguised form (the *patronato*) until 1886, when it was finally abolished.

The record of Latin American slavery in the nineteenth century, it should be noted, does not support the thesis of some historians that cultural and religious factors made Hispanic slavery inherently milder than the North American variety. In its two main centers of Cuba and Brazil, under conditions of mounting demand for Brazilian coffee and Cuban sugar and a critical labor shortage, there is ample evidence of systematic brutality with use of the lash to make slaves work longer and harder. The slaves responded with a resistance that varied from slowdowns to flight and open rebellion—a resistance that contributed to the final demise of the institution.

The Process of Modernization

The Landowners

Patriarchal family organization, highly ceremonial conduct, and leisurely lifestyle continued to characterize the landed aristocracy and Latin American elites after independence. The kinship network of the large extended family ruled by a patriarch was further extended by the institution of *compadrazgo,* which established a relationship of patronage and protection on the part of an upper-class godparent toward a lower-status godchild and his or her parents. The lower-class family members in turn were expected to form part of the godparent's following and to be devoted to his interests.

As in colonial times, great landowners generally resided most of the time in the cities, leaving their estates in the charge of administrators (but it must not be assumed that they neglected to scrutinize account books or were indifferent to

considerations of profit and loss). From the same upper class came a small minority of would-be entrepreneurs who challenged the traditional agrarian bias of their society and, in the words of Richard Graham, were "caught up by the idea of capitalism, by the belief in industrialization, and by a faith in work and practicality." Typical of this class was the Brazilian Viscount Mauá, who created a banking and industrial empire between 1850 and 1875 against the opposition of traditionalists. Mauá's empire collapsed, however, partly because the objective conditions for capitalist development in Brazil had not fully matured, partly because of official apathy and even disfavor. The day of the entrepreneur had not yet come; the economic history of Latin America in the nineteenth century is strewn with the wrecks of abortive industrial projects. These fiascos also represented defeats for the capitalist mentality and values.

After mid-century, with the gradual rise of a neocolonial order based on the integration of the Latin American economy into the international capitalist system, the ruling class, although retaining certain precapitalist traits, became more receptive to bourgeois values and ideals. An Argentine writer of the 1880s noted that "the latifundist no longer has that semibarbarous, semifeudal air; he has become a scientific administrator, who alternates between his home on the estate, his Buenos Aires mansion, and his house in Paris." In fact, few estancieros or hacendados became "scientific administrators." They preferred to leave the task of managing their estates to others, but the writer accurately pointed to a process of modernization or Europeanization of elites under way throughout the continent.

The process began right after independence but greatly accelerated after mid-century. Within a decade after independence, marked changes in manners and consumption patterns had occurred. "Fashions alter," wrote Fanny Calderón de la Barca, Scottish-born wife of the Spanish minister to Mexico, who described Mexican upper-class society in the age of Santa Anna in a series of sprightly letters. "The graceful mantilla

The family of an Indian cacique wearing Spanish dress. (From Carl Nebel, *Voyage Pittoresque et Ar-chéologique . . . [au] Mexique,* Paris, 1836. Courtesy of the Newberry Library.)

gradually gives place to the ungraceful bonnet. The old painted coach, moving slowly like a caravan, with Guido's Aurora painted on its gaudy panels, is dismissed for the London-built carriage."

The old yielded much more slowly and grudgingly to the new in drowsy colonial cities like Quito, capital of Ecuador, but yield it did, at least in externals. The U.S. minister to Ecuador in the 1860s, Friedrich Hassaurek, who was harshly critical of Quitonian society and manners, noted that "in spite of the difficulty of transportation, there are about one hundred and twenty pianos in Quito, very indifferently tuned." Another American visitor to Quito in this period, Professor James Orton of Smith College, observed that "the upper class follow *la mode de Paris,* gentlemen adding the classic cloak of Old Spain." He added sourly that "this modern toga fits an Ecuadoran admirably, preventing the arms from doing anything, and covers a multitude of sins, especially pride and poverty."

Under the republic, as in colonial times, dress was an important index of social status. According to Orton, "no gentleman will be seen walking in the streets of Quito under a poncho. Hence citizens are divided into men with ponchos and gentlemen with cloaks." Dress even served to distinguish followers of different political factions or parties. In Buenos Aires under Rosas, the

246

artisans who formed part of the dictator's mass base were called *gente de chaqueta* (wearers of jackets), as opposed to the aristocratic unitarian liberals, who wore dress coats.

By the close of the century, European styles of dress had triumphed in such great cities as Mexico City and Buenos Aires and among non-Indian sectors of the population generally. But attitudes toward clothes continued to reflect aristocratic values, especially scorn for manual labor; dress still made the man. In Buenos Aires, for example, at the turn of the century, a worker's blouse would bar entrance to its wearer to a bank or the halls of Congress. As a result, according to James Scobie, "everyone sought to hide the link with manual labor," and even workingmen preferred to wear the traditional coat and tie.

The Immigrants

After 1880, there was a massive influx of European immigrants into Argentina, Uruguay, and Brazil and of lesser numbers into such countries as Chile and Mexico. Combined with growing urbanization and continued expansion of the export sector, this helped to accelerate the rate of social change. These developments helped to create a small industrial working class of the modern type and swelled the ranks of the middle class and the blue-collar and white-collar workers.

But aside from that minority of the working class that adopted socialist, anarchist, or syndicalist doctrines, the immigrants posed no threat to the existing social structure or the prevailing aristocratic ideology; instead, many were conquered by that ideology. The foreigners who entered the upper class as a rule already belonged to the educated or managerial class. Movement from the middle class of immigrant origin to the upper class was extremely difficult and rare; for the lower-class immigrant it was almost impossible. A few immigrants made their fortunes by commerce or speculation. Their children or grandchildren took care to camouflage the origins of their wealth and to make it respectable

by investing it in land. These nouveaux riches regarded Indians and workers with the same contempt as their aristocratic associates.

Women

Independence did not better the status of women. Indeed, their civil status probably worsened as a result of new bourgeois-style law codes that strengthened husbands' control over their wives' property. More than ever, women were relegated to the four walls of their houses and household duties. Church and parents taught women to be submissive, sweetly clinging, to have no wills of their own. The double standard of sexual conduct prevailed; women were taught to deny their sexuality and believe that procreation was the sole end of sexual intercourse. But women's actual conduct did not necessarily conform to the law and ideology. Silvia Arróm has shown, for example, that the restrictions did not deter women in early nineteenth-century Mexico from engaging in extramarital affairs.

The democratic, liberal movements of the first half-century after independence stimulated some developments in favor of women. In Argentina, Sarmiento wrote that "the level of civilization of a people can be judged by the social position of its women"; his educational program envisaged a major role for women as primary-school teachers. In Mexico, the triumph of the Reforma was followed by promulgation of a new school law that called for the establishment of secondary schools for girls and normal schools for the training of women primary-school teachers. In both countries after 1870 there arose small feminist movements, largely composed of schoolteachers, that formed societies, edited journals, and worked for the cultural, economic, and social improvement of women. In the last decades of the century, with the development of industry, women in increasing numbers entered factories and sweatshops, where they often were paid half of what male workers earned, becoming a source of superprofits for capitalist employers. By 1887, according to the census of Buenos Aires, 39 percent of the paid work force of that city was composed of women.

The Church

The church, which in some countries had suffered discredit because of the royalist posture of many clergy during the wars of independence, experienced a further decline in influence as a result of increasing contacts with the outside world and a new and relatively tolerant climate of opinion. In country after country, liberals pressed with varying success for restrictions on the church's monopoly over education, marriage, burials, and the like. Since the church invariably aligned itself with the conservative opposition, liberal victories brought reprisals in the form of heavy attacks on its accumulated wealth and privileges.

The colonial principle of monolithic religious unity was early shattered by the need to allow freedom of worship to the prestigious and powerful British merchants. It was, in fact, the reactionary Rosas, who disliked foreigners and brought the Jesuits back to Argentina, who donated the land on which the first Anglican church in Buenos Aires was built. Despite the efforts of some fanatical clergy to incite the populace against foreign heretics, there gradually evolved a system of peaceful coexistence between Catholics and dissenters, based on reciprocal good will and tact.

The Inquisition, whose excesses had made it odious even to the faithful, disappeared during the wars of independence. In many countries, however, the civil authorities assumed its right to censor or ban subversive or heretical writings. Occasionally, governments exercised this right. In the 1820s, clerical and conservative opposition forced the liberal vice president of Gran Colombia, Francisco de Paula Santander, to authorize the dropping of a textbook by the materialist Jeremy Bentham from law school courses. In Buenos Aires, under Rosas, subversive books and other materials were publicly burned. According to Tulio Halperín-Donghi, however, a reading of

the press advertisements of Buenos Aires booksellers suggests that this repression was singularly ineffective. In Santiago in the 1840s, Francisco Bilbao's fiery polemic against Spain and Catholicism was burned by the public hangman. According to Sarmiento, however, it was not the content of Bilbao's book but its violent, strident tone that caused this reaction; Bilbao, he added, had been justly punished for his clumsiness.

After mid-century, with the enthronement of positivism, which glorified science and rejected theology as an approach to truth, efforts to suppress heretical or anticlerical writings diminished or ended completely in many countries. In general, during the last half of the nineteenth century, there existed in Latin America a relatively free market in ideas—free, that is, as long as these ideas were couched in theoretical terms or referred primarily to other parts of the world and were not directed against an incumbent regime. Governments were often quick to suppress and confiscate newspapers and pamphlets whose contents they considered dangerous to their security, but they remained indifferent to the circulation of books containing the most audacious social theories. By way of example, the Díaz dictatorship in Mexico struck at opposition journalists and newspapers but permitted the free sale and distribution of the writings of Marx and the anarchist theoretician Peter Kropotkin.

As a result of the ascendancy of positivism, the church suffered a further decline in influence and power. Conservative victories over liberalism sometimes produced a strong proclerical reaction, typified by Gabriel García Moreno, who ruled Ecuador from 1860 to 1875 and carried his fanaticism to the point of dedicating the republic to the Sacred Heart of Jesus. Rafael Núñez, dictator of Colombia from 1880 to 1894, drafted a concordat with the Vatican that restored to the church most of the rights it had enjoyed in colonial times. But such victories failed to arrest the general decline of the church's social and intellectual influence among the literate classes. Anticlericalism became an integral part of the ideology of most Latin American intellectuals and a large proportion of other upper-class and middle-class males, including many who were faithful churchgoers and observed the outward forms and rituals of the church. However, church influence continued strong among women of all classes, Indians, and the submerged groups generally.

The Romantic Revolt

The achievement of political independence did not end Latin American cultural dependence on Spain and Portugal. The effort of Latin American writers to find their own means of self-expression, to create national literatures, fused with the larger effort to liquidate the Hispanic colonial heritage in politics, economics, and social life. Accordingly, Latin American literature was from the first a literature of struggle; the concept of art for art's sake had little meaning for the writers of the first half-century after independence. Many writers were also statesmen and even warriors, alternately using pen and sword in the struggle against tyranny and backwardness. This unity of art and politics is expressed by the famous comment of Ecuadoran essayist and polemicist Juan Montalvo when he learned that the dictator García Moreno had been assassinated; "*Mi pluma lo mató*" ("My pen killed him"). That unity found its most perfect embodiment in the Cuban José Martí, who devoted himself almost from childhood to the struggle against Spanish rule in Cuba and died in 1895 in action against Spanish troops. He also blazed new trails in Latin American poetry and prose.

Latin American writers took the first step toward literary independence by breaking with Hispanic classic traditions and adopting as their models the great French and English poets and novelists of the romantic school. Romanticism, which Sarmiento once defined as "a true literary insurrection, like the political uprising that preceded it," seemed peculiarly appropriate for the achievement of the tasks the revolutionary young writers of Latin America had set themselves.

Victory over classicism, however, did not come without a struggle. In 1842 a famous debate took place in Chile between the Venezuelan Andrés Bello, conservative arbiter of literary taste, and the Argentine Domingo Sarmiento, who upheld a democratic freedom of expression and the superiority of contemporary French literature over all others. Their opposition was by no means absolute, for Bello was not a true reactionary in politics or literature. A distinguished poet, scholar, and educator, he had made major contributions to the development of Hispanic culture. His Spanish grammar, published in 1857, ended the domination of Latin grammatical rules and forms over the language and won acceptance by the Spanish Academy. His poem "The Agriculture of the Torrid Zone," despite its classic form, stimulated the rise of literary Americanism. He was an admirer of Victor Hugo's romantic writings and had himself translated Hugo and Dumas.

But Bello had a conservative's love for order and decorum and regarded himself as a guardian of the purity of the Castilian language. He was shocked when Sarmiento, in a review of a recently published grammar, wrote that "teachers of grammar are useless, for people learn by practical example and general discussion . . . the people are the real creators of a language, while grammarians are only the maintainers of tradition and compilers of dictionaries." Writing in a conservative journal, Bello retorted with praise of linguistic purity and academic standards; it would make as little sense, he wrote, to allow the people to make their own laws as to permit them to dictate the forms of their language. Sarmiento countered with an ardent defense of democracy in language and style. Bello, who disliked polemic, soon withdrew from the fray, but his disciples continued the debate.

Before the controversy ended, Sarmiento had silenced his opponents and converted Bello's chief disciple, José Victorino Lastarria, to his own beliefs. Romanticism soon triumphed everywhere, but Latin American romanticism was not a simple carbon copy of the European original; it bore its own vigorous stamp, displayed its own distinctive character.

Romanticism in Argentine Writing

By no coincidence, Esteban Echeverría, the founder of Argentine romanticism, gave the name *Dogma socialista* (*Socialist Teaching*) to his first important writing in which *socialism* stood for a nebulous concept of the primacy of the general interest of society over the individual interests. "Association, progress, liberty, equality, fraternity: these sum up the great social and humanitarian synthesis; these are the divine symbols of the happy future of nations and of humanity." By the time *Dogma socialista* was published in 1839, Echeverría had been forced by the Rosas terror to flee from Buenos Aires to Montevideo, where a group of young exiles combined literary activity with plots to overthrow the Rosas regime.

In his short prose masterpiece, *The Slaughterhouse* (published posthumously but probably written about 1840), Echeverría rejects one element of European romanticism, its idealized view of the common people. With unsparing realism, he describes the repellent sights and smells of a slaughterhouse that is also a gathering place of the Mazorca, the band of thugs who terrorize the enemies of Rosas. The story is also a political allegory: the slaughterhouse, with its butchers in gaucho dress and the black and mulatto women who carry away entrails, empty stomachs and bladders, and wade in blood, is a symbol of Rosas' Argentina, in which barbarous lower-class elements are given a free hand to torture and kill. The climax of the story comes when the butchers intercept a passing unitarian, a young man who wears stylish European dress and has his beard cut in the shape of a U. They tie him up, taunt him, and prepare to beat him. He scornfully replies to their taunts, breaks loose with a supreme effort, and dies from a hemorrhage before their very eyes. In the words of Arturo Torres-Rioseco, "the whole story is a sombre and terrible vignette, against a background of howling curs, bedraggled Negresses, circling vultures—a slaughterhouse that represents the real *matadero* [slaughterhouse] tyranny of Rosas."

A few years after Echeverría's death in 1851, another Argentine émigré, José Marmol, began to publish in serial form in Montevideo the first Argentine novel, *Amalia.* Again, as in *The Slaughterhouse,* literature and political attack fuse. The young unitarian, Eduardo Belgrano, tries to escape from his federalist pursuers; he takes refuge in the house of the widowed Amalia, and the two fall deeply in love. But the dictator's secret police discover Eduardo's hiding place and kill the lovers. Despite a stilted style and the artificiality of some of the characters, its intensity of feeling and the vivid descriptions of various social types and life in Buenos Aires lend portions of the book a genuine power.

Another exile from Rosas' Argentina, Domingo Sarmiento, illustrated his artistic theories in his formless masterpiece, *Life of Juan Facundo Quiroga: Civilization and Barbarism* (1845). Sarmiento offers a geographical and sociological interpretation of Argentine history, showing how the pampa had molded the character and lifestyle of the gauchos, the mass base of the Rosas dictatorship and the petty caudillos who ruled under him. From this tough, self-reliant breed of men springs the "hero" of Sarmiento's book, the provincial caudillo Facundo. Facundo was master of the Argentine western provinces and Rosas' lieutenant until the greater tyrant, who brooked no rival, had him ambushed and killed.

The ambiguity of Sarmiento's posture toward the gaucho—condemnation tempered by recognition of his admirable qualities—gave way to total defense and vindication of the gaucho and his values in the climactic work of gaucho literature, the epic poem *The Gaucho Martín Fierro* (1872) of José Hernández. Written some thirty years after Sarmiento's *Facundo,* its poignant, nostalgic mood reflects the uprooting of the old patriarchal estancia, the unfenced pampa, and the freedom of the gaucho's life by triumphant bourgeois "civilization" championed by Sarmiento. Hernández, a federalist who opposed Mitre and Sarmiento, supported the revolt of the last untamed gaucho chieftain, General López Jordán, and believed that the city, the seat of the central government, was exploiting and strangling the countryside. He portrayed the gaucho as a victim of the forces of "civilization"—judges, recruiting officers, corrupt police. The poem is strongly influenced by the folk songs of the gaucho *payador* (minstrel) and makes restrained but effective use of gaucho dialect.

Mexican National Literature

The beginnings of Mexican national literature are linked to the founding in 1836 of the Academy of Letrán, an informal literary circle whose members met to talk of literature or listen to readings of poetry and prose. Here, according to the Mexican literary historian González Peña, "was incubated the generation which later filled half a century of the history of Mexican literature." One of its founders, Guillermo Prieto, wrote that "the great and transcendent significance of the Academy was its decided tendency to 'Mexicanize' our literature, emancipating it from all other literatures and giving it a specific character." Prieto also noted that the academy "democratized literary studies, recognizing merit without regard to social position, wealth, or any other considerations." The effort to create a Mexican literature was closely linked to the struggle for political and social reform. Most major Mexican literary figures of the first half-century after independence—such men as Guillermo Prieto, Ignacio Altamirano, and Ignacio Ramírez—took an active part in that struggle.

The most serious effort to create a national Mexican literature was made by the Indian comrade-in-arms of Juárez, Ignacio Altamirano. Believing that Mexican poetry and literature should be as completely original as "are our soil, our mountains, our generation," Altamirano rejected the imitation of foreign models. He attempted to offer an example of such originality in his novel *Clemencia* (1869), set in the period of the French intervention. More successful, because of its fresh, unpretentious descriptions of life in a small Mexican village, was his *Christmas in the Mountains* (1870).

From the Academy of Letrán also issued a school of romantic poetry whose most remarkable creation was the "Prophecy of Cuauhtemoc" (1839) of Ignacio Rodríguez Galván. The poem sounds some major themes of Mexican romanticism: nationalism, anti-Spanish sentiment, and the glorification of pre-Cortesian Mexico. The magnificent coloring of the poem, its authentic romantic agony, the restless alternation in the poet's mind between thoughts of his personal sorrow and the woes of his people, make it, in the words of Menéndez y Pelayo, "the masterpiece of Mexican romanticism."

Chilean Writers

Chile lagged behind some of the other republics in the development of a national literature, perhaps—as Sarmiento suggested in his duel with Bello—because the absolute sway of Bello's classicist doctrines had created inertia, or perhaps because the relative stability of Chilean politics and the upward movement of the Chilean economy deprived its writers of the spur that the more dramatic contrasts of Argentine and Mexican life gave to creative literary activity. But if Chile lacked a Sarmiento or an Echeverría, it produced, in José Victorino Lastarria and Francisco Bilbao, two major writers on sociological topics who in their own way promoted the ideal of Chilean cultural emancipation.

Francisco Bilbao threw a bombshell into staid Santiago society with his essay "The Nature of Chilean Society" (1844), in which he declared: "Slavery, degradation: that is the past. . . . Our past is Spain. Spain is the Middle Ages. The Middle Ages are composed, body and soul, of Catholicism and feudalism." Later (1856), in his

America in Danger, Bilbao issued a powerful cry of warning to Latin America to unite under a regime of freedom and democracy. He sounded a special alarm against the expansionist designs of the United States in Latin America. In *The American Gospel* (1864), he offered much the same message: Latin America must throw off its Hispanic heritage of repression and obscurantism, and it must adopt rationalism rather than Catholicism as its guide if the Disunited States of Latin America were to achieve the place the United States had gained among the nations of the earth.

Lastarria, more moderate and scholarly than Bilbao, caused a lesser stir with his address, "Investigations of the Social Influence of the Conquest and the Colonial System of the Spaniards in Chile" (1844). Despite an occasional factual error, it remains an effective summary of the liberal case against the Spanish colonial regime. Andrés Bello undertook to review it. Conceding the general correctness of Lastarria's criticism of Spanish policy and work in Latin America, he offered a partial defense that stressed the mildness of Spanish rule and its civilizing mission in the New World. Whereas Bilbao was profoundly influenced by French left-wing republican and utopian socialist ideas, Lastarria's thought reflected the more conservative positivist teachings of the French philosopher Auguste Comte. Like Bilbao, however, Lastarria waged a consistent struggle against the backwardness he identified with Spanish civilization, which he felt was "the principal cause of our political and social disasters.... We cannot remedy these disasters except by reacting frankly, openly, and energetically against that civilization, in order to free our minds and adapt our country to the new form, democracy."

Brazilian Romantic Literature

A strong nationalism characterized the Brazilian romantic literature of the first decades after independence. In contrast with the Argentine writers of the same period, Brazilian writers expressed their nationalism in glorification of the Indian past. This Indianism reflected differences in the historical experience of the two countries: the Brazilian Indian had long ceased to pose a serious threat to white society, and Indian blood was widely diffused throughout the Brazilian people. Indianism, moreover, represented an effort to find roots for Brazilian nationalism—roots that could not be found in Portugal or Europe generally.

The greatest romantic poet of the first generation and the principal exponent of Indianism in poetry was Antônio Gonçalves Dias, in whose veins ran the blood of three races—white, Indian, and black. Basing himself on a careful study of Indian languages and culture, Gonçalves Dias conjured up the image of the defeated Indian with extraordinary emotive power in his *American Poems* (1846) and in the narrative poem "The Timbiras" (1857). He also celebrated the beauty of the Brazilian landscape in poems like the nostalgic "Song of Exile" (1846), which opens with the line: "My land has palm trees where the sabiá sings."

Indianism also found expression in the novels of José de Alencar, whose two most popular novels, *Iracema* (1865) and *The Guarani* (1856), deal with the theme of love between Indian and white. Despite the improbable plots and the sentimentality and artificiality of the dialogue and characters, Alencar's limpid, poetic style successfully evokes, somewhat in the manner of James Fenimore Cooper, the drama of the clash of Indian and white cultures and the grandeur of the Brazilian wilderness, with its majestic rivers, dense forests, and great waterfalls.

After the optimistic nationalism of the first generation of Brazilian romantic poets came the introspection, pessimism, and escapism of the second generation, which perhaps were a reaction to the defeat of the republican revolts of the 1830s and 1840s. In sharp contrast to these second-generation poets, who appeared to be sensitive to their own sufferings and misfortunes only, Antônio de Castro Alves devoted his poetic talent above all to the struggle against slavery. Because of his lofty, impassioned style, he is known as the founder of the *condoreira,* or condor school of poetry. Castro Alves's verses, read at countless abolitionist meetings and frequently published in the abolitionist press, gave a major stimulus to the growth of the abolitionist and republican movements in Brazil.

In 1867, Latin American romanticism, already in decline, produced its finest prose flower, the delicate love story *María* by the Colombian Jorge Isaacs. The story is set in a patriarchal country estate in the Cauca River Valley. Told in a simple, elegiac style, pervaded by a mood of gentle nostalgia, it relates the unfolding of an idyllic romance between a landowner's son and his cousin María. The story ends tragically when María dies during her lover's absence in London.

The Historical Novel

The romantic movement yielded an abundant harvest of historical novels, most of which dealt with episodes from the Spanish Conquest and the colonial era. Often their authors seemed chiefly concerned with exposing Spanish cruelty and the horrors of the Inquisition. Whether or not faithful to the historical facts, they generally lacked originality, talent, and psychological realism.

In 1872, however, Ricardo Palma began to publish his ironic and sparkling evocations of colonial Lima, *The Peruvian Traditions* (1872–1906). With these "traditions," Palma created a new genre: "A short sketch that was not history, anecdote, or satire, but a distillation of all three." Drawing on his immense knowledge of the colonial period (he was director of the National Library of Peru during the latter part of his life), Palma applied his own formula for the traditions: "a little bit, and quite a little bit of lying, a dose of the truth be it ever so infinitesimal, and a great deal of nicety and gloss in the style." From these elements Palma spun a long succession of cheerfully malicious tales that played on the follies and frailties of viceroys, priests, and highborn ladies

as well as lesser folk. Palma's "traditions" evoked the past far more successfully than the typical historical novel of this period.

Literature and Social Change, 1880–1910

By 1880 the romantic movement in Latin American literature had almost completed its tasks and exhausted its creative possibilities. As a result of the economic and political changes that we have surveyed, a new social reality had arisen. The growth of industry, immigration, and urbanization gave a new face to Latin American society. The ruling classes were increasingly acquisitive, arrogant, and philistine; the condition of the masses had not improved and may even have deteriorated. Latin America had become more European; in the process, it had failed to solve some old problems and had acquired some new ones.

In conformity with the specific conditions of their countries and their own backgrounds, writers responded to the new environment in a variety of ways. Generally speaking, romanticism survived as a vital force only in those countries where the old problems had not been solved. (Examples are Ecuador, the scene of a bitter struggle between liberals and conservatives, and Cuba, whose struggle for independence did not reach its climax until the 1890s.)

Poetry and Modernism

In poetry, the most important new phenomenon was the movement called modernism. Because the movement comprises an immense variety of stylistic and ideological tendencies, it is difficult to define. The common feature of modernist poets, however, was their search for new expressive means, for new stylistic forms, in reaction against the outworn language and forms of romanticism. The artistic creed of many modernist poets included rejection of literature as an instrument of social and political struggle. Turning their backs on "a world they never made," the world of shoddy and unstable prosperity ruled, in Rubén Darío's words, by *el rey burgués* (the bourgeois king), these escapists sought refuge in the ivory tower of art.

Most escapist of all was the prodigiously gifted Nicaraguan Rubén Darío (1867–1916), who defined modernism as the rejection of any explicit message in art; stress on beauty as the highest value (in Darío's poems, the swan is the recurrent symbol of beauty as an end in itself); and the determination to free verse from the tyranny of traditional forms. Not unexpectedly, in view of their conception of the artist as an outcast from bourgeois society, Bohemianism, alcohol, and drugs were elements in the lifestyle of many escapist poets, and not a few came to tragically early ends.

In their effort to achieve a renovation of poetry (and prose as well), the modernists drew on a variety of foreign sources (French Parnassianism, impressionism, symbolism, Whitman and Poe, Spain's medieval ballads). But they did not imitate; they appropriated these foreign methods for the creation of poetry and prose that were "entirely new, new in form and vocabulary and subject matter and feeling."

Escapism was a major current of modernism but not the only one. Indeed, before the movement had run its course, some of the leading escapist poets had risen to a new awareness of the continent's social and political problems and the writer's responsibility to the people. Darío himself exemplifies this evolution. If in the first, escapist phase of his poetic career he peopled his verses with satyrs, nymphs, centaurs, peacocks, and swans, in its second phase he gave voice to a powerful public poetry that reflected his new Americanism and concern with political and social themes. Darío's Americanism led him to a search for symbols in both the Spanish and the Indian past, regarded as the sources of a Latin American culture threatened by the aggressive expansionism of the United States.

Literary critics dispute whether the Cuban José Martí was a precursor of modernism or one

Rubén Darío. (Courtesy of the Organization of American States)

of its major figures and creators. Certainly, his spirit was alien to the escapist tendency of many modernist poets. Far from seeking refuge in an ivory tower, he dedicated his life to the struggle for Cuban independence; Cubans of all political faiths still call him "the Apostle." Martí's faith in humanity and progress reflected his links to Enlightenment thought, to romanticism, and to the optimistic evolutionism of the late nineteenth century. "I have faith," he wrote in the preface to his first book of verse (1882), "in the improvement of man, in the life of the future, in the utility of virtue." In a time of rampant racism, he denounced race prejudice of every kind.

From 1881 to 1895, Martí lived in exile in New York. As a correspondent for various Latin American newspapers, he wrote a vast number of articles in which he subjected political, economic, and cultural developments in the United States to searching analysis. Martí fervently admired Lincoln, Emerson, Mark Twain, and the abolitionist Wendell Phillips but expressed growing concern over the rise of monopolistic and imperialist tendencies. He especially feared and disliked the Republican leader James G. Blaine, whom he regarded as the chief exponent of North American imperialist designs on Latin America. He wrote in 1889: "What is apparent is that the nature of the North American government is changing in its fundamental reality. Under the traditional labels of Republican and Democrat, with no innovation other than the contingent circumstances of place and character, the republic is becoming plutocratic and imperialistic." In 1895 he left the United States to launch the Cuban Revolution. On the day before his death on May 19, 1895, while fighting Spanish troops, he set down his fears concerning U.S. policy toward Cuba: "I know the monster because I have lived in its lair, and my sling is that of David."

Martí's artistic ideas reflected his belief in the organic links between art and society, in the social responsibility of the artist. Art should reflect the joys and sorrows of the masses; in that sense it is a collective product. "Poetry is durable when it is the work of all. Those who understand it are as much its authors as those who make it." Simplicity and directness characterize his poems, but he was capable of using vivid, concrete imagery of great symbolic power. The very simplicity of his verse makes it difficult to render into English. In prose he achieved a genuine stylistic revolution. "The style he achieved," writes Pedro Henríquez-Ureña, "was entirely new to the language. He follows no single rhythmical pattern, but constantly varies it . . . he combines words—and meanings—in many unfamiliar ways. The effect is a constantly varied interplay of light and color. In style, as well as in what lies beyond style and becomes expression, his power of invention was inexhaustible." Dario said of Martí: "He writes more brilliantly than anyone in Spain or America."

The Romantic Revolt Continued: Ecuador and Peru

The fires of romantic revolt continued to burn in two Andean republics where small groups of intellectuals battled the rule of reactionary landowners, generals, and the church. In Ecuador, the writer Juan Montalvo, exiled by the fanatical dictator Gabriel García Moreno, leveled polemical attacks against him and claimed credit for García Moreno's assassination. Unhappy with the new rulers of Ecuador, Montalvo spent much of his life in exile from his native country. His *Seven Essays* (1882), reflecting a somewhat old-fashioned liberalism, propose the regeneration of Latin America through the formation of a model elite. His curious *Chapters That Cervantes Forgot,* a continuation of *Don Quijote,* published posthumously, display Montalvo's virtuosity in the use of sixteenth-century Castilian and express his ideas on a wide variety of topics.

The Peruvian writer Manuel González Prada advanced more radical ideas. A member of that generation of Peruvian youth that witnessed with feelings of profound humiliation the swift defeat of their country in the War of the Pacific, he initiated a new era of social unrest and intellectual ferment in Peru. He launched his "prose thunderbolts" against all that was sacrosanct in Peruvian society: the army, the church, the state, the creole aristocracy. In 1886 he founded a *Círculo Literario* (Literary Circle) with the declared aim of creating a nationalistic literature of "propaganda and attack." He proclaimed that "the people must be shown the horror of their degradation and misery; a good autopsy was never made without dissecting the body, and no society can be thoroughly known until its skeleton is laid bare."

González Prada made good his promise of dissecting the Peruvian organism by the ferocity of his attacks. Peru, he wrote, was a great boil: "press down anywhere and the pus comes out." He described the Peruvian Congress as a sewer where all the filth of the country had come together. He called for the creation of a vigorous new literature that would deal with national problems; this required writers to reject tradition and forge a new language: "Archaism implies backwardness: show me an archaic writer and I show you a reactionary thinker."

A woman writer who formed part of González Prada's literary circle and shared many of his progressive ideas, Clorinda Matto de Turner (1854–1909), wrote the first Indianist protest novel, *Birds Without a Nest* (1889). Set in an Indian village of the sierra, the novel denounces the abuses committed against the Indians by the exploitive trinity of judge, priest, and governor. "We were born Indians," declares an Indian woman, "slaves of the parish priest, slaves of the governor, slaves of the cacique, slaves of all those who hold the rod of authority." However, aside from the lesson of the personal charity and benevolence that well-disposed upper-class whites should show to the Indians, the writer offers no solution. As the novel ends, the young married couple who sought to protect the Indians return discouraged and defeated to Lima, leaving the Indians in their former state. With all its weaknesses, however, *Birds Without a Nest* was the forerunner of a genre, the Indianist novel, that had a great future.

Realism and Naturalism

Schools of literary realism and naturalism first arose in lands like Chile, Argentina, and Brazil, where capitalism and capitalist relations had struck firm roots. The Chilean writer Alberto Blest Gana began writing realist novels between 1860 and 1867. Strongly influenced by French realism—especially by Balzac—Blest Gana made the corrosive power of money on human relations the primary theme of his novels, *Arithmetic in Love* (1860), *Martín Rivas* (1862), and *A Good-for-Nothing's Ideal* (1863). Blest Gana painted broad canvases depicting a Chilean society in which merchants, landowners, army officers, and humble provincials struggled to improve their situation by marriage. In 1860, bestowing a literary award to him for *Arithmetic in Love,* a jury

that included José Victorino Lastarria and the historian Miguel Luis Amunátegui praised the novel because "the characters are Chileans, they are very like the people we know, the people we shake hands with and talk to. . . . The novel presents vivid, colorful, and accurate pictures of our national customs."

The boom of the 1880s, which transformed Argentine society, inspired the writing of some naturalist novels whose authors, however, lacked the great talent of Blest Gana. Buenos Aires, with its atmosphere of feverish prosperity and cosmopolitanism, provided the setting for most of these novels. A typical work is *The Bourse* (1890) by José María Miró, which deals with the rise and fall of a financier on the stock exchange. The novel is weakened by poor technique and xenophobic attacks on gold, Jews, and immigrants, regarded as the chief causes of the materialism that was allegedly destroying Argentina. Similar attacks on materialism and the egotism of the ruling classes characterize the naturalist novels of Eugenio Cambaceres (1843–1888).

In the urban novels of Joaquim María Machado de Assis (1839–1908), a master of ironic realism, Brazilian psychological letters display a precocious maturity. Although Machado, a mulatto, shunned involvement in the abolitionist or republican struggles of his time, his work exposes the stifling atmosphere of a society dominated by racism and the race for wealth; cynicism and disillusionment are the typical attitudes of his characters. In *Dom Casmurro* (1900), the principal character ends his melancholy story by congratulating himself that he had no children of his own and thus "transmitted to no one the legacy of his misery." The last words of the narrator of the story "The Attendant," as he is about to die, are a cynical revision of the Sermon on the Mount: "Blessed are they that *possess,* for they shall be comforted." More explicit criticism of Brazilian society appears in the naturalistic novels of Aluizio Azevedo (1857–1913), notably in *The Mulatto* (1881), in which a scheming priest and the relatives of a white girl plan the murder of her well-educated, cultured mulatto sweetheart.

At the turn of the century (1902) appeared an impressive study of rural Brazil, Euclides da Cunha's *Os sertões* (*Rebellion in the Backlands*), which deals, among other things, with the siege of Canudos in 1896–1897, when a handful of wretched backwoodsmen, led by the mystic Antônio Conselheiro, heroically resisted a federal army of some six thousand men. In his style—now lush and sensuous, now rugged; in his unsparing realism; and in his outspoken but unsentimental sympathy with the semibarbarous folk of the backlands, da Cunha blazed a trail for the regional and social novelists who would soon dominate the Brazilian literary scene.

Glossary

Adelantado* (Ah-day-lahn-tah-doh)† Commander of a conquering expedition with governing powers in a frontier or newly conquered province.

Alcabala (Ahl-cah-bah-lah) Spanish sales tax imposed by the crown.

Alcalde (Ahl-cahl-day) Member of a *cabildo* who in addition to administrative duties served as a judge of first instance.

Alcalde mayor (Ahl-cahl-day mē-yor) Royal governor of a district. See *Corregidor.*

Audiencia (Ow-dee-en-see-ah) A colonial high court and council of state under a viceroy or captain general, or the area of its jurisdiction.

Auto-da-fé (Ow-tō-dah-fay) or **auto-de-fé** (ow-tō-day-fay) The church's public ceremony of pronouncing judgment during the Inquisition, followed by execution of the sentence by secular authorities.

Ayllu (I-ee-yoo) A kinship and territorial unit of social organization, originally Inca, in the Andean region.

Cabildo (Cah-beel-dō) A municipal council in the Spanish colonies.

Cacique (Cah-see-kay) (1) An Indian chief or local ruler. (2) A tyrannical local boss.

Calpulli (Cahl-pool-yee) A kinship and territorial unit of social organization in ancient and colonial Mexico.

---

* Terms repeatedly defined or glossed in the text are not included in the Glossary.

† Aids to pronunciation of terms appear in parentheses after each term, and are phonetic approximations.

Capitão mor (Cah-pee-taow more)   The commander-in-chief of the military forces of a province in colonial Brazil.

Capitulación (Cah-pee-too-lah-syon)   The contract between the Spanish monarch and the leader of an expedition of conquest or discovery.

Chinampa (Chee-nahm-pah)   A garden or piece of arable land reclaimed from a lake or pond by dredging up soil from the bottom and piling it on a bed of wickerwork (Mexico).

Cofradía (Co-frah-dee-ah)   A religious brotherhood, originally Indian; sodality.

Colegio (Cō-lay-heeō)   A college or school.

Composición (Cōm-po-see-syon)   A settlement legalizing title to usurped land through payment of a fee to the king.

Congregación (Cōn-gray-gah-syon)   Resettlement of scattered Indian populations in order to facilitate Christianization and the collection of tribute.

Consulado (Cōn-soo-lah-doh)   A merchant guild and a tribunal of commerce during the colonial period.

Converso (Cōn-vair-so)   A converted Spanish Jew or the descendant of one.

Corregidor (Cō-ray-hee-door)   Royal governor of a district. *Corregidor de indios* administered Indian pueblos.

Cortes (Core'-tays)   The Spanish parliament.

Côrtes (Kohr-tees)   The Portuguese parliament.

Creole (Cree-ole)   An American-born Spaniard in the Spanish colonies.

Curaca (Coo-rah-cah)   A hereditary chief or ruler in ancient or colonial Peru.

Encomendero (En-cō-men-day-ro)   The holder of an *encomienda.*

Encomienda (En-cō-myen-dah)   An assignment of Indians who were to serve the Spanish grantee with tribute and labor; also, the area of the Indians so granted.

Fazenda (Fah-sen-dah)   A large estate (Brazil).

Hacendado (Hah-sen-dah-doh)   The owner of a *hacienda.*

Hacienda (Ha-see-en-dah)   A large landed estate.

Hidalgo (He-dahl-go)   A member of the lower nobility of Spain.

Inquilino (Een-kee-lee-no)   A Chilean tenant farmer.

Mayeque (Mē-ay-kay)   A tenant farmer or serf on the estate of a noble family in ancient Mexico.

Mayorazgo (Mē-yor-ahz-go)   An entailed estate.

Mestizo (Mez-tee-zo)   A person of mixed Indian and white descent.

Minga (Meen-gah)   A free Indian miner in colonial Peru.

Mita (Me-tah)   In colonial Peru, the periodic conscription of Indians for labor useful to the Spanish community. See *Repartimiento.*

Moderados (Mow-day-rah-dose)   Individuals comprising the moderate wing of the Liberal party in nineteenth-century Mexico.

Obraje (Ō-brah-hay)   A primitive factory or workshop, especially textile manufacture, often employing convict or debt labor.

Oidor (Ōee-door)   A judge of an *audiencia.*

Ouvidor (Oo-vee-door)   A royal judge who usually combined judicial and administrative duties (Brazil).

Patria (Pa-tree-ah)   The fatherland.

Patrón (Pah-trone)   Master.

Patronato real (Pah-trō-nah-toh ray-ahl)   The right of the Spanish crown to dispose of all ecclesiastical offices.

Peso (Pay-so)   A monetary unit of eight *reales.*

Quinto (Keen-toh)   One-fifth; the royal share or tax on all mine production or spoils of a conquest.

Real (Ray-ahl)   A monetary unit; one-eighth of a *peso.*

Regidor (Ray-hee-door)   A councilman in a *cabildo.*

Relacão (Ray-lah-sow), pl. **relaçoes** (ray-lah-sows)   A high court in colonial Brazil that combined judicial and administrative functions.

Repartimiento (Ray-par-tee-me-en-toh)   (1) An assignment of Indians or land to a Spanish settler during the first years of the Conquest. (2) The periodic conscription of Indians for labor useful to the Spanish community. (3) The mandatory purchase of merchandise by Indians from royal officials; also *repartimiento de mercancías.*

Reparto de mercancías (Ray-pahr-toh day mayr-cahn-see-ahs)   See *Repartimiento* (sense 3).

Residencia (Ray-zee-den-seeah)   A judicial review of a colonial official's conduct at the end of his term of office.

Senado de cámara (Say-nah-doh day cah-mah-rah)   A municipal council in colonial Brazil.

Visita (Vee-see-tah)   A judicial investigation of a colonial official's conduct, a tour of inspection, or other official visit, usually made unannounced.

Visitador (Vee-see-tah-door)   An official entrusted by the crown or the viceroy with the conduct of a *visita.*

Yanacona (Yah-nah-cō-nah)   (1) A servant or retainer of the Inca in ancient Peru. (2) An Indian laborer or tenant farmer of semi-servile status attached to a Spanish master or estate in colonial Peru.

Bibliographical Aids

Suggestions for Further Reading*

The indispensable *Handbook of Latin American Studies,* published annually since 1936, attempts to digest published material on Latin America in the social sciences and humanities. C. C. Griffin, ed., *Latin America: A Guide to the Historical Literature* (University of Texas Press, Austin, 1971), "provides a selective scholarly bibliography, accompanied by critical annotations, covering the whole field of Latin American history."

Students can also keep abreast of the most recent writing in the field by consulting the review sections of *The American Historical Review* (1895–), the *Hispanic American Historical Review* (1918–1922, 1926–), *Revista de Historia de America* (1938–), *The Americas: A Quarterly Review of Inter-American Cultural History* (1944–), *The Review of Inter-American Bibliography* (1951–), *Latin American Research Review* (1965–), and the British *Journal of Latin American Studies* (1969–).

For well-informed coverage of current events in the area, see the *Latin American Weekly Report* and the *Latin American Regional Reports,* published by Latin American Newsletters Ltd. (London). For more extended coverage of particular topics and events, see the bimonthly *NACLA Report on the Americas,* published by the North American Congress on Latin America (1967–) and focusing on the political economy of the area. The articles in *Latin American Perspectives*

---

* This bibliographical essay represents a small sample of the vast literature on Latin American history, largely limited to books published since 1970. For more thorough coverage, students are urged to consult the bibliographical aids given below, especially the *Handbook of Latin American Studies* and the Griffin *Guide.*

(1973–) offer scholarly Marxist interpretations of past and present problems of the area.

General Works

Good recent surveys of the colonial period are James Lockhart and Stuart B. Schwartz, *Early Latin America: A History of Colonial Spanish America and Brazil* (Cambridge University Press, Cambridge, Eng., 1983), L. N. McAlister, *Spain and Portugal in the New World* (University of Minnesota Press, Minneapolis, 1984), and M. A. Burkholder and L. L. Johnson, *Colonial Latin America* (Oxford University Press, New York, 1990). Stanley J. and Barbara H. Stein, *The Colonial Heritage of Latin America: Essays on Economic Dependence in Perspective* (Oxford University Press, New York, 1966), shows the continuity of Latin American economic patterns from colonial times to the present. For a compact but comprehensive collection of source materials, see Benjamin Keen, ed., *Latin American Civilization: History and Society, 1492 to the Present* (Westview Press, Boulder, Colo., fifth ed., 1991).

David Bushnell and Neill Macaulay, *The Emergence of Latin America in the Nineteenth Century* (Oxford University Press, New York, 1988), is a readable, well-informed survey of the subject. Leslie Bethell, ed., *The Cambridge History of Latin America,* 6 vols. to date (Cambridge University Press, Cambridge, Eng., 1985–), provides an authoritative collaborative history of the region from pre-Columbian times to the present.

Chapter 1
Ancient America

B. M. Fagen, *The Great Journey: The Peopling of Ancient America* (Thames and Hudson, New York, 1987), is a clear account of a complex subject; it is skeptical of datings assigning a great antiquity to man in America. Friedrich Katz, *The Ancient American Civilizations* (Praeger, New York, 1972),

remains the best synthesis, valuable for its factual content and probing questions. For new viewpoints on the Aztec and Inca civilizations, see G. A. Collier, R. I. Rosaldo, and J. D. Wirth, *The Inca and Aztec States, 1400–1800: Anthropology and History* (Academic Press, New York, 1982).

E. J. Wolf's classic *Sons of the Shaking Earth* (University of Chicago Press, Chicago, 1959) is a brilliant short account of the history and culture of Middle America. The intriguing Olmec civilization has attracted much scholarly attention; Ignacio Bernal, *The Olmec World* (University of California Press, Berkeley, 1969), is a good introduction to the subject. Nigel Davies, *The Toltecs: Until the Fall of Tula* (University of Oklahoma Press, Norman, 1977), attempts to separate fact from fiction in the shadowy Toltec history. Joseph Whitecotton, *The Zapotecs* (University of Oklahoma Press, Norman, 1977), forms a valuable companion study to John Paddock, ed., *Ancient Oaxaca* (Stanford University Press, Stanford, Calif., 1966).

Frances Berdan, *The Aztecs of Central Mexico: An Imperial Society* (Holt, Rinehart, and Winston, New York, 1982), is a concise, well-informed treatment of socioeconomic life and culture. Ross Hassig, *Trade, Tribute, and Transportation. The Sixteenth Century Political Economy of the Valley of Mexico* (University of Oklahoma Press, Norman, 1985), is an innovative study; see also his valuable *Aztec Warfare: Imperial Expansion and Political Control* (University of Oklahoma Press, Norman, 1988). Jacques Soustelle, *The Daily Life of the Aztecs on the Eve of the Conquest,* tr. by Patrick O'Brian (Macmillan, New York, 1962), is a colorful yet sound account. Miguel Leon-Portilla, *Aztec Thought and Culture: A Study of the Ancient Nahuatl Mind* (University of Oklahoma Press, Norman, 1963), is richly informative. Benjamin Keen, *The Aztec Image in Western Thought* (Rutgers University Press, New Brunswick, N.J., 1971), surveys four centuries of interpretation of Aztec culture.

Two classic surveys of the Maya are Sylvanus Morley, *The Ancient Maya,* revised by G. W. Brainerd (Stanford University Press, Stanford, Calif.,

1965), and Michael Coe, *The Maya* (Praeger, New York, 1956). For a summary of recent developments in Maya studies, see Norman Hammond, *Ancient Maya Civilization* (Rutgers University Press, New Brunswick, N.J., 1982).

E. P. Lanning, *Peru Before the Incas* (Prentice-Hall, Englewood Cliffs, N.J., 1967), is an excellent introduction to the subject. Paul Kosok, *Life, Land, and Water in Ancient Peru* (Long Island University Press, New York, 1963), is an important study of irrigation in pre-Inca Peru. Garcilaso de la Vega, *Royal Commentaries of the Inca and General History of Peru,* tr. by H. V. Livermore, is an indispensable source, but its idyllic picture of Inca rule must be viewed with caution. R. W. Keatinge, ed., *Peruvian Prehistory: An Overview of Pre-Inca and Inca Society* (Cambridge University Press, Cambridge, England, 1988), is a basic reference work. Alfred Metraux, *The History of the Incas* (Pantheon, New York, 1969), remains the best brief introduction to the subject. J. V. Murra has shed much light on Inca economic and social organization in a series of searching essays and in his doctoral dissertation, *The Economic Organization of the Inca State* (JAI Press, Greenwich, Conn., 1980).

For recent high estimates of pre-Conquest Indian populations, see Woodrow Borah and S. F. Cook, *The Aboriginal Population of Central Mexico on the Eve of the Spanish Conquest* (University of California Press, Berkeley, 1963), and S. F. Cook and Woodrow Borah, *Essays in Population History, Mexico and the Caribbean,* 3 vols. (University of California Press, Berkeley, 1971–1979). W. M. Denevan, ed., *The Native Population of the Americas in 1492* (University of Wisconsin Press, Madison, 1976), brings together conflicting viewpoints and attempts to generalize from the evidence.

Chapter 2
The Hispanic Background

For the general Hispanic background, see S. G. Payne, *A History of Spain and Portugal,* 2 vols.

(University of Wisconsin Press, Madison, 1973). On the Reconquista, see D. W. Lomax, *The Reconquest of Spain* (Longman, New York, 1978). John Elliott, *Imperial Spain, 1469–1716* (New American Library, New York, 1964), John Lynch, *Spain Under the Hapsburgs,* 2 vols., rev. ed. (New York University Press, New York, 1984), and Henry Kamen, *Spain, 1469–1714: A Society of Conflict* (Longman Group, London, 1983), usefully complement each other. J. H. Mariéjol, *The Spain of Ferdinand and Isabella,* tr. and ed. by Benjamin Keen (Rutgers University Press, New Brunswick, N.J., 1961), remains the best general account of the life, manners, and institutions of Spain under the Catholic Sovereigns. Henry Kamen, *The Spanish Inquisition* (New American Library, New York, 1965), is a clear, thorough survey of the subject. Ruth Pike shows that nobility did not exclude the practice of commerce in *Aristocrats and Traders: Sevillian Society in the Sixteenth Century* (Cornell University Press, Ithaca, N.Y., 1972).

Chapter 3
The Conquest of America

C. E. Nowell, *The Great Discoveries and the First Colonial Empires* (Cornell University Press, Ithaca, N.Y., 1954), is a concise introduction to the subject. J. H. Parry, *The Age of Reconaissance* (World, Cleveland, 1963), is especially informative in such areas as techniques of navigation, ship construction, and armaments. For the impact of the New World on the mind of the Old, see John Elliott, *The Old World and the New, 1492–1650* (Cambridge University Press, Cambridge, Eng., 1970); the subject is studied in much greater detail in Fredi Chiapelli, ed., *First Images of America,* 2 vols. (University of California Press, Berkeley, 1976). William Brandon, *New Worlds for Old* (Ohio University Press, Athens, Ohio, 1986), documents the large impact of reports from America on the development of social thought in Europe, 1500–1800.

On the background of the Portuguese outward

264 thrust, see B. D. Diffie, *Prelude to Empire: Portugal Overseas Before Henry the Navigator* (University of Nebraska Press, Lincoln, 1961). C. R. Boxer, *The Portuguese Seaborne Empire, 1415–1825* (Knopf, New York, 1969), is a masterful survey of the Portuguese colonial experience.

S. E. Morison, *The European Discovery of America: The Southern Voyages, 1492–1619* (Oxford University Press, New York, 1974), is an authoritative account. Morison's *Admiral of the Ocean Sea: A Life of the Admiral Christopher Columbus,* 2 vols. (Little, Brown, Boston, 1942), remains a standard biography, but must be supplemented by the work of the knowledgeable Italian scholar Paolo Emilio Taviani, *Christopher Columbus: The Grand Design* (Orbis, London, 1985). Kirkpatrick Sale's challenging *The Conquest of Paradise* (Alfred Knopf, New York, 1990) is very critical of Columbus and the consequences of his discovery. Tzvetan Todorov, *The Conquest of America: The Question of the Other* (Harper & Row, New York, 1984), calls attention to the distorting lenses through which Columbus, Cortés, and other Europeans saw the Indians. For the grim consequences of the discovery for the natives of the Caribbean, see Carl Sauer, *The Early Spanish Main* (University of California Press, Berkeley, 1966). J. G. Varner and J. J. Varner, *The Dogs of the Conquest* (University of Oklahoma Press, Norman, 1983), is the first study of the role played in battle by the fearsome Spanish war dogs. A. W. Crosby, *The Columbian Exchange. Biological and Cultural Consequences of 1492* (Greenwood Press, Westport, Conn., 1972), is a pioneering study of the subject. N. D. Cook, *Demographic Collapse: Indian Peru, 1520–1620* (Cambridge University Press, Cambridge, Eng., 1981), illustrates the demographic catastrophe that overtook Indian populations in the wake of the Conquest.

For the long-neglected native vision of the Conquest, see Miguel León-Portilla, ed., *The Broken Spears: The Aztec Account of the Conquest of Mexico* (Beacon Press, Boston, 1962), and Nathan Wachtel, *The Vision of the Vanquished: The Spanish Conquest of Peru Through Indian Eyes, 1530–1570* (Barnes & Noble, New York, 1977). The major Spanish eyewitness accounts of the conquest of Mexico are by Cortés himself, *Letters from Mexico,* tr. and ed. by A. R. Pagden (Grossman, New York, 1971), and by Bernal Díaz del Castillo (many editions). Díaz del Castillo wrote his book in part to correct the hero-worshiping account of Francisco López de Gómara, *Cortés: The Life of the Conqueror by His Secretary,* tr. by L. B. Simpson (University of California Press, Berkeley, 1966). R. C. Padden, *The Hummingbird and the Hawk: Conquest and Sovereignty in the Valley of Mexico, 1503–1541* (Ohio State University Press, Columbus, 1967), presents interesting new interpretations.

John Hemming, *The Conquest of the Incas* (Harcourt Brace Jovanovich, New York, 1970), supersedes all previous accounts. James Lockhart, *The Men of Cajamarca: A Social and Biographical Study of the First Conquerors of Peru* (University of Texas Press, Austin, 1972), sheds light on the backgrounds of the conquistador group. On the origins and ramifications of the El Dorado legend, see John Hemming, *The Search for El Dorado* (E. P. Dutton, New York, 1978). For the origins, motives, and occupations of the conquistadors and other Spanish settlers, see Lockhart's *Men of Cajamarca,* cited above, and James Lockhart and Enrique Otte, eds., *Letters and People of the Spanish Indies: Sixteenth Century* (Cambridge University Press, Cambridge, Eng., 1976).

Chapter 4
The Economic Foundations of Colonial Life

For the juridical and moral aspects of the struggle over Spain's Indian policy, see Lewis Hanke, *The Spanish Struggle for Justice in the Conquest of America* (University of Pennsylvania Press, Philadelphia, 1949). For messianic and utopian influences on the Conquest, see J. L. Phelan, *The Millennial Kingdom of the Franciscans in the New World* (University of California Press, Berkeley,

1956). On Las Casas, see Juan Friede and Benjamin Keen, eds., *Bartolomé de Las Casas in History* (Northern Illinois University Press, DeKalb, 1971), an anthology that presents varied points of view on Las Casas.

A growing literature shows the Indians not as passive objects of Spanish rule but as makers of their own history who resisted Spanish pressures with a variety of strategies. Examples of this trend include S. J. Stern, *Peru's Native Peoples and the Challenge of Conquest: Huamanga to 1640* (University of Wisconsin Press, Madison, 1982); Karen Spalding, *Huarochirí: An Indian Society Under Inca and Spanish Rule* (Stanford University Press, Stanford, Calif., 1984); Nancy Farriss, *Maya Society Under Colonial Rule* (Princeton University Press, Princeton, N.J., 1984); and G. D. Jones, *Maya Resistance to Spanish Rule: Time and History on a Colonial Frontier* (University of New Mexico Press, Albuquerque, 1989). Inga Clendinnen's fine book, *Ambivalent Conquests: Maya and Spaniard in Yucatan, 1517–1570* (Cambridge University Press, Cambridge, Eng., 1987), sympathetically explores the mental worlds of Spanish friars and Indian converts. Rolena Adorno, *Guaman Poma: Writing and Resistance in Colonial Peru* (University of Texas Press, Austin, 1986), shows how a great Indian chronicler used his work in a "hidden polemic" against the colonial regime.

The literature on Spanish-Indian relations is closely linked to that on Spanish colonial labor and tribute systems. J. A. and J. E. Villamarín, *Indian Labor in Mainland Colonial Spanish America* (University of Delaware Press, Newark, 1975), shows how different patterns of Indian labor management were employed in different times and places. L. B. Simpson's pioneering study, *The Encomienda in New Spain,* rev. ed. (University of California Press, Berkeley, 1950), argues that the encomienda was eventually "tamed." W. L. Sherman, *Forced Native Labor in Sixteenth-Century Central America* (University of Nebraska, Lincoln, 1979), is a careful study of a region whose labor conditions were notoriously oppressive. Indian labor, tribute, and land are major themes in Charles Gibson's monumental *The Aztecs Under Spanish Rule: A History of the Indians of the Valley of Mexico* (Stanford University Press, Stanford, Calif., 1964). Gibson's book, like that of François Chevalier, *Land and Society in Colonial Mexico,* tr. by L. B. Simpson (University of California Press, Berkeley, 1963), documents the triumph of the hacienda over the Indian pueblo in central Mexico, but W. B. Taylor, *Landlord and Peasant in Colonial Oaxaca* (Stanford University Press, Stanford, Calif., 1972), shows that Indians retained much of the land in that province. John Tutino, *From Insurrection to Revolution in Mexico: Social Bases of Agrarian Violence, 1750–1940* (Princeton University Press, Princeton, N.J., 1986), is a broad interpretive survey of the peasant struggle for land and survival. Much recent literature on the colonial hacienda features a revisionist stress on the diversity of the institution: examples of this trend include R. G. Keith, *Conquest and Agrarian Change: Emergence of the Hacienda System on the Peruvian Coast* (Harvard University Press, Cambridge, Mass., 1976); K. A. Davis, *Landowners in Colonial Peru* (University of Texas Press, Austin, 1984); and S. E. Ramirez, *Provincial Patriarchs: Land Tenure and the Economics of Power in Colonial Peru* (New Mexico University Press, Albuquerque, 1986).

For a good general survey of black slavery, see L. B. Rout, Jr., *The African Experience in Spanish America: 1502 to the Present Day* (Cambridge University Press, Cambridge, Eng., 1971). H. S. Klein, *African Slavery in Latin America and the Caribbean* (Oxford University Press, New York, 1986), surveys all aspects of the subject over a larger area. Rolando Mellafe, *Negro Slavery in Latin America* (University of California Press, Berkeley, 1975), is a concise history. Monographs on black slavery in specific colonies include F. P. Bowser, *The African Slave in Colonial Peru, 1524–1650* (Stanford University Press, Stanford, Calif., 1973), and C. L. Palmer, *Slaves of the White God: Blacks in Mexico, 1570–1650* (Harvard University Press, Cambridge, Mass., 1976). Richard Price, ed., *Maroon Societies: Rebel Slave Communities in the Americas* (Johns Hopkins University Press, Baltimore, 1979), is one of the few studies of a neglected subject. For the dimensions of the slave trade, see P. D. Curtin, *The American Slave Trade: A Census* (University of Wisconsin Press, Madison, 1969). On the trade itself, see J. C. Miller's massive *Way of Death: Merchant Capitalism and the Angolan Slave Trade, 1730–1830* (University of Wisconsin Press, Madison, 1988).

On the encomendero as businessman, see G. M. Riley, *Fernando Cortés and the Marquesado in Morelos, 1522–1547: A Case Study in the Socioeconomic Development of Sixteenth-Century Mexico* (University of New Mexico Press, Albuquerque, 1973). L. B. Simpson's important *Exploitation of Land in Central Mexico in the Sixteenth Century* (University of California Press, Berkeley, 1956), chronicles, among other things, the replacement of men by sheep. M. J. MacLeod, *Spanish Central America: A Socioeconomic History, 1520–1720* (University of California Press, Berkeley, 1973), is the story of the economic rise and fall of a region. J. C. Super, *Food, Conquest, and Colonization in Sixteenth-Century Spanish America* (University of New Mexico Press, Albuquerque, 1988), deals with, among other topics, colonial patterns of food consumption and Indian adaptation to European foods.

P. J. Bakewell, *Silver Mining and Society in Colonial Mexico: Zacatecas, 1546–1700* (Cambridge University Press, Cambridge, Eng., 1971), calls into question older views on the availability of Indian labor and silver production trends. On Peruvian mining, see P. J. Bakewell, *Miners of the Red Mountain: Indian Labor in Potosí, 1545–1650* (University of New Mexico, Albuquerque, 1984), and J. A. Cole, *The Potosí Mita 1573–1700, Compulsory Indian Labor in the Andes* (Stanford University Press, Stanford, Calif., 1985). R. M. Salvucci, *Textiles and Capitalism in Mexico: An Economic History of the Obrajes, 1539–1840* (Princeton University Press, Princeton, N.J., 1987), studies the history of an ill-famed but widespread colonial industry.

On colonial commerce, the classic study of C. H. Haring, *Trade and Navigation Between Spain and the Indies in the Time of the Hapsburgs* (Harvard University Press, Cambridge, Mass., 1918), remains the standard work. For the Italian

role in colonial trade, see Ruth Pike, *Enterprise and Adventure: The Genoese at Seville and the Opening of the New World* (Cornell University Press, Ithaca, N.Y., 1966). W. L. Schurz, *The Manila Galleon* (E. P. Dutton, New York, 1939), deals with the important silk trade between Manila and Acapulco. On the foreign challenge to the Spanish commercial monopoly, see K. R. Andrews, *The Spanish Caribbean: Trade and Plunder, 1530–1630* (Yale University Press, New Haven, Conn., 1978). For piracy, see the still valuable work of C. H. Haring, *The Buccaneers in the West Indies in the Seventeenth Century* (Methuen, London, 1910).

Chapter 5
State, Church, and Society

C. H. Haring, *The Spanish Empire in America* (Oxford University Press, New York, 1947), is especially good on the political and administrative system. Mario Góngora, *Studies in the Colonial History of Spanish America* (Cambridge University Press, Cambridge, Eng., 1975), the work of a great Chilean scholar, sheds light on themes ranging from the organization of conquests to "the institutions and founding ideas of the Spanish states in the Indies." J. H. Parry, *The Spanish Theory of Empire in the Sixteenth Century* (Cambridge University Press, Cambridge, Eng., 1940), is an important background study. Peggy Liss, *Mexico Under Spain, 1521–1556* (University of Chicago Press, Chicago, 1975), fills a gap in the literature on Spanish rule in Mexico. Two valuable audiencia studies are J. H. Parry, *The Audiencia of New Galicia in the Sixteenth Century* (Cambridge University Press, Cambridge, Eng., 1948), and J. L. Phelan, *The Kingdom of Quito in the Seventeenth Century: Bureaucratic Politics in the Spanish Empire* (University of Wisconsin Press, Madison, 1967). R. H. Vigil, *Alonso de Zorita: Royal Judge and Christian Humanist, 1512–1585* (University of Oklahoma Press, Norman, 1987), traces the career of a Spanish judge of rare integrity and social conscience. For the functioning of the early cabildo, see J. P. Moore, *The Cabildo in Peru Under the Hapsburgs* (Duke University Press, Durham, N.C., 1954). J. I. Israel, *Race, Class, and Politics in Colonial Mexico 1610–1670* (Oxford University Press, New York, 1975), and K. J. Andrien, *Crisis and Decline: The Viceroyalty of Peru in the Seventeenth Century* (University of New Mexico Press, Albuquerque, 1985), explore the processes of economic and political change in the neglected seventeenth century.

R. E. Greenleaf, ed., *The Roman Catholic Church in Colonial Latin America* (Knopf, New York, 1971), is a collection of informative texts with a useful introduction. Robert Ricard, *The Spiritual Conquest of Mexico,* tr. by L. B. Simpson (University of California Press, Berkeley, 1966), is a classic work, but its confidence in the reality of the "conquest" is questioned by many modern scholars; see, for example, the negative conclusions of L. M. Burkhart, *The Slippery Earth: Nahua-Christian Moral Dialogue in Sixteenth Century Mexico* (University of Arizona Press, Tucson, 1989). Serge Gruzinski, *Man-Gods in the Mexican Highlands: Indian Power and Colonial Society, 1520–1800* (Stanford University Press, Stanford, Calif., 1989), illustrates the survival of pagan religious notions in the colonial period. On the colonial Inquisition, see two works by R. E. Greenleaf, *Zummáraga and the Mexican Inquisition, 1536–1543* (Academy of American Franciscan History, Washington, D.C., 1961), and *The Mexican Inquisition in the Seventeenth Century* (University of New Mexico Press, Albuquerque, 1969).

On the Jesuits, see Magnus Morner, *The Political and Economic Activities of the Jesuits in the La Plata Region: The Hapsburg Era* (Institute of Ibero-American Studies, Stockholm, 1953). On the church and its wealth, see J. F. Schwaller, *Church and Clergy in Sixteenth-Century Mexico* (University of New Mexico Press, Albuquerque, 1987), and *Origins of Church Wealth in Mexico* (University of New Mexico Press, Albuquerque, 1985).

On the structure of class and caste, see Magnus Morner, *Race Mixture in the History of Latin America* (Little, Brown, Boston, 1967). L. S. Hoberman and S. M. Socolow, *Cities and Society in Colonial Latin America* (University of New Mexico Press, Albuquerque, 1986), is an important collection of essays on the groups composing urban society. On the lives of the so-called inarticulate masses, see the pioneering collection of essay-biographies edited by D. G. Sweet and G. B. Nash, *Struggle and Survival in Colonial America* (University of California Press, Berkeley, 1981). For conflicting views on the condition of colonial blacks, see Eugene Genovese and Laura Foner, eds., *Slavery in the New World* (Prentice-Hall, Englewood Cliffs, N.J., 1970), and D. W. Cohen and J. P. Greene, eds., *The Freemen of African Descent in the Slave Societies of the New World* (Johns Hopkins University Press, Baltimore, 1972). A valuable pioneering study of colonial medical history is Donald B. Cooper's *Epidemic Disease in Mexico City, 1761–1813: An Administrative, Social and Medical Study* (University of Texas Press, Austin, 1965).

For Spanish immigration to the Indies, see Peter Boyd-Bowman, *Patterns of Spanish Immigration to the New World, 1492–1580* (State University of New York at Buffalo, 1973). James Lockhart's *Spanish Peru, 1532–1560* (University of Wisconsin Press, Madison, 1968) is a "collective biography" of the first generation of Spanish settlers. Two notable works on Latin American women are a collection of essays edited by Asunción Lavrin, *Sexuality and Marriage in Colonial Latin America* (University of Nebraska Press, Lincoln, 1989), and Patricia Seed, *To Love, Honor, and Obey in Colonial Mexico, 1574–1821* (Stanford University Press, Stanford, Calif., 1988). We now have a full-scale study of Hispanic women in colonial Peru, Luis Martin's *Daughters of the Conquistadores* (University of New Mexico Press, Albuquerque, 1983).

Chapter 6
The Bourbon Reforms and Spanish America

Richard Herr, *The Eighteenth-Century Revolution in Spain* (Princeton University Press, Princeton,

N.J., 1958), lucidly describes the Bourbons' effort to reconstruct Spain. On the intendant reform, see John Lynch, *Spanish Colonial Administration, 1782–1819: The Intendant System in the Viceroyalty of the Rio de la Plata* (Athlone Press, London, 1958), and J. R. Fisher, *Government and Society in Colonial Peru: The Intendant System, 1784–1814* (Athlone Press, London, 1970). M. S. Burkholder and D. S. Chandler, *From Impotence to Authority: The Spanish Crown and the American Audiencias, 1687–1808* (University of Missouri Press, Columbia, 1977), traces changes in the composition and functioning of the audiencia. S. M. Socolow, *The Bureaucrats of Buenos Aires, 1769–1810* (Duke University Press, Durham, N.C., 1988), is a case study of the new Bourbon colonial bureaucracy. Studies of Bourbon changes in military policy and the rise of a colonial military elite have proliferated; for two good examples, see C. L. Archer, *The Army in Bourbon Mexico, 1760–1810* (University of New Mexico Press, Albuquerque, 1978), and L. G. Campbell, *The Military and Society in Colonial Peru, 1750–1810* (American Philosophical Society, Philadelphia, 1978). J. K. Chance, *Race and Class in Colonial Oaxaca* (Stanford University Press, Stanford, Calif., 1978), shows how "passing" from casta to creole status modified the formal hierarchy of race and class; his *Conquest of the Sierra. Spaniards and Indians in Colonial Oaxaca* (University of Oklahoma Press, Norman, 1989) studies the impact of Spanish trading practices on Indian social organization.

G. G. Walker, *Spanish Politics and Imperial Trade, 1700–1789* (Indiana University Press, Bloomington, 1979), skillfully traces the growing crisis and ultimate collapse of the Spanish fleet system. S. M. Socolow, *The Merchants of Buenos Aires, 1778–1810* (Cambridge University Press, New York, 1978), is a case study of a class of growing importance in the Bourbon era. Doris Ladd, *The Mexican Nobility at Independence, 1780–1826* (University of Texas Press, Austin, 1976), studies the make-up, social linkages, and attitudes of a small but powerful group.

For some economic trends in the late colonial period, see David Brading, *Miners and Merchants in Bourbon Mexico, 1763–1810* (Cambridge University Press, Cambridge, Eng., 1971); B. R. Hamnett, *Politics and Trade in Southern Mexico, 1750–1821* (Cambridge University Press, Cambridge, Eng., 1971); and J. R. Fisher, *Silver Mines and Silver Miners in Colonial Peru, 1776–1824* (University of Liverpool, Liverpool, 1977). Eric Van Young's important *Hacienda and Market in Eighteenth-Century Mexico: The Rural Economy of the Guadalajara Region, 1675–1820* (University of California Press, Berkeley, 1981), documents, among other findings, the growing domination of the great estate. John Kicza, *Colonial Entrepreneurs: Families and Business in Bourbon Mexico City* (University of New Mexico Press, Albuquerque, 1983), is an extraordinarily informative work. Ann Twinam, *Miners, Merchants, and Farmers of Colonial Colombia* (University of Texas Press, Austin, 1982), explores the colonial roots of the entrepreneurial spirit traditionally associated with the province of Antioquia. Jay Kinsbruner, *Petty Capitalism in Spanish America: The Pulperos of Puebla, Mexico City, Caracas, and Buenos Aires* (Westview Press, Boulder, Colo., 1987), is an innovative study of grocery stores in the late colonial and early national periods. On labor relations in the late Bourbon era, see the notable work of Doris Ladd, *The Making of a Strike: Mexican Silver Workers' Struggles in Real del Monte, 1766–1775* (University of Nebraska Press, Lincoln, 1988).

On colonial culture, see the basic study by J. T. Lanning, *Academic Culture in the Spanish Colonies* (Oxford University Press, London, 1940), and Mariano Picon Salas, *A Cultural History of Spanish America, From Conquest to Independence,* tr. by Irving Leonard (University of California Press, Berkeley, 1962). Irving Leonard combines literary and social history in his *Books of the Brave* (Harvard University Press, Cambridge, Mass., 1949), and *Baroque Times in Old Mexico* (University of Michigan Press, Ann Arbor, 1959). George Kubler studies the interplay of economics, society, and art in *Mexican Architecture in the Sixteenth Century,* 2 vols. (Yale University Press, New Haven, 1948). For the dawning of creole national consciousness and its religious expression, see Jacques Lafaye, *Quetzalcoatl and Guadalupe: The Formation of Mexican National Consciousness,* tr. by Benjamin Keen (University of Chicago Press, Chicago, 1976); on creole efforts to refute European charges of the New World's inferiority, see Antonello Gerbi, *The Dispute of the New World: The History of a Polemic, 1750–1900,* tr. by Jeremy Moyle (University of Pittsburgh Press, Pittsburgh, 1973).

L. E. Fisher surveys the revolt of Tupac Amaru in *The Last Inca Revolt, 1780–1783* (University of Oklahoma Press, Norman, 1966); for the revolt of the Comuneros, see the work of J. L. Phelan published posthumously, *The People and the King: The Comunero Revolution in Colombia* (University of Wisconsin Press, Madison, 1977).

Chapter 7
Colonial Brazil

Caio Prado Junior, *The Colonial Background of Modern Brazil,* tr. by Suzette Macedo (University of California Press, Berkeley, 1967), stressing economic and social aspects, remains the best general survey. A series of authoritative studies by the British Brazilianist Charles Boxer spans almost the whole course of Brazil's colonial history; see especially *The Dutch in Brazil, 1625–1654* (Clarendon Press, Oxford, Eng., 1957), and *The Golden Age of Brazil, 1695–1750* (University of California Press, Berkeley, 1962). Dauril Alden, ed., *The Colonial Roots of Modern Brazil* (University of California Press, Berkeley, 1972), is a valuable collection of essays on socioeconomic topics. James Lang, *Portuguese Brazil: The King's Plantation* (Academic Press, New York, 1979), is a useful synthesis, with a stress on the distinctive features of Brazil's colonial history.

Stuart B. Schwartz, *Sugar Plantations in the Formation of Brazilian Society: Bahia, 1550–1835* (Cambridge University Press, New York, 1985), is a masterful study of the economy and society that arose on the foundation of sugar and slavery. For the backgrounds of colonial officials and their relations with other social groups, see Schwartz's *Sovereignty and Society in Colonial Brazil: The High Court of Bahia and Its Judges, 1609–1745* (University of California Press, Berkeley, 1973). Dauril Alden, *Royal Government in Colonial Brazil* (University of California Press, Berkeley, 1968), focuses on the problems faced by an able viceroy of Brazil in the eighteenth century. K. R. Maxwell, *Conflicts and Conspiracies: Brazil and Portugal, 1750–1808* (Cambridge University Press, New York, 1973), surveys the emerging conflict between mother country and colony. On Portugal's Indian policies, see John Hemming, *Red Gold, The Conquest of the Brazilian Indians, 1500–1760* (Macmillan, London, 1978), which records "an appalling demographic tragedy of great magnitude."

Gilberto Freyre, *The Masters and the Slaves,* tr. by Samuel Putnam (Knopf, New York, 1946), is a literary and historical masterpiece, but its nostalgic portrayal of race relations must be viewed with caution. For a corrective, see Charles Boxer, *Race Relations in the Portuguese Colonial Empire, 1415–1825* (Clarendon Press, Oxford, Eng., 1963).

Chapter 8
The Independence of Latin America

John Lynch, *The Spanish-American Revolutions, 1808–1826* (Norton, New York, 1973), is an admirable synthesis, based on thorough research and supplied with a comprehensive annotated bibliography. T. A. Anna, *Spain and the Loss of America* (University of Nebraska Press, Lincoln, 1983), argues that that loss was due above all to Spain's incorrect or incoherent policies for dealing with the crisis. For the trail-blazing revolution in Haiti, see T. O. Ott, *The Haitian Revolution, 1789–1804* (University of Tennessee Press, Knoxville, 1973), and C. L. R. James, *The Black Jacobins: Toussaint L'Ouverture and the Santo Domingo Revolution,* 2nd rev. ed. (Vintage, New York, 1963). The best life of Bolívar is Gerhard Masur, *Simón Bolívar,* 2nd ed. (University of New Mexico

Press, Albuquerque, 1969). On Miranda, see the standard work of W. S. Robertson, *The Life of Miranda,* 2 vols. (University of North Carolina Press, Chapel Hill, 1929). There is an adequate short life of San Martín by J. C. Metford, *San Martín the Liberator* (Longmans, Green, London, 1950). John Street, *Artigas and the Emancipation of Uruguay* (Cambridge University Press, London, 1959), is an excellent study of the Uruguayan hero and the process of Uruguayan independence. For that process in Chile, see Simon Collier's thorough study, *Ideas and Politics of Chilean Independence, 1808–1833* (Cambridge University Press, 1969), and Jay Kinsbruner, *Bernardo O'Higgins* (Twayne, Boston, 1968). On Brazil's transition to independence, see A. J. R. Russell-Wood, ed., *From Colony to Nation: Essays on the Independence of Brazil* (Johns Hopkins University Press, Baltimore, 1975).

John Tutino, *From Insurrection to Revolution in Mexico: Social Bases of Agrarian Violence, 1750–1940* (cited above), offers a carefully reasoned explanation for Mexico's peculiar road to independence. B. R. Hamnett, *Roots of Insurgency: Mexican Regions, 1750–1824* (Cambridge University Press, New York, 1986), focuses on the local or regional roots of revolutionary discontent. J. E. Rodriguez, ed., *The Independence of Mexico and the Creation of the New Nation* (UCLA Latin American Center Publications, Los Angeles, Calif., 1989), presents some revisionist views on the transition to independence. H. M. Hamill, Jr., *The Hidalgo Revolt: Prelude to Mexican Independence* (University of Florida Press, Gainesville, 1966), is important for understanding Hidalgo and the course of his revolt. W. H. Timmons, *Morelos of Mexico, Priest, Soldier, Statesman* (Texas Western Press, University of Texas at El Paso, 1963), is a competent study. On Iturbide's short-lived reign, see T. A. Anna, *The Mexican Empire of Iturbide* (University of Nebraska Press, Lincoln, 1990).

The social and economic results of the revolutions still await intensive study. Tulio Halperin-Donghi ably discusses some of these results in *The Aftermath of Revolution in Latin America* (Harper & Row, New York, 1973); he examines in depth the changes wrought by the revolution in the Plate region in *Politics, Economics, and Society in Argentina in the Revolutionary Period* (Cambridge University Press, Cambridge, Eng., 1975).

Chapter 9
Dictators and Revolutions

David Bushnell and Neill Macaulay, *The Emergence of Latin America in the Nineteenth Century,* and Tulio Halperin-Donghi, *The Aftermath of Revolution in Latin America* (both cited above), provide good overviews of developments in the first half-century after Independence. E. Bradford Burns, *The Poverty of Progress: Latin America in the Nineteenth Century* (University of California Press, Berkeley, 1980.) A provocative, but not altogether convincing, work argues that modernization put an end to a traditional, harmonious Latin American society.

M. C. Meyer and W. L. Sherman, *The Course of Mexican History,* 4th ed. (Oxford University Press, New York, 1990), supersedes all previous general histories of Mexico. C. A. Hale, *Mexican Liberalism in the Age of Mora, 1821–1853* (Yale University Press, New Haven, Conn., 1968), is a thorough analysis of the Mexican liberal creed. On the chronic financial problems of early Mexican republican governments, see Barbara Tenenbaum, *The Politics of Penury: Debts and Taxes in Mexico, 1821–1856* (University of New Mexico Press, Albuquerque, 1986). R. N. Sinkin, *The Mexican Reform, 1855–1876: A Study in Liberal Nation-Building* (Institute of Latin American Studies, University of Texas, Austin, 1979), argues that the Liberal leaders succeeded in establishing a nation-state, but at the expense of their professed libertarian ideals. For the key church issue, see Jan Bazant, *Alienation of Church Wealth: Social and Economic Aspects of the Liberal Revolution, 1856–1875* (Cambridge University Press, Cambridge, Eng., 1971). On the Caste War, see Nelson Reed, *The Caste War of Yucatan* (Stanford University Press, Stanford, Calif., 1964).

For the first half-century of Argentina's independent existence, see the reliable survey by H. S. Ferns, *Argentina* (Praeger, New York, 1969), and Miron Burgin, *The Economic Aspects of Argentine Federalism, 1820–1852* (Harvard University Press, Cambridge, Mass., 1946). On Rosas, see the fine biography by John Lynch, *Argentine Dictator: Juan Manuel Rosas, 1829–1852* (Oxford University Press, New York, 1981). For the social and political content of the liberal-conservative cleavage, see David Bushnell, *Reform and Reaction in the Platine Provinces* (University Presses of Florida, Gainesville, 1983). J. C. Brown, *A Socioeconomic History of Argentina, 1776–1860* (Cambridge University Press, New York, 1979), is an excellent history of trade and agriculture, but underestimates the emerging pattern of a new dependency. R. A. White, *Paraguay's Autonomous Revolution* (University of New Mexico Press, Albuquerque, 1978), is an important revisionist study of the Francia era.

For the first decades of independent Chile, see the relevant sections of Brian Loveman, *Chile: the Legacy of Hispanic Capitalism* (Oxford University Press, New York, 1979), and consult again Simon Collier, *Ideas and Politics of Chilean Independence, 1808–1833* (cited above). On the Chilean great estate and its social consequences, see Arnold Bauer's thorough study, *Chilean Rural Society from the Spanish Conquest to 1930* (Cambridge University Press, New York, 1975).

For independent Brazil's early history, see E. B. Burns's excellent *A History of Brazil* (Columbia University Press, New York, 1970). Leslie Bethell deals with a crucial issue in *The Abolition of the Brazilian Slave Trade: Britain, Brazil, and the Slave Trade Question, 1807–1869* (Cambridge University Press, Cambridge, Eng., 1971). Gilberto Freyre, *The Mansions and the Shanties: The Making of Modern Brazil,* tr. by Harriet de Onis (Knopf, New York, 1963), carries his study of Brazilian society and race relations into the period of the empire. On the crisis of slavery in this period, see the revisionist study of Robert Conrad, *The Destruction of Brazilian Slavery, 1850–1888* (University of California Press, Berkeley, 1973). Conrad's *The African Slave Trade to Brazil* (Lou-

isiana State University Press, Baton Rouge, 1986), is a moving account of this detestable traffic. On the condition of slaves, see Katia M. de Queiros Mattos, *To Be a Slave in Brazil, 1550–1888* (Rutgers University Press, New Brunswick, N.J., 1986). Stanley Stein, *Vassouras: A Brazilian Coffee County* (Harvard University Press, Cambridge, Mass., 1957), is a model socioeconomic study. On Dom Pedro see Harry Bernstein, *Dom Pedro II* (Twayne, Boston, 1973). C. J. Kolinski, *Independence or Death! The Story of the Paraguayan War* (University of Florida Press, Gainesville, 1965), is a good account of the war's military aspects.

Chapter 10
The Triumph of Neocolonialism

On the emergence and flowering of the neocolonial economy, see Celso Furtado, *The Economic Development of Latin America,* tr. by Suzette Macedo (Cambridge University Press, New York, 1970), and Roberto Cortes Conde, *The First Stages of Modernization in Spanish America* (Harper & Row, New York, 1974). For a study of peasant resistance to capitalist transformation of the countryside, see Florencia Mallon, *The Defense of Community in Peru's Central Highlands: Peasant Struggle and Capitalist Transformation, 1860–1910* (Princeton University Press, Princeton, N.J., 1983).

There is a good brief discussion of the Díaz era in M. C. Meyer and W. L. Sherman, *The Course of Mexican History* (cited above). J. K. Turner, *Barbarous Mexico* (C. H. Kerr, Chicago, 1910), is a blistering contemporary assessment of the result of Díaz's rule. J. M. Hart, *The Coming and Process of the Mexican Revolution* (University of California Press, Berkeley, 1987), has an illuminating background discussion of the Porfiriato, stressing foreign economic influence on the rise and policies of the regime. The Northern Illinois University Press has published a series of monographs on the Porfiriato; they include R. J. Knowlton,

Church Property and the Mexican Reform, 1856–1910 (Northern Illinois University Press, DeKalb, 1976), R. D. Anderson, *Outcasts in Their Own Land: Mexican Industrial Workers, 1906–1911* (Northern Illinois University Press, DeKalb, 1976), L. B. Perry, *Juarez and Díaz, Machine Politics in Porfirian Mexico* (Northern Illinois University Press, DeKalb, 1979), and J. H. Coatsworth, *Growth and Development: The Economic Impact of Railroads in Porfirian Mexico* (Northern Illinois University Press, DeKalb, 1981). For an excellent survey of intellectual dissent in the late Porfiriato, see J. D. Cockcroft, *Intellectual Precursors of the Mexican Revolution, 1900–1913* (University of Texas Press, Austin, 1968). For the mutations of positivist thought and other ideological developments in Porfirian Mexico, see Charles Hale's exemplary study, *The Transformation of Liberalism in Late Nineteenth-Century Mexico* (University of Princeton Press, Princeton, N.J., 1990). Monographs on particular regions or provinces have proliferated in recent years; two good examples are Mark Wasserman, *Capitalists, Caciques, and Revolution: The Native Elite and Foreign Enterprise in Chihuahua, Mexico, 1854–1911* (University of North Carolina Press, Chapel Hill, 1984), and Allen Wells, *Yucatan's Gilded Age: Haciendas, Henequen, and International Harvester, 1860–1915* (University of New Mexican Press, Albuquerque, 1985).

On Argentina in the same period, see H. S. Ferns, *Argentina* (Praeger, New York, 1969), and especially Thomas McGann, *Argentina, the United States, and the Inter-American System, 1880–1914* (Harvard University Press, Cambridge, Mass., 1957), for an excellent account of oligarchical politics in the period from 1880 to 1914. For the British connection, see H. S. Ferns, *Britain and Argentina in the Nineteenth Century* (Clarendon Press, Oxford, Eng., 1960). James Scobie, *Argentina: A City and a Nation* (Oxford University Press, New York, 1971), is especially good for economic and social developments; see also his *Revolution on the Pampas: A Social History of Argentine Wheat* (University of Texas Press, Austin, 1964). On the rise of Radicalism, see David Rock, *Politics in Argentina, 1890–1930*

(Cambridge University Press, New York, 1975).

On the political and economic evolution of Chile in the same period, see again Brian Loveman, *Chile: The Legacy of Hispanic Capitalism* (cited above). On the agrarian structure, consult A. J. Bauer's excellent *Chilean Rural Society from the Spanish Conquest to 1930* (Cambridge University Press, New York, 1975). R. N. Burr, *By Reason or Force: Chile and the Balancing of Power in South America, 1830–1905* (University of California Press, Berkeley, 1965), studies Chile's international relations. For the War of the Pacific, see William Sater, *Chile and the War of the Pacific* (University of Nebraska Press, Lincoln, 1986). For opposing interpretations of the civil war of 1891, see Harold Blakemore, *British Nitrates and Chilean Politics, 1886–1896* (Athlone Press, London, 1974), and Maurice Zeitlin, *The Civil Wars in Chile (or the Bourgeois Revolutions That Never Were)* (Princeton University Press, Princeton, 1984).

For Brazil in the period under review, see especially E. B. Burns's *A History of Brazil* (Columbia University Press, New York, 1970). On the decisive slavery issue, again see Robert Conrad, *The Destruction of Brazilian Slavery* (cited above). Euclides da Cunha, *Rebellion in the Backlands,* tr. by Samuel Putnam (University of Chicago Press, Chicago, 1957), portrays the defeat of a major religious protest movement. P. L. Eisenberg, *The Sugar Industry in Pernambuco, 1840–1910* (University of California Press, Berkeley, 1974), studies the transformation of a major industry. Richard Graham ably discusses British economic and cultural influence in *Britain and the Onset of Modernization in Brazil, 1850–1914* (Cambridge University Press, New York, 1968). Warren Dean, *The Industrialization of São Paulo, 1880–1945* (University of Texas Press, Austin, 1969), is an important work on early Brazilian industrialization and its social aspects. On the so-called social question, see June Hahner, *Poverty and Politics: The Urban Poor in Brazil, 1870–1920* (University of New Mexico Press, Albuquerque, 1986). On the very different lifestyle of the elite, see Jeffrey D. Needell, *A Tropical Belle Epoque: The Elite Culture of Turn-of-the-Century Rio de*

Janeiro (Cambridge University Press, New York, 1986).

Chapter 11
Society and Culture in the Nineteenth Century

Tulio Halperin-Donghi's book, *The Aftermath of Revolution in Latin America* (cited above), is excellent on social and cultural change in the post-independence period. For the process of social and cultural Europeanization, again see Richard Graham's book on British influence on Brazil, *Britain and the Onset of Modernization in Brazil* (cited above), and Frank Safford's excellent study, *The Ideal of the Practical: Colombia's Struggle to Form a Technical Elite* (University of Texas Press, Austin, 1976). The literature on nineteenth-century Latin American women is meager, but Silvia Arrom, *The Women of Mexico City, 1790–1857* (Stanford University Press, Stanford, Calif., 1985), is a valuable case study.

J. L. Mecham, *Church and State in Latin America: A History of Politico-Ecclesiastical Relations,* rev. ed. (University of North Carolina Press, Chapel Hill, 1966), is the standard work on the subject. The Mexican philosopher Leopoldo Zea ably discusses Latin American nineteenth-century thought in *The Latin American Mind* (University of Oklahoma Press, Norman, 1963) and *Positivism in Mexico* (University of Texas Press, Austin, 1974); see also Charles Hale, *The Transformation of Liberalism in Late Nineteenth-Century Mexico* (cited above). For a source book on the subject, see R. L. Woodward, Jr., ed., *Positivism in Latin America* (D. C. Heath, Lexington, Mass., 1971). On the rise of racist ideology, see Richard Graham, ed., *The Idea of Race in Latin America, 1870–1940* (University of Texas Press, Austin, 1990).

On Latin American literature in the nineteenth century, Jean Franco, *An Introduction to Spanish American Literature* (Cambridge University Press, London, 1969), is especially recommended for its perceptive treatment of the relations between literature and society. For a case study in the relations between historiography and politics, see Allen Woll, *A Functional Past: The Uses of History in Nineteenth-Century Chile* (Louisiana State University Press, Baton Rouge, 1982).

Index